CONSUMING RELIGION

VINCENT J. MILLER

CONSUMING RELIGION

Christian Faith and Practice in a Consumer Culture

continuum
NEW YORK • LONDON

2004
The Continuum International Publishing Group Inc
15 East 26th Street, Suite 1703, New York NY 10010

The Continuum International Publishing Group Ltd
The Tower Building, 11 York Road, London SE1 7NX

Printed in the United States of America

Library of Congress Cataloging-in-Publication Data

Miller, Vincent Jude.
    Consuming religion : Christian faith and practice in a consumer
culture / Vincent J. Miller.
        p. cm.
    Includes bibliographical references.
    ISBN 0-8264-1531-8 (hardcover : alk. paper)
    1. Consumption (Economics)—Religious aspects—Christianity. 2.
Christianity and culture. I. Title.
BR115.C67M55 2004
241'.68—dc22
                                                    2003019542

Contents

Acknowledgments

I THANK, FIRST OF ALL, EILEEN, MY WIFE, FOR HER COMPANIONSHIP AND support. This book is a product of her labor as much as my own. My colleagues in the Theology Department at Georgetown provided a home for research and teaching. Colleagues there and elsewhere provided advice, criticism, and conversation that helped me refine my ideas. They include Matt Ashley, John Cavadini, Nancy Dallavalle (who provided comments on the entire manuscript), Rick Gaillardetz, Tony Godzieba, Tony Keaty, Dustin Kidd, Arthur Jones, Dolores Leckey, Charles Mathewes, Sandra Yocum Mize, Bruce Morrill, Joseph Murphy, Tom O'Meara, Tom Ryan, Christopher Steck, Terrence Tilley, John Wright-Rios, and Abraham Velez. I thank as well my students over the years for their enthusiasm about the topic, their hard questions, and their demands for clarity.

Presentations of portions of the research for the book at scholarly venues provided helpful criticism and feedback: the College Theology Society, the Contemporary Theory and Constructive Theology group at the Catholic Theological Society of America, the Louisville Institute Winter Seminar in 2001, an interdisciplinary seminar at the Center for Religion and Democracy at the University of Virginia, and the Woodstock Theological Center. The earliest version of these ideas was presented at my parish, Our Lady Queen of Peace. I thank that community for both its support and its witness. An earlier version of chapters 2 and 3 appeared as "Taking Consumer Culture Seriously" in *Horizons* 27 (2000): 276–95.

Student assistants Mythri Jegathesan and Sarah Grandfield provided much help with research. Tara Dankel was profoundly generous with her time and energy, checking citations and diligently tracking down sources at times only dimly (and sometimes incorrectly) remembered. Thanks as well to my editor, Frank Oveis, for his encouragement, support, and good humor throughout the writing process. I thank Georgetown University, the Carl Landegger fund, and the Louisville Institute for grants that provided research time for the conception and completion of this project.

This book is dedicated to Thomas "Buddy" King (1942–2002), who opened business late one ordinary day so he could help an old woman plow her garden.

Introduction

T HIS IS NOT A BOOK ABOUT RELIGION *AGAINST* CONSUMER CULTURE; IT IS a book about the fate of religion *in* consumer culture. The two topics are related but distinct. Frustrated with the banality of consumerism, many turn to religion seeking more compelling and authentic values and ideals. Any number of religions offer just that, and so it is worthwhile to contrast religion and consumer culture. Sociologist Robert Bocock concludes his influential book on consumption by invoking the great potential of religious traditions and communities for countering consumerism. In light of the destruction being wreaked by advanced capitalism, they "may be more important to the future of the planet earth than has been realized so far."[1] Yet he also notes that the United States, the world leader in consumption, is the most religious of the developed capitalist societies. Not only that, American religion is deeply informed by a Puritan religious tradition highly critical of consumption and indulgence. Clearly there is a serious disconnect between religious belief and practice at work here. This disconnect is the concern of this book.

What is it about consumer culture that renders religious critique less potent than theologians, believers, and sociologists such as Bocock would hope? I will argue that consumer "culture" is not merely a particular set of ideologies: for example, believing that driving SUVs, having plastic surgery, or watching *American Idol* are good and worth pursuing. It is primarily a way of relating to beliefs— a set of *habits of interpretation and use*—that renders the "content" of beliefs and values less important. Any theological engagement with consumer culture must consider this formal aspect of consumer culture if its critiques and counternarratives are to have a practical impact, and that is what we undertake here. This book maps the ways that consumer culture domesticates critique so that religious engagements with it might be more effective.

Although it is beyond dispute that consumer culture is marked by pernicious ideologies, such a description is ultimately insufficient. Consider the most commonly critiqued tenet—selfish materialism, the belief that human happiness is found in the accumulation of things. Against this belief one could argue for material simplicity in order to focus on the more important things in life: family, community, the contemplative life. The "voluntary simplicity" movement has been mounting such a critique for some time with help from religious believers from a

1

variety of traditions. The response is informative. There have been a few counter-attacks from the world of pundits: James Twitchell's apologetic defense of the joys of high-consumption materialism, *Lead Us into Temptation*; conservative media star David Brooks's ironic celebration of the excesses of America's ruling class, *Bobo's in Paradise*, and so on. While these public thinkers have been peddling their ideologies, the real forces behind consumer culture have been deployed in an entirely different and more subtle strategy, one that suggests that the frontal defense of material consumption is little more than a ruse.

This other response is both broader and more pervasive. The voluntary simplicity movement hit a nerve. Many members of consumer societies are tired of glitzy gluts of ever more stuff. Marketers respond not with worry but with appreciation. They want to know where the nerves are so they can position their products to hit them. A stroll through the supermarket illustrates this marketing strategy. Foodstuffs and personal care products are packaged as plain, simple, honest. The color schemes of labels as well as the products themselves are muted. Beige, lavender, and pale green provide the palette for iced tea and shampoo, risotto mixes and aroma therapy candles. At the checkout, we encounter this color scheme again, this time on the cover of a magazine that includes articles on getting organized, simplifying family life, and making Campari-grapefruit compote. It is full of glossy photo spreads of food, interiors, and clothing. A soft, minimalist aesthetic dominates these images—a hybrid of Martha Stewart and Zen Buddhism. The target audience of this magazine is professional women with incomes above $65,000 a year. Its title? *Real Simple*. Examples could be multiplied. There are also more severe color schemes that appear: the angry black and red of anticapitalist, anarcho-marxists is aimed at the children of those professionals, who are equally tired of endlessly consuming ever more stuff. Consumer culture seems endlessly capable of turning critique into a marketing hook.

There is no reason to believe that religion is any different in this regard. We can readily list any number of Christian theological themes that run counter to the implicit anthropology of consumerism: creation, unmerited grace, the paschal mystery, charity, sacramentality, the preferential option for the poor, forgiveness, denial of the flesh, and so on. But these challenges are no more guaranteed a critical foothold than the voluntary simplicity or anticorporate movements. We note in saying, however, that these movements have been effective as well. While their aesthetics have been exploited to sell candles and T-shirts, they have also formed communities that foster different forms of life and engage in significant political action. Clearly, having one's symbol system exploited for marketing purposes is not the same as being politically neutralized. The relationship of beliefs, narratives, and symbols to concrete practice is always complex. In consumer cultures it is particularly so, owing to advanced capitalism's protean power to exploit critique. This ability to encompass dissent is a serious concern for theology, because it presumes that the beliefs, narratives, and symbols that it stewards inform the life and politics of the Christian community.

This book explores how consumer culture changes our relationship with religious beliefs, narratives, and symbols. After a preliminary chapter on method, chapter 2 will present the core of the analysis. The basic idea is the "commodification of culture." This grows from Karl Marx's account of how ordinary commodities present themselves to us. Commodities appear on the scene, as if descended from heaven, cloaked in an aura of self-evident value, saying nothing about how, where, and by whom they were produced. As the market has become ubiquitous—the means by which we satisfy most of our needs—everyday existence has become a constant exercise in taking this abstraction for granted. Our eating, clothing, shelter, labor—all confirm us in this abstraction. We nourish ourselves on food from nowhere and dress in clothes made by no one. As consumer capitalism has expanded, corporate production has encompassed cultural goods as well as material ones. Here the same rules apply. While cultural objects' auras of value often include reference to their exotic origins, we feel perfectly comfortable consuming them like exotic fruit. Consider the 1994 song "Return to Innocence" by Enigma. The techno dance music of the song framed repeated, haunting samples of Difang Kuo singing a traditional Ami harvest song.[2] Millions bought the album, and countless millions more heard and enjoyed the music of this obscure indigenous culture in Thailand. The example is noteworthy for illustrating how readily people could engage music sung in a language that few even knew existed. We enjoy the melody and rhythms of a song without concerning ourselves about its origins. We treat it as a commodity, valuable in itself, sundered from the cultural associations and practices that give it meaning. Who sang it? What did it mean to him or her? It could have just as easily been a birthing song, a song of mourning, or a ritual chant by a priestly caste cursing outsiders who dare to listen in. Whether ignoring the sounds of grief or dancing to our own curse, we enjoy the music nonetheless.

Chapter 2 will also consider the host of practices, structures, and infrastructures in contemporary American society that support and reinforce the commodification of culture. Our cultural habits are formed by the way in which we work under the guidance of modern labor management, the way in which we live together (and apart) in single-family homes. Our imagination and desires are formed by advertising and marketing structures. These concrete historical factors and structures must be considered if we are to work against the tide of commodification that they reinforce.

Chapter 3 will apply this analysis of consumer culture to particular religious traditions. Commodification has two interrelated consequences for religion. First, elements of religious traditions are fragmented into discrete, free-floating signifiers abstracted from their interconnections with other doctrines, symbols, and practices. This abstraction of elements from their traditions weakens their ability to impact the concrete practice of daily life. Deprived of their coherence with a broader network of beliefs, they are more readily put to other uses, as shallow signifiers of whatever religious sentiment we desire. The second consequence concerns practices. When abstracted from their conditions of production—that is, from their communities of origin—practices are deprived of their links to the institutional and communal setting in which they shape the daily lives of religious practitioners.

Tibetan prayer flags provide an example. They look good on my neighbor's veranda, fluttering in the wind, the way I imagine they do at Dharamsala, and once did throughout Tibet. Simple cotton cloth flutters in a rainbow of muted colors, imprinted with Tibetan texts and symbols which I find attractive, but about which I know next to nothing. I like the idea of constant prayer as they flutter in the wind, somewhat like the vigil candles of my own tradition. I would very much like to fly them on my own front porch. Should I? There are two sets of questions here. The first is familiar. It concerns the politics of cultural appropriation. What is my relationship to Tibetan Buddhism? What right do I have to use the symbols and practices of that religion? There are many serious North American practitioners of Tibetan Buddhism, but their numbers come nowhere near the number of flags sold, whether in hip dharma shops supporting the work of Tibetan exiles or even hipper music, T-shirt, and smoking paraphernalia shops. Does such informal popular use help preserve an endangered culture or contribute to its erosion? These are important questions, but a second set of issues is of more consequence to the fate of religion in consumer culture. What would flying Tibetan prayer flags do to my relationship with the symbols of my own Roman Catholic tradition? By displaying the symbols of another tradition with so shallow an engagement with them, I draw my own traditional symbols into competition with them. They compete on common ground where they are all gauged in terms of their visual impact rather than the traditional practices associated with each. The modernistic bronze crucifix over the front door holding this year's palms and the Eichenberg print join the faux ivory Infant of Prague languishing in a drawer somewhere in being evaluated in terms of their impact in display, having more to do with my choice of paint color than with any particular religious discipline that forms my life.

This presents a problem for theology because it is a serious threat to the integrity of religious practice but it does not directly challenge the meanings and symbols with which theology is most comfortable. The most profound challenge of consumer culture is neither a heretical corruption of doctrine (not that examples of such are lacking in the religious discourse of consumer cultures), nor a theology or ontology implicit in particular practices. Such problems are familiar ground for theology. It has well-developed interpretive and analytical methods for addressing such crises. For this reason it is always tempting to lure cultural problems such as consumerism into this familiar territory—the seminar room, the heresy trial—where their implicit doctrines, values, and anthropologies can be evaluated, found wanting, and declared anathema. The problem faced in consumer culture is of an entirely different order and thus calls for a fundamentally different response. Here theology is faced with a cultural system that shows little interest in censoring, editing, or corrupting the contents of religious belief. Any belief, even those most radically critical of capitalism, are embraced with enthusiasm.

This is a crisis for hermeneutical methods in theology since it has to do with the function rather than the content of meanings. Hermeneutical methods have been expanded to deal with issues of power insofar as they distort the tradition. Hermeneutics of suspicion look behind the text for the traces of lost voices to prevent retrieval from becoming an exercise in the legitimation of the status quo. Contemporary critical perspectives struggle to include marginalized voices in the current moment of the ongoing conversation/argument of living tradition. Consumer culture presents a related but distinct problem. It is not a matter of misunderstanding born of historical distance, the forgetting of suppressed voices and experiences, or of the marginalization of such voices today. All of these meanings, even the most radical and decentering, are welcomed. The problem lies not in getting the tradition right, or being open to any voice, but in how the contents of tradition are engaged and put to use.

A consideration of the impact of the Disney Corporation (obligatory in any book on religion and consumer culture!) illuminates the problem theology faces. It is not difficult to find any number of problematic ideologies in Disney films: pernicious gender and racial stereotypes, individualism, bloodless violence, and so on. Beyond that, we might note the mass-market dumbing down the films inflict on complex and ambiguous myths and fairy tales (e.g., the replacement of the christological ending of *The Little Mermaid* with a male-centered climax out of an action-adventure flick that involves crashing a ship into a monstrous female villain who then dutifully explodes). Disney's most profound effects, however, are at once much more visible and much less noticed. Whatever lessons our children learn from the content of these films—whether respect for the "circle of life" or distrust of women who wear false eyelashes—they learn something much more powerful from the very act of consuming them. From preschool on, children know the characters and story lines of whatever Disney film is *au courant*, whether they have seen it or not. They enact the roles on playgrounds and in backyards; they debate about which character they like best. They learn about the films through the marketing that is omnipresent in their world. Fast food kids' meals include toy characters, and the characters appear on cereal boxes and in commercials during television programs aimed at children. More sophisticated dolls, action figures, and props are available in toy stores. Add to this costumes for Halloween, underwear, pajamas, clothing, lunch boxes, backpacks, watches, pencils, notebooks, stickers, and on and on. Merchandising revenues dwarf box office receipts.

This use of narrative to sell merchandise gives rise to the most profound cultural impact of Disney and other producers of commercial popular culture: the formation of our habits of interpretation and appropriation. Children learn to quickly accept narratives, to enjoy the roles and symbol systems of the stories, to locate themselves within the tales, and to consider their heroes, conflicts, and ideologies. While children are learning to do all of this, they are simultaneously learning to treat these narratives, roles, and symbols as disposable commodities: things to be played with, explored, tried on, and, in the end, discarded. Although this book will argue against the excesses of elite denunciations of the shallow narcissism of religious seekers, and of individualist "spirituality," we see here in germ the interpretive habits of that form of religious life.

Since my daughter was two years old, she has been intrigued with our nativity set. She has often wanted to play with the figures. Ours are abstract carvings of olive wood sturdy enough to endure the curiosity of toddlers. My mind misty with recollections of the Dutch theologian Edward Schillebeeckx's earliest christological memory—his father telling him as he looked at his nativity set, "That baby is God"—I welcomed her enthusiasm. She was interested in the stories the went with the figures: Jesus, Mary, Joseph, the shepherds, the animals, the Magi positioned still at a distance . . . just as she was interested in the stories that went with more brightly colored figures a few feet away: a pink baby pig, a blue donkey, a honey-colored bear, and a young boy named Christopher Robin. As a theologian, I was more or less prepared to expound on the meanings of the nativity figures, but my training offered little help in addressing the fact that the narratives of God's incarnation in Jesus of Nazareth might have the same status for her as those of a silly old bear named Pooh. The problem here has to do with the context and framing of religious discourse, not with the content of that discourse itself. I'm confident that Luke can out-narrate A. A. Milne. He is not, however, given the chance, because the context of consumer culture does not construct the relationship between the two as conflict. We are certainly incited to choose, but choices are not exclusive. Choose and choose again. Jesus, Pooh, and the Lion King as well. *Gloria in Excelsis Deo! Hakuna Matata!*

A theological response to these problems must move beyond the level of meaning to address the structures and practices through which meanings are engaged. Chapter 3 will consider particular forms of religious belief and practice associated with consumer culture. These include the religious "seeker" who moves from community to community and tradition to tradition, as well as "spirituality," a form of religious belief that is detached from religious institutions and communities, where believers construct their own religious syntheses from diverse traditions and sources. I will argue that these forms of religious practice can be understood in terms of the commodification of culture. It is not that people are necessarily shallow and narcissistic as the "therapeutic culture" critique would have it. Rather they encounter religion in a commodified form, where doctrines, symbols, values, and practices are torn from their traditional, communal contexts. In such a setting it is quite easy to construct hybrid religiosities abstracted from particular communities (such syncretism has always taken place; it is simply infinitely more easy to do now). Such deinstitutionalized forms of religious practice have come to prominence amid a broader transformation of religion. Changes that were once understood as the inevitable decline of religious belief in the face of secularization have in recent years been reconsidered. Sociologists now speak of the "decline of religious monopolies" or of religious "deregulation" in which religious belief and practice remain strong, but traditional religious authorities and institutions lose their power to influence both society at large and their own believers.

This "decline" suffered by religious leaders is, however, paradoxical. What they lose in traditional power and authority, they gain in media celebrity. Religious leaders such as John Paul II, the Dalai Lama, and Mother Teresa now enjoy enormous popularity and global celebrity. The consequences of religious celebrity correspond perfectly with the commodification of culture. Religious celebrities are broadly, if vaguely, admired. A poll in an undergraduate class tells the tale. Students were unanimous in admiring and respecting John Paul II. A majority of them simultaneously considered the Vatican's policies on sexuality and the treatment of women to be fundamental obstacles to either joining or remaining in the Catholic Church. Not a single one associated John Paul with any of these issues. Similarly, conservative American Catholics had little difficulty negotiating the contradiction between their devotion to John Paul II as a man of historic genius, sanctity, and wisdom and their complete disregard of the substance of his condemnation of the United States' war of choice against Iraq.

Religious celebrity raises the broader question of religious use of the secular corporate media. I will argue that, while use of popular media brings major advantages, it also entails significant costs. When religious leaders use secular media, they risk being engaged in the same way as other "new cultural intermediaries"—media stars, lifestyle experts, and the like. This inclines believers to bring the interpretive habits they develop in consuming popular culture to their engagement with their own religious leaders and elements of their own religious traditions.

Chapter 4 considers desire, an unavoidable topic for any theological consideration of consumer culture. Here again the conflict between consumer culture and Christianity is not a matter of explicit opposition. The problem arises not from conflicting goals of desire, for example, the love of God versus the love of things, but rather from the focus and texture of desire. Consumer desire is, surprisingly, not really about attachment to things, but about the joys of desiring itself. It is the joy of endless seeking and pursuit. Actual consumption always comes as something of a disappointment, as the object can never live up to its promise. This form of desire is hauntingly similar to Christian portrayals of desire as an endless, unquenchable seeking after an infinite God. This similarity in form presents the danger of a subtle derailing of fundamental Christian desires such as the desire for God and the desire for justice. It also tends to erode our ability to focus desire on the singular. This formation of desire thus weakens our ability to commit to others and to accept the suffering that their mortality brings with it. It lessens our ability for thankfulness and sacrifice, both of which are likewise bound to the particular.

The notion of the commodification of culture provides insight into the negative consequences of consumer culture. There is, however, more to the story. Chapters 5 and 6 turn to a complementary perspective that provides a more optimistic reading of the activities of religious consumers. As illuminating as the narrative of commodification is, one notices anomalies that challenge its portrayal of unremitting decline. A conversation with colleagues about students writing term papers on popular music reveals a striking correlation between an interest in the band U2 and the pursuit of nontraditional, politically committed career paths. A woman comments on her choice of wall paint. "I think I chose the color because it had 'Aztec' in the name. I liked the association with indigenous cultures." Her choices in interior design thus express her political solidarity. Shallow indeed . . . were it not for the fact that she has committed her life to peace activism, teaching courses in nonviolence at regional churches and schools, and she regularly makes lengthy trips to third-world countries to learn in detail the plight and needs of indigenous peoples. Stranger still, the advertising exploitation of countercultural values may not have arisen as former hippie boomers sold out and began to spend like their establishment parents. Thomas Frank has noted that the great Doyle Dane Bernbach ad campaign for Volkswagen not only preceded the sixties counter-culture but may have aided in its formation.[3] Corporate culture had established the Volkswagen Van as a sign of nonconformity long before they appeared at anti-war protests painted with flowers. Here we begin to glimpse the other side of consumer culture. People accomplish socially and politically significant things through consumption. Perhaps they accomplish important religious tasks as well.

The rise of consumer culture overlaps with the rise of widespread literacy. The doors to the archives of tradition are no longer open only to those with specialized training. A higher percentage of believers than ever is reading more theological writing than ever. This is not limited simply to popular works (whether this term is understood pejoratively or not). The *Classics of Western Spirituality* series by Paulist Press is a provocative example. The connotation of "classic" in the series title probably lies somewhere between the term "classic rock" (coming into existence around the time of its founding) and the Harvard Classics series. It was originally marketed by subscription, like a record club or knickknacks from the Franklin Mint. The focus on "spirituality" is, as we have seen, susceptible to critique in terms of its consonance with consumer culture, all the more so given the very clear pluralism of the series, which encompasses a breadth of Christian spiritual traditions, other Abrahamic faiths, even *Native North American Spirituality of the Eastern Woodlands*—something for everyone. That said, the series consists of scholarly translations of serious sources accompanied by sophisticated and lengthy introductions written by experts in the field. With the possible exception of a handful of authors such as Augustine, Aquinas, or the author of the *Cloud of Unknowing,* most of these editions were the largest print runs of the texts ever offered. At a time when there are more literate, educated religious believers than ever, there are more sources for them to read than ever. Lay people (in both the religious and scholarly sense of the term) are reading weighty works by Julian of Norwich, Meister Eckhart, John Ruusbroec, Catherine of Siena, George Fox, and others. Clearly, an economy that produces such a series and a culture where it is popular cannot be all bad.

Our age is witnessing an explosion of agency and authorship. New media technologies—the rise of cable networks, low-cost publishing, and above all the Internet—call for and make possible publication by the masses. But questions remain. What is the status of this agency? The pessimistic marxist account presumes that it is as superficial as the mass culture offerings of the commercial culture industries. The word used to describe this creativity is frequently dismissive: shallow *bricolage*, ill-informed syntheses that contribute nothing to religious traditions because they are, in the end, merely ignorant misuses of beliefs and symbols. A spirituality that blithely combines reincarnation and resurrection is perhaps the canonical example.

But the word *bricolage* has a more respectful use. Michel de Certeau regards it as an important form of practical knowledge, a form of cultural practice that supports a politically potent popular culture. We will apply de Certeau's analysis to popular production in consumer culture and consider its political and religious potential. Understanding this potential will require a rethinking of one of the most oft-used dismissals of consumer culture: conspicuous consumption. Thorsten Veblen coined the term not only to describe the morbid excesses of the leisure class but to highlight the social significance of their consumption, which provided a way to establish class identity amid the fluid social boundaries of the United States. In the intervening century, conspicuous consumption has spread to the masses. As culture has been exploited to sell commodities, commodities have become important cultural expressions. We will pursue Pierre Bourdieu's much more refined account of conspicuous consumption as a means by which individuals and subgroups establish social identity and status. Many examples leap to mind: *kente* cloth and African American identity, college leftists wearing Palestinian *kaffias*, Amish plain dress, and the like. While these are easily dismissed as shallow display, they provide the basis for establishing real social identity and solidarity. They have real political significance and power.

These two insights will form the foundation for our consideration of popular religion in consumer culture. I will argue that bricolage is not necessarily shallow. Indeed, anonymous, popular production is responsible for the bulk of our cultural and religious traditions. The problem with consumer culture is not that the masses are encouraged to develop their own religious syntheses but that believers encounter the elements of tradition in an abstract, fragmented form and are trained to engage them as passive consumers.

The explosion of agency that has accompanied consumer culture precludes turning back. The only way forward is through consumer culture, by embracing grassroots agency. Restricting popular religious production will only reinforce the widespread reality of the contemporary passive believer as a postmodern peasant who takes what she finds useful or desirable from official religion and pays little attention to the demands for consistency from church authorities, who are largely irrelevant to her faith and practice. The only response to such passive, shallow bricolage that is likely to succeed is to encourage and deepen religious agency, to give people the formation and responsibility necessary to engage their traditions creatively as mature practitioners.

The final chapter of the book turns from diagnosis to prescription. Using the analysis of the first six chapters, it will chart a critical engagement with consumer culture. If the fundamental problem is how consumer culture transforms the way we practice beliefs, then any adequate response must attend to the level of practice. Michel de Certeau's distinction between strategic and tactical practices provides a way of conceiving of the status of practices in consumer culture. In the pluralistic world of consumer culture, religious communities seldom exercise strategic control of the field of action. Rather, they are limited to tactical actions that must locate themselves in a world dominated by foreign logics. For that reason, they work not by directly enacting their visions of how the world should be but by disrupting the workings of the dominant order and turning them to their own ends and desires.

If the abstraction and fragmentation of religious traditions are the result of cultural habits learned in other practices of consumption, then challenging the abstracting effects of commodification on the general level will be helpful for countering it on the explicitly religious level. While this discussion involves many tactics for countering consumerism, that is not its primary goal. Our interest here is not consumption, but the cultural dynamics of commodification. A variety of tactics are considered for countering the most culturally significant effect of commodification: abstraction. In addition to general tactics for countering commodification, we will also consider the tactical use of specifically Christian beliefs and practices to counter commodification (e.g., the notion of sacramentality and the Roman Catholic eucharistic liturgy). This section does not develop full-scale ontologies or liturgical theologies, but considers how these beliefs and practices provide a tactical challenge to the workings of commodification.

The second half of the chapter turns to the related question of countering the commodification of religion in particular. Generalized talk of "religious traditions" is itself consonant with commodity abstraction. Thus, this question must be addressed from the perspective of a particular religious tradition. Each tradition faces particular challenges, because religions have internal communal and theological attractions to the structures and practices of consumer culture. Likewise, each religious tradition has its own peculiar resources for responding to commodification. Roman Catholicism is particularly interesting in both regards. It has, perhaps more than any other religious tradition, a robust communication infrastructure with a global reach. This provides a potential alternative to the corporate media that can be used to counter the abstraction of religious culture and to deepen the agency of religious consumers. The use of this media, however, is informed by Catholicism's long history of conflict between clerical elites and the popular religion of the masses. This leaves it ill prepared to face the rise of an educated laity and the erosion of popular religion in a consumer culture.

We will consider two groups of tactics. The first concerns reinforcing the interconnections among doctrines, symbols, and practices. This aims to stabilize both their meanings and their connections with practices that inform the shape of daily life. Catholicism's rich array of communication structures, such as administrative offices, the liturgy, and its vast media and communication networks, appear as very valuable alternatives to the corporate culture industries as a means of communicating religious beliefs, symbols, and values. The goal of these tactics is not to prevent unauthorized use of religious traditions but to strengthen popular agency by preserving more complex religious building blocks for it to work its bricolage upon. The second group of tactics considers ways to strengthen and facilitate popular agency. If the explosion of culture agency that has accompanied the rise of consumer culture is not likely to go away, then it should be embraced and brought into the ongoing dialogue of the living tradition. This section considers how to do this by providing authorization, practices, and spaces in which believers can act as agents of the Catholic tradition.

There are a number of caveats that must be made at the start of this work. The most important we have already seen several times. Although this book is motivated by a profound concern about the corrosive and destructive consequences of consumption, it is not primarily a book about consumerism. High-consumption lifestyles are the norm in the advanced capitalist societies, and many of us are seriously conflicted about our levels of consumption in the face of the economic injustice and environmental destruction it causes. Since consumption is so overdetermined, people frequently misread any discussion of the topic as a lifestyle indictment. As necessary as that task may be, this book focuses on a different topic: how the habits of consumption transform our relationship to the religious beliefs we profess. Our analysis of the carryover of these habits into religious practice will, of course, require an extended consideration of the origins and characteristics of high-consumption societies. Our account of the dynamisms that drive high-consumption societies will not, however, focus on critique. From the perspective of the allocation of resources and labor, conspicuous consumption— whether that of gilded-age barons or inner-city youth—is a hideously expensive means of establishing social stratification. Levels of consumption in America alone are environmentally unsustainable. Throw in the burgeoning middle class across the world and it is clear that this system cannot continue for long. Our analysis, however, will focus on the social, political, and religious potential of consumption, on its significance and potential within the consumer societies we inhabit, as economically and environmentally unsustainable as they may be. Although the suggestions for a practical response to the commodification of religion will make use of tactics relevant to a more general countering of high-consumption lifestyles, this overlap should not obscure the central focus of this work on the practice of religion in consumer culture.

A second caveat is theological. This book will likely be criticized for lacking a thick, overarching theological narrative. It consistently avoids stark contrasts between Christian theological beliefs and values—ontologies, anthropologies, accounts of the good—and those of consumer culture. I do not propose the retrieval of some overlooked element of the tradition that will address the problems of consumerism by healing desire or restoring a proper sense of relationship with others. I avoid such moves for a considered reason. Consumer culture is best diagnosed not as a deformation of belief but as a particular way of engaging religious beliefs that divorces them from practice. I assume that any number of religious doctrines, anthropologies, and narratives provide resources for human flourishing that are infinitely better than the menu of titillation, selfishness, jingoism, and mindless pablum that dominates contemporary popular culture and politics. But in consumer culture, even the most brilliant and timely retrieval of Augustine, Gregory of Nyssa, or Catherine of Siena must face the problem of how people receive and practice the theological insights they provide. Theology is in the business of offering accounts of human existence from the perspective of revelation as mediated in various traditions. This book aims to contribute to that broader task both by mapping the likely pitfalls that theological discourse will face in its contemporary reception and by developing tactics to help it avoid them.

A third caveat concerns the focus on commodification. It has been a profoundly important cultural dynamism since the dawn of high consumption societies in the late eighteenth century. This period in the West has been marked by profound social and cultural upheavals. But, commodification, is, of course, only one dynamism among many. Our exclusive focus on the cultural consequences of this economic dynamic is not meant to deny that other important social and cultural dynamisms are at work in the world. They are so numerous that only a partial list can be offered here: modernization, secularization, detraditionalization, functional specialization, the rise of literacy, global migration, pluralism, globalization, the rise of communication, information, and other technologies, etc. Many of these dynamics have effects that are intertwined with those of commodification. This book will focus solely on commodification, making reference to the others as they are relevant to it. This does not mean of course that those other factors are necessarily subordinate to commodification.

Lastly, something must be said about nostalgia. Nostalgia haunts this work, just as it haunted Marx's account of the commodity where exchange value obscured the more honest and authentic "use value" of things. It has haunted romantic criticisms of the shallowness of consumer culture from eighteenth-century Germany, through the neo-medievalism of the Arts and Crafts movement, the mid-twentieth-century critique of the Frankfurt school, to contemporary critiques of consumerism from the voluntary simplicity movement and environmental activists. Accusations of nostalgia come on several levels. One often heard against any criticism of contemporary capitalism is that the critic must offer an alternative to the system that currently feeds, shelters, and educates many (but certainly nowhere near all) people. Critics are accused directly or indirectly of biting the hand that feeds them. It should be needless to say that offering a comprehensive alternative to capitalism is not a necessary condition for analyzing its negative consequences. But there is another nostalgia critique that must be taken more seriously for our project: cultural and religious nostalgia. Pick a golden age and place: medieval Europe, immigrant urban Catholicism in early-twentieth-century America, small-town community life anywhere, anytime. Each of these hovers behind contemporary frustrations with the rootlessness and isolation of contemporary American culture. Medieval Europe holds perennial fascination for anti-modernists, especially Catholic ones. As Jacques Delemeau has observed, accounts of the Middle Ages as the Age of Faith usually tell us more about the concerns of those waxing nostalgic than about actual life in medieval Europe.

The foundational analysis of this book—commodification—is an account of decline and loss. When we relate to cultural and religious traditions as commodities, they lose their power to inform the concrete practice of life. This account of the particular ways in which religious beliefs, narratives, symbols, and practices are disarmed in the culture of advanced capitalism does not necessarily presume that there was a time when these elements of religious traditions directly informed the practice of daily life. One need not be an expert in the social history of Christianity to realize that Christendom was seldom transparent to Christian doctrines. Examples of past power regimes that distorted or hindered religious belief can be easily compiled: imperial Rome after Constantine, Germanic feudalism, the power struggles between the papacy and political authorities, the wars of religion, modern European colonialism, and so on. Beyond these monumental political distortions of Christianity lies a more fundamental problem. The application of doctrine to communal practice is never a straightforward affair. There are certainly connections to be made between one's theology of creation or understanding of the incarnation and the practice of daily life, but such correlations are seldom direct applications. They involve a host of factors that, in addition to theological doctrines, include cultural factors as well as plain chance. Mourning the desire for a golden age or a perfect community where daily life is organically informed by religious belief, I will nevertheless seek to understand the particular ways in which Christian belief is hindered from influencing the politics of daily life in consumer cultures. This understanding will be used to plan a tactical response to the specific problems posed by consumer culture for religious faith and practice. The tactical goal of the book to some extent precludes nostalgia. It aims not to reestablish some golden age of Christian culture but to provide guidance for living a more authentically Christian life in a culture that is neither entirely Christian in its logic nor entirely alien.

CHAPTER 1

How to Think
about Consumer Culture

IT'S ABOUT MORE THAN VALUES

THIS BOOK IS CONCERNED WITH THE WAYS IN WHICH CONSUMER CULTURE transforms religious belief and practice. This differs somewhat from the approach most commonly employed by religious critics of consumerism, which tends to view consumer culture as a set of beliefs and values. John Paul II's forceful critique of consumerism in his 1999 "World Day of Peace" address is exemplary. He labeled consumerism an outlook "no less pernicious" than racism, "Marxism, Nazism, and Fascism." If the intensity of his critique was unusual, the form of his argument was not. His choice of language—"outlook," "myth," and "ideology"—follows the conventional form of critique as a set of values, beliefs, or ideas.

John Kavanaugh, S.J., has offered an extended account of consumer culture from this perspective in his widely read book *Following Christ in a Consumer Society*. He contrasts a vast repertoire of consumer values of the "Commodity Form" of life with the Christian values of the "Personal Form"of life.[1] The Commodity Form is marked by the reduction of persons to things. Kavanaugh associates it with an absence of empathy and the ability to sustain interpersonal commitments, abortion, euthanasia, capital punishment, militarism, ethical relativism, and instrumental rationality. He also notes how other values and experiences (e.g., friendship, love, intimacy, pride) are reduced to objects of consumption.

The problem with these approaches lies in their assumption that beliefs drive our behavior. Elements of John Paul's address provide a clear example of the problem. He describes consumerism as an ideology in which "the selfish satisfaction of personal aspirations" becomes the ultimate goal of life, and the resulting "negative effects on others are considered completely irrelevant."[2] Many, if not all, of us make decisions every day that are consistent with at least the second half of that statement. The selfish sociopathic yuppie—Patrick Bateman in *American Psycho* or Gordon Gekko in the film *Wall Street*—is a cultural icon. The latter at least was a true enough portrayal of the excesses of Ivan Boesky and Michael Milkin. While excessive consumption is widespread, however, such crass selfishness is not. Relatively few of us avow anything of the sort, however excessive our consumption may be.

Consider the relation between our overconsumption and the economic exploitation it rests upon. We begin in a cluttered middle-class American household with children. A friend has a word for it: "sh...tuff"—an amelioration of the word for excrement—to describe the drifts of toys that litter the floors, bank up to the walls, pile in the corners of our houses. Gifts given to our cute children by everyone. Many of these are stuffed animals. Long ago these were costly enough to limit their number. That was the age of the prized teddy bear saved to adulthood, providing memories of childhood or the subject for a father's literary life's work. Today children have so many that no one in particular gets worn down out of affection. The Velveteen Rabbit's quest to be "real" is foreclosed to these hordes. Now, unless they are part of the Ty corporation's carefully controlled supply-and-demand system for Beanie Babies™, they are almost free; cheap enough to be the substrate for gestures that hover between thoughtful and thoughtless. They serve as gifts to young children from grandparents' acquaintances during the penumbral days of glutted holiday giving. They were sent by the thousands to Arlington in the wake of September 11 to comfort victims' children. Schools had closets full, not knowing what to do with them. We joke about the senseless slaughter of so many "polyesters." What to do with them? Give them to charity? Poor children in this country have just as many. It seems wrong to just throw them away, and since they are made from synthetics, they cannot be composted (in that sense, more trouble than excrement), so they pile up in corners, fill bins and baskets, and clutter our lives.

Now we turn to China. A few weeks before Christmas, in November 2001, a nineteen-year-old toy-factory worker, Li Chunmei, collapsed to the floor of her dormitory and died of what muckraking Chinese newspapers call *guolaosi*: "overwork death." She worked at the Bianan toy factory in Songang, in the Chinese enterprise zone in the Pearl River Delta near Hong Kong. She worked as a "runner," the lowest skill job in the factory. Runners take partially completed stuffed animals from work station to work station. They are on their feet all day and earn about twelve cents an hour. Runners were responsible for keeping the work moving between twenty-five work stations. During peak production season, there is illegal (and underpaid) mandatory overtime. As a result, Chunmei had been working from 8:00 A.M. to midnight, with only two hours of break time for meals for sixty days straight, seven days a week when she collapsed and died. She had complained of illness and exhaustion, but her manager's only response was to dock her three days' pay (about two dollars) when she skipped an evening overtime session to rest.[3] She was worked to death making things that we try not to call shit.

As I see this story in the newspaper, I force myself to read it, to regard the photographs of an unhappy young Chinese woman. A voiceless knot of grief forms in my throat. Did Chunmei work on any of the animals I am tripping over this morning? The shell game of corporate outsourcing makes it impossible to know. I feel implicated, but what to do? Divest? Participate in campaigns against such factories? Both are worthwhile. But the quest for an adequate response (or even an inadequate one for that matter) only highlights the mindlessness of it all. The contractor who ran the factory could triple wages (an insignificant portion of the final cost of most such items) without significantly raising their price. What drives this? Certainly not focused desire. Chunmei's death, like consumerism more broadly, was not caused by the conscious selfish demands of American children or their parents' desire to spoil them. If faced with the choice, absolutely no one would demand Chunmei's sacrifice for their ability to buy more cheap toys than they could ever enjoy. Although explicit, reflexive selfishness is likely to come into the picture with forms of consumption more directly tied to quality of life (e.g., cheap transportation, living space, warmth, etc.), it is still significantly the case that people would never explicitly choose such high levels of consumption if they were to face the privation of others. Many of those who enjoy a high standard of living in advanced capitalist societies still curse the injustices upon which their comfort depends. Thus, in dealing with consumerism, to accuse people of narcissistic selfishness where "negative effects on others are considered completely irrelevant" misses the mark significantly.

Perhaps it is simply a case of denial and self-deception. Our dislike of the consequences of our decisions does not disprove our selfishness. We accept the values of the culture around us, even if we refuse to admit the fact. John Paul has argued that such implicit values must be taken seriously.

> The manner in which new needs arise and are defined is always marked by a more or less appropriate concept of man and of his true good. A given culture reveals its overall understanding of life through the choices it makes in production and consumption. It is here that the phenomenon of consumerism arises. In singling out new needs and new means to meet them, one must be guided by a comprehensive picture of man which respects all the dimensions of his being and which subordinates his material and instinctive dimensions to his interior and spiritual ones.[4]

A number of theologians have undertaken a criticism of consumer culture from this perspective. Craig Gay argues that the shallow excesses of contemporary consumerism are merely a manifestation of the broad enactment of the modern values of autonomous self-determination and secularization. The former manifests itself in our endless desire for self-expression, experience, and fulfillment; the latter in the strangely circumscribed range of material objects through which we seek fulfillment and self-expression.[5] We may disavow the egregious examples of the social cost of these values such as Chunmei's death, but we continue to firmly hold them. People who drive SUVs that get fewer than twelve miles per gallon may not like the consequences of their choices, but they make them nonetheless. Others have offered similar criticisms of consumer culture from an ideological perspective. Graham Ward and D. Stephen Long have both argued that unlimited consumer desire is a manifestation of the heretical ontology of "lack" at the heart of modernity.[6] These theological projects rightly critique the implicit values, anthropologies, and ontologies of societies and economic systems. They are necessary if we are to discern what is wrong with consumerism and consumer cultures. Yet they do not quite get at the problem. While life provides no shortage of examples of shallow, narcissistic, selfish consumers—whether culpably or cluelessly so—there are many other people, whose sincerely held beliefs and values are deeply informed by Christianity and other profound traditions, who are frustrated with the excesses of consumption and would like to live another way, but simply do not know what to do.

When it comes to formulating a response to these problems, such approaches are less helpful. The quotation from John Paul makes explicit what these approaches generally presume, that the answer lies in developing, retrieving, or promulgating a more adequate anthropology or ontology. If the problem is best diagnosed on the level of ideas, the answer lies there as well. There are two problems with such a response. First, it does not adequately attend to the nonintentional aspects of social and economic systems, how they frequently work without any supporting ideology or implicit ontology. Second, and more importantly, such a response runs headlong into a problem specific to consumer cultures: the commodification of dissent. Jeremiads against the excesses of capitalism sell quite well as consumer goods, as do evocative accounts of more properly orthodox ontologies or anthropologies. Advanced capitalism has shown itself to be strangely immune to ideological criticism. It seems capable of selling anything, including the values of its most committed opponents. It turned the 150th anniversary of the *Communist Manifesto* into a marketing opportunity. In minimalls throughout the land stacks of glossy paperback editions were placed next to cash registers in major chain bookstores to tempt impulse purchases. If capitalism's greatest critic is so easily defused, it seems unlikely that these alternative religious anthropologies and ontologies will fare much better.

Capitalism has long responded to its critics with such mercantile enthusiasm: from William Morris, the utopian and founding member of the British Labour Party now best remembered (and even then most appreciated) for designing easy chairs and wallpaper, to Kurt Cobain, the suicidal lead singer of Nirvana, whose scathing critiques of popular culture—"Here we are now, entertain us/I feel stupid and contagious"—proved enormously marketable, as did his grunge antiaesthetic, which became a fashion fad.[7] It is important to note for the thesis being pursued by this study that the popularity of Nirvana was not a result, as is often suggested, of listeners not "getting" Cobain's irony. Far from it; they could not get enough of it. What could be more deliciously ironic than mindlessly moshing to a song about the mindlessness of popular music fans? Like other critical perspectives, irony is easily encompassed by consumerism.

January 26, 2000, promised a major event in the confluence of radical politics and popular culture. The avowedly anticapitalist group Rage Against the Machine asked Michael Moore (of *Roger and Me* fame) to direct a video for their new album *The Battle for Los Angeles*. Moore was enthusiastic about the project, which, in his words, shed light on "the evils of our economic system and the era of greed in which we live." Extras at the shoot, held in front of the New York Stock Exchange on Wall Street, were divided into "fans" and "suits," who were instructed to "love" and "hate" the group respectively. The extras followed their cues, but to Moore's consternation, the many real "suits" working in the exchange did not. As word spread that Rage was performing, many young traders left the floor to watch the filming, at one point chanting "Suits for Rage!"[8] According to Amazon.com, who knows who you are and what you buy, *The Battle for Los Angeles* was the second-best-selling CD among students at Georgetown University in May 2000. I leave it as an exercise for the reader to decide whether the average Hoya is best classified as a "suit" or a "fan."

Classroom experiences are particularly illuminating because they involve open discussion of theological doctrines with a significant level of complexity. I have now taught at two elite Catholic universities, both of which churn out thousands of "well-rounded" Catholic members of the professional managerial class each year. Troubled by the legitimating role that the theology requirement likely plays in this (and to convince myself that, appearances notwithstanding, I have not sold out to "the Man"), I emphasize in my teaching aspects of the Catholic tradition that might disrupt the easy assimilation of Catholicism with students' career plans in the status quo. To my dismay, they never seem much troubled by these things. In fact, they quite like them. They eagerly absorb the most radical reconstructions of Jesus' politics, the preferential option for the poor, and Catholic social teaching—all of which their life plans preclude them from acting upon. While there is likely some miming of the professor's politics at work here, their enthusiasm (not something they display capriciously) suggests that their interest is sincere. They very much want a religion that cares about the poor, stands against injustice, and so on. The ease with which we are able to negotiate such disconnects between belief and practice is the central concern of this study.

These two sets of examples make clear that something more complex than values and beliefs is driving excessive consumption. On the one hand, the system runs contrary to the sincerely held values of many of those who benefit from it. On the other, critical denunciations of the system are such attractive values that they easily become commodities in themselves. Clearly something else is at stake in consumerism than a pernicious set of values. While an emphasis on beliefs and values will remain useful for clarifying the conflicts between the gospel and the form of life fostered by consumer culture, it does not provide an adequate guide for responding to the problem because it ignores the deeper cultural dynamics of consumerism. Unless we attend to these deeper workings of culture, theological reflection will miss the most profound challenge of consumerism—the commodification of culture—the reduction of religious beliefs, symbols, and values to objects of consumption.

CULTURE AND BELIEF

The problem arises from a simplistic conception of culture as a system of beliefs. Such an approach comes easily to theologians and pontiffs, who are accustomed to arguing the vital importance of conceptual distinctions for the life of the Christian community. The default approach to culture of theologians and religious critics of consumer culture closely resembles Clifford Geertz's anthropology. (Hence, Geertz's influence among theologians—from Tracy to Lindbeck —is no surprise.) Geertz's understanding of anthropology is primarily hermeneutical. It is, according to his famous definition, an "interpretive [science] in search of meaning."[9] Within this definition lies the assumption that human action is fundamentally meaning based. His use of the notion of "thick description" presumes just that. Human interactions are intentional. They can be understood only by closely attending to the meanings agents intend through them. Thus, the classic example of the wink. What distinguishes it from an involuntary twitch of an eyelid is the winker's intentional use of the gesture within a context where it has a recognized cultural meaning. To twitch one's eye in such a context is to enact the associated meaning. Culture itself is "an historically transmitted pattern of meanings embodied in symbols, a system of inherited conceptions expressed in symbolic forms by means of which men communicate, perpetuate, and develop their knowledge about and attitudes toward life."[10] For Geertz, religion concerns particular sorts of meanings: a worldview or ontology—"conceptions of a general order of existence" and an ethos—"moods and motivations" concerning how life is to be lived. These include morals as well as more general attitudes toward existence such as how to face adversity or express joy. These meanings are conveyed by a system of religious symbols and narratives, especially through their ritual use. Symbols bear a worldview; they "express the world's climate and shape it" and inform our ethos "by inducing in the worshipper a certain distinctive set of dispositions (tendencies, capacities, propensities, skills, habits, liabilities, pronenesses) which lend a chronic character to the flow of his activity and the quality of his experience."[11] For Geertz, meanings are the cause of our actions.

Talal Asad criticizes Geertz on this point for "inadvertently . . . taking up the standpoint of theology."[12] He argues that it is not at all clear that the meaning-content of religious symbols necessarily informs the practice of a religious community or that worldview and ethos are necessarily consistent. He traces the assumption that there must be such a continuity to the clerical exercise of power within Christianity. Church authorities "exercised the authority to read Christian *practice* for its Religious Truth."[13] This assumption that practices can be interrogated for their orthodoxy lives on in Geertz's assertions that symbols and rituals generate religious conviction. This assumption, however, obscures much of importance, namely, "the occurrence of events (utterances, practices, dispositions), and the authorizing processes which give those events religious meaning, and embody that meaning in concrete institutions."[14] The relation between religious meanings and the practices of the believing community is complex. Religious traditions are constituted by myriad beliefs, symbols, and rituals. These have varied influences on the shape of the religious community's life. Some are revered as fundamental doctrines yet have little impact on practice, while others that are held to be theologically secondary have a disproportionate impact on the daily life of the religious community. (For example, in many Christian traditions, theologies of ordination have much more impact on the communal form of life than trinitarian doctrine.) This disconnect between beliefs and practices is manifest also in the contemporary social impotence of religious symbols. Asad asserts that "a deeply committed Christian surely cannot be unconcerned at the existence of truthful religious symbols that appear to be largely powerless in modern society." For this problem, the understanding shared by Geertz and traditional Christian theology of the culture as a system of meanings offers little help. To address it, Asad asserts that we must consider other questions. "What are the conditions in which religious symbols can actually produce religious dispositions? How does (religious) power create (religious) truth?"[15]

These questions are influenced by Michel Foucault, whose theoretical perspective is helpful for thinking about how our actions are formed by forces that lie beneath and can run contrary to our consciously professed beliefs and values. By bracketing the question of meaning, Foucault's cultural analysis is able to focus on the function and effects of discourse aside from its content, or what it says. This perspective will help us clarify how religious belief and practice are transformed in consumer culture.

With his research into the penal system, Foucault became increasingly fascinated with the role of power in discourse. The "surface of discourse" is not a two-dimensional plane of signifiers, but deeply convoluted and fissured, linked as it is to practices, disciplines, institutions, and, thus, the power struggles of human history. Foucault spoke of "discursive régimes"—the structures, rules, and power relations that construct and constrain discourse below the level of meaning. These underlying structures render discourse opaque to our intentions. At times they even cause our utterances to have effects directly opposed to what we intend to accomplish through them. Two of Foucault's better known historical examples of this dynamic illustrate the point. In *Discipline and Punish* he studied eighteenth- and nineteenth-century penal reforms, where he found a contradiction between the content of discourse and its effects. Foucault opens the book by juxtaposing an account of the torture and dismemberment of the regicide Damiens in 1757 with the daily regimen for a house of reform eighty years later. These symbols are readily reconciled with the standard account of penal reform: that things were bad and got better. The methods and language of the reformers suggest only a humane desire to reorganize the penal system, basing it upon rehabilitation rather than spectacles of torture and punishment. Foucault argued, however, that beneath its laudable goals and rhetoric, the reform was a refinement and expansion of the exercise of power that corrected the inefficiencies of the previous model whereby the sovereign's will was imposed on the masses. The very language of "reforming the individual" was part of a civilization-wide creation of the individual that made possible a program of disciplinary monitoring that spread beyond the prison walls to factories, schools, and homes. In all of these, individuals could be monitored and dossiers could be compiled on their performance and behavior. Rather than decreasing repression, the reformer's discourse was part of an explosive extension of social control.

Similarly, in the first volume of *The History of Sexuality*, Foucault argued that the distinction frequently drawn between the repression of the Victorian era and the supposed sexual freedom of the present ignored a similar contradiction. He suggested that our open discourse of sexuality, far from being a manifestation of freedom, is in fact a form of confessional coercion that denies us the ruses afforded by silence. Celebrations of contemporary sexual openness ignore the omnipresent imperative that we make our "sex speak."[16] Our open sexual discourse is not about pleasure, excess, or hedonistic freedom; it is yet another manifestation of the construction of the self-monitoring individual. As these examples show, the effects of discourse are not a direct function of content, because discourse is constructed and constrained by underlying structures, practices, and power relations in culture. We cannot assume that what our statements *do* is consistent with what they *say*. It is this notion of practice—as social actions that have a profound power to form us as persons in ways in which we are not aware—that this book will use.[17]

Foucault provides two important insights for our attempt to understand the ways in which consumer culture transforms religion: the materiality of discourse and its relation to power. By bracketing meaning, Foucault's discourse analysis is able to attend to the materiality of discourse, the ways in which it is deployed and functions in culture. Discourse need not be internally consistent or coherent in order to have important effects. This alerts us to the fact that elements of the Christian tradition are often appropriated or employed in ways that work counter to their interior logic. Furthermore the notion of the changing rules of discursive regimes suggests that even when elements of a tradition are coherent among themselves, the structure of the new regime may make them function in ways fundamentally opposed to the meanings they bear. The key to addressing such situations lies not in calling for greater consistency or retrieving meanings (tasks with which theology is familiar) but in attending to the structures, institutions, and practices whereby a given religious tradition is reenacted. Thus, we will need to consider how the underlying structures and practices of consumer culture transform the function of Christian symbols and practices.

The second great contribution of Foucault to our question has a similar pedigree. It is found in precisely that aspect of his thought that is most often excoriated: his Nietzschean contamination of truth with power. While there is an extensive scholarly critique of this aspect of his thought, a caricature of it has a broader influence. Foucault and those who employ his methods are dismissed for reducing all knowledge to power, thus rendering their own arguments (and criticisms of them) futile. Foucault was not particularly eager to alleviate the anxieties of his critics in this regard, but he clearly rejected the simplistic reduction of knowledge to power.[18] Foucault sought not to identify the two but to explore their relation. In so doing, he disrupted comforting dichotomies that ensconce reason, freedom, and meaning in a placid realm beyond the agonistic struggles of history. Herein lies the value of his genealogical perspective for exploring the effects of consumer culture on religious belief and practice: it helps us avoid the temptation to set aside or sacralize cherished concepts, practices, and traditions (e.g., authenticity, personalism, countercultural communities, gospel values, proper ontologies, and so on) as immune to the contaminations of this culture. Deprived of the false comfort of these options, we can develop an analysis of the ways in which Christian faith and practice are affected by consumer culture.

RELIGION AND CULTURE

Kathryn Tanner has engaged such concerns about culture from a specifically theological perspective. Her analysis provides a number of insights and questions relevant to theology's relation to culture and to the roles of meaning and structure in culture. Her reflections on whether religious communities constitute proper cultures help clarify the relation between Christianity and consumer culture.[19]

Tanner reviews postmodern critiques of modern anthropological assumptions that culture is a coherent set of meanings that consistently inform social practices. Modern conceptions of culture, such as Geertz's, have come under heavy criticism for projecting onto culture the anthropologist's need to find a coherent order. The ethnographer's project of writing a text describing a given culture freezes a living, developing culture in a snapshot where historical processes such as internal conflicts and external influences cannot appear. Cultures are seldom unified, coherent, self-contained units. Similar metaphors, such as culture as "language" or "grammar," are misleading as well. These oversimplify the relation between cultural meanings and social practices, reducing agency to a matter of application. However problematic it may be to assume that such cultures existed in the past, this "integrated" ideal of culture is an increasingly unlikely occurrence. Cultures today and in the future are more likely than ever to be marked by mixture, change, and conflict, as geographical boundaries that allowed previous cultures to develop somewhat independently of others are increasingly weakened.[20]

Contemporary anthropology emphasizes the unsettled and dynamic character of cultures. The influence of culture on social practice is always in process. Consistent with the postmodern emphasis on the polysemy of texts and thus the importance of interpretation, culture "produces meaning through the struggle over the definition of signifying forms—a struggle that conveys the sense people make of history in their desires to preserve, alter, or revolt against the terms in which it appears to them."[21] The relation between culture and social practices is not something that an observer can simply "read off" the culture itself; it is something that is determined and constantly contested in the actions of social agents within that culture. These more recent descriptions of culture attempt to balance previous emphases on cultural stability and coherence with attention to change, hybridity, conflict, and process. If modern conceptions of culture focused on culture as an ordered system of meanings informing social practices, postmodern ones counter that the relevance of cultural meanings for social practices is a constantly shifting affair. Meanings inform practices only insofar as agents employ them in their actions.

Tanner finds that the modern conception of culture appears "repeatedly in contemporary discussion of a surprisingly large range of theological questions."[22] Theology frequently presumes that the beliefs, symbols, and practices of the believing community are a culture in this modern sense. When theology conceives of itself as theoretical reflection on Christian culture, it assumes that the implicit theological rules can be read off of Christian social practices. But in reality, the "cultural dimension of a whole way of life never offers of itself the sort of clarity and consistency that academic theology pursues." As a result, the very act of analysis is itself already an exercise in *poesis*. When theologians "try to dig underneath the messy surface of Christian practice" to find meaning and order, they are often enough producing their own idealized order.[23] Just as the genre of ethnography informs the culture being studied, so the disciplinary requirements of theology inform the theologian's presumptions about Christian culture. Christian culture is presumed to be logically coherent among its various beliefs and to consistently apply them to its social practices. The subject position of the theologian is, of course, different from that of the anthropologist. The theologian does not claim to write as an outsider, but as an authoritative insider. Thus, theologians also expect to find incoherence and inconsistency between Christian beliefs and practices. When these inconsistencies are discovered, it is the task of theology to correct them in order to bring Christian social practices in line with a coherent set of Christian beliefs.

Other criticisms of the modern anthropological conception of culture apply to its theological use. Christian communities are marked by the same instabilities that postmodern anthropologists find in other cultures. They too are marked as much by change as by continuity, as much by disagreement as by harmony, and as much by conflict as by order. Above all, however, Christian communities fail to conform to the anthropological ideal of a self-contained, coherent culture. As much as Christian communities may wish to define themselves over against the outside world, the line between the two is enormously difficult to draw. As Francis Schüssler Fiorenza notes in a similar vein, the "overlapping of traditions and horizons is neglected by a view of Christianity that isolates Christian traditions from modern traditions, as if they were polar opposites, or that regards Christian traditions in isolation from other religious traditions, as is sometimes done in the writings of George Lindbeck, John Milbank and Stanley Hauerwas."[24] Tanner argues that Christian communities simply do not function as complete cultures. They inevitably borrow much of their worldview, structures, and practices from the culture around them. Even the most geographically isolated sectarian communities borrow their language, dress, gestures, kinship relations, and so on, from other cultures. This is true not only for contemporary Christianity but also for its earliest forms. There is no original, pure form of Christianity. Syncretism and cultural mixture mark it from the beginning. Even practices that would seem to be unique to a given form of Christianity, such as not eating meat on Fridays, depend on broader culture for their significance. Friday abstinence stood out well in the meat-and-potatoes days of mid-twentieth-century America. When it is practiced today, it is less conspicuous because of changes in American cuisine. It would function utterly differently in a predominantly vegetarian culture, where the distinctive Christian practice would be consuming meat Saturday through Thursday. Rather than speak of a distinctive Christian culture, taking a cue from the postmodern anthropological emphasis on process, Tanner prefers to speak of this "Christian parasitism" as a distinctive set of "operations" that Christians carry out on the cultures in which they dwell. "Christian practices are always the practices of others made odd."[25] Christian theological discourse rearticulates and uses the contents of broader culture such as marriage or child-rearing in a way that gives them its own "spin."[26]

Tanner's discussion of the difficulty of classifying Christianity as a culture is relevant to our project in a variety of ways. Much of our concern will be with the ways that consumer culture erodes the stability of religious traditions. Her account of culture cautions against a nostalgia for a lost moment of cultural coherence when Christianity organically informed the social practices of believers. Concern about the erosions of commodification does not, however, require us to posit an earlier time when Christianity functioned as a coherent and consistent culture. Consumerism joins the many other cultural dynamisms—nationalisms, ethnic identities, colonial domination, and class divisions—that have encumbered and encompassed Christian communities' attempts to live their faith and continue to do so. Although we will analyze religious traditions and communities in cultural terms, we will not presume that they form coherent cultural wholes, either at present or in the past.

Tanner redirects our attention to another source of difficulty. The problem is not that some coherent, holistic Christian culture has been shattered but that believers practice and use Christian doctrines and symbols in a way that prevents them from influencing their everyday social practices. They are instead engaged with habits of interpretation and use drawn from consumer culture which treat cultural objects as consumable decoration for the preexisting structures of everyday life. If Tanner's analysis redirects our search for the problem, it also directs us toward a solution. Stemming the tide of the commodification of culture must involve addressing the ways that believers use and practice what they draw from their religious traditions.

A WORKING MODEL OF CULTURE

We began our discussion of culture by noting that a strictly meaning-based conception was misleading for understanding the problems posed by consumer culture because it could not address how the function of meanings changes in such a setting. The genealogical account of culture used by Asad and Foucault provided a way to think about how cultural meanings function within structures of power and practices that work largely below the level of awareness. To this, Tanner's review of postmodern anthropological conceptions of culture brought a different notion of practice, one that emphasized culture as a system of processes in which individuals and groups employ meanings to serve their needs and goals in a somewhat intentional manner. Throughout these various revisions, meaning has remained a fundamental part of culture, but one that is situated within other cultural dynamics. Humans locate themselves in the world through meanings and engage meanings in their action, but this engagement is seldom transparent and straightforward. Our analysis of the fate of religion within consumer culture will have to pay attention precisely to this gap, to these misdirections in human engagements with meanings. If cultural action is not simply a matter of the direct application of meanings to practice, then theology must consider the specific ways in which meanings are related to practice in consumer culture.

Wendy Griswold offers a sociological model of culture that is helpful for focusing our attention in this regard. Griswold speaks of a "cultural diamond" that consists of four interconnected elements. Each impacts the other. The model is communicative. It considers the various factors at work in the relation between cultural creators and cultural receivers. The first element is the "cultural creator." This includes not just individual agents but the organizations, institutions, and infrastructures that produce and distribute cultural objects. Thus, it includes not just script writers but the entire system of film production and distribution. Or in religious terms, not just the church leader or the theologian but the whole of a religious community's system of communicating and inculcating its doctrine. "Cultural objects" are the symbols, beliefs, values, and practices that are communicated and received. Griswold defines them as "shared significance embodied in form."[27] Although they are distinct objects, as bearers of significance they relate to broader cultural systems of meaning. Status as a properly cultural object depends on the object's being understood in relation to such systems of meaning. Thus, a quilt only becomes a proper cultural object when, in addition to being used as means of warmth, it is considered as a work of craft within a particular tradition.

The relation between cultural objects and broader systems of meaning is, obviously, not something an object accomplishes itself. The relation depends on the activity of both creators and receivers. Authors work from a particular context toward particular goals and with a particular audience in mind. The intentional creation of a cultural object does not, however, completely define its meaning. "Receivers" are active as well. In order for cultural objects to function as bearers of meaning they must be interpreted and correlated with a broader horizon of meaning. The receivers that do this may or may not be the intended audience and therefore may interpret the object within a context that the author did not foresee and put it to uses the author did not intend. The agency of the authors and receivers implies the fourth point of Griswold's cultural diamond—the "social world."

The social world is the aspect of culture with which we will be most concerned in this book because this is precisely what changes in consumer culture. The change is not in the content of beliefs but in the way in which they are disseminated, interpreted, and practiced. Theology is familiar with thinking about the changes of interpretation that arise from historical distance. Griswold's sociological account helps us better consider the impact of changes in communication structures and interpretive practices. We will consider four factors that constitute the social world of a cultural object: the horizon of its production, the authority given its creator, the infrastructures through which it is shared, and the practices of interpretation and use by which it is engaged.

The social world is implicit in the origins of a cultural object. The creator fashions a cultural object from the elements of one or more cultural archives or traditions, composed of symbols, narratives, beliefs, and practices. These provide the material with which she works, as well as the motivations and goals toward which she aims. The object has its intended meaning within this cultural horizon. Here we cross over from the social world's presence in the creation of an object to its role in its reception. A cultural object's effects are not confined to its intended audience and use. Ideas, texts, and symbols cannot be easily controlled. They may spread and have impacts far beyond that intended by their creators. As they live on in history, they may outlive the cultural horizon in which they were produced. Thus, their meaning changes as they are associated with different constellations of beliefs and put to unforeseen uses.

The social world is also implicit in the social location of the cultural creator. Different positions (pope, theologian, popular author) bring different senses of authority, goals, and rules of proceeding. Papal statements make certain assumptions about warrants and argumentation that theologians do not, and vice versa. These assumptions appear in the process of reception as much as creation. Closely related to this is the system of distribution or communication infrastructure through which the cultural object is shared with others. Papal encyclicals and popular books on spirituality are disseminated through very different channels. Cultural receivers' approaches to these cultural objects are highly informed by the channels through which they receive them. An article in a professional journal invites critical and skeptical engagement. A book on spirituality encountered while browsing at a chain bookstore with a cup of coffee in one hand elicits a more casual response.

One of the defining characteristics of consumer culture is comercially produced culture. Our concern in this book will not be primarily with the quality of the content that is marketed. Both the Frankfurt school's criticisms of the banality of "mass culture" and theological, scholarly, and pastoral exhortations for openness to the potential cultural and religious profundity of "popular culture" have their validity. We will use the term "corporate cultural production" not in the Frankfurt sense of an industry devoted to disseminating a particularly mind-numbing content, but to designate its significance as a vast infrastructure for the distribution and marketing of cultural objects. This encompasses the range of modern media: newspapers and magazines, film, radio, music, television, the Internet, and so on. This infrastructure is global in scale and is increasingly replacing previous communications infrastructures from state and public media to religious infrastructures such as denominational presses and even the communications systems of specific religious institutions. In addition to replacing formal institutional systems of communication, the infrastructure of corporate cultural production has become a deeply rooted part of our socialization processes over the past several generations in the United States and elsewhere. The culture industries divide us into age cohorts and subcultures that become fundamental to our identity.

The notion of "cultural object" as an analytic category is problematic. For all its emphasis on the relation of a given object to a cultural horizon, this theoretical perspective may presume the fragmentation of cultural and religious traditions into discrete objects. From a sociological perspective Mike Featherstone expresses anxiety about the erosion of religious systems into tool kits of "cultural resources" that individuals use willy-nilly. He fears that this compromises the classical sociological functions of religion to provide social cohesion and to address "core existential questions."[28] Theological anxieties are even more profound. To speak of Christianity as a collection of cultural objects that are engaged by subjects within a social setting may be about as literal an instance as can be imagined of John Milbank's concern about theology being positioned by secular reason.[29] My fascination with this problem is no doubt reinforced by such theoretical perspectives, but its origins lie in repeated experiences of the disconnect between belief and practice. If we are to understand the fate of religious belief and practice in a consumer culture we must employ an analysis that can consider the various factors that influence the social function of religious symbols, beliefs, and practices. As we shall see, such a theoretical perspective will enable us to think about the factors that insulate the practice of everyday life from being impacted by religious beliefs. The ideas of Griswold and the other sociological and materialist analyses employed in this study provide a way to think of how this is happening: how the elements of religious traditions—beliefs, symbols, and practices—are fragmented in consumer culture; how they are lifted from their traditional contexts and thrown into a cultural marketplace where they can be embraced enthusiastically but not put into practice.

An example of the problems posed by the rise of corporate cultural production can be found in the question: What happens when a papal text is engaged in the setting of Barnes and Noble? The current pope is prolific. Not only are the number and length of his encyclicals unprecedented, but he has also written mass-market books in an attempt to reach a broader, popular audience. *Crossing the Threshold of Hope* sat piled alongside other best-sellers in chain bookstores—near the writings not only of the Dalai Lama but also of Tom Clancy and V. C. Andrews. This example embodies one of the fundamental concerns of this book. The social world includes the interpretive habits and dispositions of cultural receivers. For the majority of people in advanced capitalist societies (the United States, Europe, Japan, and others) and for the middle and upper classes just about everywhere else, these habits and dispositions are now formed by the consumption of commercial popular culture. The interpretive habits fostered by commercial popular culture are tailored to its project of marketing consumable cultural commodities. This project is fundamentally different from the goals of other communities—religious and not. Of course those goals are too diverse to be reduced to a tidy summary, but there are several goals common to traditional cultures that do not match those of corporate cultural production. They are more interested in stability and continuity than in sheer volume of production and distribution. That is to say, although they may engage in massive projects of propaganda and indoctrination, these projects remain mere means to the more fundamental goal of maintaining continuity on the level of society, institutions, and culture. Franciscan and Dominican preachers, Jesuit missionaries, and Methodist circuit riders are certainly involved in massive forms of cultural dissemination, but they do so not simply for sake of such activity in itself, but to counter perceived threats to orthodoxy, to bring the gospel message to those who have not heard it or who need assistance in living it, and so on. Corporate cultural production has no goal beyond profiting as much as possible from the goods it can distribute.

The rules for interpretive practices involve questions of both *who* may engage in such activities and *how* they may do it. Our task in the next three chapters will be to consider how consumer culture transforms both of these aspects of interpretive practices. Both are important. For a variety of reasons, consumer culture involves a great expansion in *who* may exercise cultural agency. It constructs every person as the author of his or her own identity, expressed aesthetically through the consumption and display of commodities. This shallow understanding of agency is tied to a more profound one. Consumer culture accompanies an explosion in literacy and, more recently, in technologies that make it possible for the masses not only to consume culture but to produce and share it as well. This eruption of agency poses a fundamental challenge to the more carefully controlled systems of authorization and production in religious traditions such as Catholicism. I will argue that the positive potential of this aspect of consumer culture must be taken seriously. There is nothing intrinsically wrong with broad cultural agency. The problem in consumer culture arises with the question of *how* people exercise this agency—that is, with the interpretive habits and dispositions it instills. We will see that consumer culture encourages a shallow engagement with the elements of religious traditions because we are trained to engage beliefs, symbols, and practices as abstract commodities that are readily separable from their traditional contexts. The cost of this form of engagement is that when elements of religious cultures are deprived of their interconnections with one another and of their ties to particular communal practices, our interpretations and applications of them become less likely to impact our own practice of life. They are reduced to shallow bricolage, not because such popular cultural production is necessarily shallow, but because members of consumer cultures encounter cultural objects shorn of their connections to traditions and communities and are trained by their consumption of commodified culture to treat them in a shallow manner.

This book will use the term "consumer culture" to refer to these cultural habits of use and interpretation that are derived from the consumption of commodified cultural objects. We will not use the term to refer to a specific culture. These habits and operations are present in the cultures of many advanced capitalist societies. Despite sharing these characteristics, England, Japan, Sweden, and the United States remain distinct cultures. These habits are properly cultural because they are instilled through a process of socialization and inform people's relationship to cultural material. We will distinguish it from two related terms: "consumerism" and "consumer society." Consumerism is the most general term. It refers simply to the high levels of consumption in advanced capitalist societies and the great significance and importance that it is given in these societies. Consumerism speaks of the fact that consumption is profoundly overdetermined, but it does not imply any particular explanation for this fact. The term "consumer society" more directly addresses this concern. Consumer societies are societies in which consumption plays an important role in establishing social identity and solidarity. These tend to be marked by high levels of consumerism because the consumption of commodities is linked to such fundamental social functions. This concept will play an important role in our analysis of the political significance of consumption in chapter 5. The bulk of our reflections, however, will focus on consumer culture as an analysis of how the habits and dispositions formed in consumption of material and cultural commodities can spread and colonize other dimensions of human life. Thus, it is essential for answering our question: How do religious faith and practice change in consumer cultures?

CONCLUSION

This chapter has discussed how to consider the relation between religion and consumer culture. It rejected a simple contrast between the two based on an understanding of culture that focused solely on meanings or values: consumer culture proposes one set of values, Christianity another. Such an approach cannot attend to the changes the take place in consumer culture concerning *how* people relate to cultural meanings and values. We supplemented such a meaning-centered approach to culture with one that took more seriously the role of nonintentional aspects of culture: power relations, structures, and practices. This provides a way to conceive of how the practices of consumer culture may reorient the meanings of a given religious tradition, rendering our most heartfelt acts of religious avowal incapable of transforming the practice of our daily lives. Kathryn Tanner's and Wendy Griswold's analyses provide an emphasis on process and agency in culture. Cultural meanings are related to practices only insofar as groups and individuals apply them. Thus, although our theological enthusiasm for meaning is chastened, meanings remain a fundamental, although not determinative, aspect of culture.

In our analysis of religion and consumer culture, we will think of religious traditions as akin to but not identical to proper cultures. Religious traditions consist of religious beliefs, symbols, values, and practices. The meanings of the cultural objects that constitute traditions are rooted in their interrelations. These systematic interrelations and coherences are familiar territory for theology. Religious traditions also consist of particular institutions and practices that relate beliefs and symbols to the practice of daily life. This less familiar territory is the focus of this book. We must explore how consumer culture transforms religious belief and practice by transforming the way that people avow, interpret, and employ the beliefs, symbols, values, and practices of their religious traditions.

Our analysis will be undertaken in two stages. In the next chapter, we will consider the rise of consumer culture and how it shapes the relation between beliefs and practice. We will use various marxist accounts of the rise of commodification and its effects on culture. Then in chapters 3 and 4, we will apply this perspective to contemporary changes in religious practices. This stage of the analysis will emphasize how changes in the social world impact the way we engage cultural objects. For that reason, it will downplay the active agency of consumers and will tend toward a rather pessimistic, if disturbingly illuminative, account of commodification as decline. In chapters 5 and 6, in order to balance the analysis, we will turn to a fuller consideration of the agency of cultural receivers. We will consider how, within the constraints placed upon them by consumer culture, consumers still exercise meaningful cultural creativity in their consumption, including their "consumption" of religious cultural objects.

CHAPTER 2

The Commodification of Culture

NOW THAT WE HAVE DEFINED AN APPROACH TO CULTURE THAT ADDRESSES the complex ways in which religious belief and practice can be influenced by consumer culture, we can now consider specific accounts of the cultural shifts that accompany the rise of consumer capitalism. This chapter will consider various cultural dynamisms, structures, and practices of consumer culture that emerged in the twentieth century. The most important of these is the commodification of culture, a process in which the habits and dispositions learned in the consumption of literal commodities spread into our relationships with culture. This results in the liquidation of cultural traditions whereby the elements they comprise (beliefs, symbols, practices, and so on) are abstracted from their traditional contexts and engaged as free-floating signifiers, put to decorative uses far removed from their original references and connections with other beliefs and practices. This is the central problem consumer culture poses for theology. When beliefs are readily embraced in abstraction from their traditional references and contexts, it is less likely that they will impact the concrete practice of life.

We will attempt to balance broad theoretical accounts of the cultural dynamics of commodification with more detailed accounts of particular economic arrangements. These "hard" materialist portions of the analysis are important; they highlight how cultural shifts are rooted in concrete structures—the way people work, obtain food, and live together (or apart). Otherwise we will be left with broad materialist accounts of the inexorable unfolding of the logic of the commodity fetish or even broader idealist accounts of the errors in thought or belief implicit in our current forms of life. Such cultural critiques, while valuable for highlighting what is wrong, are much less helpful for mapping a path to a better form of life, especially in consumer culture, where ideas are so easily abstracted from practice. Our attention to the nitty-gritty materialist details of these cultural shifts will be better able to guide a response by (1) calling attention to the ways in which the structures of everyday life form us in certain ethically, politically, and religiously significant ways, and (2) providing a map of the places where such unwitting formation is taking place so that such influences may be more consciously resisted.

We will consider Marx's account of alienation and the commodity fetish in relation to various accounts of the "Fordist" era of capitalism, which dominated the Western capitalist societies in the middle third of the twentieth century. This will link consumerism to particular forms of labor and the structure of the single-family home and give us many of the most critiqued aspects of consumerism: inefficient mass consumption, selfish individualism, political passivity and disengagement, and so forth. We will focus in particular on the rise of the single-family home and pay careful attention to how this institution transforms our relationship with cultural traditions.

We will then turn to more detailed critiques of the shape of capitalist society and culture during the latter half of the century, such as those of Henri Lefebvre, Guy Debord, Jean Baudrillard, and Fredric Jameson. These critics describe how commodification colonizes more and more of life. Cultural symbols and beliefs become increasingly shallow, free-floating postmodern signifiers. We will correlate these theoretical critiques with the particular shape of global capitalism that began to emerge in the mid-1970s, an economic system characterized by greater flexibility regarding labor, capital investment, and production. Fordist era economic growth was fueled by replacing the traditional production of the home with mass-produced items. As this path of growth became ever more saturated, mass production and marketing were replaced by a different strategy that was better suited to this "post-Fordist" era. Instead of pushing corporate production into the domestic sphere, post-Fordist expansion is driven by tying ever more aspects of existence to consumption. This required not mass markets but sophisticated market segmentation, so that products could be tailored and marketed to ever smaller niche markets to provide for every possible lifestyle. Post-Fordism coincides with the explosion of electronic media such as cable television and the Internet. This quantum increase in bandwidth required ever more "content" for marketing. As a result more and more culture is drawn into corporate cultural production and people are increasingly formed to engage culture with the same habits they employ in consuming the commercial popular culture.

COMMODIFICATION

The first general theoretical approach to the topic of consumerism we will consider can be termed "productivist." It considers the practice of consumption as an effect of the economic system of production in which it takes place. While such an approach is in danger of falling into a "crude, one-sided economistic" analysis, which reduces the complexities of human culture to a reflex or superstructure of the economy, it is nonetheless essential for any adequate analysis of consumerism. The issue, as we conceive it, arises in cultures influenced by capitalism. Consumption is necessary for modern capitalism, "for the simple and obvious reason that, unless products could be sold in return for money, there would be no profits."[1]

A productivist approach characterizes thinkers as diverse as the Frankfurt social theorists, the economist John Kenneth Galbraith, and the theorist of the postmodern Fredric Jameson. While, as the examples suggest, these approaches are diverse, they share common emphases. First and most obviously, they give great consideration to the interests of manufacturers, the wiles of marketers, and the increasing variety of things that can be bought and sold. They also share a set of concerns that—to use the vocabulary of some—can be grouped under the heading of "alienation." Each presumes some form of "authentic" existence or "true" need against which consumer behavior can be evaluated. This provides the basis for a critical evaluation of the false or artificial desires and needs that are elicited in consumer capitalism.

Although he was not the first to view human culture this way, Karl Marx is undoubtedly the seminal thinker for the productivist approach. Although his work has been endlessly criticized from both the right and the left, his reflections on "alienation" and the commodity as "fetish" remain touchstones for productivist critiques of consumerism. His materialist analysis will help us to see how, despite the ease with which we can associate consumerism with problematic values, it is deeply rooted in a particular form of human labor as well as in the ways we meet our most fundamental needs such as food, clothing, and shelter.

Alienation

Marx's notion of alienation is a central concept in his critique of the cultural consequences of capitalism that takes us immediately to a consideration of structures and practices. It has several related but distinct meanings.[2] The most fundamental of these is the systematic alienation of men and women from their creative power as human beings. It is the root of Marx's understanding of how false consciousness keeps the proletariat from realizing their revolutionary power by systematically depriving them of a sense of their own power and agency. Alienation is driven by two concrete economic factors. The first, "objectification," is quite simple. It concerns the legal status of the goods that workers produce. In preindustrial economies, craftsmen were the owners of the work they produced and were free to dispose of it as they chose (within the often dire economic conditions). In the capitalist system, the product of the worker's labor belongs not to the laborer but to the employer. This brings about the second aspect of alienation— the estrangement of workers from self-realization in their labor. Because they do not own the products of their labor, the relation between effort and creativity is shattered. Labor is reduced to time and energy exchanged for wages. This is accelerated by the progressive "deskilling" brought about by industrialization and the division of labor. Engineers and managers take over the design of products and the manufacturing process, further sundering laborers from creative involvement in their work. Marx termed the resulting form of labor "external labor," which does not belong to the worker's "essential being." The worker therefore "only feels himself outside his work, and in his work feels outside himself." Such labor is under-taken only out of necessity or because of force; it is a "labor of self-sacrifice, of mortification."[3] The wage labor system systematically masks the workers' creative power. Labor becomes drudgery.

This loss of meaning and potential for self-realization has been the topic of extensive criticism by commentators ranging from John Ruskin and William Morris to Peter Maurin, Jacques Ellul, and John Paul II. Our primary concern here is its relation to commodification and the rise of consumerism. These dynamics of alienation combine to create consumption as we know it today in two ways. The first of these is the wage system of labor. Individuals work for wages in order to pay for their essential needs—food, shelter, clothing. This is an inevitable conse-quence of any highly specialized division of labor that must be evaluated in tan-dem with the prosperity brought by specialization. Nevertheless, there is a second, deeper dynamic at work here. Alienated labor is undertaken only because it is nec-essary to fulfill the worker's basic needs for survival. Humans have always sought to fulfill these needs, but under this system their exertions are sundered from the direct fulfillment of their needs, achieving that only indirectly through exchange. Thus, the understanding of human needs becomes increasingly passive. Marx argued that this eroded the nobility of human needs, reducing them to brute, ani-mal desires.[4] Elaborate rituals of planting, harvest, preparation, and sharing are stripped to their elemental form, reduced to the crude consumption of purchased foodstuffs. The same flattening affects other central human needs such as cloth-ing, shelter, and reproduction.

The shallow conception of human needs that characterizes consumerism is therefore tied to a particular practice of labor and not simply to an inadequate conception of what is good. This is important because if these values arise from a particular form of labor, they cannot be adequately addressed by compelling counterarguments or passionate preaching. They are reinforced daily as people expend themselves in their work. (Of course, not all labor is so alienated. Although the quest for a "meaningful" career is certainly one of the cruel chimeras of con-temporary capitalist ideology, many occupations—from the helping professions to service employees such as bus drivers and educators—retain an explicitly social referent that militates against alienation.) Insofar as industrial laborers, post-industrial service workers, and white collar office workers pour their lives into alienated labor, they will be inclined to seek just the sorts of shallow fulfillments that consumerism provides. This account also suggests that there is more to our myths of domesticity than a cover for selfish consumption. It is the one place where we readily find nonalienated labor without going to look for it (with obvi-ous caveats concerning gender inequalities).

Now, let us turn to a second portion of Marx's analysis: the commodity fetish. This will take us from a consideration of the ways in which we engage the world through our labor to the ways in which we meet our needs for food, shelter, and clothing.

The Commodity Fetish

Marx believed that the commodity contains the form of life of capitalism in germ.[5] Understanding it is, however, a difficult task. At first glance commodities seem simple enough. They are valuable objects that are exchanged. Marx argued that the very obviousness of their value, which we so take for granted, was in fact quite mysterious. Indeed, to understand a commodity's value one must penetrate its "religious fog." Marx's understanding of the commodity rests upon a fundamental distinction between "use value" and "exchange value." He considered the former to be "clear as noon day."[6] For millennia, humankind has fashioned things for use from the materials at its disposal. Marx offered the example of a table: fashioned from wood to serve a specific purpose. As long as it is made for use, its value is easily understood: it provides a stable surface at the necessary height, and so forth.[7] For our concerns, it is important merely to note that, when an object is evaluated according to use value, there is a fundamental continuity between the "essence" of an object—its social function—and its appearance in use value. This continuity is ruptured when an object is produced for exchange.[8]

A profound transformation takes place in the table once it is produced for exchange rather than for use by its maker. "It not only stands with its feet on the ground, but, in relation to all other commodities, it stands on its head, and evolves out of its wooden brain grotesque ideas far more wonderful" than if it were to begin dancing of its own free will.[9] The commodity appears to us as intrinsically valuable, when in fact its true value is dependent on a number of factors that do not appear with it. In addition to its use value, the commodity's value depends on an economic system in which commodities can be exchanged and on the labor that produced it. These sources of value, however, do not appear in the commodity. They are obscured by the aura of self-evident value. Marx termed this the "commodity fetish." He described it using language evoking idolatry. Objects of imagination appear to us as "independent beings endowed with life" that enter "into relation both with one another and with the human race."[10] We are duped into locating value in the commodity itself rather than in the human needs that drive exchange, the social systems that allow exchange to take place, or the labor necessary to produce them. We are trained to locate value in the appearance of the commodity, in abstraction from these other factors. This habit of abstraction has profound consequences.

The presumption built into the commodity, that things are valued in exchange, was evident in some people's response to the Y2K crisis. At the end of 1999, many of those most fascinated with the impending end of civilization prepared for the event by withdrawing cash from their bank accounts. People obsessed with the imminent collapse of civilization went on assuming that greenbacks would hold their value. The commodity, it seems, can survive the end of the world. The example clarifies the nature of commodity fetishization. It is not simply that we are deluded into valuing what is valueless, but that we tend to misplace value—which arises within a certain social system—onto the things themselves. Exchange value is real value, but it exists only within the system that makes exchange possible and in relation to the concrete needs that drive exchange. Commodity fetishization inclines us to mistakenly attribute the value of the object to its appearance, to "*naturalize* a *social* process."[11] Thus, it is no surprise that Federal Reserve notes would seem capable of surviving the collapse of the government that issues them.

Our consumption of commodities trains us to presume the hidden social agreement: that all things will be valued in exchange. Labor, deprived of its meaning in sustaining the community, is reduced to the production of objects for exchange and, eventually, to the exchange of portions of one's life for wages. Our very lives become objects of exchange. In Guy Debord's words, Marx sensed a fundamental shift in the mode of human existence from "being" to "having."[12] We will call this progressive dynamic "commodification."

Commodity logic is insidious. It preinterprets dimensions of our existence that we consider separate from economic calculus. I once overheard a young man's response to a criticism of his fiancée's appearance. In defense of his *choice* of spouse, he noted the many other things that she offered: intelligence, psychological depth, compatibility, companionship, and so on. While these are likely better measures of a potential spouse than appearance, the response shared with the challenge the same crass logic of exchange. Physical attractiveness and psychological compatibility are of course perennial factors in romantic desire, but this logic transforms them. Love is reduced to a calculus of maximum returns, relationships to an exchange of emotional commodities, persons to things. It is not a question of consciously choosing such evaluative criteria. This logic is our cultural default, the form in which we are most likely to cast our deliberations. The question of why we love someone is reflexively translated into a question about what we love about them.

The second element of commodity abstraction has equally profound consequences. The commodity hides the conditions of its production. In contrast to systems where social relations were more explicit, in capitalist societies, "producers do not come into social contact until they exchange their products," thus "the specific social character of each producer's labor does not show itself except in the act of exchange."[13] Value appears only in exchange, in relation to other commodities. We can see how the fascination with things, the tendency to fetishize them as intrinsically valuable is a function of this system of exchange. Since their value appears only in the moment of exchange, "a definite social relation between men ... assumes, in their eyes, the fantastic form of a relation between things."[14] This provides a deeper insight into the workings of abstraction. The tendency to locate value in things, in their appearance, is a function of this system of exchange, in which the conditions of a product's manufacture (who produced it, under what conditions, using what resources, and so on) simply do not appear. The commodity appears naked in the marketplace, shorn of all the communal references that would give it meaning. As Sut Jhally argues, this systematic evacuation of meaning provides the void that advertising fills. This way of perceiving the value of things based on shallow appearances easily overruns the banks of commerce and floods into our cultural hermeneutics. It is implicated in our comfort with consuming fragments of cultures abstracted from their "conditions of production"—the traditions and institutions in which they have their coherent meanings and are connected to a particular way of life.

The materialism of Marx's analysis is crucial. As wrongheaded or heretical as these cultural tendencies may be, they are rooted in the way we carry out fundamental practices of human existence: feeding, clothing, and sheltering ourselves. A trip to the supermarket trains us in the mental habits of commodification. We choose our food from a vast array of items that compete with each other for our attention. They call to us with their appearance and packaging. Glistening meats and colorful produce are arrayed in a spectacle of plenty. Deeper into the store, manufactured items call out from the shelves with their carefully designed packaging. No salesperson explains their quality and origins; they speak for themselves. There is a profound rhetoric of things here. The commodities offer themselves up to our credulous gaze. But like all seductions, they veil as much as they reveal. The meat in the counter, a paradigm of reduction to passive objectivity, refuses to tell of its origins. Glistening boneless, skinless chicken breasts say nothing of the dangerous production lines on which they are processed. Gleaming filet mignons say nothing of the cow whose loins they were, of the slaughter that was necessary to remove them or of the food and space it took to raise the cow. Was it a high-plains feedlot in the isolated stretches of Nebraska or a field recently slashed and burned from the rainforest in the Amazon basin? Simply gazing at the meat counter trains us in abstraction, in valuing things without asking such questions. How many times do we repeat this practice during our shopping trip? Fifty, a hundred, a thousand times? Certainly more than the number of beads on a rosary. We take these items home for more intense (ritual?) practices. We open, prepare, and consume a can of beans without thought of the calloused hands and stooped backs of the workers who harvested them in the hot sun. We toss kiwis in a balsamic vinaigrette, mindless of the global stretch our salad enacts. These are practices. They form us as we eat, wear clothes, listen to music, sit at a desk, use a computer. They form us to think in a way that shows up in our relationship with culture and with religion. We toss kiwis with balsamic; we believe in resurrection and reincarnation. Our steaks arrive without violence; in the United States we preach endlessly, everywhere, about God's forgiveness of everyone for everything, but this chief doctrine of contemporary Christianity is all but absent from the religiously supersaturated response to September 11. We eat beans from nowhere; more than three-quarters of respondents in a recent survey identify social justice as a necessary requirement for being a "good Catholic," yet fewer than 9 percent report having participated in any organized justice activity in the past year.[15]

Marx's analysis proved prescient—much of what he described did in fact come to pass. For all its illuminative power, however, this account of alienation and commodification remains profoundly abstract. Because of this abstractness, the concept of the commodity fetish is always in danger of being reduced to an evocative trope. Its redolence of idolatry makes it particularly attractive to Christian critics of consumerism. If it is to function in more than an evocative manner in our analysis, we must consider the concrete economic and social events of the twentieth century that brought Marx's dystopian vision to fruition. This analysis will also consider the ways in which the events of the past century went beyond what Marx could imagine.

TWENTIETH-CENTURY CAPITALISM

Marx's account of the alienation of labor and the commodity fetish found concrete historical realization in the shifts that took place in industrial capitalism in the first half of the twentieth century. These shifts gave rise to consumption as we know it today and laid the foundations for the commodification of culture that is a central part of consumer culture. A narrative of labor and consumption runs through the twentieth century. It begins with "Schmidt," whom we will meet shortly as the laborer who loaded tons of pig iron a day but also had the skill and energy to build his own house during mornings and evenings. His home was a center of production as much as consumption. His wife worked as hard as he did: growing a garden, buying only basic foodstuffs, doing most of the preparing and preserving of the food they ate. By mid-century, a very different type of home dominated the American landscape: the suburban single-family home. It was supported almost entirely by wages. Little or no production took place here. The housewife was still given responsibility for its management, but now her energies were devoted to managing consumption. By the end of the century, these gender roles had changed again. Both members of conventional households now work outside the home to provide income to fuel ever-increasing levels of consumption.

Frederick Taylor and Fordism

How did we get from the first type of home to the last? A primary concern for productivist accounts of consumerism is the relation between production and consumption. How do particular forms of production give rise to particular forms of consumption? Various arrangements are possible. They arise from a variety of factors, including technology, culture, and class competition. An enormous shift took place in Western capitalism in the first few decades of the twentieth century. Productive capacity exploded; the types of goods produced changed dramatically; and the nature and degree of consumption were transformed profoundly. Michel Aglietta argues that just before this revolution, "early modern capitalism" was not concerned greatly with the life of the worker. Surplus labor supplies fed by the migration of workers to the industrialized cities enabled workers to be exploited as sources of "absolute surplus value" to be used up and discarded. At this point, production was concentrated on major capital goods—machinery, railways, and the like. Mass production had not yet penetrated far into daily life. The domestic realm was still a significant site of production for shelter, food, clothing, and culture.

Aglietta coined the term "Fordism" to describe the new economic-cultural equilibrium that replaced this earlier form of capitalism.[16] Fordism describes two coincident and related historical shifts in production and consumption. An analysis of the former, the ways in which new technologies and management practices changed the nature of human labor, can help us better understand not only the nature of the shifts in consumption that followed but also why they took place. Our interest in culture will, however, require us to go beyond Aglietta's productivist account to consider the cultural and political factors in this transformation.

The changes in the nature of industrial production that took place at the turn of the century can be conveniently marked by Frederick Taylor's attempts to develop a scientific approach to the management of labor. Taylor brought the disparate reflections on the rational organization of work and the division of labor articulated by classical economists such as Adam Smith and later thinkers of the Industrial Revolution such as Charles Babbage into a systematic approach which he termed "scientific management."[17] The essence of his approach was to divide work into discrete, measurable elements that could be experimentally modified to maximize output. Taylor reads like the inverse of Marx. The reduction of human creativity to "labor power," which Marx so lamented, was axiomatic for Taylor. He deliberately sought to obliterate all legacies of craft labor culture. A scion of a wealthy Philadelphia family, destined to study at Harvard, Taylor rejected his family's plans, scandalously opting for an apprenticeship in machining. After completing this training, he worked as a laborer in a machine shop, quickly advancing to boss of the machining department, at which point he ruthlessly exploited the insider knowledge he had gained in the service of management.[18] He sought to disrupt what he called the "systematic soldiering" of craftsmen working under the piecework system. They held to conventional estimates of what was a reasonable amount of work that could be accomplished in a day and were united in opposing any attempt to increase quotas. Taylor considered any recuperation during the workday beyond the bare necessity required to maintain the maximum work pace to be wasted potential labor. Fighting the productivity conventions of the craft system required fighting the craftsman's status as a skilled expert. Taylor spoke baldly of removing "all possible brain work from the shop."[19] Management would instead gather "all of the traditional knowledge which in the past has been possessed by the workmen" and evaluate and administer it scientifically.[20] For Taylor, not only would this lead to greater efficiencies; it would also prevent the worker from exploiting his own knowledge against the employer, should he or she dis-cover an innovative labor-saving procedure. This system of labor management led to the obliteration not only of craft traditions in the workplace but also of the intellectual and scientific culture that the workers supported. In the middle of the nineteenth century, there were more than 1,200 "Mechanics Institutes" in England with at least 200,000 members.[21] These organizations held lectures and offered courses in science and technology. The great inventors of the industrial revolution were mechanics whose scientific knowledge flowed from their practical knowledge.[22] After the revolution Taylor unleashed, the engineer became the great administrator of this knowledge. This resulted in the progressive intellectual impoverishment of industrial workers. In 1915, a report from a congressional investigation into corporate use of Taylor's principles lamented the decline in the knowledge of the labor pool in just two decades.[23]

This "deskilling" had consequences that went far beyond the shop floor. Combined with the ever more complete exhaustion of the worker's energy in the course of the workday, it helped transform the home from a site of domestic production into a place increasingly dependent on mass consumption. An anecdote from Taylor is fascinating in this regard. It concerns a campaign to quadruple workers' quotas for hand loading "pigs" of iron from 11.5 to 47 tons per day. (The numbers surprised Taylor's contemporaries as well. He offered a detailed explanation of how a worker could indeed carry 1,156 pigs of iron weighing 92 pounds each in the course of a ten-hour workday.)[24] Taylor's description of how he "scientifically" selected a worker who possessed both sufficient strength and sufficient interest in money to abandon traditional work practices gives a glimpse into the lives of workers at the time. He selected "Schmidt," a "little Pennsylvania Dutchman" known to be "exceedingly close" with his money. Taylor was certain of his ability to do additional work during the day because he had "been observed to trot back home for a mile or so after his work in the evening, about as fresh as he was when he came trotting down to work in the morning. We found that . . . he was engaged in putting up the walls of a little house for himself in the morning before starting to work and at night after leaving."[25] For his quadrupled workload, the man received a 60-percent increase in wages. With less of their energy available for domestic labor at the end of the day, industrial workers became increasingly dependent on manufactured goods to maintain their households. Thus, instead of building stone hearths in their free time, they now bought stoves on credit, paying the bills with their wages.

Henry Ford found great success by applying Taylor's system of labor management. Ford's use of Taylor was so influential that scholars speak of "Fordism" to describe the shifts in management and labor practices as well as broader shifts in the relation between industry and labor and in patterns of consumption. In addition to Taylor's management practices, Ford's success relied on technological advances that made the automated production line possible and a new form of labor relations that made labor and management partners in maintaining the stability of the workplace. The automated production line further fragmented and deskilled labor. The rhythm of work was now completely determined by machines. The new alliance between management and labor also led to the epochal rise in living standards and consumption (not the same thing) in Western industrial nations in the postwar period.

Ford's revolution unleashed an explosive growth of productivity. The first plant where he implemented the automatic production line in Highland Park, Michigan, saw a 1,200-percent increase in productivity within four years.[26] As this revolution spread throughout the economy, the vast increase in productive capacity collided with the inertia of cultural habits of consumption. Henry Ford's own values marked this contradiction. He demanded rigorous discipline from his workers, which was enforced by his infamous "Sociological Department" in home visits that documented everything from alcohol use and sexual habits to hygiene and the use of leisure time.[27] Ford's values exemplified Max Weber's Protestant "worldly asceticism," so consonant with the needs of early capitalism—first among the bourgeoisie, then among the workers themselves. Workers who lived up to Ford's demands and were parsimonious with their wages would find their reward in the ownership of one of the cars they produced. The increased efficiency brought by the mass production that Ford championed, however, rendered delayed gratification counterproductive. An excess of productive capacity changed frugality from a virtue to a vice and made consumption a social responsibility. In a 1907 book aptly titled *The New Basis of Civilization*, the economist Simon Nelson Patten opined that "the new morality does not consist in saving, but in expanding consumption."[28] This built upon a shift that had been under way for more than a century. "Consume" in its earliest senses was essentially destructive, as in devour, waste, destroy, exhaust, and so on. Its meaning in English began to shift in the mid-eighteenth century academic discussions of political economy, which used "consumption" as the economic complement to "production."[29]

Fordist Culture

The relation between production and consumption is complex. In good marxist fashion, Aglietta argued that these shifts in production transformed the family, the community, and the law. The nuclear family of parents and children living in their own detached home functions well as the fundamental social unit in a high-consumption society. This living arrangement became the norm, supported by law, and the basic demand for the assimilation of the working class into American culture.[30] Social welfare legislation can be read as a way of ameliorating not only the damage caused by poverty but also the fundamental volatility of the small family unit—for both the families themselves and the consumer economy for which they are an indispensable source of demand. Thus, social welfare programs were one of the tools employed in the maintenance of demand by Keynesian economics.

Inevitably, productivist accounts such as this oversimplify the nature of cultural change, tending to make "highly generalised claims in which the dominant cultural sensibility of a mass-consumption norm is simply 'read off' from the impact of certain material and economic changes in the lives of ordinary people."[31] While the economic precariousness of industrial workers left them little choice but to conform their lives to the revolutions in industrial work, shifts in civilization as massive as those that marked the first half of the twentieth century inevitably have complex cultural and political dimensions.[32] As E. P. Thompson observed concerning the formation of the English working class, "there is no such thing as economic growth which is not, at the same time, growth or change of a culture."[33]

For a variety of reasons, the increased pay and shorter work hours offered by employers such as Ford did not automatically lead to an increase in consumption. Not least among these was the fact that workers continued to live on the edge of poverty. Even significant increases in their wages did not give them the wherewithal to plunge into luxury consumption. Although this problem was addressed somewhat by the rise of consumer credit, there were more intractable cultural obstacles blocking the emergence of mass consumption. Domestic production was as much a set of cultural practices as an economic necessity. Beyond providing nonmarket means of obtaining the necessities of life, these were practices that sustained a form of life. They were cuisine, costume, and dwelling as much as food, clothing, and shelter.

> Indigenous networks of social structure . . . carried premises and values which generated mistrust or open opposition to the corporate monopolization of culture. Traditional family structures, agricultural lifestyles, immigrant values which accounted for a vast percentage of the attitudes of American working classes, and the traditional realms of aesthetic expression—all these were historically infused with an agglomeration of self-sufficiency, communitarianism, localized popular culture, thrift and subjective social bonds and experiences that stood, like Indians, on the frontiers of industrial-cultural development.[34]

Despite the rise of productive capacity, these factors remained an obstacle to the emergence of a high-consumption society and had to be fought on the level of culture. Here we face an instance of what that determined marxist opponent of economic reductionism Antonio Gramsci termed "hegemony"—the processes by which a dominant class elicits the consent of those it dominates. This involves negotiations between various groups within a society (e.g., the Fordist concord between management and labor) as well as dispersed practices, symbols, and ideas (often enough not explicitly political) that support the status quo. In the case of Fordist culture, these ranged from broad evocative concepts such as "progress," "hygiene," "modernism," "automation," and "power" exploited in advertising to the aesthetics of product design.

Stewart Ewen has documented how in the 1920s business leaders and advertisers developed strategies to address these problems systematically. This program required that they be not only "captains of industry" but "captains of consciousness." They challenged the worth of goods produced at home by emphasizing the superior quality and safety of modern methods of production. Concerns about food safety were exploited with advertising references to the "scientifically" monitored and controlled production of prepared foods, which were often enough produced under conditions not significantly cleaner than home kitchens. Standardized products in elaborately sealed containers were presented as inherently superior and safer than homemade foods. Health concerns were similarly exploited by endless cleaning and hygiene products. Ads directly challenged the communitarian social bonds of local culture by portraying isolated individuals whose status was solely dependent on their individual attributes. As a Cutex advertisement put it in 1920: "You will be amazed to find out how many times in one day people glance at your nails. At each glance a judgement is made. . . . Indeed some people make a practice of basing their estimate of a new acquaintance largely upon this one detail."[35] Appearance, hygiene, and comportment were constantly being scrutinized in the marketplaces of employment, society, and relationships. "Each portion of the body was to be viewed critically, as a *potential bauble in a successful assemblage*."[36] The various commodities on offer (from soaps and cosmetics to cars and grammar courses) were offered as solutions to the inadequacies of the self, which had now become the fundamental commodity. Whereas Gramsci emphasized the role of civil society (the family, religion, unions, etc.) in the maintenance of hegemony, Ewen's analysis makes clear that in the twentieth century, many of these functions were coopted by advertising. The hegemony of the Fordist era was not, however, limited to the intentional manipulations of advertisers. It was dispersed aesthetically in the style of industrial design.

The stereotype of Fordist industrial design is, naturally, the Model T, "available in any color you want as long as it's black."[37] There is much truth to the stereotype. The large-scale production of the era depended on standardized design. It is, however, equally misleading. Product design could equally well be described in terms of "Sloanism." Alfred P. Sloan, the head of General Motors, competed with Ford by offering a highly differentiated line of cars available in a range of colors (as were Fords after 1926).[38] In the beginning, mass-produced commodities had to compete with well-entrenched markets for craft-produced objects. As long as the infrastructure of craft (organized and quasi-industrial by this time) production was still intact, industrial producers could not market unattractive, utilitarian goods. The hand tools produced by the Stanley Rule and Level Company are a case in point. Their earliest tools were elegantly designed and elaborately decorated because they had to compete not only functionally but also aesthetically with handmade wooden tools. Only after cast iron tools had achieved market dominance were they able to simplify the design and decoration of their tools in order to cut production costs.

The presence of high design values in Fordist commodities was not, however, simply an issue of competition with the fading glories of hand-worked objects.

This was also the golden age of industrial design: the age of Bauhaus and Stream-lining. The Bauhaus reacted against the aesthetic impoverishment of modern life. As part of its program to reintegrate craftsmanship with artistic design, its students were required to study with both an artist and a master of a given craft. For a variety of reasons (chief among them its dependence on revenues from the design of industrial prototypes), the curriculum and ideology of the Bauhaus grew to emphasize industrial design.[39] Along with other renowned aesthetic movements, such as the Arts and Crafts movement, whose leftist politics were fundamentally opposed to industrial capitalism, the Bauhaus unwittingly aided and abetted the commodification of all dimensions of life by emphasizing aesthetics and style in design. Both Morris's neo-medievalism and Walter Gropius's stark minimalism are the direct forebears of the style-is-everything advertising campaigns of today. Target carries on this tradition with mass-produced brio in recent ad campaigns that feature models wearing household items (lampshades, ironing boards, wrapping paper) as high-fashion clothing.

Modernism was "harnessed and used as a form of expression by the very forces against which it was initially responding" in other important ways. Its minimalist functionalism—"form follows function"—provided an aesthetic to challenge the dominance of older cultural styles that were both inefficient to produce and out of harmony with the values of modern industrial capitalism. "Unbridled . . . from the constraints and expectations of older, relatively static and undynamic forms of representation, capital could now freely develop its own unique brand of aesthetics through which the concepts of progress, speed, efficiency and functionalism could all be accommodated appropriately."[40] This is particularly evident in the "streamline" or "streamform" aesthetic, which began as a functional design to minimize the drag caused by air resistance on a moving airplane. In the 1930s, this aeronautical form was applied to almost all consumer goods—from automobiles to toasters. America's great industrial designer, the French emigré Raymond Loewy, is responsible for the look of this age more than his high-culture contemporaries Gropius, Le Corbusier, or Constantin Brancusi. He designed the body of the Pennsylvania Railroad S-1 locomotive that pulled the Broadway limited, a form so stunning (and widely advertised) that most people know it intuitively without being able to name it. It was displayed at the New York World's Fair in 1939 and serves as a near archetypal expression of the aesthetics of the age. Loewy's vision is ubiquitous in American culture. He designed the Coke bottle and the Greyhound bus, the logo for Lucky Strikes, as well as Texaco and Shell. In this style, Ewen reads physics "transformed into a cultural allegory" for industrial, technological culture rushing through modern civilization with minimal resistance from traditional culture.[41] Awkward inspirational copy from a discarded 1936 high school yearbook rescued from the garbage confirms the association: "Streamline: frictionless passage between the air . . . produced an eagled swiftness . . . gave this fast-moving civilization travel like an arrowflight, and tomorrow's generation an undreamed sweeping swiftness." Ewen's insight is consonant with

Loewy's design maxim, "Most advanced, yet acceptable."[42] The style communicates the triumph of technology. Its endless progress will not only replace what had been lost as traditional culture was swept aside but will also provide health, prosperity, and leisure hitherto unimaginable. This salvation is distributed sacramentally in the form of the consumer commodity.

The Single-Family Home

The cultural hegemony of the Fordist era was not solely a matter of design aesthetics and advertising rhetoric; it rested upon very specific transformations in the economic structures of daily life. Aglietta's materialist argument highlights the importance of one structure that has become fundamental to our culture: the single-family home. Aglietta calls attention to the correlation of the greater extraction of workers' energy during the workday with the decline of the homestead as place of production and the rise of the single-family home, where the nuclear family depends on wages to support a consumption-centered lifestyle. This new form of domestic consumption was particularly commodity-centered. In contrast to previous forms of consumption that were enmeshed in a complicated division of labor among the extended family (e.g., small garden plots, maintaining livestock and poultry, and so on), standardized housing (now more spatially distant from the workplace) created a home sustained by the workings of technology and appliances (e.g., plumbing, cooking, light, heat, entertainment devices) that replace the labor of the extended family. These new technologies and appliances are also commodity-intensive because their functioning depends on an infrastructure of goods and services (e.g., coal, lamp oil, gasoline, electricity, plumbing, wiring, repair shops, and the like), that must be provided from outside as well. The rise of the consumption-centered single-family home parallels the deskilling that took place in the industrial labor world. The fact that the initial purchase of such durable goods was far beyond the means of the working class resulted in the revolution of consumer financing.[43] Here is the birth of "normal" consumption in the United States, where simply living involves owning and maintaining a home, regular improvements to maintain its market value, owning one and then two cars for transportation to work, shopping, and so on.

Structures as ubiquitous as the single-family home are so deeply ingrained in the fabric of our lives that their profound significance (and contingency) is overlooked. The presence and impact of this or that ideology can be debated, but, as the fundamental structure of our dwelling, the single-family home forms our lives profoundly. The corporate motto of the Federal National Home Mortgage Association—"We're in the American Dream Business"—communicates how important the single-family home is as a social ideal. Other politically powerful myths, such as "family values," Betty Friedan's feminine mystique, and the innocence of childhood are linked to it as well. In the United States, the single-family home builds upon an earlier potent ideology: the independent hardworking farmer of rural republicanism. The emphasis on order and good stewardship of the land that marked the mores of farming communities is translated into responsible homeownership. The quality of the home and the appearance of its landscaping become expressions of the homeowner's good character. As they are translated into the nonproductive locus of the single-family home, however, they lose their concrete references and become primarily symbolic. It is indeed important for a farmer to prevent brush from encroaching upon a pasture or crop field. The same cannot be said for lawn edging and broadleaf weed control.

The single-family home along with the automobile provided the infrastructure for the emergence of the modern nuclear family. More physically distant from the support and shared labor of the extended family, the nuclear family was forced to become increasingly autonomous. The single-family home requires a whole range of appliances to replace the labor of the extended family. This has given rise to what Albert Borgmann terms the "device paradigm," whereby automated systems insulate us from each other and the refractory realities of the world.[44] His central metaphorical example is the replacement of the hearth with centralized heating systems (which took place in the same period of time we are considering). The thermostat-controlled furnace evened out the cyclical rhythms of life: the banking of the hearth before bed, coaxing the fire back to life in the morning, the periodic need to refuel with wood or coal, watching the supply of cut wood diminish through the cold season. All of these cycles are flattened as the automatic thermostat stabilizes the temperature. Borgmann fears that such devices insulate us from the world. It is, for example, much easier for us to ignore the relation between our desire for warmth and the consumption of natural resources when one chooses a temperature by turning a dial on the wall rather than through repeated trips to the woodpile or coal bin. Borgmann links devices such as this with a certain sense of "commodity," understood in terms of the root meaning of "commodious" or convenient. The furnace produces the good—heat—in abstraction from the manifold practices and engagements associated with the hearth.

Borgmann is easily criticized for being overly romantic. The mediating effects of devices do more than sunder us from a vital connection to our environment; they protect us from it as well. Consider droughts. In highly developed nations, technological infrastructures limit their effects to brown lawns and loss of income for farmers. In less developed nations, droughts cause famine. Whatever its problems on the macro-scale, Borgmann's analysis is deeply illuminating when applied to the single-family home. Devices replace both the physical labor and social supports of the extended family. The first is obvious enough. It is embedded in countless claims for products that provide "convenience." ("Automatic" has disappeared from product descriptions and ad copy because of its shear ubiquity.) The second requires further attention. The emergence of the single-family home and the nuclear family rendered families increasingly dependent on income as the sole determinant of security and flourishing. Wages and benefits replaced extended family and community relationships as the source of security. Borgmann identifies insurance and retirement pensions as economic "devices" that provide the good of "security" in an abstracted commodified fashion.[45]

The emergence of the single-family home accompanied a vast increase in the standard of living, security against risk, retirement planning, and so forth. It brought problems as well. We will consider three: social isolation, narrowed political and social concern, and the fragmentation of culture. The single family, while supported by a host of market devices, is socially isolated and particularly vulnerable to instabilities in income. This is a particularly cash-intensive form of life, which makes it difficult for extended family members and friends to support one another in times of crisis. Former acts of communal support such as barn raising or providing labor to run a farm or business are difficult to reproduce in the contemporary setting. Sustaining a single-family home requires a level of cash flow that few can afford to assume for friends or family in need. This isolation puts significant stress on couples. A middle-class existence generally requires that both members of a couple work, and the economic stability of the home depends greatly on the stability of their relationship. This burden might lie beneath the appeal of the hysterical violence of such films as *Fatal Attraction* and *Unfaithful*. While these films clearly engage anxieties concerning gender, sex, and betrayal, their catastrophic portrayal of wayward sexual desire is deeply consonant with the emotional and economic precariousness of the nuclear family in its single-family home.

The transformation of the home from a site of domestic production to one centered on consumption involved a complex change in gender roles. Patriarchal privilege was displaced into the workplace and women's newfound political power was honored by advertising appeals to their wisdom in overseeing domestic consumption.[46] This appeal to women as consumers can be read either as an ideologically driven strategy to roll back the political gains women had made during the latter half of the nineteenth century, or as an unintended consequence of the commercial displacement of domestic production. Either way, women were deskilled in much the same way that skilled laborers had been by Taylor's scientific management. Scientific experts in hygiene and home economics functioned as parallel figures to the engineers and managers who administered the deskilling of industrial laborers. Both women and industrial laborers suffered a corresponding loss in social status and political influence. In Mary McClintock Fulkerson's words, "it is no surprise that by the twentieth century [a woman's] link to the public sphere is altered in relation to the idealization of mid-nineteenth-century domesticity. No longer producing, she is 'produced' as a consumer, and the crafts for which she was once admired are no longer valued, at least as the fruit of her labor."[47] The homemaker was reduced from an active craftsperson to a passive consumer.

Consumption, however, replaced not only the competences and status that accompanied domestic production but also the comradery involved in such work.

While devices replaced domestic servants and family labor, they could not fill the vacuum of social isolation. Barry Levinson's 1990 film *Avalon* portrays this shift in the lives of a Jewish immigrant and three generations of his descendants. Two scenes from the marriage of the second generation are contrasted pointedly. Living with parents during the first years of their marriage, they are shown passionately engaged, arguing in whispers in their cramped bedroom, the sounds of the other household members audible through thin walls. Years later, successful, living in their own spacious suburban home, they lie mute, side by side in bed. One sullen, the other glaze-eyed, slack-jawed, watching the Jack Parr show on the television at the foot of their bed.

This social isolation brings with it the atrophy of certain psychological skills. Chief among them is the ability of adult children to live with or close to their parents. Intergenerational tensions may be near universal (dishonoring parents is classed with murder and adultery in the Ten Commandments). Perhaps it is therefore inevitable that as economic resources rise, children will seek to live apart from their parents and to seek professional care for their parents when old age makes them incapable of caring for themselves. Devices such as pensions and long-term care insurance replace the familial burden of caring for an infirm family member. Nevertheless, this living arrangement results in the loss of the ability to live in close proximity with one another. Two generations ago, it was not uncommon for families to raise five or more children in small, two- or three-room houses. Our inability today to imagine how this was possible is a testament to the psychological skills we have lost. Now it is a common expectation that each child should have her or his own room. This social arrangement requires an enormous amount of resources and renders us less able to share our dwellings with others in hospitality. The social isolation of the single-family home is evident in another Fordist-era device, the benzodiazepine tranquilizers (e.g., Valium), "Mother's little helpers." Whatever the value of the many modern conveniences that make the single-family home possible, raising a family and running a household remain an enormously demanding task. Whether the isolated housewife of stereotypes past or the two-income family of the present, the nuclear family faces an enormous amount of work with little outside assistance.

The social isolation of the single-family home led to increased consumption for another reason. The single-family home is merely one advance in the long-standing erosion of traditional markers of identity by modernity. As clan, family, profession, and other sources of ascribed identity have faded in significance, consumption has become the major means by which people establish, maintain, and communicate their personal and social identities.[48] Juliet Schor describes this acceleration of conspicuous consumption as the emergence of a "new consumerism." This social use of consumption leads to a particularly intensive form of consumerism. Because the status goods employed in conspicuous consumption have only a relative value, the social consumer faces an unavoidable inflationary economy. This was accelerated by several other factors, including mass-market advertising on television, which exposed those with lower incomes to products targeted at upper-income brackets, and the increasing gulf between high and low incomes since the 1980s. In such an atmosphere of constantly rising expectations, John Kenneth Galbraith's "keeping up with the Joneses" has become an endless task. To stand still is to fall behind. Thus, the rise of the single-family home is a milestone in the shunting of the need for social standing into consumption in a way that ensures the endless perpetuation of consumer desire.[49] (Chapter 5 will consider the social significance of consumption in a more positive light.)

The social isolation of the single-family home corresponds to narrowed practical and moral concerns. Although late-twentieth-century free-market conservatism arose from a complex of historical factors, its blindness concerning the common good and its suspicion of public investment and social safety nets correspond well to the narrow concerns encouraged by the single-family home. Each family works to purchase the various devices necessary to support itself materially and socially. There is less direct experience of extended-family or intergenerational purchases (e.g., equipment for a farm or family business). Taxes are easily perceived as part of a zero-sum equation where every dollar given to various levels of government is one dollar less for the family to use to pursue its own goals and display its standing. Despite the fact that the isolated nuclear family has much to gain from social safety nets, public services, and education, antitax rhetoric will always find a hearing in a social arrangement where so much depends on income. The individualism and materialism rightly condemned by papal encyclicals, ethicists, and cultural critics have their foundation in the very material social structure of the single-family home.

This results in a truncation of Aquinas's *ordo caritatis*. We may rightly have a greater moral obligation to our immediate family members than to those less directly related to us, but this social arrangement threatens to transform that gradation of obligation into a stark distinction. Social isolation and the burdens of maintaining a family in this system make it unlikely that other people's needs will ever present themselves. If and when we do encounter them, we are likely to be so preoccupied with the tasks of maintaining our immediate families that we will have little time and resources to offer. The geography of the single-family home makes it very likely that we will care more about the feeding of our pets than about the millions of children who go to bed hungry around us.

In his discussion of the politics of the Catholic suburban exodus, Mark Massa derides former Catholic Workers for becoming preoccupied with the finer details of lawn maintenance—a cheap shot, but accurate enough.[50] As empty-nesters who move into condominiums learn and celebrate, there are many less demanding ways to live. The single-family home makes significant demands on the family's time and money, not only to maintain the building itself but also for other ritual tasks such as yardwork, the heir of the dual traditions of rural republicanism and European formal gardens. These tasks are not undertaken with any particular enthusiasm, as though people prefer the solitary pleasures of time spent with lawn mowers, hedge trimmers, and leaf blowers to political and communal engagement. They are simply an accepted, unchosen, and unquestioned part of our social architecture that requires us to act as if we prefer such solitary labors to more communitarian pursuits.

Maintenance of the consumer homestead is not, of course, a joyless task. The twentieth century witnessed not only the emergence of the single-family home but also the rise of the "gentleman carpenter," the "family handyman," the "weekend warrior," the "do-it-yourselfer." At each stage, the movement has emphasized the joys of craft labor over against the fragmented work of the factory laborer and the physically desiccated existence of the white-collar office worker. (A similar movement and ideology center on the home gardener.) The joys and value of such avocations should not be dismissed; however, they remain significantly tied to the structures and interests of the single-family home. The do-it-yourself ethos includes a strong economic component. A thousand-dollar paint job can be accomplished in a weekend with a few gallons of paint. Indeed, the ethos has long been capital intensive. Tool manufacturers have catered to this market for more than a century by offering less expensive versions of their professional tools and heavily marketing top-of-the-line tools to home enthusiasts. Part of the calculus of the ethos involves being able to accomplish a job for less than a professional would charge *and* being able to add the required tool to one's holdings. The basement or garage shop has always been as much a focus of do-it-yourself literature as the jobs themselves. This reached its video apogee in Norm Abrams's *New Yankee Workshop,* where relatively simple woodworking projects are completed with a dizzying array of power tools. Norm's fetish was parodied in Tim Allen's television comedy series *Home Improvement,* about the host of a fictional show called *Tool Time,* whose typical refrain was the demand for "more power." This ethos is of a piece with the single-family-home ideal of device-centered self-sufficiency. It appears in a host of contexts besides male power-tool paraphilia: in kitchen appliances and "professional" cookware; in sports "gear" made with space-age materials such as titanium, boron, and carbon fiber; and above all in the myth of independence so long employed in car advertisements that has found its apogee (one can hope) in the SUV craze.

Home improvements bring us to another aspect of how the single-family home focuses our concern in a politically significant manner. We account for consumption linked to home improvement differently from other luxury consumption. Walnut panels and leather upholstery in a car are generally seen as self-indulgent luxuries that quickly depreciate in value. The opposite is true for household improvements. Granite countertops, Jacuzzis, and stainless steel kitchen appliances, while clearly extravagant, are accounted for as long-term capital investments that will enhance a home's resale value. Indeed, their ostentatious high quality contributes to their being counted on the investment side of the family balance sheet rather than on the consumption side. The home is, for many people, their primary investment. There is a profound social metaphor in the fact that the single-family home building is itself the primary source of retirement security for many. In other cultures and in our recent past, the primary investment was not so purely financial; it was instead one's relationship with one's children. (We must avoid being overly romantic here. That too included a financial component—investing in children's education or job training—and a clear economic expectation of repayment.)

The importance of real estate for financial security has political consequences that are readily apparent: "NIMBYism." "Not in my back yard!" is not merely an expression of a shallow unwillingness to live with others who lack the sense and good taste to be like ourselves; it is also an expression of significant economic interest. The siting of social-service agencies and halfway houses in residential areas has a negative effect on property values. Clearly there are reprehensible motives at work in such reductions of value, but the economic costs are real enough for those who bear them. These economic factors reinforce and exacerbate the suspect selfishness of the NIMBY argument. Likewise, the financial importance of property values impacts the rhetoric of neighborhood politics by transforming moral and political goods such as justice and diversity into economic calculus to elicit interest. Supporting a thriving school that successfully educates a diverse population or preserving retail space for small, family-owned businesses is promoted as "good for property values." This economic structure provides a specific reason for the translation of moral solidarity into self-interest. While small ethnic restaurants may succeed in these calculations, homes for young single mothers and drug-rehabilitation centers, whatever their large-scale social benefits, have little to offer to the local bottom line.

Our analysis thus far has unearthed the profound moral and political consequences of the institution of the single-family home. We have seen how on a very literal, economic or materialistic level this institution encourages the typical behaviors and decisions that are criticized as consumer values. People are encouraged to act selfishly, not primarily because they are infected by some faulty anthropology or ontology, but because of very significant personal economic costs. This supports our thesis that an adequate encounter with consumer culture requires attending to such structures as much as to values or beliefs. We must probe further here, considering not simply what sorts of ethical behavior the single-family home encourages but also the habits it fosters in our relationship to culture.

The most significant effect of the rise of the single-family home for our topic is its impact on the mediation of culture from generation to generation. As the single-family home and the nuclear family replace the extended family as the basic unit of society, the process of socialization into traditional beliefs and practices is weakened. In an extended family, patriarchs and matriarchs continue to exercise profound influence into their old age. In a nuclear family, people become heads of households at a younger age, and parents' influence on the lives of their children declines precipitously once the children reach adulthood and start their own households. The smaller and more volatile social unit of the single-family home accelerates cultural change. Each generation is freer to make its own choices regarding cultural and religious practices from the options they encounter. These choices of culture are increasingly drawn from commercial offerings as consumption becomes a means of establishing and expressing identity. The rise of generational marketing niches further erodes the intergenerational mediation of culture, as each new generation forms its identity using commercial popular culture and styles of which its parents know little or nothing. Thus, parents and grandparents have little wisdom to offer younger generations on how to dress, what music to listen to, what to read, what to eat, and the like. Culture is thus constructed as something one learns from peers' appropriations of commercial popular culture, not wisdom handed down from elders. Not only do we dress nothing like our grandparents and eat very few of the foods they did, but we also do not approach relationships or child rearing as they did. The next chapter will discuss the experts we now learn from. For now, it is sufficient to note how the rise of consumer culture profoundly weakens the handing on of cultural and religious traditions between generations.

The single-family home becomes the fundamental unit of culture as well as society. Neighborhoods cease to be culturally or religiously homogeneous, and people are welcome to express whatever religious convictions they desire within the bounds of (a still quite Waspish) good taste. My grandparents knew the religion, ethnicity, and political affiliation of just about everyone on their block. Not only do I have no idea about my neighbors, but without asking them, I have no way of knowing. Short of an occasional bumper sticker, religious or political convictions are not particularly manifest in people's lifestyles. The decor inside their homes provides more clues. The single-family home serves as a principle of individualization that sets the boundaries for religious practice. One can profess anything one wants within its bounds.

There is another cultural consequence of the rise of the single-family home that is more directly related to consumption. It is part of the broad transformation of the social system that, in Zygmunt Bauman's words, results in our being constructed "first and foremost as consumers rather than as producers."[51] This is evident enough in the decline of domestic production discussed above. This shift affected cultural as well as material production and involved the rise of commercial cultural offerings such as music, theater, and film, which certainly helped bring the habits of consumption into the cultural realm as they replaced folk music, storytelling, and other forms of entertainment. It was, however, even more profoundly driven by the invasion of commercially produced products into the home. This was not simply a replacement of material goods and a specialization of labor. Foodstuffs are cuisine, clothing is costume. The work involved in their production is cultural as much as physical. Making cheese, sauerkraut, and pasta, or beer and wine was an act of tradition. Whatever the drudgery of much of this labor, it required knowledge of the proper methods and training in skill. These made the home a place for learning and handing on cultural traditions. Their replacement by commercial offerings eliminated an important locus of cultural agency. The decline in the status of homemaker discussed above can be generalized to folk culture in general. As people spent less time in the skilled, traditional labor of domestic production, they had less experience as active producers and more as passive consumers. This had consequences for their ability to function as active agents of tradition, which affected their engagement of religious traditions as well.

This account of Fordism gives us much of what is familiar in religious criticisms of consumption. We see an explicit system of values that was actively disseminated through advertising. After centuries of negative connotations, consumption not only became a necessary dimension of the economy but was promoted in service of the common good. Acquisitiveness became a virtue. Individualism was intensified in a variety of ways. The nuclear family in its single-family dwelling became the new fundamental unit of society. The social isolation this brought was assuaged through consumption. Appliances stood in for the labor once exchanged as part of the lives of extended family or neighborhood relations. Individualism was also intensified through the narcissism elicited by advertising. Deprived of communal sources of identity, people were encouraged to invest in commodity-based self-enhancements. The economic structure of the single family forms political and ethical choices in a way that corrodes a sense of the common good. Finally, we considered how the shift from the extended to the nuclear family weakened our relationship to cultural traditions. Having discussed the rise of a culture of commodities, we must now consider the development of the commodification of culture.

THE COMMODIFICATION OF CULTURE

These deeper transformations are more difficult to map. As commodities have achieved more cultural significance, the commodity form has overrun its banks, flooding into broader culture. We have seen this at work in the our discussion of advertising and appearance. As advertisers exploited the alienation and anomie of urban existence in order to peddle products that could enhance appearance, they were simultaneously remaking the person in the form of the commodities they were selling. In this section we will consider how advertising and the rise of the modern media drove the commodity form toward what one commentator has termed "the total occupation of social life." Two French cultural critics of the mid-twentieth century, Henri Lefebvre and Guy Debord, offered extended analyses of the cultural shifts that took place during the Fordist era. Lefebvre began his work in the period of reconstruction after World War II; Debord was a decade younger and was influenced by Lefebvre. Their reflections will help us chart the transformations that began early in the twentieth century whose increasing momentum through mid-century would issue in postmodernity at its close.

Henri Lefebvre:
"Everyday Life" in the Modern World

Writing in postwar France, Henri Lefebvre was a firsthand witness to the social and cultural upheavals that accompanied the rise of Fordist industrial production. He offered an analysis of urbanism and everyday culture that explicitly anticipated—in both content and language—discussions of postmodernism that would not come into their own for nearly half a century. His research is deeply marked by two aspects of his biography: his marxist politics and his experience of growing up in Provençal France. As a member of the Communist Party, he was well versed in marxist social analysis but was frustrated by its materialistic tendency to undervalue the importance of culture. Lefebvre and his peers had hoped that the postwar reconstruction in France could be undertaken along revolutionary lines, but this did not come to pass. Lefebvre believed that the failure was caused by the absence of a "worker consciousness" to enable the workers to participate in the process as an effective political voice.[52] This sense of "worker consciousness" was rooted in more than marxist strategies for class politics; it arose as well from experience. Throughout his life Lefebvre moved between his Provençal home in southwest France and Paris, the city of modernism and consumption on whose streets Baudelaire's *flâneurs* strolled in dandyish self-display. Living between these two worlds, Lefebvre was attuned to their differences, conflicts, and ultimately the triumph of the one over the other. The postwar period was a time of revolution, but not the one for which he had hoped. The decades following the war witnessed the final penetration of folk culture by commercialism, the final supplanting of peasant craft traditions by industrial production, and the flattening of the rural cyclical temporality of work, seasons, and festivals into the linear temporality of modernity. Born at the turn of the century, Lefebvre was at once romantic and cold-eyed about what was being lost. He could both wax rhapsodic about how the peasantry, unlike the dour bourgeoisie, had maintained their taste for good food and wine, and note the burdens of material poverty, the real risks that peasants undertook in the festival excesses whose loss he lamented. He evoked the hidden depths beneath the "banality" of peasant (*cum*-working-class) culture. "In the heart of poverty and (direct) oppression there was *style*; in former times *labours of skill* were produced, whereas today we have (commercialized) *products* and exploitation has replaced violent oppression."[53] The consumer revolution brought both material comforts and cultural impoverishment. The combination of the two defused the sense of identity that could give workers political unity and power.

Lefebvre described this new culture using the term "everyday life." The French *quotidien* connotes banality, the humdrum experience of the workaday world. It is the word used to describe the daily newspaper. As in his analysis of the peasant culture which it supplanted, he saw "everyday life" as a "diptych" of both dignity and burden, involving both the mundane ingenuities that the masses employ to both "get by" and even flourish (this more romantic meaning of the term would dominate subsequent usage) and the real privations that modern existence exacts from people. This book reserves the term "everyday life" to refer to Lefebvre's definition. The generic sense of ordinary, lived existence will be referred to as "daily life." Everyday life is the routine that provides the necessary continuity for people to negotiate the endless upheavals of modernity, where "all that is solid melts into air."[54] Lefebvre developed the notion of the *quotidien* to correct the economism of marxist thought, which he believed undervalued culture as the evanescent superstructure of the economic base. He wanted to retrieve the richer, more cultural understanding of production held by the younger Marx. Orthodox marxist analyses tended to reduce social reproduction to the mere physical maintenance of the labor pool and thus could not adequately address the ways in which a given economic system transforms the nature of human existence. His notion of everyday life attempted to mediate between economic production in the strict sense and the culturally complex realities of consumption. Everyday life is both an ideological system and a set of practices.

Lefebvre evoked the banality of everyday life by contrasting it with the "style" of past cultures. "Style gave significance to the slightest object, to actions and activities, to gestures; it was a concrete significance, not an abstraction taken piecemeal from a system of symbols."[55] The varied career of the Latin root *prosa* provides a clue to the contrast: nothing was "prosaic, not even the quotidian; the prose and poetry of life were still identical."[56] What distinguishes style in this sense is its ability to influence the form and practice of life. The cultures of the past were capable of great collective works: temples, cathedrals, monuments, and the like. They shared powerful symbols and collective wisdom. While all of this sounds beautiful, it was not necessarily pretty. Much of the greatness of these cultures, their ability to produce *aristoi*, depended on exploitation and repression. Their great works are monuments both to their achievements and to the suffering of those coerced to build them. Style was a matter of cruelty and power as much as of wisdom and myth.

Everyday life in the modern world lacks such an overarching symbolic realm. It is burdened by a series of estrangements: from labor, from community, and from nature. Upon this standard marxist lament, Lefebvre developed an extended analysis of shifts in the symbolic realm of culture. Lefebvre's assertion about the absence of style is not simply an antimodern aesthetic judgment. It describes a fundamental shift in the relationship between humans and culture. Our lives are no longer formed or given meaning by an explicit cultural-aesthetic whole.

This impoverishment was driven by the progressive invasion of money and exchange, "the prose of the world," into more and more dimensions of human existence. Lefebvre argued that the profane had "displaced" the sacred, but could not replace it, leaving a fundamental lack at the heart of human existence. As a result, everyday life is marked by an endless, unfulfilled quest for style. Georg

Simmel described modernity as the time of "no-style."[57] We purchase and pilfer elements of past cultural styles, which, sundered from their lived context, lose their power to inform life. This observation is not as contradictory to our discussion of the style of modernism as it first seems. We noted how its formalism functioned both as an expression of technological enthusiasm and as a program for dispensing with the cultural inertia of traditional aesthetic sensibilities—style in Lefebvre's sense. Without style, culture loses its ability to inform daily life. Rather than a stable system of reference for identity and action, culture is reduced to a weary task for the hollowed-out subject—to construct private meaning amidst the flux of modern life. It is a necessary burden. Humans require meaning, but the alienated work and social relations of capitalism do not provide it. People must therefore construct their own cultural syntheses to give meaning to lives whose essential forms are established and nonnegotiable. As with decorating the interior of an apartment, they are free to choose whatever they want to hang on the walls, but this freedom is constricted by the layout of the walls themselves. Lefebvre described the result as a society of "bureaucratically controlled consumption."

This cultural impoverishment was facilitated by the rise of advertising and what Lefebvre called "the realm of make-believe." Twentieth-century advertising differed fundamentally from that of the nineteenth century. Early advertising emphasized the usefulness of the object. It elicited desire by fitting the product into the consumer's already constituted world. Whatever the legitimacy of the solutions it offered, the desires it elicited arose more or less from the person's experience (e.g., frustration with the difficulty of various labor tasks, health concerns, and so on). Twentieth-century advertising emphasized not the life of the consumer but the "imaginary lives" of the products themselves. "A display window in the Faubourg Saint-Honoré or a fashion show are rhetorical happenings, a language of things."[58] Graphic advertisements (the classic French ones Lefebvre discussed are now reproduced as decorator elements) of street and arcade signs and glossy magazine ads played an important role in the final colonization of rural life by urban consumer culture.

As this rhetoric of things gradually "invades experience," it brings about two effects. First, value becomes a function of being signified. What began as an attempt to ascribe value to things, ends by overshadowing them. "There is nothing, whether object, individual, or social group—that is valued apart from its double, the image that advertises and sanctifies it. This image duplicates not only an object's material, perceptible existence but desire and pleasure that it makes into fictions situating them in the land of make believe, promising 'happiness'—the happiness of being a consumer."[59] The second effect follows upon the first. Consumption is transformed into an "imaginary" act. People are no longer primarily interested in the goods themselves, but in their images. Consumption becomes an imaginary activity whose object is the advertisement as much as the product itself. This, one might say, is Victoria's *real* Secret. The practices associated with this new form of consumption—for example, window shopping and ad "reading"—are highly visual. They condition and discipline our ways of seeing. The reading of ads becomes part of the flow of reading magazines and watching television.

There is an inevitable frustration built into this way of relating to the world because these signs cannot fulfill the desires they elicit. Frustration and disappointment cannot be avoided "if people have nothing more substantial than signs to get their teeth into."[60] Lefebvre sketches a world where alienation becomes nearly total, where the quantitative explosion in the symbolic realm effected by advertising accompanies and accelerates the increasing shallowness of symbols in general. It is marked by "anguish arising from a general sense of meaninglessness." No matter how great "the proliferation of signs and signifieds," they can never compensate "for the general lack of significance."[61] The disappointment with consumption also depends on the overvaluing of the act of consumption that advertising elicits.

The cultural shift illuminated by Lefebvre is of concern for theology because theology desires strong symbols of the sort that Lefebvre associates with style—symbols that inform a way of life. Consumer cultures fracture the unity of style. They do not attack the symbols themselves; rather, they erode the systems that support their cultural power. Thus the defense of the meaning of symbols is ineffective. People are free to adorn their worlds with symbols drawn from one or many cultural systems. In some respects this is undeniably liberating. The unified cultures of style marked some as outcasts and consigned others to slavery. This freedom is bought at the cost of the political "traction" of symbols. They provide meaning "content" for everyday life, but the symbolic realm is no longer able to determine the concrete shape of our daily lives or even to challenge its dominant form.

Guy Debord: The Society of the Spectacle

Guy Debord, a generation younger than Lefebvre, offered a more radical account of this cultural shift in more extreme language. Debord wrote as one engaged in radical political action. If Lefebvre's account of the final eclipse of organic peasant communities by a bureaucratic society of controlled consumption is rhapsodic and wistful, Debord's is angry, snide, and marked by his search for a way to subvert this oppressive regime. Guy Debord was a member of a post-marxist radical group called the "Situationist International" (SI). It flourished in Paris with its own peculiar blend of obscurity and notoriety from 1957 through 1969 and during those years published a journal *International Situationniste*. Influenced as much by the avant garde, Dada, and surrealist movements as by marxism, the SI sought to bring about a revolution in everyday life. Their writings were the source of many of the infamous slogans scrawled on Parisian walls during the 1968 student uprising—"Free the Passions," "Never Work."[62] Debord's impassioned combination of critique and activism secures his continued attractiveness to contemporary activists. The "culture jamming" and "adbuster" movements draw their inspiration from Debord, and his vocabulary and categories are still employed by contemporary anticorporate and antiglobalization activists.

If Marx's analysis of early capitalism described a shift from "being to having," Debord sensed an equally profound shift under way around him, this one from "having to appearing."[63] He named and critiqued this new form of civilization in his 1967 work *The Society of the Spectacle*. In its most obvious sense, Debord's notion of the "spectacle" describes the further acceleration of the influence of media noted by Lefebvre. The vast explosion of visual media from print and outdoor ad images and, above all, the rise of television change our perceptions and sense of reality. The sense of sight becomes hypertrophied, and visuality becomes the dominant measure of significance. "That which appears is good, that which is good appears." Human experience is transferred into a hyper-reality; "everything that was directly lived has moved away into a representation."[64]

But this notion of shallow media culture is only the "crudest definition" of Debord's notion of the "spectacle." "More generally, it refers to the vast institutional and technical apparatus of late-capitalism, to all the means and methods power employs, outside of direct force, to relegate subjects to the critical and creative margins of society and to obscure the nature and effects of its distorting power."[65] "The spectacle is not a collection of images, but a social relation among people, mediated by images." Thus, for Debord, it was the result of the ongoing unfolding of the logic of commodification. "The spectacle is the moment when the commodity has attained the *total occupation* of social life." Indeed, the spectacle is capital itself, "to such a degree of accumulation that it becomes an image." Commodity fetishism comes to "its absolute fulfillment in the spectacle, where the tangible world is replaced by a selection of images which exist above it, and which simultaneously impose themselves as the tangible *par excellence*."[66] It is the "materialization of ideology," where the particular perspective of the bourgeoisie becomes the dominant "objective" worldview.[67] The form of the commodity triumphs over culture; "the content of life is swept aside by the commodity form in which it appears."[68]

Debord believed that the spectacle was a form of ideological control, a "permanent opium war," or "enriched privation" that distracted people from the real politics of their lives.[69] This insight is borne out by the de facto priorities manifest in what our society provides. How poor do you have to be to not be able to afford a television? Homeless? Televisions are present even in shelters and in areas where seemingly much more essential elements of social infrastructure (e.g., education, healthcare) are sparse and inadequate. In a poverty-ridden Appalachian state, satellite dishes sit alongside the trailers that dot the unpaved back roads. A local joke identifies them as the "state flower." Along with sporting events, rock concerts, shopping malls, and magazines, television provides images of the good life that bring virtual, vicarious fulfillment. In the face of a spectacular world with which our everyday lives could never compete, we are reduced to passive spectators, consumers of illusions.

This reduction of persons to passive spectators is the triumph of alienation. In addition to critiquing it, Debord and the SI were committed to challenging it. Debord was as critical of the totalitarian regimes of communist states as he was of Western capitalist societies. For this reason he did not advocate traditional marxist revolution (although he did write admiringly of workers' and farmers' councils as means for restoring the creative consciousness of the alienated working class). Afraid of falling into the communist/totalitarian version of the spectacle, the SI hesitated to provide a comprehensive counterideology. Rather, they employed a range of anarchist cultural guerilla tactics to engage the spectacle. Through street actions, workplace disruptions, and graffiti, they sought to awaken people to the alienation they were accepting. They advocated a program of *détournement,* or "twisting," which employed dadaist tactics to subvert the messages of ads by defacing them or by modifying their slogans to highlight the flawed logic of their rhetoric.[70] Each of these tactics aimed at sabotaging the smooth workings of the spectacle. Debord and the SI trusted in the survival of an inchoate consciousness of alienation among the masses, that the images of fulfillment offered by the spectacle could not, in the end, gloss over the privations (whether basic or "enriched") that people suffered. People "wear designer jeans yet remain lonely and unhappy; the spectacle is ubiquitous but people are still bored; everyday life is shit *and people know it."*[71]

Lefebvre and Debord offered pessimistic accounts of how these transformations arose from the unfolding logic of the commodity fetish. They considered this emergent culture to be an ideological distraction from the violence of class exploitation. However pessimistic their accounts may have been, they were not hopeless, inasmuch as each was an exercise in ideology critique. A few short years after Debord published *The Society of the Spectacle*, another author would offer an account of the same dynamics so dystopian as to make Debord's indictments seem almost blithe in comparison.

Jean Baudrillard and Simulation

If for Guy Debord spectacle was the latest grand diversion in a long history of ideological controls that rulers had used to pacify potentially unruly masses—that is to say, a massive *dis*simulation—Jean Baudrillard argued that civilization had entered an utterly new era of pure simulation. In this new era, the opening lines of Dubord's *Society of the Spectacle*—"everything that was directly lived has moved away into a representation"—were so literally true as to render any talk of "reality" over against its dissimulation meaningless.

Baudrillard began as a neo-marxist but came to conclude that the cultural effects of capitalism had progressed to a point where they could no longer be adequately comprehended by analyses of political economy. Marx had correctly fore-seen the progressive stages of commodification and had correctly understood the cultural consequences of the shift from use value to exchange value. But Marx had erred by considering the further commodification of culture to be merely a *quantitative* expansion of this dynamic. For Baudrillard, the emergence of "sign value" was a *qualitative* revolution as fundamental as the emergence of exchange value. In this third stage the commodity fetish grows from a misrecognition of the value of particular commodities to a fetishization of the entire system of consumption.[72] The "conspicuous consumption" that Thorsten Veblen associated with the "leisure class" extends to all members of the economy; ostentation grounds the value of things. The Bauhaus heralded the emergence of this new commodity form; the human environment took on a life of its own as a system of signs. The design of everyday objects was intended to express their place within the rationally planned whole of modern living. This marked the emergence of a "semiurgic society" as fascinated with the manipulation of signs as the "metallurgic" one that preceded it had been with the manipulation of matter.[73] A sign-drenched culture unfolds: designer clothing progresses from an emphasis on form and style to the literal wearing of signs—stylized G's, A's, DKNY, Tommy, and so on. The "use value" of objects is their sign value. Consumption becomes a cultural system of signification possessing its own logic, unmoored from the system of production. Human subjects do not play much of a role in Baudrillard's structural linguistics, nor in his account of the culture it describes. The cultural codes of this system of signs construct our needs and desires. Human agency is reduced to choosing between the fulfillments proffered by the system. The spectacle has become total. Human experience is so completely determined by it that there are no surplus needs or experiences of contradiction left upon which one could build a subversive politics.

In his subsequent writings, Baudrillard enacted the shift he described. Economic and class analysis disappeared, and, after encountering the work of Marshall McLuhan, he turned to the institution most consonant with his views—the media. Modern media are both the condition of the full emergence of the sign economy and a cultural space that takes on immense importance because of its success. In accordance with his understanding of the passivity of consumers vis-à-vis the cultural code of signs, Baudrillard has spoken of humans being constituted as the "terminals" of the media networks, reduced to consuming eyes, shallow reflections of the television screens in front of which they are constituted. But his analysis of media goes beyond any simple consideration of the media as a tool for pacifying the masses. The media are a "black hole of signs." The explosive proliferation of signs in the media swamps signification and dissolves stable meanings, devouring both communication and the social.[74] The poles of communication are short-circuited, and the sender is fused with the receiver. While media still serve as tools for massification, they are themselves absorbed into the masses. The demands of the masses control the media as much as vice versa. The public penetrates the private, and the private becomes public as the "obscene" details of our lives are disseminated by the media for mass consumption. This implosion brings about a world of simulation where the boundary between reality and simulation becomes increasingly irrelevant, and cherished notions such as "depth" and "authenticity" are meaningless.

Before dismissing this as an instance of the rhetorical exaggeration for which faddish French intellectuals are renown, consider a recent obscene media spectacle. Which of Bill Clinton's impeachment trials was more important: the one he underwent in the media during the first three weeks of the scandal or the official one conducted by Congress after the fact? Which was the "real" trial? Surviving the first made the second redundant.

Baudrillard's dystopic scenario inspired the Wachowski brothers' film *The Matrix*, which paid homage to Baudrillard by giving a cameo to his book *Simulacra and Simulation*. Ours is the age of the "third order simulacra." Unlike earlier eras, where simulations were parasitic on a dominant cultural system (e.g., feudal social hierarchy) or the automated production of endless copies of a design, in this third era, simulation engulfs reality and becomes its own "hyper-reality," which refers to nothing beyond itself. The most important illusion about Las Vegas or Disneyland is their boundaries. We shudder at Disney's completely manufactured community *Celebration,* where a Norman Rockwell world is recreated in minute detail, down to selectively burnt-out bulbs in the marquee of the town theater. This is not a theme park but a residential community. Perhaps this is disturbing not because it is so odd but because it is all too familiar. Does the Disney Corporation run the schools there? God forbid that a media giant should be entrusted with the formation of our children!

Talk of giant media corporations and shallow culturescapes makes an easy case for Baudrillard's dystopia. Simulation appears in other more problematic realms of life. On the eve of the allied bombing of Iraq, Baudrillard notoriously declared, "The Gulf War will not take place."[75] While this and his subsequent essays on the topic have deservedly become the focus of excoriations of the culpable political naïveté of postmodern intellectuals, they make a disquieting point.[76] Although the absorption of war into simulation was not evident to the tens of thousands of Iraqis who were killed, for the rest of the world, the "event" of the Gulf War took place as much on the media networks as in the Middle East. Video footage from the guided bombs provide the metaphorical shape of the entire event. These "smart" weapons tell only one story—the triumph of technology—as they transmit back images of their inexorable approach to their target. This "information payload" is the mirror of their explosive payload, unleashed as the signal ends. Outside of representation, absent in the awkward static on the videotape when the signal ended, dead bodies were not part of this war. Like war, contemporary politics is pulled into simulation. Voters participate in democracy primarily in the form of polling and focus-group data that are endlessly run through simulation models of the electorate by candidates. Messages and policies are tweaked to maximize support among mathematically modeled demographic groups. Party infra-structures fade in significance. The networks of relationships, favoritism, and graft that ward bosses and district chairs once provided have been replaced by virtual constituencies that are served by the new political "machine"of the media.

With Baudrillard we pass into postmodernity. While earlier theorists had fore-seen its emergence and sketched its characteristics with eerie prescience (from Marx's "all that is solid melts into air" to Lefebvre's 1947 concern about the shal-lowness of signs), Baudrillard draws it into the heart of analysis itself. His extreme account of the abstracting cultural effects of commodification sketches the limit of the problem: a situation where the elements of culture are so drawn into sys-tems of distribution and marketing that culture becomes completely frictionless, unable to impact the politics of daily life. If Baudrillard helps us understand how consumer culture has brought us to the carnivalesque morass of postmodernity, he provides little guidance for engaging it. Douglas Kellner argues that Baudrillard so emphasizes the formal workings of media technology that there is no "real the-ory or practice of cultural interpretation in Baudrillard's media (increasingly anti-) theory."[77] The structuralist bias which emphasizes the working of signs over the agency of persons is so ingrained in his thought that he cannot imagine a counterpolitics. Culture, however, only exists as practiced by persons regardless of the images circulating on cable networks. Thus, culture can become frictionless only if people practice and engage it in a way that makes it so. Baudrillard sketches a cultural trajectory in terms of media and technology, but pays little attention to the habits and dispositions of the postmodern subjects he presumes are consti-tuted in front of the video screen. For this we must turn to another thinker.

Fredric Jameson:
The Cultural Logic of Advanced Capitalism

The marxist literary critic Fredric Jameson is well known as a key interlocutor in the debates concerning postmodernism that took place in the 1980s and early 1990s. Jameson's contribution, heavily indebted to Baudrillard, grew out of a career-long insistence that literary criticism ought to consider not only the inner workings of texts but also their connections with their cultural historical contexts. Criticism, as Jameson conceives it, can thus contribute to political action by pro-viding a map of the cultural territory. In *Postmodernism, or, the Cultural Logic of Late Capitalism*, Jameson examined the emergence of this new "cultural domi-nant" in a range of elite and popular aesthetic and cultural movements. Jameson sees postmodernism as an inchoate "cognitive mapping" of social, cultural, and personal experience in a time of multinational capitalism. Jameson's account is dialectical, acknowledging both the "baleful" and liberating potential of this cul-tural shift.[78] This analysis is particularly useful for theological reflection because Jameson writes as a committed leftist, seeking to map the cultural political terrain as a guide for radical politics. Thus, he rejects the postpolitical resignation and cultivated nihilism of Baudrillard.

Jameson describes the postmodern era as a time when capitalism penetrates the precapitalist enclaves of nature and the unconscious, reducing all human action, including politics, to some variation of consumption.[79] Advertising imagery and the commodification of culture take their toll by stripping everything of depth. Jameson evokes the depthlessness of postmodern aesthetics by contrasting the deep interpretations that Van Gogh's paintings of a peasant's shoes have elicited (e.g., Heidegger's *Der Ursprung des Kunstwerkes*) with Andy Warhol's *Diamond Dust Shoes*, a technicolor photo negative of a jumbled array of women's dress shoes floating in a contextless, shallow foreground. The latter confounds hermeneutic readings, evokes no life world, summons no reponse: "Nothing in this painting organizes even a minimal place for the viewer, who confronts it at the turning of a museum corridor or gallery with all the inexplicable contingency of some natural object. . . . There is . . . no way to complete the hermeneutic gesture and restore to these oddments that whole larger lived context of the dance hall or the ball, the world of jetset fashion or glamour magazines."[80] The centrality of fetishized commodities in Warhol's works suggests that they "*ought* to be powerful and critical political statements," yet they are produced and received in a manner that seems to have made them anything but. Warhol's shoes signal a "fundamental mutation in both the object world itself—now become a set of texts or simulacra—and in the disposition of the subject" who is now inclined to relate to it as such.[81] Jameson describes the consequences of this shift in terms of pastiche, nostalgia, and schizophrenia. We will consider these in turn.

In advanced capitalism, aesthetic production and much of everyday culture are integrated into economic production. Cultural change accelerates with the consumption to which it has been yoked. In an age marked by "stylistic and discursive heterogeneity without a norm," an age that lacks any shared project or language, the oppositional, subversive strategies of high modernism—irony, satire, and negation become powerless. In such an age, parody is reduced to pastiche.[82] The form of subversion remains, but without a stable symbolic status quo it deteriorates into the endless adoption and juxtaposition of styles, a form of "blank irony." Since cultural elements have become shallow and weightless, unmoored from the politics of people's lives, their subversion has little effect. Transgression and subversion are absorbed into the spectacle with little remainder.

The cultural consequences of the simulacrum run deeper than this shift in artistic style. Pastiche finds its expression in retro and nostalgia in popular culture. The lack of depth in style, the "iron law of fashion change," the separation of the signifier from the signified sunder us from any organic relationship to our own past. History becomes a collection of dead styles that we can only plunder, not understand. The other side of this retro nostalgia is our inability "to focus on our own present, as though we have become incapable of achieving aesthetic representations of our own current experience."[83] Jameson explicitly excludes from his definition of the term the deep, affective longing so central to romantic nostalgia. This retro nostalgia is shallow, an ahistorical appropriation of past symbol worlds, "a depersonalized visual curiosity," as in his alternate phrase "nostalgia-deco."[84]

The scintillating cascade of cultural symbols and practices is driven by the voracious appetite of capitalist production, not by the dynamisms of the traditions from which they are drawn. Commodities and cultural objects are best suited to their task when their conditions of origin are masked. Traditional resonances are welcomed only insofar as they deepen their aura of desirability. Commodification drives both the postmodern circulation of cultural wares and their evisceration. It demands ever more and ever shallower things.

If abstraction of the commodity from the conditions of its production was necessary for widespread exchange in early capitalism, it becomes even more important in the high-consumption world of advanced capitalism. We consume so many things that we simply do not have the mental energy to consider their origins. This abstraction has effects that go far beyond providing "moral insulation" for the gluttonous postmodern consumer. This abstraction of the commodity from its production simultaneously sunders consumption from production, further reinforcing alienated passivity. The hieroglyphic postmodern commodity confronts us as a sheer face of facticity transcending any context. The "product somehow shuts us out even from a sympathetic participation, by imagination, in its production. It comes before us . . . as something we could not begin to imagine doing for ourselves."[85] Indeed, there may be a much deeper dark side than we dared imagine to the widespread inability of consumers to program their VCRs. This fabulous world of the dancing, glistening surfaces of postmodern commodities reduces us to stunned passivity.

This is Jameson's central concern. He elucidates the problem using Jacques Lacan's structuralist understanding of schizophrenia as a language disorder. A breakdown in the chain of signifiers causes meaning by intersignification to crumble into "a rubble of distinct and unrelated signifiers."[86] Schizophrenia gets at the simultaneous splendor and terror of consumer culture: a world awash in unmoored signifiers—children's backpacks adorned with the huge face of Elmo on glistening vinyl, gonzo brand "No Fear" T-shirts with "Bosnia" written where other brands would have a fashion capital such as Paris or New York, *Zippy the Pinhead's* fascination with the nostalgic tremendum of giant ad statues. This schizophrenia involves more than overwhelming experiences of visual intensity. The collapse of the chain of signification brings the collapse of the temporal unity that constitutes personal identity. The self is reduced to a series of unsynthesizable presents where experience is dominated by the brute materiality of depthless signifiers. Its political consequences parallel those of schizophrenia. The "breakdown of temporality . . . releases [the] present of time from all the activities and intentionalities that might focus it and make it a space of praxis."[87] Deprived of the ability to hold on to the past or project into the future, the subject floats adrift, a passive consumer of intensities, no longer an agent of historical change. In Terry

Eagleton's words, advanced capitalism has deconstructed the subject much more than any postmodernist theoretical program could ever hope to, reducing the contemporary subject to "a dispersed, decentered network of libidinal attachments, emptied of ethical substance and psychical interiority, the ephemeral function of this or that act of consumption, media experience, sexual relationship, trend or fashion."[88]

Jameson helps us tie the account of the commodification of culture to particular habits and dispositions. Pastiche, in high and low culture, both expresses the liquidity of culture in advanced capitalism and trains us to engage culture in such a fashion. Political praxis is reduced to nostalgia and schizophrenia in a world where symbols have no cultural friction. This is a profound problem for theology, which desires that its retrievals, interpretations, and syntheses of doctrines and symbols will impact the life of the believing community. When cultural elements are encountered and engaged in commodified fashion—as floating, shallow postmodern signifiers unrelated to one another or to particular communities and practices—interpretation and syntheses, no matter how sophisticated, will have little practical impact. Thus, in addition to its more traditional tasks, theology must consider the systems that present elements of tradition in a commodified fashion and the formation of believers' interpretive habits that incline them to engage tradition as a commodity.

The four theorists we have considered, for all their indebtedness to materialist analyses, still offer decidedly abstract accounts of the commodification of culture. For that reason we will conclude the chapter with a discussion of an economic transformation that took place in the last third of the twentieth century: the crisis of mass-market Fordism. The system that replaced Fordism has had a profoundly different, but equally significant impact on culture.

POST-FORDISM

In the early 1970s, the economies of the advanced capitalist nations entered into a prolonged period of crisis. While an increase in energy costs resulting from the organization of OPEC is frequently cited as the cause, internal tensions within Fordism were equally important to the crisis. The stability of the Fordist economy depended on two factors that were becoming increasingly difficult to sustain: the expansion of domestic consumption and the increase in productivity through Taylorian management. By the end of the 1960s the domestic market had begun to reach saturation. It was not that there were no people left who had yet to buy into the Fordist lifestyle, but that the massive expansion of markets the industrial juggernaut required to maintain momentum had become a thing of the past. Large-scale markets were required to recoup the massive costs of developing products and maintaining distribution networks. At the same time, productivity increases leveled off as the Taylorian fragmentation of labor tasks inevitably reached the point of diminishing returns. The alienation of labor that resulted also took its toll through decline in quality, absenteeism, and high injury rates. The effects of this deceleration of productivity were exacerbated by the strength of organized labor in the Fordist economy. Keynesian control of economic demand had ensured economic stability by linking wage increases to growth in productivity. Accustomed to decades of steadily rising standards of living, labor was not inclined to accept cutbacks in salary increases as the economy slowed. These two factors contributed to the economic crisis of the 1970s as much as did the oil crisis. Western capitalism was transformed as a result.[89]

As with the debate on things postmodern, consensus is easier to find concerning the nature of the Fordist era that has putatively come to an end than on what is replacing it. Numerous models, ranging from the discussions of economic minutiae to starry-eyed musings on the glories of the coming "postindustrial" or "information age," vie to describe the "post-Fordist" era.[90] Such speculation is particularly susceptible to overheating because of the marketability of the issue in the world of corporate guru-dom. This discordant diversity of views notwithstanding, there is a sufficient commonality among competing scholarly positions to sketch a rough consensus, which reveals a number of changes that accelerate the cultural effects of commodification.

A common theme among accounts of post-Fordism is flexibility, which is contrasted to the inertia of the massive, integrated institutions of mid-century capitalism. Information and communication technologies have made possible fundamental changes in labor, production, and marketing. They have allowed an explosion in the "outsourcing" of production, which has resulted in a "vertical disintegration" of the monolithic corporations that had relied on an extended system of subsidiary divisions to produce all the parts and services for their final products.[91] This outsourcing had both geographical and institutional dimensions. Globalized communication and transportation allowed capital to move production to locations with lower labor costs and fewer environmental regulations. Flexibility is evident in the trend in labor management in the advanced capitalist nations away from assigning a worker a single, fragmented task to a model that assigns workers a variety of tasks and encourages and rewards workers for knowledge and innovation.[92] This flexibility was accomplished in part through the systematic disempowering of organized labor. The decline of the significance of the nation-state and the rise of transnational corporations completed the disruption of the trilateral equilibrium (management, labor, and state) of the Fordist economy. Flexibility is evident also in the productive apparatus itself: multi-use tooling and small-batch and "just-in-time" production.

These changes in production fostered the emergence of new business strategies. Whereas firms had previously engaged in a battle for mass-market share, flexibility in production combined with information technology made it possible for businesses to attend to smaller niche markets. Mustard tells the story as well as any commodity. The H.J. Heinz Company, famous for its 57 varieties, illustrates the older system. Heinz's mustard was packaged in their hallmark faceted jar (a squattier version of the ketchup bottle), with their standard label. It was thus presented to the consumer on the reputation of the company; Heinz sold an entire product line. Post-Fordist mustard arrived, fittingly enough, in a Rolls Royce. "I say, would you happen to have any Grey Poupon?" The singular desire of a yuppie shopping in a recently gentrified neighborhood in the late 1980s expresses well the post-Fordist consumer *Zeitgeist:* "All I want is a place where I can buy twelve kinds of mustard."[93] Grey Poupon embodies the contradictions of post-Fordist consumer production. While its name nostalgically evokes the ancient manufactory founded by Mssrs. Grey and Poupon at 32 Rue de la Liberté in Dijon, it is manufactured and, more importantly, marketed by the American consumer product giant R.J. Reynolds Nabisco. Its "niche" is maintained by the massive corporation's marketing power and ability to secure retail space in supermarkets.

Our appreciation of the significance of cultural nostalgia and niche marketing will be aided by a consideration of changes in the "ideal type" of commodity that happen as a result of the crisis of Fordism. Martyn Lee contrasts the dominant strategies of growth in Fordist and post-Fordist economic systems: "expansion" and "intensification." As we saw, Fordism was driven by the expansion of commercial production into spheres previously served by domestic production. In the post-Fordist era, economic growth is secured by a recursive reworking of the consumption habits of extant market populations, or "intensification," rather than seeking new markets. Put simply, growth depends on changing the nature of the commodity rather than selling commodities to new populations. Miniaturization is a telling trope for this process. Physical miniaturization and the rise of multiuse products allow for greater levels of consumption. Compare today's small home theater systems with the bulky console units of yesteryear. Now it is possible to have an audio system, television, video game system, and computer in one room. Even more to the point, it is now possible to have fully functional versions of these devices in many rooms of the house—family rooms, kitchens, and bedrooms. This provides the opportunity for near-constant consumption of media: during meals, while getting dressed, when gathered together, and while separated. Lee sees a similar dynamic at work in what he terms "temporal compression." This is a continuation of the labor- and time-saving impulses that marked the Fordist era. By reducing the amount of time required for daily tasks, more time is freed up for consumption. While the microwave meal is the primary example cited by Lee, the literal temporal compression of commodities should also be noted. If the feature film that requires an evening to consume corresponds well to the production system and pace of the Fordist era, the three-minute music video distributed via cable is a paradigmatic example of the post-Fordist commodity. Even though cable television makes it possible, it would make little sense to watch a few minutes of a feature film while brushing one's teeth. But this is plenty of time in which to enjoy a music video, catch the current headlines on CNN or MSNBC, or see what's brewing on the Weather Channel.

Both aspects of miniaturization point to another element in the intensification of commodities—an increasing emphasis on complexity and content. The personal computer exemplifies how this new complexity is different from sophisticated commodities of the past. Swiss watches can be bought with built-in mechanical chimes, multiple chronographs, perpetual date systems, and the like. Although such devices are quite expensive, they hold their value for generations. Computers can be expensive as well, but their value is solely a function of the speed with which they can run the latest software. A microprocessor chip that sold for a thousand dollars five years ago is virtually worthless today, and computer hardware only serves as a substrate for software. It is not surprising that old computers have about as much value as old software packages. This reality is evident in the changing construction of computer chassis. In the beginning of the PC market, IBM products were distinguished from cheaper clones by their heavy-gauge steel chassis and cases. Because of constant innovations, computers now become obsolete within three years, and so such material quality is pointless. Now the chassis of even the most expensive brands are made of plastic. This is not to say that computer cases are no longer relevant to value. The enormous success of Apple's stylish I-Mac line, however, proves the point. Its added aesthetic value is more a matter of information than material.

Lee suggests that this "dematerialisation of commodities" addresses the crisis of market saturation caused by the durability of consumer goods.[94] This new style of commodity can be described in terms of information or experiential content, and the key here is "content." As the corporate media buying frenzy of the 1990s made clear, increasingly it is such content that turns the wheels of commerce. Corporations that had become enormously successful by selling infrastructure realized that gadgetry such as DVDs and the Internet were only interesting insofar as they had content to provide. Thus Sony acquired Columbia and AOL merged with TimeWarner to ensure future success by having something to distribute through their media.

What is this content? In one form or another it is culture. These acquisitions sought the massive archives of popular culture possessed by the media organizations. Although this explains the rise of new cable classic movie channels such as TMC and Bravo, it goes deeper than this. Commercial media conduits offer an ever-widening range of cultural objects, and factors other than the explosion of inexpensive media bandwidth drive this commodification of culture. We have seen how early-twentieth-century advertising and product design increased demand by challenging the authority of traditional cultures. In the process, print, radio, and television media were established as important cultural loci. If these Fordist-era events tended toward a homogenizing mass culture, the later turn to niche marketing has shown that commercial exploitation of culture need not disdain difference. Cultural objects from global ethnic cuisines and aesthetics to the interests and concerns of contemporary lifestyle subcultures (urban black youth, gay and lesbian, evangelical Christian, and so on) provide both market segments and treasure troves of symbols that can be utilized in product design and marketing. In addition to exploiting such identities, this marketing system encourages and creates them as well.

Here lies the strange fate of the mass-culture critiques of the 1950s and 1960s. If Fordist-era commercial culture had to offer a homogenized mass culture that catered to the lowest common denominator (which was white and politically conservative), post-Fordism provides the opportunity for an enormous broadening of commercial popular culture. Thus, the assimilation of the Latino immigrants who have arrived in this country over the past several decades is likely to be very different from the earlier waves of immigrants, who became Americans by giving up their original cultural identities. A distinctive Latino identity will likely survive because the current marketing networks can cater to it as a lucrative cultural niche. There is now room in marketing structures and media bandwidth to recognize and give voice to different and dissenting voices, but their particularity or dissent is treated as a cultural product that is marketed like any other. A broad pan-Latin identity is being created by networks such as Univision and Telemundo targeting Latinos. But the existence of space in the media for a variety of voices does not necessarily mean that corporate media will offer truly diverse material. The explosion of media bandwidth in the past two decades has also been accompanied by an epochal concentration of media ownership. Cultural differences and minority perspectives are preserved at the cost of being commodified. (Chapter 5 will explore this dynamic in greater detail.)

Post-Fordist economic structures have cultural impacts just as Fordist ones did. The fragmentation of Fordist mass markets into niches contributes to the decline of cultural stability that Jameson associates with postmodernism. Whatever its manifest shortcomings, the mass-market, three-network television establishment that preceded the cable era provided the basis for a common culture. Mini-series in the late 1970s such as *Roots* or *The Holocaust* were shared cultural referents; millions watched the same thing at the same time. Post-Fordist explosions in media bandwidth, which make narrowcasting and on-demand programming possible, make it unlikely the media will provide such politically significant shared referents again.

Post-Fordist marketing structures build on and intensify the cultural impact of the single-family home by targeting nuclear families. In recent years technology and age segmentation have made possible finer units of marketing. The size of the basic social unit has been further refined from the nuclear family in its single-family home to each individual member of the family as a discrete consumer. Media access provides the metaphor for this shift. With the intensification of consumption, televisions and computers are present throughout the home. Families no longer need to negotiate what to watch on television together; each individual can withdraw to a different room to watch a program of choice.

The centrality of the single-family home for Fordist culture encouraged generational thinking. Mass markets created the notion of a coherent "youth" market and thus of a coherent generational identity. Wade Clark Roof notes the link between marketing strategies and the strong generational identity of the "baby boomers." They "were the first generation of children defined by Madison Avenue by means of television as having distinct needs and wants."[95] The niche marketing of post-Fordism might be resulting in a corresponding disappearance of generational identity. The much ballyhooed Gen-X was the last stable generational marker, and it was characterized by a curious lack of group identity. (It is interesting to note in that regard how so much of the interest concerning the differing opinions of so-called "young theologians" is found among aging boomers. Younger theologians frequently do not think of themselves as part of a generation.)

If the nuclear family was freed to construct its own cultural and religious beliefs and practices as it set up its home with little interference or oversight from grandparents, in post-Fordist culture each individual family member is now freer to make his or her own cultural choices. Children choose from a range of niched youth cultures in media consumption, fashion, and room decor. The experience of baby boomers choosing the culture for their families from the many on offer becomes an expectation for their children and grandchildren. It is not uncommon to hear parents express discomfort with forming their children—especially regarding religion—viewing their responsibility instead as facilitating their children's choices by exposing them to various options. All of this further accelerates cultural change. As culture and religion increasingly become matters of individual choice, the familial, cultural, and institutional networks that stabilized their meanings diminish in strength. As a result, cultural symbols, beliefs, and values lose their semantic mass, in exactly the manner Jameson described.

CONCLUSION

Neither consumerism nor consumer culture can be adequately understood in terms of a particular set of values. Both high levels of consumption and the transformations in cultural habits that mark consumer cultures are rooted in structures and practices that are seldom chosen and frequently unnoticed. Our systems of labor, commodity exchange, the single-family home, marketing, and advertising have profound impacts on the way we live our lives and how we relate to culture. The commodity fetish in particular emerged as a fundamental factor in both consumerism and consumer culture. Our countless acts of consumption and evaluation of commodities large and small train us daily to value things out of their contexts. The same habits of valuation are at play in our deciding whether seventy-nine cents a pound is a fair price for bananas in a produce section two thousand miles from where they were grown, whether we "like" a piece of music that samples an indigenous folk song without saying anything of its origins, or—

to consider a more directly religious example—whether Buddhist Vipassana meditation or Jewish Midrash is a good "fit" for our personal spirituality.

The commodity fetish is linked to a number of fundamental aspects of advanced capitalist societies as we saw with Lefebvre's notion of everyday life, Debord's idea of media spectacle, and Jameson's account of the depthless liquidity of postmodern cultural symbols. These cultural structures and habits are reinforced by a host of practices such as shopping, considering advertisements, constructing an identity, and consuming cultural products.

The broad range of factors contributing to consumerism and consumer culture gives a picture of a multifaceted problem, which therefore calls for a variety of responses to counter the pernicious effects of consumer culture. Although theology is most familiar with the task of clarifying meanings and encouraging believers to act accordingly, there are other practices involved in the preservation and handing on of a religious tradition. Ecclesiology has always been significantly about the organizational details of the stewardship of the Christian message; for example, determining who is authorized to interpret, hand on, and judge the content of the tradition, and delineating how the community should be structured. The details of consumer culture call for engagements of this sort. The relationship of the nuclear family to the larger community and questions concerning the dissemination of the tradition stand out as particularly important.

At this point, we can offer a basic definition of consumer culture as a situation in which elements of culture are readily commodified. Cultural commodities, like literal products, are characterized by abstraction and reification; they are abstracted from their conditions of production, presented as objects valuable in themselves, shorn of their interrelations with the other symbols, beliefs, and practices that determine their meaning and function in their traditional contexts. Unmoored from these contexts, their "semantic mass" is greatly reduced. Cultural commodities become more susceptible to manipulation and misappropriation, free-floating signifiers that can be put to uses unrelated, indeed contradictory, to the meanings they bear. The commodification of culture is not adequately understood as the inevitable unfolding of the logic of the commodity fetish; it has arisen in a particular set of structures and practices. Contra Baudrillard, the weightless signifiers of consumer culture can be understood only in terms of the particular habits and dispositions of human agents engaging culture in a commodified manner.

This chapter has not exhausted the characteristics of consumer culture nor the factors that drive consumption. The next chapter will consider advertising and media infrastructures in greater detail. Chapter 5 will balance the economistic account of this chapter by taking the active agency of consumers more seriously and determining the role of conspicuous consumption in establishing social identity and solidarity. The task to which we now turn is to apply our analysis of consumer culture to contemporary religious belief and practice.

CHAPTER 3

Consumer Religion

Eclecticism is the degree zero of contemporary general culture: one listens to reggae, watches a western, eats McDonald's food for lunch and local cuisine for dinner, wears Paris perfume in Tokyo and "retro" clothes in Hong Kong.
— Jean-François Lyotard, *The Postmodern Condition*

Kids in Boston, Leningrad, and Santiago, Chile, all wear the same blue jeans and listen to the same music, so why can't we have one universal catechism?
— Bernard Cardinal Law, address to Synod of Bishops, Rome, 1985

T HE USE OF RELIGION IN RECENT POPULAR MUSIC WILL PROVIDE AN ENTRY TO our topic. From there, we will go on to assess how the effects of commodification illuminate contemporary religious sensibilities. The rest of the chapter will connect this general sketch of sensibilities to specific issues and practices. Here we will contextualize cultural criticism and cultural history of the therapeutic needs of consumers and their effects on religion within discussions of the changing nature of the social and institutional aspects of religion, such as the rise of "spirituality" as the dominant form of religious belief and the so-called "deregulation" of religion. Whatever the decline in respect for "institutional" religion, religious leaders such as the Dalai Lama and Pope John Paul II have achieved unprecedented levels of international celebrity, but religious celebrity accelerates the commodification of religion in general and has important consequences for religious institutions. As religious leaders use the media to spread their message, they gain broader audiences and more direct access to members of their own communities, but this access comes at a very high cost. By using corporate media, religious leaders encourage their followers to engage religious beliefs and symbols with the interpretive habits and dispositions they use for commercial popular culture. This chapter will show that, whatever the accuracy of denunciations of shallow narcissistic religious seekers flitting from one tradition to another in an attempt to get their needs met, such behaviors are undergirded by a host of structural causes. Rather than condemn the seekers and narcissists, we pursue an understanding of the broader cultural tides upon which they are borne.

GREGORIAN CHANT, HERMAN MELVILLE'S NEPHEW, AND THE MARQUIS DE SADE

How does commodification affect religion? We can begin our consideration with a few examples drawn from popular culture. The abundance of examples from which we have to choose suggests that religion is very marketable indeed. It is tempting to begin with the album *Chant,* which earned the Benedictine Monks of Santa Domingo more than $70 million in its first year of sales. Its cover art of simulacra monks floating in a Daliesque sky amid clouds and randomly scattered stone blocks (bricolage from a dismantled monastery?) seems a tailor-made target for critique. Since this was a re-release, however, of material first produced in the 1970s—its phenomenal success in 1993 was due in large part to its marketing and cover art—it is better to begin with a more contemporary popular album that employs religious material (and, one might note, was more likely actually to be played by those who bought it). The album *Play,* by the DJ artist Moby, was nominated for two Grammy awards in 1999 and has sold nearly ten million copies. On it Moby combines digital samples of African American singers of spirituals, the blues, and gospel with techno and electronica dance music.

African American music has long been a source of inspiration for white people—from artists such as George Gershwin, Elvis, the Rolling Stones, and Joe Cocker to contemporary blues enthusiasts among middle-class whites. The very depths of experience and resistance described by James Cone in *The Spirituals and the Blues* are mined as sources of emotional intensity and "pure authenticity" (to quote the liner notes of a Joe Cocker album.) Moby (born Richard Melville Hall—his stage name refers to his distant ancestor Herman Melville) took this to new levels with his song "Natural Blues."[1] The song opens with a haunting *a cappella* refrain. Vera Hall, her voice sampled from a recording made in her kitchen by Alan Lomax in 1959, intones, "Oh Lawdy, trouble so hard" and "Nobody knows my troubles but God." Hall's voice—the only human voice on the song—is "chopped" to fit a dance beat that is gradually introduced while the sample of her voice is repeated rhythmically. One could read the composition as a sobering metaphor for the transformation of religious culture by capitalism. The content remains the same but is employed in a context so alien as to seem (at best) earnest mockery.

In order to understand what Moby has done, however, we must consider the nature of his work. As a DJ musician, a large share of his creative work involves remixing the music of others into extended versions more suitable for dancing. A great portion of his discography consists of remixes for club use, which are available only on twelve-inch vinyl. Thus, his extensive sampling of the artists on Alan Lomax's *Sounds of the South* should be understood as an extension of his skills into another genre. That said, unwittingly or not, the work continues the long history of white artists and producers profiting more from the work of black artists than do the artists themselves. The album's success went beyond the music market. The songs were featured on a number of television programs, and, most lucratively, they proved enormously attractive as a source for ad soundtracks. *Every* song on the album was eventually licensed for use in a commercial.[2] In these ads, emphasis was generally given to the sampled music. "Natural Blues" was used as part of a Calvin Klein campaign. Another song, "Find My Baby," which sampled Boy Blue (a.k.a. Roland Hayes) singing the plaintive refrain of "Joe Lee's Rock," a classic blues meditation on infidelity, provided the soundtrack for an American Express commercial featuring Tiger Woods golfing through Manhattan.

The problems with the politics of cultural appropriation notwithstanding, the music is provocative and moving. Although it derives much of its power from samples of Lomax's collection and from contemporary black artists, Moby's compositions are clearly artful. He has spoken of how moved he was upon encountering this music, and his compositions manifest this. His meditative electronica compositions—both part of the sampling songs and independent compositions—suggest that there is much that deserves serious consideration in the ritual practice of club dancing for which it is produced. Undeniably, similar "misappropriations" are often at work in retrievals within mainstream religious traditions.

The samplings share enough to merit comment. Deeply expressive cries of suffering or pain—"trouble so hard," "why does my soul feel so bad?," "gonna find my baby"—serve as carriers of emotional intensity. It is informative to contrast Moby's mechanical reproduction of gospel singers with Steven Reich's serial composition "It's Gonna Rain," which samples an emotional street preacher. Reich's work materializes the sampled voice by dismantling it into its composite sounds and repeating them on slightly different cycles. Strange melodies emerge as the sounds of the human voice move in and out of sync, in and out of intelligibility. Moby pulls his samples in another direction. Although equally torn from their context, they are preserved intact as elements of meaning which are then subsumed into the structure of a new composition. Solitary voices uttering their pain and crying out to God are played as notes within the broader whole of the compositions. Repeated rhythmically they work almost as mantras, creating intense feelings of loss and need in the context of trancelike dance music.

Bracketing the question of cultural piracy (copyrights are acknowledged, the Lomaxes and even Jesus Christ are thanked in the liner notes, Vera Hall and the other artists are not), let us assume the good will of listeners and consider the political effects of the songs. As with World Beat music, giving ear to Hall can be an expression of solidarity. As a colleague suggested, perhaps this could lead people to buy an album of Hall's music. While buying an album from preservation labels such as Rounder or Folkways is perhaps a laudable exercise of consumer choice, whatever sentiments of solidarity we may attach to it, the underlying act is consumption.

Such "virtual" solidarity is hamstrung by the abstraction inherent in commodification. Moby's song tears Hall's music from the cultural matrix that produced it, reducing its laments to floating symbols of intensity, religiosity, and authenticity. At best, such music provides catharsis of the political sentiments of the audience; at worst, its abstraction reinforces the listeners' unreflective distance from similar injustices in their own lives.

This abstraction impedes the translation of ethical concerns into action, reducing ethics to sentiment. The virtual becomes a substitute for concrete political solidarity, or to put it another way, a fundamentally different act—consumption—is substituted for political action. The uncomfortable, challenging, disruptive aspects of face-to-face, shoulder-to-shoulder solidarity are eliminated. These disembodied voices ring with challenging otherness but are, in fact, completely domesticated. They are about as likely to cause a political disturbance as a digital keyboard is to go out of tune. This virtual solidarity does not disrupt; instead, it legitimates the subjectivity of the consumer through the payoff of moral sentiment. Katherine Bergeron has offered a critique of the album *Chant* along these lines. The use of chant is particularly informative, as this music forms part of the ritual prayer of the monastic community. There it is tied to a host of practices and institutions that link it as a cultural object to the life of the community. She argues that such nostalgic uses of religious music remove it from its liturgical context and transform it into "virtual" rituals that make no demands on the listener.[3] They do, however, make one demand: "consume"—a long way from *"ora et labora"* (although, as Tom Beaudoin has noted, such a critique must be careful not to assume too much about the demands "real" liturgies place upon participants).[4]

This critique of the effects of such music does not presume shallow motives on the part of artists. Moby, for example, has demonstrated great willingness to alienate his fan base, as he did with his previous album, *Animal Rights.* Rather, the commodification of culture strips such works of their subversive potential. Another recent popular use of chant exemplifies this disarmament of culture. The 1993 release of *Chant* did not mark the reemergence of Gregorian chant into popular culture. It was preceded by Enigma's 1990 album *MCMXC A.D.* One popular song on the album, "Sadeism" interspersed the chant for the final sending forth of the mass, *Procedamus in Pace,* with dance music and a conversation (whispered in sibilant French) with the Marquis de Sade. (This album provoked a plagiarism lawsuit with the Munich Kapelle Antiqua, whose performance was sampled on the album).[5] "Sadeism" and many of the other songs on the album lie somewhere between subversive modernist attempts at ironic juxtaposition and flat-out postmodern pastiche, where the decadence implied is merely another passing source of intense experience.

These examples make clear that there is still a substantial interest in things religious. The predictions of the late 1960s of progressive secularization have not come to pass. Critics of secularization theory speak now of the decline of religious institutions leading not to the disappearance of religion but to its revitalization after the decline of institutional monopolies in a newly "deregulated" market. We will have to consider the consequences of this shift of infrastructures. Religion inhabits new spaces, is mediated by new classes of people, and is practiced in new ways. We have already alluded to club dancing as a ritual practice, and it is not too much of an exaggeration to see Moby as a quasi-clerical figure; he clearly retrieves, presents, and interprets religious material. We must consider not only how members of the new class of cultural mediators resemble classical religious leaders but also how leaders in classical religious traditions are recast in the mold of pop-culture celebrity. The mass-marketing of classical religious material such as *Chant* also alerts us to the changing spaces of religious practice. Katherine Bergeron incisively notes that religious nostalgia is nothing new. She argues that the monks of Solesmes who did such painstaking work to recover the traditions of Gregorian chant, were imbued with romantic nostalgia for a lost golden age. She describes Solesmes as "a kind of tourist site for *fin-de-siècle* types seeking spiritual thrills."[6] However, decadent spiritual tourists such as Claude Debussy and J.-K. Huysmans still had actually to travel to the abby to hear the monks chant. Today, monasteries and churches still exist but are joined by the concert hall and the dance club. If these latter seem evanescent in contrast to their venerable predecessors, they appear as bedrocks of solidity when compared with the locations for encountering religious culture we charted in the previous chapter: the single-family home, the car radio, and the portable CD player. These are the spaces where postmoderns construct themselves, and we will consider the sorts of identities favored by these spaces and this system of engagement with religious tradition.

THE DUAL DYNAMISMS
OF COMMODIFICATION IN RELIGION

In chapter 2, we discussed the two tendencies of commodification that seemingly work in opposite directions despite the fact that they are intrinsically related. On the one hand, there is consumer capitalism's insatiable hunger for marketable stuff, which creates a world where everything is transformed into a commodity that can be brought to market, exchanged, and consumed: selves, others, culture, religion. On the other hand, we witness a great hollowing out. Exchange demands interchangeability, equivalence. Anything that stands in the way of exchange becomes a problem. Rough edges must be smoothed. Objects must now function outside of their original contexts. Both dynamics are evident in the music described above. Artists ransack cultures for material, which they then use in ways that thoroughly domesticate the objects. African American spirituals, Gregorian chant, and long-dead libertines are combined into a swirling pastiche served up on the dance floor or through the Walkman. We will consider the effects of these dynamics upon religion in turn.

The Insatiable Desire for "Stuff"

The first of these dynamics, the insatiable desire for things, arises from the fact that commodification requires material on which to work. As commodification expands through culture, it focuses on those elements of culture that can most readily be made into discrete elements of exchange. Cable television, one of the key infrastructures of the culture industry, is an illuminative example. With more than 120 channels available in conventional systems and upwards of 500 on digital, there is an enormous need for "content."

This infrastructural shift undergirds and reinforces the tranformations of post-Fordism, bringing about a shift in taste. Here the produce section provides an allegory for religion. If Fordist America ate millions of tons of iceberg lettuce, as it slid into a generalized Judeo-Christian theistic civil religion, the taste for mixed exotica in post-Fordist religion resembles the organic mesclun bin—an assortment of greens drawn from various European and Asian cuisines that likely never appeared together on a salad plate until the 1990s. The post-Fordist religious market, like cable television, needs content. This commodification of religion works on a number of levels. Most obviously, it spawns an interest in the material aspects of religion. There is particular interest in paraphernalia of a size suitable for mass marketing—prayer beads (Buddhist prayer beads were a recent marketing sensation), jewelry and body adornments (*bindis*, henna tattoos, and the like), images and statuary, religious vessels, and so forth. A company called Accoutrements, which bills itself as an "outfitter of material culture," offers a line of novelty items ranging from the humorous to the oddly, ironically serious. These include a wind-up "Nunzilla toy," a "Jesus action figure," "Hindu God finger puppets" and glow-in-the-dark statues of St. Clare and St. Isadore, the patron saints of television and the Internet, respectively. Each comes on a standard plastic bubble card. On the back of the packages are brief essays on the historical and theological significance of the figure, that—with the exception of Nunzilla—are factual and serious.

The media provide other avenues for commodification. Sacred music constitutes a part of the enormously popular "World Music" repertoire offered by numerous small studios such as Amiata, March Hare, and Waterlilly as well as larger studios and labels for major music studios such as Windham Hill, Shakti, and Ellipsis. A character in Don DeLillo's *Underworld* jogs along a drainage canal, listening to Sufi chants on "wireless" headphones while savoring the marketing thoughtfulness embodied in the design of his velcro ankle wallet.[7]

Visual media are important in this regard as well. Televangelism comes quickly to mind: televised worship services with high production values—from the liturgies of the "Hour of Power" to the high-energy revival preaching of Jimmy Swaggart (notoriously, Jerry Lee Lewis's cousin).[8] Commodification in the most literal form is clear in the (age-old) promises of healings or blessings in return for seed money, or pulp spirituality books available in exchange for "love offerings." Less crass religious offerings such as *Touched by an Angel* are probably more significant. In addition to televised religious programming, one could also note the literal marketing of religious practices, such as videos on Tantric sexual practices or the *Kama Sutra*. (For the latter, Amazon.com lists sixteen videos, sixty-nine books, and hundreds of paraphernalia ranging from massage oils to Kama Sutra "honey dust.") Christian shock jock Bob Larson offered a video on the threat of satanism in the United States as a premium gift to supporters. He promised that, unlike competitors, his video showed a real, satanic ritual in all of its shocking detail—violence, blood, nudity! While certainly satanism, as the shadow religion of Christianity, was of particular interest to his audience, it is clear that other religions they might consider equally unsaved do not lend themselves to video exploitation. Sales and rentals of videos of Quaker prayer meetings have been disappointing in all markets.

Although these examples do not represent particularly large markets, the same dynamic is evident on a much broader scale. Religions that lend themselves to visual intensity and symbolism have greater appeal in consumer culture.[9] Much has been written concerning the religious vision and gender politics of Madonna videos. From a formal perspective, there is a clear consonance of Catholicism with the other elements employed in her early videos: her overt sexuality signaled in a range of fetish objects, her exposed navel, the kitschy beauty mark, the decadent overlayering of lingerie and lace, and so on. Her video for the song "Like a Prayer" had plenty of interesting plot dynamics and narrative twists. Andrew Greeley enthusiastically welcomed her assistance in his lifelong mission to help Catholics appreciate sex. The title of his piece conveyed his theological admiration: "Like a Catholic: Madonna's Challenge to Her Church."[10] It no doubt challenged those who understood its religious symbolism and were accustomed to sundering sexuality from the sacred. If shown in parishes, at episcopal conferences, and in Roman consistories, this video could perhaps have functioned as the powerful challenge for the Catholic Church to accept its sacramental vision of human sexuality that Greeley believed it was. Extreme Augustinian anxiety about sex was not, however, a particular hangup for MTV's primary audience—males (and to a lesser extent females) between the ages of fourteen and twenty-four. Whatever merits this video may have had for challenging the perduring Jansenism within Christianity, it was amply successful for its target audience. Its various transgressions—religious, sexual, and racial (the video featured a Martin de Porres character)—provided plenty of visual and sexual intensity for a three-minute music video. Rosaries worn as necklaces, the crucifix hovering where the eye is drawn for other reasons, fingered with black-lace gloves, provide the perfect elements for the genre. Madonna explained her interest in the crucifix, although her consummate commercialism and the location of the statement (in an interview that accompanied the 1985 publication of nude photos of her in *Penthouse*) might call for a grain of salt: "Crucifixes are sexy because there's a naked man on them."[11] Non-sacramental and aniconic traditions have a hard time competing with that. Madonna has subsequently drawn from other symbolically rich religious traditions. She appeared in an MTV performance with a troupe of Indian dancers, wearing the forehead decoration of a Brahman priest. The 1998 album *Ray of Light* included a song with Sanskrit lyrics drawn from a Yogic text, and a video for that album used kabbalistic symbolism and imagery. A friend once observed how poorly the United States Conference of Catholic Bishops exploits its television coverage: men in black suits with pectoral crosses hidden discreetly in their breast pockets. Catholics like Madonna and Fulton J. Sheen could teach them a thing or two.

All of this spills over into religion away from the tube. The rising dominance of video as a genre ties in with and reinforces the visual hypertrophy of consumer culture. It is not simply a question of religion being marketed as video content, but of the sensibilities of video consumption informing religious tastes more broadly. Stark modernist aesthetics or their Protestant predecessors do not signify in this culture so hungry for spectacle. Religions that provide symbol-rich content have an advantage in such a setting that goes deeper than the mere presence of visual material. One could say that if a distorted Protestant piety was useful to capitalism in an earlier stage, perhaps a hypertrophied form of Catholic sacramentality conforms nicely with the needs of an epoch where the consumption of things and signs has become a cultural imperative.[12] (However, nonsacramental religions may have an advantage in legitimating consumption in other areas by making fewer specific demands, allowing for religion to be a better commodity, as we shall see below.)

This interest in "stuff" is evident also in a broad shift in religious sensibilities that spans ideological divides between liberals and conservatives and is manifest across traditions: a widespread interest in the particularities of cultures and religious traditions. It appears in a variety of ways. Religious believers manifest an increased interest in the distinctive identities of their religious traditions and the folkways left behind in the great suburban exodus. There is a striking parallel in the development of scholarly interest in material culture and the movement of kitsch items into what were once called antique stores. Theological scholarship has also been marked by this shift. Waves of narrative, postliberal, and radical orthodox scholarship that emphasize the particularity of Christian tradition have swept through the academy along with historical, textual, and cultural analyses by scholars fascinated with the embarrassing details of biblical texts and religious traditions and practices.

The advantage enjoyed by more visual and sacramental religious traditions comes at the cost of being assimilated into the forms of commercial popular culture. We will consider below how this transformation of sensibility spills over into religious traditions, changing the nature of religious rituals and the way people relate to religious leaders. For now, a brief example will serve to clarify the dynamic and its costs. Neotraditionalist forms of Catholicism that repudiate the Second Vatican Council seem almost perfect illustrations of commodified nostalgia. Rejecting the council's attempts to engage modernity critically, they dwell in the Catholicism of the recent past, revering its practices, beliefs, decor, and costume. Such nostalgic retrievals inevitably idealize the past by abstracting it from the particularities that created it and sunder it from any organic relation to the present. But we cannot dwell in the past. Inevitably, such "traditionalist" retrievals are not only innovative but also deeply contemporary. Fundamentalism is a thoroughly modern phenomenon. Traditionalism is deeply marked by the contemporary in that it easily conforms to the logic of nostalgia described by Fredric Jameson. Like souvenirs brought home from distant lands, the religion of the past is excised from its cultural political context and used to decorate the everyday life of our own time.

Clearly, neotraditionalist retrievals can function as more complex engagements with contemporary culture. For example, William Portier argues that the retrieval of preconciliar practices and dress among contemporary seminarians is not adequately described as "conservative." Rather, this retrieval provides the material for a Catholic form of evangelical visible witness.[13] Past moments of the Christian tradition provide abundant material for such tactical engagements as well as more substantive resources for contemporary problems. What we must notice, however, is the crucial importance of *how they are retrieved*. When treated according to the norms and practices of consumer culture, they are not critical engagements with contemporary culture; they are mere window dressing for capitulation to the status quo of everyday life.

Abstraction: Only Certain Kinds of Stuff

Here we cross over into the second dynamic of commodification, the flip side of nostalgia. If there is an endless appetite for stuff in consumer culture, there are very specific restrictions placed on how this stuff can function. Cultural products must be disciplined for market, much the way agricultural produce has been. Do you like tomatoes full of flavor, juicy, nutritious? Agribusiness has nothing against such things, but economic calculus demands commodifiable produce: plants that set fruit quickly and all at once, with thick skins that can travel well. When new varieties are developed, these qualities are given priority. Taste and nutrition follow. If the first dynamic of commodification endlessly seeks the exotic and new, giving us *habañeros*, this one brings the unobjectionableness of McDonald's french fries, tailored to the need for widespread acceptance. This does not preclude making reference to the transcendent, placing demands on the believer, or calling for subversive action, but it does place serious parameters around these aspects of religion.

While the explicit disciplining and censoring of religion into a bland, common civil religion may be most characteristic of the Fordist period, this dynamic is amply present in our own period as well. It was certainly clear in the earliest days of religion in the media. Witness the explicit censoring and evaluating of which religious voices were worthy and permissible to have access to the airwaves in early radio. Stations gave air time to religious preachers and teachers as a way of satisfying community service requirements. They frequently employed boards of evaluators to select appropriate figures for these programs. R. Laurence Moore notes that, as a result, these were generally educated pastors from rather wealthy communities. He quotes a manual for religious broadcasters from the time that discourages moral critiques of society and advises ministers against speaking "dogmatically." "Remember, its normality we're all striving for."[14]

These dynamics continue today. Jim and Tammy Fay Bakker were members of the Assemblies of God, a Pentecostal denomination that practices speaking in tongues. The Bakkers regularly engaged in this practice behind the scenes of their program but never on camera. While it would have provided exquisite spectacle, it was deemed too bizarre for a mass audience.

Consider the differing fortunes of religions in the corporate world. Imagine the likely response of a corporate recruiter to a practitioner of Zen as opposed to a member of a Pentecostal community that practices snake handling. Would the candidate's religious practices be equally respected? Certainly both religions would contribute much to one's ability to function under stressful conditions. Contemporary popular culture is profoundly marked by a default preference for a generalized, nonspecific religiosity, from the vague theism of "From a Distance" to the expressly nonchristological evangelical Christianity of *Touched by an Angel*.[15] The same pattern is observable in the more exotic niches of the religious market. Religious music sales tend toward genres more easily engaged in a shallow manner, such as rhythm and chants, rather than lengthy, complex musical works such as Indian Ragas or operatic narrative works such as Indonesian Gamalon or European opera.

Like the first dynamic (nostalgia and the insatiable desire for stuff), abstraction spills over into broader religious practice as well. This dynamic provides a balancing, opposed attitude to the desire for particularity. If particular elements of religious culture are desirable, the equally particular exclusivity of their interrelationships is not. The moniker "nondenominational" for evangelical Christian churches is appealing for side-stepping the historical "baggage" of traditional denominations.[16] The universality of monotheism signifies in such a situation, but overly particular monotheistic accounts of God do not. Thus, we witness a preference for nonpersonal accounts of God. While this accounts for the appeal of explicitly nonpersonal traditions (e.g., Hindu notions of Brahman), it is manifest more widely in implicit form (e.g., belief that the same God is worshiped in all religions). Neil Gaiman skewers this tendency in a scene in *American Gods*, a novel about a conflict between the old, forgotten gods who were brought to America by past immigrants and the new gods of technology, money, and the media. Traveling cross-country in an attempt to rally the old pantheon for one final battle with the new, Odin meets the Celtic Oestre of the Dawn. She is doing better than most of the old gods because once a year people still ritually consume foods sacred to her—decorated eggs and candy bunnies. He attempts to rouse her interest by challenging the sincerity of these rituals. The first person he questions about the holiday responds that she thinks Easter has something to do with Jesus (although she is not sure). The second person he questions seems more promising. She professes to be a "pagan." The aged gods grow excited, inquiring whom she worships, what sorts of rituals she performs. The young pagan grows angry, believing she is being mocked. There are no particular rituals. She worships "the female principle. It's an empowerment thing."[17]

Such abstraction is evident not just in the uneducated retrievals of contemporary neopagans, but also in some of the most influential scholarly theology of the past century. Much of the appeal of the transcendental and existential theologies of figures such as Karl Rahner and Paul Tillich can be traced to their projects distinguishing the essence of Christian faith from the cultural particulars of traditions that had become increasingly unintelligible to modern believers. This task is, whatever the nuances and differences between their particular projects, essentially one of abstraction. Eugene McCarraher describes Tillich's project as an attempt to develop an "absolute faith that" could "supposedly flourish outside the confines of symbol and ritual."[18] Catholic philosopher John Caputo brings this antitradition to a contentless apophatic apotheosis in his influential adaptations of Derrida, offering apocalyptic without apocalypse, messianism without a messiah, religion without religion.[19] Francis Schüssler Fiorenza argues that contemporary attempts to advocate and respect religious pluralism and cultural otherness by both theologians and scholars of religion may, in fact, be "an expression of a Eurocentric market economy in which ideas, including religious ideas, are reduced to commodities."[20]

These conceptions of the deity are a sign of the deeper changes in how people engage religious traditions. Much has been said concerning the "cafeteria" mentality among contemporary religious believers. The metaphor obviously resonates with consumerism. We are now in a position to consider the details of this connection. The logic of the consumption of culture militates against the maintenance of the deep coherence of religious and cultural traditions. The vast appetite for things described above requires that symbols, beliefs, and practices be removed from their original contexts. Their retrieval enables them to live on, but they are enacted within a fundamentally different logic.

Joseph Campbell provides a perfect example of how the first dynamic (reification) coincides with this second (abstraction). His enormous success (enough to warrant a conference entitled "The Joseph Campbell Phenomenon" in the early 1990s) wasn't due to his originality. Much of his thought was borrowed from Carl Jung and Mircea Eliade. Much more, however, than skill at popularization drove his success. The format of his most successful publication—the multivolume *Power of Myth*—tells the tale. They are large-format, glossy books crammed with snippets of mythology and the spiritual practices of the world's religions, the text woven in and out of myriad symbols and images. Campbell's publications fed a hunger for things religious. As William Dinges has noted, however, for all its encyclopedic presentation of traditions, it is a profoundly antitraditional work. Campbell's debts to Jungian psychology and the *philosophia perennis* incline him to reduce all traditions to manifestations of fundamental archetypes, all religious figures to another instance of the "hero with a thousand faces." This approach is appealing because of what it enables religious believers to do. Focusing on the particular attraction that Campbell held for Catholics, Dinges observed that he provided believers with a "way to re-appropriate (and de-parochialize) the symbolism of their own tradition."[21] In the process of retrieval, symbolism is freed from its communal and institutional infrastructure. As a consequence, religion is rendered increasingly private and individual. "Modern men, incapable of strict fidelity to a single religion, would find their own heroism in a therapeutic piracy that ransacked the world's spiritual treasures."[22] This is manifest not simply in the location of interpretation but also in the perception of the content of the religious life. Individual concerns increasingly swamp questions of communal obligation and broader questions of justice. Campbell's popular success is a perfect illustration of the effects of the dual dynamics of commodification upon religion. Traditions are pillaged for their symbolic content, which is then repackaged and recontextualized in a way that jettisons their communal, ethical, and political consequences. Traditions are valued as sources of "poetic and imaginative imagery," while their logics, systems of doctrine, and rules of practice are dismissed for their rigidity and exclusivity.[23] But it is precisely these connections that enable religion to inform the practice of life.

Thus, the commodification of culture causes a number of problems for religious belief and practice. The dual dynamics we have just sketched comprise the most fundamental of these: a dissolution of the coherence of religions reducing them to a palette of "cultural resources" that can be employed in any number of ways—even ways fundamentally at odds with the basic logic of their original religious tradition. This fragmentation also divorces faith from practice. Symbols, beliefs, and even spiritual disciplines become free-floating cultural objects ready to be put to whatever use we desire. Buddhist meditation serves as a stress management tool in a capitalist business world devoted to endless acquisition; Yoga is reduced to a physical fitness regimen; the crucifix becomes a brand symbol for the niche marketing of Catholic education. These dynamics do not, however, simply float in the air. When we introduced them in the last chapter, we were careful to observe the particular economic, social, and cultural changes that brought them about. We will now gauge their effect on religious faith and practice.

THE CONSUMER SELF
AND RELIGIOUS TRADITIONS

There are many competing accounts of the interests and activities of consumers. Neoliberal economists celebrate the sovereign wisdom of consumers, while despondent Frankfurt theorists lament how happily the masses are duped by marketing and mindless commercial culture. This disparity is an indication of the complexity of the topic. We begin here with a pessimistic account of the activity of consumers that sees contemporary society as gripped by a fragmenting narcissism that transforms everything, including religion, into a self-centered, therapeutic exercise. Some theorists attribute this therapeutic sensibility directly to consumer culture and the social forces of commercial marketing. While this sort of cultural critique often verges on either moralistic diatribe or hand-wringing, it nevertheless corresponds well to recent sociological literature on the changing nature of religious identity and belief. We will consider studies of the religious dispositions of the postwar "seeker" generations as well as broader sociological accounts of changes in the institutional nature of religion.

The Therapeutic Self

The terms of the critique are immediately familiar: contemporary religion has been transformed into a narcissistic, therapeutic enterprise by generations of rootless "seekers" who lack allegiance to religious institutions or communities. "So long as there is a consumer market to cater for, especially in its postmodern cultural form, spiritual Disneylands will thrive. Ignoring tradition-based limits to consumption, they cannot operate as religion. The payoff, however, lies with what can therefore be offered—provisions for those intent on 'narcissistically pleasing themselves.'"[24] Paul Heelas's comments continue a criticism now (at least) four decades old. In the mid-1960s Philip Rieff spoke of the *Triumph of the Therapeutic*, where, deprived of any transcendent good or even shared communal values, human existence is reduced to "an intensely private sense of well-being."[25] Focusing on the work of psychoanalytic writers such as C. G. Jung and D. H. Lawrence, he charted the reconfiguration of Western Christianity into a therapeutic enterprise. Christopher Lasch's influential account *The Culture of Narcissism* contrasts this therapeutic sensibility with traditional religion. People no longer hunger for salvation or an era of justice, but for "the feeling, the momentary illusion, of personal well-being, health, and psychic security."[26] He attributes the genesis of this sensibility to the bureaucratic complexities of modern existence, which erode peoples' "everyday competence." The resulting dependence is manifested psychologically as narcissism, where a "grandiose, narcissistic, infantile, empty self" depends on others to validate its existence.[27] Morality is replaced with a shallow ideal of psychic equilibrium. Shorn of its disruptive challenge, religion becomes a mere coping mechanism employed to smooth the contradictions of the middle-class status quo.

T. J. Jackson Lears has offered an account of the emergence of this *mentalité* within the history of twentieth-century advertising. He locates it within the broader upheavals of modernity that unmoored the bourgeois self from traditional sources of identity. Urbanization removed people from the ties of smaller communities and released them into an anonymity that was at once exhilarating and debilitating. Technology increasingly removed the traditional sources of suffering and struggle (at least among the leisure class) against which human existence had perennially identified itself. The rise of interdependent national markets deprived people of a meaningful sense of autonomy. They were increasingly placed at the whims of market forces beyond their control. In America, this was particularly destabilizing in light of the rural republican myth of the industrious, self-sufficient landholder. The secularization of mainstream Christianity furthered this disorientation by removing the transcendent goals and sanctions that had previously set the bounds for acceptable behavior.[28]

These erosions of the stability of the self gave rise to the therapeutic ethos. In the wake of the collapse of traditional frameworks of meaning, the modern self faced an increased demand to perform and be productive. This instrumentalized and commodified self was expressed in a shift in emphasis from character to "personality." In a social world reconfigured in terms of market competition, individuals were forced to market themselves by cultivating "winning" personality traits as well as appearance, hygiene, and health. A host of cultural elites—physicians, psychologists, and Christian ministers—offered an ideology of the self to assist people in accomplishing these tasks. These therapeutic programs portrayed security, vitality, and harmony as personal concerns and responsibilities that could be achieved without social change. Despite the great variety of programs and prescriptions, they all shared the "tacit assumption that self-realization was the largest aim of human experience . . . commitments outside the self shrank to meet the seeker's immediate emotional requirements."[29] "Growth," "becoming," and "self-realization" became ends in themselves, divorced from broader social or transcendent goals. The eighteenth-century and early-nineteenth-century literature Jackson Lears surveys sounds eerily contemporary in its promises of "unlimited growth" achieved by "unlocking human potential."

These therapeutic assumptions are evident across popular literature, psychology, and religion. In 1908, the Emmanuel movement offered a program that combined mind-cure techniques such as autosuggestion and hypnotism with Christianity, which, in the words of its founders, possessed "the greatest of therapeutic agents" for unlocking one's potential. Jesus was portrayed as the archetypal vigorous, winning personality. In the words of influential liberal Protestant moralist Harry Emerson Fosdick, the foundation of Christianity is faith in "man's personality, with all its possibilities and powers."[30]

Most significant for our project, however, Jackson Lears argues that the emergence of the therapeutic sensibility is best understood in the context of the rise of consumer capitalism. While it clearly served the needs of the corporate world and reinforced the authority of cultural professionals (physicians, psychologists, clergy, and so on), capitalism's rise was not simply a matter of class interest or bureaucratic dominance. Any such widespread cultural dominant is inevitably sustained by a complex range of forces and interests. Jackson Lears pinpoints advertising as an essential factor in the emergence, dissemination, and continued vitality of the therapeutic ethos. Both the form and the content of advertising reinforced the perspective of the therapeutic self and exploited its anxieties.

Print advertising underwent a seismic shift in the 1890s. The sheer number of ads for a growing range of consumer goods rendered text-based ads increasingly ineffective. Advertising trade journals noted the need to capture the reader's attention, and technical advances in printing provided the means for doing so with images. The rhetoric of advertising shifted from providing information about products to more sensational, attention-grabbing forms. This rise of sensational advertising paralleled the growth of other forms of popular spectacle such as cabarets and amusement parks, which provided "commodified titillation" for harried city dwellers.[31] These forms of popular culture were consonant with the therapeutic quest for intense experiences, and the content of ads was equally well suited to the therapeutic milieu. Claude Hopkins and Albert Lasker revolutionized advertising with their "reason why" approach. Instead of describing the qualities and virtues of the product being sold, they conjured visions of the ways in which the product could transform the consumer's life. Medicines were not simply effective cures; they bestowed vitality and vigor. Hygiene products brought romantic success; clothing, esteem. This new form of marketing aroused "consumer demand by associating products with imaginary states of well-being" and by exacerbating the social anxieties of the therapeutic self. This shift in marketing fundamentally changed consumption by transforming commodities into symbolic markers for deeper fulfillment. A 1928 ad for Drano featured a nude woman standing in a bathtub, marveling at her free-flowing drains. Ad images promised "therapeutic feelings of emotional or sensuous excitement," but because of the disconnect between products and ads, fulfillment was invariably deferred.[32] Most uses of Drano likely fell short of the voyeuristic pleasures the ad promised and provided.

Advertising's use of the therapeutic had three significant effects: it increased social insecurities, further eroded the meaning of cultural symbols, and promoted a relation between consumption and fulfillment. The most obvious critique of this advertising program was its exploitation of human insecurity. Whatever the merits of various products for facilitating social success (and these cannot be dismissed out of hand), the cumulative cultural effect of these ads exacerbated insecurity by creating an atmosphere in which every aspect of the anxious self—personality, appearance, hygiene, parenting, and housekeeping—was subjected to ruthless surveillance. There was a deeper, less obvious dynamic in advertisements that furthered these unsettling effects. The use of attention-grabbing images and the juxtaposition of symbols and evocations of fulfillment with consumer goods eroded the stability of these images, symbols, and concepts in a manner consonant with Jameson's account of postmodernism. "Under capitalism, visual and verbal signs become detached from all traditional associations and meaning in general is eroded. The world of advertisements gradually acquired an Alice-in-Wonderland quality."[33] Hence, this paleo-postmodern comment, penned by a cultural critic in 1915, "American culture grows more Heiroglyphic by the day."[34]

Grounding the critique of therapeutic culture in advertising is important not just because it ties that literature to scholarship concerning transformations in

religious belief and practice. It is valuable because it relates these cultural dispositions to a particular material infrastructure and practice, which is essential for our
analysis. The exploitation of the therapeutic paradigm in marketing was a water-
shed in the commodification of culture. It engendered a profoundly important
change in the practice of consumption by associating it with psychological and
social needs that were previously fulfilled through nonmarket means such as community and religion. It is impossible to overstate the importance of this shift. The
massive cultural force of advertising directed people to fulfill their needs for
meaning, wholeness, and belonging through consumption—a practice in which,
in the course of the twentieth century, more and more people engaged more and
more often. Thus, the excesses and irrationalities of our consumer society are not
simply a matter of shallow, ignorant greed, of people choosing the comforts of
luxury vehicles over committed relationships or spiritual pursuits. This advertising program exploited the dislocations suffered by modern persons and systematically proposed consumption as the remedy.

There are two complementary dynamics at work here that are relevant to religion. The first is relatively obvious. By exploiting the human desire for meaning
and belonging, marketers could be said to be positioning their products to compete with religion. What is perhaps less obvious but much more important is that
the pursuit of fulfillment was transformed in the process as well. As people were
being trained to find fulfillment in consumption, they were also, in effect, being
trained to bring the habits and dispositions of the realm of consumption to more
traditional sources of meaning, including religion.

In its desire for self-fulfillment and freedom of choice to meet its own needs,
the therapeutic self is precisely the consumer self. Its engagement with the world is
one of choosing the goods most consonant with its own particular life*style*. In this
culture, religion, like other commodities, serves to fill in the identity of the consumer. It can do this only insofar as it confirms the fundamental form of the self as
consumer. Thus, the form of religion we have been discussing—abstracted sentiment divorced from practice—is ideally suited to this world. It supplies the veneer
of meaning and conviction of which modern existence so often deprives us, without disrupting the underlying form of our lives—our obligation to consume.

The rise of the therapeutic took place amid a host of other transformations of
religion in the twentieth century. Sociological literature on religion in postwar
America addresses these other forces that have contributed to changes in religious
faith and practice.

Sheila, the Seekers, and Spirituality

Concern about the reconfiguration of religion in terms of individual therapeutic
needs was perhaps most famously expressed by Robert Bellah and his collabora-
tors in *Habits of the Heart* with the term "Sheilaism"—named for the interview
subject Sheila Larson, who described a faith in God mediated by her "own little

voice," heavily influenced by her experiences in psychotherapy and independent of traditional religious communities. The authors used her as an emblem of "a kind of radical individualism that tends to elevate the self to a cosmic principle."[35] Although they were careful not to reduce this individualized selection of religious belief to a self-centered lack of concern for others, the authors did raise the specter of a nation divided by "cancerous" individualism, where each person is isolated in her or his own vague, personal creed, lacking resources to relate his or her individual concerns to broader communities. Some have come to Sheila's defense. As for the cancerousness of her individualism, we should note that Sheila was neither a corrupt chief financial officer nor a drug dealer, but a nurse. Wade Clark Roof argues that Sheilaism has taken an undeserved "beating" as a scapegoat for a host of social anxieties about the fragmentation of belief and community.[36] Roof has undertaken several extended studies of religious belief and practice among the postwar generations. His account of the "seeker" as the "spiritual style" of the baby-boomer generation helps to balance denunciations of the influence of therapeutic concerns upon religion.

Members of the boomer generation "value experience over beliefs, distrust institutions and leaders, stress personal fulfillment yet yearn for community, and are fluid in their allegiances."[37] Along with Catherine Albanese, he finds this religious style present in the religious lives of people with very different levels of commitment to very different sorts of religious traditions—from conservative evangelical Christians and women whose feminist consciousness has alienated them from traditional Christianity to practitioners of New Age spiritualities.[38] Henri Nouwen's prolific production serves as a model of the peregrinations of the seeker generation. After living a particular lifestyle or in a particular culture for a few years, he would publish a journal or a book on the topic, eventually producing volumes on Trappist monasticism, liberation theology, Latin American spirituality, and finally Jean Vanier's *L'Arche* community. Robert Wuthnow argues that there has been a fundamental shift in the form of American religious life, from a church-based "dwelling" in the immediate postwar period, where allegiance to congregations was strong and stable to the "seeking" unleashed by boomer spirituality.[39]

Roof does not reduce the emergence of quest culture to consumerism but notes that they are deeply intertwined in their origin and continued development. The boomer generation grew up being catered to and courted by marketers. If the quest for identity has its roots in this marketing program, it in turn serves as a theme for further marketing. Quest, Odyssey, Discovery, Explorer, Pathfinder—all likely if not actual names of religious formation or retreat programs—were also names of best selling SUVs and minivans in the 1990s.[40] Roof argues, however, that all this materialism and consumption have given rise to a "postmaterialist" culture.[41] Growing up in an era of abundance, many members of this generation now seek deeper spiritual and communal sources of fulfillment.

This generation's signal contribution to American religious culture has been the reorientation of religion in terms of "spirituality," which has come to denote the personal, experiential dimensions of religion in opposition to its institutional forms. Believers increasingly relate to religious traditions as repositories of insights and practices that they appropriate for their own personal syntheses. Roof finds that people across traditions consistently default to individual language concerning religious agency. This is dismissed by the narcissism critique, and it is deeply suspect in many theological circles. But, for all its many detractors, there is no denying that this is a particularly active form of religious engagement. People presume that they must find a form of religious belief and practice that is right for them and be able to justify their choice. This is a particularly intentional form of belief. In Susan Harding's words, there has been a shift "from a world in which beliefs held believers to one in which believers hold beliefs."[42]

Even when commitment involves a particular tradition or community, the individual has responsibility to choose and evaluate that commitment. In this sense, seekers must be taken seriously. While there is much that happens under the guise of "seeker-friendly" or "seeker-driven" church outreach that sorely tempts theologians and others to adopt tones of snide mockery (a corporate food court in the narthex?!), seekers themselves are too easily dismissed. Their low commitment to particular institutions and communities can be understood as driven by the seriousness of their searching. What is often dismissed as self-centered, consumerist evaluation of religious communities (e.g., "What do you have to offer me?"), can be equally understood as posing serious and challenging questions to these institutions and communities. Seekers want to know precisely why a particular community exists. What does it stand for? What is its mission? How is that accomplished? A culture of choice is not necessarily antithetical to commitment. Wade Clark Roof argues that it may, in fact, strengthen it. In such a context, people are certainly likely to report more caveats and hesitations when describing their religious affiliation than in situations where religious identity is ascribed as a marker for class, ethnicity, or the like. This does not necessarily represent a decline in religious seriousness; indeed, it may signal an increase. Such caveats can be read as an indication that people are carefully and thoughtfully negotiating the terms, conditions, and limits of their affiliation with a given religious group rather than accepting it as a social given like ethnicity.[43]

Nancy Ammerman's research into the practices of "Golden Rule" Christians should also be noted in this regard. While this group is not identical to Roof's seekers, it shares a lower level of institutional commitment and an ambivalence concerning overly doctrinaire formulations of faith. If members of this group score low on conventionally accepted scales of religious commitment, they possess a stable religious orientation that informs a range of practices—from mutual support and neighborliness to care for the poor and hungry.[44] There may indeed be much of value in these more institutionally fluid forms of Christianity, including more commitment than we are inclined to think in the life of a wandering seeker.

Seekers are, of course, nothing new. They are present in one form or another in many religious traditions. They are often associated with moments in the life of communities when extant forms cease to be adequate. There is no theological reason to assume that contemporary seekers are any less (or more) sincere than those of days past. Nor is there any reason to assume that their spiritual syntheses are necessarily less profound than those found in the many established religious traditions both great and small.

There are, however, serious problems inherent in spirituality as a religious formation. Roof's description of spirituality very closely resembles commodified habits of cultural consumption. Elements of tradition are interpreted, engaged, and used in abstraction or disembedded from "their traditional moorings—from historic creeds and doctrines, from broad symbolic universes, from religious community."[45] These connections stabilize the meanings of religious elements and connect them to practices. Shorn of these, elements of religious traditions pose less of a challenge to the status quo; they can be more easily made to conform to the default assumptions and practices of the dominant culture. Thus, in our culture, such a reception of any religious tradition is easily coopted to the therapeutic paradigm. A second, related problem concerns the difficulty of sustaining religious commitment. While there is no particular reason to assume that contemporary seekers develop syntheses that are necessarily less profound than their predecessors, the emphasis on individual agency and religious experience renders sustained commitment to a religious vision extremely difficult. Without the support of a community of shared belief, commitment hinges to a great extent on the willpower of the individual believer. There is a third problem related to the first two: the difficulty of connecting a religious synthesis to a concrete form of life. Great spiritual traditions are the work of generations. Much of this work involves connecting symbols and beliefs to practices that form a way of life. These connections are seldom obvious or straightforward. It is this particular connection that is most challenged by the commodification of culture, where beliefs and commitments are easily reduced to a decorative function of providing private meaning to fill in the voids left by the structures of everyday life.

The Decline of Religious Monopolies

While the religious "style" of spirituality fits nicely with our account of the rise of consumer culture, it is clearly also a result of other cultural shifts of the past century. A range of transformations have taken place during the lives of the postwar generations—from the anti-establishment upheavals of the 1960s to the rise of pluralism as a fact of life in North American culture. These built upon the more fundamental upheavals of modernity in general to render communal and traditional sources of identity and meaning unstable, leaving individuals increasingly responsible to negotiate their own meanings and identities in an ever-changing world.

These reflections on the changing forms of religion in the modern world come in the wake of the decline of an earlier analytical narrative: secularization. A generalized account of the progressive decline of the social and personal influence of religion once not only dominated sociology but also approached the givenness of common sense in both theological circles and in broader culture. At the beginning of the twenty-first century, it is clear that expectations of the ongoing, progressive decline of religion were mistaken. While Western scientific rationality dominates many spheres of human existence, a vast majority of Americans still profess religious beliefs, and religion continues to inform political rhetoric and policy. Although the United States has long been a "religious hothouse," there is ample evidence from around the world attesting to the widespread continued vigor of religion. Islam is a potent political force, and Catholicism played a pivotal role in the end of communism in Poland. Pentecostalism is remaking the face not only of Latin American piety but also of its politics.[46] Orthodox marxist predictions of the disappearance of religion do not seem to alleviate the anxieties of Chinese authorities, who violently struggle not only to secularize what they consider the medieval anachronism of the stubbornly religious culture of Tibet but also to repress a new religious movement, Falun Gong, which has emerged in the heart of an officially irreligious nation.

Although some facts of secularization, such as disestablishment and the laicization of church property, are undeniable, religion clearly continues to thrive in other venues. If we distinguish the decline of institutional religion from the role of religion in people's lives, we are alerted to an important shift. The decline once described in terms of an all-encompassing secularization appears, rather, to have been a decline in the social and cultural power of religious institutions. The symbols, practices, and myths that they once stewarded continue to inform people's lives, but religious authorities and institutions exercise less control over how these are used. Some writers employ metaphors drawn from economics to describe this shift. They speak of the "deregulation" of religion or the decline of religious institutional monopolies.[47]

Roof cites changes in immigration law and Federal Communications Commission regulations as factors contributing to this deregulation. The latter ended the free air time given to religious programming administered through local boards of established religious leaders. Bland establishment broadcasts could not compete with the aggressive, attention-grabbing style of what would become televangelism. Although despised by mainstream churches, radio and television evangelists were successful enough with audiences to pay their own way on the airwaves. Mainstream religious institutions lost further social influence as sectarian, denominational, and parochial institutions (e.g., community centers, colleges, publishing houses, and hospitals) were replaced by state-sponsored public and private commercial institutions.[48] This process of replacement was the result not simply of the further expansion of the secular state into civil society but also of commercial interest in the market for religious goods (e.g., secular publishing houses competing with denominational presses).[49]

While much of this decline has to do with internal crises within particular religious traditions, the general erosions of modernity, and the rise of pluralism, it can also be usefully compared to the decline of the power of the state in the global economy that has emerged over the past several decades. As modernity slides into postmodernity, the modern state joins its former rival, institutional religion, among the social structures that are being eroded by global communications, travel, migration, and market exchange.

This notion of deregulation provides a helpful corrective to the excesses of the secularization hypothesis. Both, however, can be oversimplified. The deregulation thesis is susceptible to a romanticized view of the history of religion. The baseline for comparison is important. Religious leaders have struggled to control the beliefs and practices of lay believers, from the earliest spreading of the gospel through medieval Europe to Revolutionary-era America. Thus, we may be witnessing not an unprecedented period of decline in the cultural influence of religious elites but rather a return to the mean after a period of highly organized control of religion that took place during the emergence of widespread literacy among believers.

R. Laurence Moore sees this deregulation as nothing new. Following an insight of Matthew Arnold, he argues that, in the absence of government establishment, religions inevitably compete for followers according to a market model. He charts the venerable history of American religious leaders' use of commercial marketing techniques and pointedly notes how this often resulted in a complicity with commercial interests, which compromised the prophetic power of religion.[50] This analysis is interesting in light of the common observation that the United States has long had rates of religious belief and activity far above those of Europe. Lyon and Roof both agree that deregulation, far from leading to the decline of religion, has contributed to its ongoing vitality.[51] In a similar vein, Mike Featherstone speaks of how the locus of the sacred has moved from the traditional institutions that preserve religion to consumer culture. Lyon describes this as a new way of engaging religion as a "cultural resource" that individual believers appropriate and integrate into their own personal syntheses. There is much about this shift that can be considered positive, which will be addressed in chapter 5. As we have seen, Featherstone and others are more pessimistic about this transformation. They worry that this change erodes the classical sociological functions of religion to provide social cohesion and a horizon of meaning and to address "core existential questions."[52] These are important sociological questions, but they are not our primary concern.

The sociological identification of religion with social cohesion does not address the equally primordial prophetic component of religion. Indeed, the Hebrew prophetic tradition identified itself against the establishment faith of the monarchy. Thus, Moore's concern that the challenging voice of prophecy is silenced in marketed religion (in contrast to established religion) misses the mark as well. In a situation where there is little elite control over the interpretation and appropriation of religion, people may or may not tend to edit out the prophetic challenge. That question is not only sociological but theological. Different theologies of grace, of the fall, and of the church will come to different conclusions. Pessimistic Protestant theological anthropologies and clerical-centered Catholic ecclesiologies tend to assume the worst about believers. In contrast, low-church Protestant ecclesiologies and the Catholic understanding of the *sensus fidelium* are much more optimistic about the workings of God's grace among the faithful. Giving choice to the Christian faithful is not necessarily a recipe for shallow bourgeois religion.

Apropos of our concerns, the deregulation of religion and its transformation into a cultural resource reinforce the fragmenting effects of commodification. This fragmentation of traditions does not automatically mean a loss of religion's prophetic challenge, it does, however, certainly corrode the broad coherence of systems of doctrine, as people pick and choose from the offerings of religious traditions to produce their own syntheses. Thus believers are less likely to be confronted by the complex interrelations of beliefs, values, and doctrines. In a situation of such fragmentation, it is simply harder to see the political demands of the gospel because people encounter it not as a coherent narrative or system, but as a set of discrete elements of meaning. Under such circumstances, it is easier for religion to become an empty myth than to be the bearer of uncomfortable challenges. In addition to fragmenting systems of beliefs, deregulation reinforces the abstraction of belief from practice. Religious institutions provide places for practices that incarnate beliefs in particular forms of life. The decline in their influence furthers the dominance of the spaces and practices of everyday life, reducing the function of religion to decoration of its spaces. Particular beliefs survive, but they are less able to inform action.

The deregulation thesis is helpful for connecting the broad dynamics of commodification with related changes in the institutional aspects of religion. We would be misled, however, if we were to conclude that the decline of institutional religion necessarily means a similar decline in the social standing and visibility of religious leaders. Paradoxically, as religious elites have lost control over the interpretation and appropriation of religious traditions, they have continued to enjoy high social status. Indeed, as the significance of religious institutions has declined, many of their leaders have achieved unprecedented global celebrity.

RELIGIOUS LEADERS AND THE MEDIA

No consideration of the commodification of religion would be complete without examining the impact of celebrity upon religious leadership. Whatever the popular evaluation of their particular doctrines, religious figures remain attractive subjects for media coverage. This interest seems a perfect example of the dynamics of commodification. Revered by people outside of the communities they lead, they are living symbols who share the same fate of other postmodern symbols, being susceptible to interpretation and use according to logics outside of their own traditions. This applies to both institutional leaders and holy figures past and present who form an important component of religious traditions as exemplars of their ideals. We will consider the fate of such figures in consumer culture in two ways. We will begin with Guy Debord's notion of spectacle, because it provides an illuminating key for understanding the fate of religious leaders in a media-saturated culture. The media provide greatly expanded access to the public, but this comes at the risk of being reduced to abstracted media content, interesting primarily as exotic or moralistic nostalgia. We will consider how religious traditions change when the media supplement or supplant traditional community structures. The quip that Moby is a one-man religious movement touched on the rising importance of what Pierre Bourdieu has termed the new class of cultural mediators. We will consider not simply the rise of new figures such as Mother Angelica and Dr. Dobson but also how this new sort of cultural authority feeds back into the structures of traditional religions. When traditional religious leaders exploit this new social position, they import with it the habits and dispositions their followers use to interpret popular media content.

Spectacle and Celebrity

Once the scene would have been surprising, perhaps even disorienting: the pope celebrating mass in Yankee Stadium, Camden Yards, or Maracana Stadium in Rio de Janeiro. Thirty years into John Paul II's papacy it is something to be taken for granted. Despite his increasing physical frailty, the former actor can still mesmerize crowds numbering in the hundreds of thousands. Close-ups of his preaching and celebration of the Eucharist are amplified on the DiamondVision screens, just as close-ups of players at bat or Mick Jagger or Madonna are at other times. What would have been unimaginable four decades ago has become routine. The pope's aggressive use of global travel and the modern media make his the first postmodern papacy. With the Dalai Lama and Mother Teresa, John Paul has joined a late-twentieth-century media pantheon of religious figures. As was the case with Christianity's much earlier appropriation of Roman imperial spectacle, modern media spectacle both benefits and deforms Christianity.

What is the problem? Certainly, the ability to attract media attention is not a bad thing in itself. On the positive side, these leaders are interesting and compelling people; on the negative, their distinctive dress and exotic beliefs make them particularly media-genic. Each of these figures has used her or his personal charisma to further their message. What could be the problem? Recall Debord's description of the society of the spectacle. The dominance of the visual accompanies a disconnection between what is represented and what is going on in people's lives. "Everything that was once directly lived has moved away into a representa-tion."[53] The spectacle is a realm of virtual fulfillment abstracted from the political forces that shape people's lives. The price for access is playing by the rules of media, not one's tradition. Chester Gillis notes the symbolism of John Paul's appearance at Camden Yards in Baltimore—the first of the current wave of retro-nostalgia ballparks. While American Catholics enjoy such pageantry and continue to revere and respect the pope as a religious figurehead, many question or ignore the moral and doctrinal positions that he has so forcefully asserted and defended during his pontificate.[54] Leaders of religious communities are transformed into media celebrities; no longer the Fourteenth Incarnation of Avalokiteśvara, the Bodhisattva of Compassion; the 262nd Bishop of Rome; or the foundress and superior of the Missionaries of Charity, but proper names—the Dalai Lama, John Paul II, Mother Teresa—like other celebrities. In addition to being able to offer a universalist religious message, each is notable as a personality: John Paul's grand-fatherly mix of playfulness and sternness, Teresa's simple speech and garb, the Dalai Lama's aura of wisdom and playfulness. Each has a distinctive vocal style: the thickness of Eastern European (Polish or Albanian) accents, the Dalai Lama's Tibetan musicality. The list of candidates for the next spot in this pantheon of media religious figures is informative. If Princess Diana fits better than Desmond Tutu, it is because the latter is associated with the quite particular politics of South Africa. Figures too closely associated with particular communities and particular interests are not susceptible to abstraction and are not attractive as celebrities.

The Dalai Lama is an obvious example of religious celebrity for reasons more profound than his association with Richard Gere. The 14th Dalai Lama has become an international religious celebrity whose dress includes Western projec-tions of oriental exoticism as much as the saffron robes of the Tibetan monk. In the minds of many, he is the relitious leader of Western myths of *Shangri-La* more than the particular, historical nation of Tibet. The Dalai Lama represents peace, innocence, ancient tradition, environmental harmony—and vegetarianism. In the liner notes of the album discussed earlier, Moby quotes the Dalai Lama in a col-lection of texts supporting veganism. Yet Tibetan Buddhism never embraced veg-etarianism, because of the harsh climate of Tibet (notably harsher than *Shangri-La*). Modern environmental concerns do not appear in Tibetan literature until 1985.[55] As for ancient tradition, the current Dalai Lama has undertaken a number of significant innovations in response to the exile. He has expanded his office to become the political representative of the nation in exile and protector of its cul-ture. His religious role is much expanded as well. Historically, the Dalai Lama was not the leader of all Tibetan Buddhists, but was more properly associated with one particular sect within Tibetan Buddhism, the Geluk. Theologically, the Dalai Lama is an advocate of "Buddhist modernism," which, like its Christian counter-part, emphasizes those aspects of Buddhism that are most amenable to universal-istic interpretation and downplays its cultural and national particularities.[56] Thus, much of the universalism and abstraction surrounding the Dalai Lama is due to his particular religious doctrine and policies. Nevertheless, as Donald Lopez argues, the cause of Tibet continues to be held prisoner to the Western, romantic image of *Shangri-La*. Its power as an abstracted symbol of nostalgia hinders pragmatic consideration of its particular problems. "To the extent that we continue to believe that Tibet prior to 1950 was a utopia, the Tibet of 1998 will be no place."[57] The character of the Dalai Lama puts it well in Martin Scorsese's *Kundun*. At the end of his journey into exile, he is asked by an Indian border guard, "Are you the Lord Buddha?" He replies. "I think I am a reflection, like the moon on water. When you see me and I try to be a good man, you see yourself."

Clearly, the Dalai Lama's modernism and promotion of an abstract "Tibetan culture" are considered responses to a desperate political situation, but his policies are well suited to his success as a religious celebrity. Were he actually to reign in an autonomous Tibet, the Western myth of *Shangri-La* would likely be tempered by criticisms of medieval religious theocracy and obscurantism of the sort that are currently issued by the Chinese government to justify its occupation. The same sorts of criticisms are frequently heard concerning the Vatican's political standing in the United Nations. If the Dalai Lama did reign in Tibet, his celebrity standing would likely be reduced to that of a patriarch of a nationalist Orthodox church.

A similar tension between celebrity and abstraction is evident in the career of Pope John Paul II. His extensive "theology of the body" is frequently criticized for employing evocative metaphor to gloss over the concrete problems that married couples face regarding sexuality and reproduction. This theology is evident in his 1988 Apostolic Letter *Mulieris Dignitatem,* "On the Dignity and Vocation of Women." While John Paul repeatedly condemns sexism as a sin in both society and the church community, he made very few concrete changes in ecclesial discipline to address the historical legacies and ongoing presence of this problem. His call for full acceptance of women into the positions permitted under canon law rests upon previous revisions in the code.[58] His permitting women as altar servers—perhaps his most significant reform in this regard—is notable for its concession to local gender norms, allowing bishops to decide against the practice, and the subsequent Vatican decision granting any individual priest the right to refuse to celebrate the Eucharist with female altar servers. Here the disconnection between his evocative, romantic rhetoric concerning the "genius of women" and his concrete policies is of a piece with the generalized abstraction of belief from practice in consumer culture.

Mother Teresa can be criticized in a similar way. The austere poverty she demanded for her community made for striking television. Malcolm Muggeridge and Richard Attenborough's *Something Beautiful for God* featured a powerful sequence where the sisters systematically dismantled the Western conveniences in a new convent they were occupying in San Francisco. Mattresses and plumbing fixtures were stripped from rooms and flung out a window into a waiting dumpster. Less inspirational, however, was Teresa's insistence that the missionaries use equally primitive practices in their clinics, severely diminishing the care they offered their patients. Her insistent refusal to address the politics of poverty, in service of an emphasis on "charity," is a textbook case of abstraction.

Again, media attractiveness is not a bad thing in itself. The problem lies in the abstracting effects of commodification that accompany it. Stripped of their traditions and practices, religious figures are more readily made objects of consumption, ready to signify whatever sentiments we need. John Paul II and the Dalai Lama are widely known and much admired, but the particularities of their beliefs are either unknown or ignored. Both hold views on sexuality that would be considered quaint, if not unintelligibly bizarre, by many of their admirers. The transformation of religious leaders into celebrities directly parallels the abstraction of doctrines and belief from practice. Religion does not disappear but is reduced to commodified consumer content. Lopez finds a metaphor for this problem in the Dalai Lama's visit to Madame Tussaud's wax museum to inspect his own image. Religious celebrity strengthens the power of the nostalgic simulacrum over against the real leaders of concrete religious communities. During his visit, the Dalai Lama would have had the opportunity to view wax figures of Mother Teresa and John Paul II . . . as well as Princess Diana.

The Catholic Church and the Media

Analyzing religious celebrity in terms of spectacle is helpful for calling attention to the ways in which religious leaders are drawn into the commodification of culture. Religious leaders do not, however, only use the media to increase their influence and support outside of their own religious communities; they increasingly use the modern media as part of the internal governance of their own communities. In the Roman Catholic Church, this embrace of the media comes in the wake of more than three decades of reflection on the changes taking place in, and being wrought by, the modern media. It has done so in documents stretching from the Vatican II Decree on the Means of Social Communication (*Inter mirifica*), through annual papal declarations on World Communications Day since 1967, to the recent documents "Ethics and the Internet" and "The Church and the Internet." These documents have generally taken an instrumental view of the media as a "means" for spreading the gospel message and enhancing the common good. Michael Budde criticizes this approach for a naïve "sacramental liberalism" that concludes from the goodness of creation that "all natural and human projects can in principle be revelatory of God and useful for divine purposes."[59] As a result, the media is considered a benign, neutral infrastructure that can be put to any use. I suspect that optimism regarding ecclesial use of the media is grounded equally in centuries of centralized Roman administration of the church. The Roman Catholic Church has been a global institution for at least four centuries and thus has confidence born of long experience that it can wield such infrastructures to its own ends. That said, all of the documents also acknowledge the destructive potential of the media, and more recent Vatican documents have been even more critical. The Pastoral Instruction *Aetatis Novae* in 1992 demonstrated awareness of the problem of the globalization of the media and the erosion of local culture as well as the related problem that has since become known as the "digital divide." The documents on the Internet have also been critical of the destructive potential of the media. Nevertheless, the nature of this critique does not alleviate Budde's concern.

Earlier distress about the misuse of the morally neutral media has been replaced with more systematic questions about the "culture" of the media. The thickest considerations of culture appear in the repeated assertions that the new media constitute a culture that must be taken seriously as a field for evangelization like any other. Thus, John Paul identifies the media as the "new Areopagus," which should not only be used as a means for communication but also be engaged in its own right.[60] The new media are "part of an unfolding culture whose full implications are as yet imperfectly understood."[61] Thus, there is need for "the development of an anthropology and theology of communication."[62] The depth of the notion of culture markedly thins, however, when these documents shift to critique. The document "The Church and the Internet" provides a number of examples. "Media culture," it warns, "is deeply imbued with a typically postmodern sense" that rejects the existence of absolute truths.[63] Likewise, the document warns that the Internet can "plunge" the young into "consumerism, pornographic and violent fantasy."[64] No attempts are made to link these cultural tendencies or particular temptations to the structures of the medium itself. There are more developed reflections on the nature of the Internet, however, in discussions of its likely ecclesiological impact. The interactivity of the medium fosters an expectation of enhanced multidirectional communication in the church (something the document takes care to defend and situate in the ecclesiology of Vatican II and canon law). The ease of choice on the Internet may spill over into religion and reinforce the tendency toward selective adherence to doctrine, which is a "recognized problem in other contexts."[65] (In this case, as the reference to an address by John Paul II in Los Angeles suggests, the "other context" is the United States.) The document also expresses concerns about virtual reality. It lauds the potential of the Internet for fostering religious affiliation and global solidarity, but warns of the isolating tendencies of the medium, contrasting it with "flesh and blood human community." Furthermore it contrasts virtual reality with the Real Presence, asserting that there are "no sacraments on the Internet."[66]

These concerns about the negative aspects of the new media have not prevented the church from engaging the media as an instrument for the dissemination of its message. John Paul II made an explicit decision to update Vatican media relations in 1984 when he appointed Joaquín Navarro-Valls as the first lay leader of the Holy See press office, the *Sala Stampa*. Under his leadership, the Vatican has broken somewhat with its traditional secrecy and has sought positively to craft the impact of the pope's message in the media, to use the media both as a tool "for

reformation . . . in the Church" and "for shaping the world." Navarro-Valls illustrates the success of his strategy by telling the story of an encounter between a
young boy and the pope in Bogotá, Colombia. The boy called out to John Paul, "I
know you; you're the pope. You're the same one I saw on television." For Navarro-
Valls, the boy's recognition shows that the policy has not achieved mere
"ephemeral celebrity," but a "ministry of global presence from the Church and
from the priesthood."[67] We will consider the impact of such uses of the secular
media on the internal lives of religious communities in order to judge whether
Navarro-Valls's confidence is well founded.

The New Cultural Intermediaries

Deregulation suggests that the "new channels of communication" provided by the
modern media lessen the power of traditional religious leaders.[68] A careful consideration of the intracommunal consequences of leaders' use of the media reveals
a more complex reality. When religious leaders use the media to communicate
with members of their communities, they are to some extent trading their traditional institutional infrastructures for those of the contemporary media.
Although this does not necessarily mean that they abandon or abdicate their traditional networks of power, it does change those traditional structures. This has
paradoxical effects. On the one hand, as Lyon suggests, it reduces their impact by
forcing them to compete with the myriad other voices in the media. On the other,
it also enhances the authority of leaders within their own communities over
against the ranks of lower authorities that once mediated their contact with rank-
and-file believers. It is a shift in mediating structures—from traditional religious
institutions to the modern media.

When religious leaders employ the infrastructure of the popular media, they
function as members of what Pierre Bourdieu has termed the "new cultural intermediaries." The term is related to other well-known attempts to describe a "new
class" and its particular interests—such as the "service," "knowledge," or "professional middle class" and popular terms such as "yuppie." Roof has offered a
"demand-side" analysis of how the interests of this new class have encouraged the
emergence of new types of religious "suppliers" to cater to their interests.[69] We will
pursue a contrasting "supply-side" analysis that considers how the "cultural intermediaries" associated with the rise of this new middle class are fostering commodified habits of interpretation that religious believers then use to engage the
leaders of traditional religions. These new cultural intermediaries work in professions that produce symbolic goods; they are marketers, advertising agents, public
relations professionals, radio and television producers, presenters, magazine journalists, fashion writers, and members of the helping professions (social workers,
marriage counselors, sex therapists, dieticians, play leaders, and so on).[70] In addition to providing knowledge for developing personal taste in the maelstrom of

consumption options (e.g., Martha Stewart or *Playboy*) they also provide guidance for life choices in the post-traditional culture where the heads of each nuclear family are expected to make their own choices concerning sexuality, child rearing, meaning, and so on. Family and community traditions are replaced by advice from professionals such as Drs. Spock, Ruth, Laura, and Phil distributed through radio, television, books, and magazines.

A New Hierarchy?

The problem with religious leaders being assimilated to this class involves more than a negative judgment of the value of these figures or others like them. Here, again the issue is form, not content. Just as these mass-mediated professionals replace traditional communal and kinship sources of guidance, religious leaders' use of these media replace local communal and generational mediations of religious traditions. We have noted how media celebrity has reinforced the other historical factors that have led to the consolidation of the office of the Dalai Lama. The case is similar with Pope John Paul II. One of the key characteristics of his papacy has been the resurgence of Roman centralization. Collegial decision-making structures such as national and regional conferences of bishops and the International Commission on English in Liturgy have had their power greatly diminished. Such ultramontane strategies are nothing new for Roman Catholicism. What is new, however, is the way in which these dynamics have been reinforced by the pope's use of the media. Consider again his celebrity as pope. He is instantly recognized the world over. Even the sound of his voice is known widely enough to support imitation both admiring and comic. But more than this, like the Dalai Lama, he enjoys direct access to believers in a way his predecessors would have found unimaginable. Both write books that are purchased by millions (and likely even read by a fair percentage of purchasers). Alfred A. Knopf paid a $9-million advance for John Paul's *Crossing the Threshold of Hope*.[71] His commercial publishing builds upon his singularly prolific production of papal documents. His innovations in papal writings are qualitative as much as quantitative. He has transformed the genre of the encyclical letter from relatively diffident, unelaborated magisterial interventions and judgments to extended, creative theological reflections. These offer not just judgments and decisions but extended treatises on controverted theological and moral topics such as the persons of the Trinity, gender, the nature of moral norms, and the relationship between faith and reason. John Paul has transformed the office of pope into something of a theologian to the world. His documents are widely read not just by theologians, ministers, and church bureaucrats but by large numbers of laity as well.

John Paul's increased access to believers has, to some extent, replaced or "leapfrogged" more traditional institutional channels of communication. Gone are the days when papal decisions and initiatives were handed down through diocesan and parish infrastructures, mediated through the interpretations of national or diocesan theological professionals. Some theologians speak of the decline of hierarchical control over the reception of church teaching in tones that echo Lyon. David Power notes, "The Vatican can put the latest papal discourse on the Internet, with very little control over how it is received or how it is treated when placed there."[72] This decline of traditional controls is not, however, a slide into an empty vacuum. Media infrastructures replace religious institutions. Now Catholic laity learn of Vatican decisions through the news media—both secular and religious. The latter play an increasingly influential role in the reception of papal teaching. Mother Angelica's Eternal Word Television Network claims to reach as many as fifty-four million homes.[73] It maintains an online archive of church documents and commentary on them. These resources consistently appear near the top of internet searches for topics related to the Catholic Church.

Angelica's clash with Cardinal Roger Mahoney, archbishop of Los Angeles, in 1998 illustrates the growing ecclesial influence of the new cultural intermediaries. In 1997, she sharply criticized the eucharistic theology of the cardinal's pastoral on the liturgy, "Gather Faithfully Together: A Guide for the Sunday Mass," in terms that the archdiocese contended amounted to accusing the cardinal of heresy. Mahoney protested to her local bishop and to several Vatican offices. In addition to demanding an apology, the cardinal challenged Angelica's contention that she was "not responsible to the National Conference of Catholic Bishops or to any of the individual bishops" in terms of Canons 753 and 1373, which establish the authority of the local bishop and reserve correction of this episcopal teaching solely to the pope.[74] Aside from a grudging apology (accompanied by her proclamation of a miraculous healing by Mary and Jesus), Mahoney's petition had little public effect. Whatever the ideological biases of Roman officials who may favor Angelica's perspective over Mahoney's, one cannot help but notice their disproportionate impact on believers. Mother Angelica's network reaches thirteen times the number of people Mahoney leads in the largest archdiocese in the United States, in a manner much more direct than any pastoral letter a bishop could ever write.[75] Tens of thousands tune in daily to watch "Mother Angelica Live," whereas bishops' pastoral letters are read mainly by pastoral ministers and an occasional highly motivated layperson. Likewise, Mother Angelica's impact also far outweighs that of trained theologians. In an article calling attention to what he terms the new "E-Magisterium," Richard Gaillardetz observes that the EWTN Web site likely gets more hits in a single day (more likely hour or minute) than the original press run of 750 copies of Tissa Balasuriya's book *Mary and Human Liberation,* for which he was (temporarily) excommunicated.[76] Studies confirm the importance of religious media for contemporary Catholics. While more than half of young Catholic adults surveyed report listening to religious programming on radio or television, they are much less likely (from 7 to 28 percent) to report participating in church-related groups such as those devoted to scripture study, prayer, faith sharing, or social justice.[77]

The example of Mother Angelica clearly illuminates the intradenominational power of this new social position, but her neotraditionalism may obscure an equally important dynamic—how religious use of the media diminishes denominational identities. The study of young Catholics just cited found interviewees just as likely to "refer to popular writers and spiritual authors as diverse as M. Scott Peck, Joseph Campbell, Laura Schlessinger, and James Dobson" as to Catholic authors such as Thomas Merton or Henri Nouwen.[78]

Thus, the growth in the importance of the new cultural intermediaries can either enhance or erode the authority and power of traditional religious leaders. This results in significant power shifts within communities. In addition to creating new positions such as Mother Angelica's quasi-episcopal status, it shifts the balance of power among traditional religious authorities to those best positioned to exploit the media. Thus, John Paul's media celebrity reinforces the ultramontane tendencies of his pontificate. This comes at a significant cost. It furthers the corrosive effects of commodity abstraction by eroding local mediating structures such as episcopal conferences, dioceses, and parishes. Religious beliefs are further drawn into the virtual realm of the contemporary media as the local communal structures that are necessary to connect them to lived practices fade in importance. There is a deep irony here. Use of the popular media to augment the authority of church leaders ends up eroding the traditions they hope to strengthen.

STYLE AND RECEPTION

We can better understand these negative consequences of religious use of the media if we consider the dominant styles within the media and their impact on habits of reception and engagement. Shifts in media influence the relationships between senders and receivers. Insofar as religious leaders disseminate their message and attempt to maintain their authority through the infrastructures of contemporary media, their message will be recoded and received by their audience in a manner consistent with those media. In the present context of the corporate culture industries, this brings a series of problems associated with the particular class interests and practices of the new cultural intermediaries.

Bourdieu associates the shape and style of these new intermediaries' cultural production with the need for social markers of identity for the broader new middle class. Traditional markers of social status are not useful for this group; thus the culture they produce is biased against the construction of a coherent, integrated vision of life. This produces a style that favors challenging symbolic hierarchies and systems of distinction.[79] Bourdieu cites as an example the index from a resource guide to adolescent culture which ranged from "Akido" to "Zen," with entries on "basket-making," "hallucinogens," "ongoing education," "therapy," and "trekking." Such seeker appropriations meet the needs of a new *petit bourgeois* employed in new professions such as cultural production and therapeutic and professional services that do not fit into traditional class hierarchies.[80] He associates their willingness to appropriate cultural traditions willy-nilly to their *déclassé* location. The anti-institutional and antisystematic temperaments of seekers express a "dream of social flying, a desperate effort to defy the gravity of the social field." Yet this projection of an attitude of disinterest in social status is for Bourdieu a classic example of the misrecognition involved in the creation of the "symbolic capital" with which social groups establish their legitimacy. Attitude here is (almost) everything. Their disdain for traditional constraints on cultural consumption displays the profound importance of culture for establishing social standing. An anti-institutional temperament legitimates a style of cultural appropriation that establishes a social identity for this new class.[81]

Mike Featherstone associates this stylistic sensibility with the problems of establishing social status in a situation of "inflation produced by an oversupply and rapid circulation of symbolic goods and consumer commodities." Since status is established only differentially, such markers are always unstable. Thus, the new cultural intermediaries have a natural interest in furthering the demonopolization of cultural and religious traditions. Thus, like Fredric Jameson, these sociologists arrive at pastiche as a fundamental style, but for different reasons. Traditions are viewed as depositories of resources that can be "ransacked" for cultural production, with what Michael Budde has aptly termed "blender-like effects."[82] This style trains audiences to engage culture in abstraction from traditions, communities, and institutions. As a result, when contemporary believers encounter traditional religious leaders and symbols in the media, they are likely to engage them with the same habits of shallow engagement.

We have considered "cultural ransacking" in our analyses of the pop artists Moby and Enigma. We noted, however, that such practices cannot be completely dismissed as shallow, commercial exploitation. Ransacking is not simply the crass production of whatever pastiche one can sell (although at times it may be exactly that). When these wide-ranging appropriations are considered in terms of establishing identities and worldviews in a changing society, we can begin to see how well many respected spiritual authors function precisely as new cultural intermediaries. Contemporary authors such as Kathleen Norris, Thomas Moore, and Karen Armstrong recognizably continue the work of similar figures in the past, from Thomas Merton to Henri Nouwen. They introduce a literate, popular audience to venerable religious and spiritual traditions in a manner that is easily detached from traditional, institutional, and communal infrastructures.

I am hesitant to dismiss the quest for identity and meaning in a posttraditional world as shallow and immature and cannot therefore regard the work of these authors as mere pandering. That must not, however, prevent us from noting how the stylistic norms of the new cultural intermediaries recode traditional material as it is distributed through popular print and electronic media. The figures discussed above occupy a space between the world of traditional religious institutions and the broader cultural marketplace, offering their wares through the new infrastructures but relying on lingering allegiances to traditional religious institutions for market share.

Mark Massa's account of Thomas Merton's role in postwar American Catholicism conveys well the ambiguous effect of even the most respected of these figures. Massa argues that Merton "offered a model of post-immigrant, post-working-class spirituality to newly arrived middle class Catholics looking for role models in the strange suburbs." This abstract version of Catholicism provided the means of maintaining Catholic identity for a generation seeking to distance itself from the perceived kitschy excesses of urban, ghetto Catholicism. The result was not that one thick religious culture was replaced by another. Rather, immigrant Catholicism was replaced by a system of virtual beliefs that addressed the immediate needs of believers without influencing their broader habits of living. "In this final ironic sense, Merton 'legitimized' the possibility of a sophisticated, accessible Catholic spirituality for a middle-class, suburban constituency without really 'converting' them to the radical implications of Cistercian or Benedictine spirituality."[83]

As the model of culture we adopted from Wendy Griswold in chapter 1 would predict, when traditional elements of religious culture are received through new media and enacted in new contexts, they function in unexpected ways, sometimes at odds with the logic of their originating traditions. Thus, a literate modern American monk's retrievals of the wisdom of ancient monastics serves as a symbolic resource for suburban Catholics to differentiate their faith from that of their ancestors and thus better assimilate in the suburbs. In this regard we return to Navarro-Valls's certainty that the little boy met the "same pope" in person that he had seen on TV. The boy may recognize him as the same pope, but in what context? Who does he associate him with? If the boy saw him on TV as part of televised coverage of the papal visit, perhaps he appeared flanked by leaders of the local church whom the boy knew. This indeed might give the boy a sense of the global ministry of the pontiff reaching to his own parish. The pope's appearance on television placed him in other constellations as well. On North American television, he would share the company of Oprah and Barney. This would certainly confer significant status, but would give the boy a very interesting ecclesiology to say the least.

CONCLUSION

Far from being immune to the dynamics of commodification, religion is as susceptible to abstraction and reification as other aspects of culture. Religious beliefs and practices are in danger of being extracted from the complex cultures, institutions, and relationships that enable them to inform the shape of daily life. As a result, they are in danger of being reduced to abstracted, virtual sentiments that function solely to give flavor to the already established forms of everyday life or to provide compensations for its shortcomings. We have traced these tendencies across a range of scholarship on religion. Spirituality as the emergent form of religious life is consonant with the workings of commodification. I argued that the narcissism and therapeutic critiques too quickly presume the shallowness of spirituality, but they correctly connect it with the modern, socially isolated individual. This isolation, not the motivations of practitioners of spirituality, is the source of the problem. Commitments to visions of the spiritual life, no matter how profound, are difficult to sustain without a community of shared belief. Furthermore, if religious syntheses are to inform the practice of daily life, they require some articulation in disciplines and practices. This again is difficult to achieve on the individual level.

The same issues appeared in the consideration of religious use of the media. Religious leaders' use of secular media bypasses their traditional communal information and organizational structures. While this may serve well a program of centralization, it comes with a significant cost. It erodes the communal mediating structures that link the authority of the leader and the doctrines and symbols they steward to the life of the local community. Thus, such use of the media present religious leaders, doctrines, and symbols in a manner that directly parallels commodification. Furthermore, it assimilates traditional religious office to the status of the new cultural intermediaries, whose class interests produce a particularly shallow engagement with cultural and religious traditions. Religious communities can exploit the mass media as a means of communication with great success, but this comes at the cost of welcoming these habits of interpretation and use into their own traditions, where they supplant traditional hermeneutics and systems of formation. Awareness of these particular dynamics and structures provides the detailed diagnosis necessary to guide a practical, critical program to counter them, which will be the task of the final chapter. Next we turn to a more theological consideration of the relationship between consumer culture and Christianity by considering the similarities and differences of their constructions of desire.

CHAPTER 4

Desire and the Kingdom of God

Never to reach satiety of desiring is truly to see God.
—Gregory of Nyssa

When I'm drivin' in my car and a man comes on the radio
Tell me more and more about some useless information
Designed to fire my imagination
I can't get no . . . satisfaction.
—Mick Jagger

I N THE WORDS OF TIM EDWARDS, IN BOTH ACADEMIC AND POPULAR CIRCLES consumer society "is simply desiring society."[1] Advanced capitalist societies are marked by some of the most sophisticated systems for forming and inciting desire that the world has ever seen. This concern about the cultivation of desire is something that capitalism shares with Christianity. But, as the juxtaposition of these texts from an early Christian theologian and a rock and roll paean to priapism suggests, while the cultivation, control, and fulfillment of desire are concerns central to the Christian tradition and to consumer culture, the particulars of the formation and focus of desire require consideration. At the same time, this juxtaposition troubles easy distinctions between Christian and consumer desire. Both know endless, insatiable longing.

Again, our purpose is not to critique consumer culture but to explore how religious belief and practice are transformed by its structures and practices. Christian desire is in danger of being distorted and exploited by consumer culture. The conflict between the two is not, however, as direct as one might think, or indeed, hope. Consumer culture poses a particularly vexing problem for Christianity because the shape and texture of the desires that it cultivates are profoundly similar to Christian forms of desire. Our analysis of this similarity will focus on form, not content. Consumer desire will be portrayed not as arising from a coherent anthropology that can be contrasted with Christianity or challenged as a heresy or parody but as a system of formation that structures desire in a manner similar enough to Christianity to sidetrack it in subtle but profound ways. The metaphor of the railroad is apt. The conflict between Christianity and consumer culture lacks the definitiveness of a head-on collision; rather it has about as much drama as a train switching tracks and going in a slightly different direction. This deflection is of a piece with consumer culture's capacity to exploit any narrative, belief, or value. Just as it can turn any culture into content to be marketed, it can yoke just about any desire to the task of furthering consumption. Although any number of reprehensible values are exploited by marketers to hawk merchandise, these will always be intermixed with laudable ones as well. Thus, easy contrasts between the object or telos of consumer and Christian desires will fail us.

This brings us to another comforting dichotomy that will, unfortunately, fail us as well: the contrast between "real" needs and "false" desires. Certainly there is much in this distinction that is correct. As levels of affluence rise in consumer societies, people do not cease desiring ever more things. As family sizes have decreased, the size of our homes has increased. We fill these larger houses with more and more appliances and increasingly large wardrobes. Possessing more than many of our grandparents could ever imagine, we obsess about the things we don't yet have. Certainly most of these desires must be false, superfluous, over and above our "basic human needs." This contrast provides an essential measure for evaluating the injustice and environmental destruction that high-consumption lifestyles require and ignore. The United Nations Food and Agriculture Organization estimates that 840 million people are undernourished and that 6 million children under the age of five die each year from causes related to hunger.[2] The United States has 5 percent of the world's population, yet it consumes 20 to 30 percent of many important natural resources (fossil fuels, timber, metals, and so on).[3] In spite of this disproportionate control of the world's bounty, 18 percent of American's under the age of eighteen live in poverty and 16.2 percent of households with children are classified as "food insecure."[4] In comparison to this crying need, most consumer desires are clearly obscene; in the fantasy lands of consumer desire, the needs of the starving are *literally* obscene—kept far offstage. A critique of consumer culture based on a contrast between Christian desire and consumerist desire can easily employ such an approach to great effect, as does John Kavanaugh. It provides an essential reality check against the occupational hazard of analyses of consumer culture—the temptation to become so enchanted with narratives, beliefs, and symbols as to ignore issues of poverty, class, and environmental degradation.

Although it is essential for contextualizing any discussion of desire and consumer culture, the distinction between real needs and false desires does not provide much help for analyzing the details of the relation between consumerist and religious forms of desire. Once we begin to consider religious forms of desire, we are no longer speaking of "basic human needs" but of complex, culturally constructed desires.[5] Even desires for distributive justice are grounded in complex visions of human flourishing. This is evident in John Paul II's call to evaluate the impact of consumerism in terms of whether it produces "new and higher forms of satisfying human needs" or "artificial new needs which hinder the formation of a mature personality," a position very similar to that of Marx, who envisioned a world where people not only had the bare necessities but were also "rich in needs."[6] The question in consumer culture is how these complex desires are formed. Don Slater argues that the issue is really "that the mediation of need by market exchange and corporate interests is undemocratic and gives people little opportunity to publicly discuss and collectively control decisions about what their real needs are and, therefore, about how social resources should be used and allocated."[7] The failure of the project of distinguishing between the necessary and the frivolous does not throw us back into the value neutrality of neoliberal economics, which assumes the consumers desires are sovereign and rational (an assumption that comes into conflict with the presumably rational choice of producers to spend enormous sums of money on advertising that makes decidedly nonrational appeals). It is clear that our desires are shaped, encouraged, and manipulated. We will therefore focus not on the content of desire, for example, whether or not Coke is the "Real Thing," but on the shape, scope, and rhythm of desire as it is constructed in consumer culture.

Our consideration of desire in consumer culture will begin with recent theological evaluations of consumer desire that emphasize its intellectual origins. These portray consumer desire as a consequence of heretical distortions of Christianity, the inadequate ontology or anthropology implicit in modernity, or the presuppositions of modern economics. These analyses can be compelling, and they are particularly appealing to theologians because they draw consumer culture into their territory. They suffer, however, from the shortcomings inherent in analyses that contrast consumer culture with Christianity. They overplay the coherence of consumer behavior with specific beliefs and do not give adequate attention to the social structures and cultural habits that threaten to reorient legitimate religious desires into the service of furthering consumption.

The mid-portion of this chapter will develop an alternative approach by exploring the structures and habits that form consumer desire. Modern marketing and advertising constructs consumer desire in two complementary ways: seduction and misdirection. Seduction concerns our relationship to objects of desire. Contrary to what is generally assumed, consumer desire is not focused on particular objects but is instead stretched out across an endless series of potential objects. Seduction spurs consumption by prolonging desire and channeling its inevitable disappointments into further desires. Misdirection is the term I give to the advertising strategy of associating commodities with needs, desires, and values that are not directly related to the given product. Misdirection encourages consumers to fulfill more profound needs and desires through consumption. This is not to say that it attempts to substitute material for more profound fulfillments, as critiques of consumer culture's "materialism" generally have it. Misdirection works by encouraging consumers to think of consumption as a way of enacting profound values and fulfilling serious desires. It is about the substitution of a practice, not the substitution of values. Seduction and misdirection combine to produce a particularly fragmented form of desire that is consistent with the abstraction inherent in commodification discussed in chapters 2 and 3. This sketch of the shape and texture of consumer desire provides the basis for considering the relation between Christian and consumer desires in the final section of the chapter.

To attempt to say anything about so profound a topic as desire and theology is daunting. Desire has been discussed, scrutinized, and cultivated in myriad ways by theological schools and spiritual movements and traditions in Christianity. A sustained treatment of any one of these is far beyond the scope of this chapter. Desire appears in several places within the Christian tradition. The first is its most ultimate meaning, and Augustine long ago provided its most lasting expression in the opening lines of the *Confessions*. "You have made us for yourself and our hearts are restless until they rest in thee." Developed in countless theologies and spiritualities through the present day, this insight holds that the human spirit cannot be satisfied with any finite thing. It always yearns for a fullness that only fellowship with the divine can give. Augustine's distinction between "use" and "enjoyment" can help us see the significance of the rise of consumer culture for desire. If God alone is truly to be enjoyed, and other things are merely to be used to further this fundamental affective orientation to God, then consumer culture with its endless proliferation of idolatrous attachments seems a profound obstacle to our union with God. But things are not so simple. Close examination of the texture of desire in consumer culture reveals that is not simply about fixing one's heart on material things or sensual pleasure. Indeed, it is about never being satisfied with them. This is a much more complex problem. Augustine and Gregory may be prophetic voices of psychological clarity, but the clarity of their solution is clouded today by its very similarity to the problem. We are trained from infancy to never cease desiring. Does this lead us to God?

Desire for God is the ultimate form of desire in Christianity, but it is tied to a host of other important desires, including the desire for the kingdom of God, the coming of God's justice on earth both for ourselves and for others. Concern for the other is particularly endangered in consumer culture by the commodification of alterity. This chapter will explore the ambiguity of this desire—to save and consume the other at once. Any consideration of desire and the kingdom of God must address eschatology and temporality. Aspects of Christian eschatology proclaimed as intrinsically subversive, such as apocalyptic expectation, look somewhat different in the context of consumer culture. They seem curiously similar to the endlessly deferred desires of a consumer market driven by endless innovation.

The final locus of Christian desire we will consider is vocational desire, what the Ignatian tradition calls "great apostolic desires"—the focused commitment of our lives. This sort of sustained commitment, along with all the allied forms of what the Benedictine tradition calls "stability" are particularly undermined by the fragmented nature of consumer desire. We are endlessly encouraged to desire everything all at once. This will provide the opportunity to revisit the issue of consumer "narcissism." The notions of misdirection and the fragmentation of desire will provide an alternative way of evaluating the instability of spiritual commitment in consumer culture that is less condemning and dismissive and, I will argue, more adequate. This analysis of the structures and practices that form consumer desire will bear fruit in final chapter, where they will provide the basis for planning a practical response to the pernicious effects of consumer culture.

THE ORIGINS OF CONSUMER DESIRE

That contemporary consumerism is marked by a dysfunctional excess of desire is a widely shared assumption among Christian ethicists and theologians, several of whom have attempted to account for the origins of consumer culture by exploring the development of the history of ideas. The emergence of one idea or another is offered as the origin of the *mentalité* that undergirds consumerism.

The Radical Orthodoxy movement is a leading contemporary proponent of diagnosing social and cultural ills in terms of the history of metaphysics. Graham Ward has offered one of the most developed ontological and anthropological accounts of the construction of consumer desire. His analysis is founded on the radical orthodox critique of the twin foundations of modernity in ontotheology and nominalism. These destroy both the relationship of the world to a transcendent God and the subject's relationship to the world. The dynamic relationality of the analogical cosmos is reduced to the empty extension of Cartesian time and space. While Ward locates the social atomism of contemporary urban existence within technological and economic changes, for him these structural changes develop the implicit logic of this modern ontology and anthropology.[8] He traces the development of ideas of community, the individual, and desire through Hobbes, Spinoza, Hegel, Freud, and Lacan. He finds here a series of "parodies" of Christian notions of community that reduce the self to an isolated monad, tragically longing for the wholeness promised in its fiction of self-sufficiency. Sundered from relationships to others, the self can never desire them in their complex alterity, only as they conform to its narcissistic needs. Relationships are reduced to acts of consumption, a consumption that, because it is completely determined by the monadic self, can never free it from itself. Everything is reduced to what Martin Buber would term an "I–it" relationship. Because of its self-orientation, this desire has no tolerance for the bodily particularities of others. Time is as closed as space; thus fulfillment is trapped in the present, reduced to the experience of *jouissance*. The difficult struggle for intimacy is degraded to the simplistic pursuit of orgasm. Thus, the modern self is implicated in an "economy of lack," which reduces desire to mere libido. Because this form of desire is literally unfulfillable, it engenders endless nihilistic longing.

Ward contrasts this with Christian desire, which he locates within an analogical account of the universe. Desire arises not from the lack of the desiring subject but from a call from beyond the self. The self is incomplete, not in nihilistic closure but in its relational openness to the world and God. Thus, Christian desire calls us to transcend ourselves. Our encounters, both with personal others and things, lead us ever onward to additional relationships with others and, ultimately, with God. Rather than being trapped in the empty extension of Cartesian space and time, the desiring self is constantly drawn forward into a fullness that exceeds every location and moment, rendering each moment eschatologically open to the gift of salvation.

Ward's account of the modern economy of lack emphasizes the ontological aspects of the construction of consumer desire. This is shown in his distinct preference for psychoanalytic accounts of human subjectivity. The link between metaphysics and culture is established through psychoanalytic narratives of the origins and predicament of the desiring subject. Social, institutional, and economic structures are generally portrayed as the macro corollaries of this anthropology. The fantasy worlds of these myriad dispersed selves are replicated in social atomism and the virtuality of culture. For this reason, while Ward recounts the economic and technological changes that accompany the rise of the postmodern city, he does not devote much attention to examining the causal role of specific institutions and infrastructures of consumer culture. As a result, his analysis does not provide much guidance for responding to the particularities of consumer culture as such.

Daniel Bell offers a similar account of the origins of desire in an ontology of lack in his *Liberation Theology after the End of History*, a book in the same series on Radical Orthodoxy as Ward's. Drawing from Gilles Deleuze, Bell argues that ontologies are constructed within particular forms of life. This connection allows him to pursue a more concrete analysis of the origins of capitalist desire using Deleuze's notion of "social machines" and the concepts of "governmentality" and "technologies of the self" from the later work of Michel Foucault. His analysis focuses on broad dynamics such as the interplay between various forms of state power and the deterritorializing effects of capitalist economy. While this serves his critique of liberationist notions of justice well, it does not offer a specific enough analysis of the particular structures and technologies of desire in contemporary consumer cultures for our purposes here.[9]

Another volume in the Radical Orthodoxy series, D. Stephen Long's *Divine Economy*, undertakes a more specific engagement with the particular economic underpinnings of consumer culture. Long applies the critique of modernity's ontology of lack to the axiomatic status of "scarcity" in contemporary economics. (Economics is commonly defined as the study of the allocation of scarce resources to competing needs.) He argues that this disciplinary assumption can only be viewed as heretical by Christian theology. For this reason, he warns that theological engagements with economics must proceed with caution. The economic formulation of the calculus of human action in terms of opportunity costs "contains a complex metaphysics that assumes all human action and language takes place in a tragic world of scarcity."[10] The "infinite desire" of the consumer is a manifestation of the frustration of the Enlightenment subject's attempt to enact its unlimited will within the constraints of a finite world. "Faced with myriad possible consumable choices that could satisfy me, once I choose one I have foregone all others. . . . Thus my choice at any historical moment is always already connected with lack."[11] Our countless daily calculations of maximum return train us to view the world in terms of this ontology of lack. These calculations presume the abstract equivalence of all goods, which "reduces everything which is good, true and beautiful to a formal value based on usefulness and substitutability, flattening all hierarchies into formal equivalences."[12] This threatens to leave us bereft of means to distinguish between objects of desire, to be unable to see our ultimate telos of fellowship with God as anything but one possible good among others. Thus, our desire for the infinite is shunted into an insatiable desire for the finite.

Long's analysis gives greater attention to the more proximate origins of consumer desire than Ward's by considering how the practice of exchange forms us in a certain metaphysics. While he provides a trenchant theological critique of the discipline of economics, this engagement is less useful as an account of consumer desire. Scholarly discussions of consumer behavior repeatedly call into question precisely those presuppositions of liberal economics that Long criticizes: its assumptions that values are private and that individuals can easily abstract from their particular wants to a generalized measure of utility for which they can then rationally calculate the cost they are willing to incur for a given good. Long rightly criticizes this for eroding particular hierarchies of values. However, the silence of classical economics on substantial notions of the good hides much more than a means/end bureaucratic rationality. It also ignores the massive deployment of marketing and advertisements aimed at directing, eliciting, and inciting consumer desire.

There are two levels to this problem. First, as we saw in our discussion of need and desires above, there is the problem of the "democratic" formation of these desires. Marketing and advertising fundamentally skew social consensus. Thus, as a society we currently seem more concerned about obtaining ever larger SUVs and luxury kitchen items than about education and health care. This commercial influence on the formation of desire led John Kenneth Galbraith to argue that business was now in control of the "private" realm postulated by classical economics, and for this reason the celebrated rationality of markets of classical economics ceases to exist in advanced capitalism.[13] The second level of this problem is even more vexing than the first. Marketing latches onto any value—no matter how profound or banal—to sell merchandise. Thus, to some extent Long's thesis is confirmed. As unrelated values are exploited to sell goods, we are disciplined to pursue values through the abstract exchange of the market, but far from being reduced to instrumental rationality, our decisions become ever more irrational. These other values are used to distract us from making rational calculations of relative value. We spend exorbitant sums on superfluous items—whether all at once, or in the daily dose of piddling impulse purchases. Indeed, one of the strategies offered by Joe Dominguez and Vicki Robin in their popular anticonsumerist guide to finance, *Your Money or Your Life,* is to calculate carefully one's actual hourly wage (discounting for the various lifestyle expenses, such as wardrobe and convenience foods that are incurred in the process) in order to assign a value in life-hours to a contemplated purchase.[14] Thus, a textbook case of classical liberal economic calculations of maximal return, firmly grounded in an ontology of lack (you only have so many years of life to live), serves as a tactic for countering unfettered consumer desire.

A fourth scholar, ethicist Peter Sedgwick, has offered an account of the emergence of consumer desire that is grounded in much thicker historical research. He draws from the work of historians such as Neil McKendrick and Colin Campbell, who argue that consumerism was firmly entrenched in England by the end of the eighteenth century.[15] For this reason, Max Weber's account of the role of Puritanism in the success of the Industrial Revolution in England is inadequate because it tells only half of the story. Worldly asceticism may explain the discipline of capitalist firm owners, but it cannot account for the widespread demand for the consumer goods that their firms produced. This widespread "consumerism justified everything which Puritanism condemned."[16] Sedgwick argues that consumer demand developed from an "alternative Protestant ethic" that originated in the Arminian reaction to Calvinism, which would eventually develop into Romanticism. If consumerism was financed by utilitarian "bankers and business men," it "drew its moral justification from Romanticism."[17]

Sedgwick traces the development of the emergence of feeling, sensibility, and aesthetics in ethics during the seventeenth and eighteenth centuries. What began with the Cambridge Platonists' accounts of the pleasure that accompanied doing good developed within a century into an account of moral "sensibility" that was coterminous with taste. Virtue was manifested in the display of good sensibility or taste. Here Sedgwick finds the roots of consumerism in this practice of imagining the self. In modern societies, the self is constituted in its display.[18] While he takes issue with Veblen's simplistic account of class emulation, he agrees with his insights into the importance of display for social identity, adding from his own genealogy its parallel importance in individual self-imagination. Consumer desire is very different from classical hedonism. It is not focused on sensual pleasure. It is not particularly attached to objects of consumption. As Sedgwick notes, consumerism is about "disacquiring as much as possessing."[19] We differ from our premodern forebears in being able to take pleasure in constant innovation. Each new object brings the possibility of new self-imagining. This account of the origins of desire leads Sedgwick to argue that any adequate response to consumerism must take into account its role in the formation of identity. Unless these underlying needs are met, the symptom of consumerism cannot be successfully remedied. We will return in the next section to his insight that consumerism is as much about losing interest in goods as it is about acquiring them.

Each of these accounts explains the origins of consumer desire in terms of the history of thought and culture. Although these transformations in thought and imagination are relevant to considerations of the origins of consumer culture, they do not provide an adequate account of the formation of consumer desire in the present. One need not embrace a strong materialist perspective that presumes culture is completely determined by economic and social structures in order to see the inadequacy of these approaches. Whatever the origins of consumer desire in modern metaphysics and anthropology, it is currently sustained not primarily by an incorrigible commitment to pernicious ideas but by a host of economic, social, and cultural structures and practices. Analysis of these will give a more adequate account of the nature of consumer desire. Equally important, it will help us better to conceive the predicament posed by consumer culture—not that Christian desires are colonized and infiltrated from within by heretical distortions but that they are deflected and deformed from the outside by the structures, practices, and habits of consumer culture. The next section will consider in detail the character of desire that is elicited by contemporary marketing and advertising.

Before moving to an analysis of consumer desires, however, we must first note a fact that is both obvious and surprising. In many ways contemporary consumption is not driven by desire at all. On the level of the obvious, we have become unable to obtain the most basic necessities of life outside of the market. Concern about consumerism, however, is focused more on the excesses of conspicuous consumption, and this is an area of consumption that is, surprisingly, driven less by desire than we would think. It is, as we have seen, motivated by the need to form and communicate an identity in a dynamic and competitive social setting. Here the Radical Orthodox critique of the ontology of lack at the heart of modernity finds a sociological corollary. Whatever one concludes concerning which is the symptom and which the cause, further exploration of the details of the social construction of lack are worthwhile.

As consumption has expanded into more and more areas of human civilization, its meaning as a human act has become less and less about the literal acquisition of things. In the second chapter, we discussed the emergence of the single-family home as a milestone in the history of consumption. The emergence of this institution resulted in the replacement of communal and kinship structures of production and support by market alternatives. Domestic production by extended-family labor was replaced by domestic appliances and a range of more highly processed and manufactured consumer goods from foodstuffs and clothing to entertainment and music. Likewise, support structures were exchanged for market-based alternatives such as various forms of insurance, and family career paths were replaced with our education-based (and economically driven) "meritocracy." As the extended family was being paired down into the nuclear family in its single-family home, individuals were increasingly on their own in competitive urban society. As previous markers of social identity such as class and ethnicity as well as traditional systems of patronage changed, individuals were increasingly dependent on factors such as appearance and "personality" to prosper socially. All of these factors have been exploited by marketing and advertising. People spend money on personal-appearance products and services, clothing, and luxury items such as watches and cars, not simply out of a desire for those particular products, or even because they enjoy reimagining and recreating themselves, but to maintain their status in a competitive society. Although it may be hard to summon much sympathy for their plight, young professionals often do not feel free to buy economy cars and inexpensive clothes, because to do so would mark them as not being "players." As traditional markers of social solidarity have been replaced with conspicuous consumption, keeping up with the Joneses has become a full-time job. Thus, life within the gilded cage of advanced capitalist societies, for all its material extravagance, is driven as much by social necessity and anxiety as by desire.

THE NATURE OF CONSUMER DESIRE

Granted that consumption is driven by much more than desire, it is undeniable that desire is fundamental to consumer culture. Although strategies for stimulating and sustaining desire are deployed to motivate consumption of particular products, their effects go far beyond the cash register. They overflow the banks of marketing to influence the focus, texture, and temporality of desire across the range of human experience. There are two fundamental dynamisms to contemporary consumer desire. The first is what Zygmunt Bauman terms "seduction." This works by offering an endlessly renewed series of objects to desire. The second comprises a host of related dynamics that I will label "misdirection." Misdirection evokes and sustains desire for commodities by associating them with unrelated human needs and desires. This section will outline the workings of these two dynamisms and conclude by considering their combined effects.

Seduction

Building on an insight of Pierre Bourdieu, Zygmunt Bauman has developed an extended account of the role of "seduction" in advanced capitalist societies. Bauman locates the rise of seduction in a historical trajectory that accompanies the rise of the modern state. In its earlier moments, the modern state struggled with traditional political, cultural, and religious structures that were an obstacle to the expansion of its control on the local level. In this stage of its formation, it employed strategies of legitimation to gain the allegiance of the populace. It did this through intellectual challenges to traditional authorities and defenses of new, centralized state authority. As state power was consolidated, it developed more sophisticated techniques of maintaining social order. Chief among these were the "twin techniques of panoptical power and seduction." Over time, the latter became increasingly dominant; the "paramount vehicle of systemic control and social integration" in consumer societies.[20]

The contrast between seduction and more ideological forms of legitimation is important. It is not a matter of being "seduced" by a particular worldview or being offered a particular set of rewards for subordinating one's will to a greater collective. Seduction does not work by offering a specific, organized set of compensations and pleasures; it offers instead the "straightforward sensual joy of tasty eating, pleasant smelling, soothing or enticing drinking, relaxing driving, or the joy of being surrounded with smart, glittering, eye-caressing objects."[21] This evocation of dispersed pleasures leads us on to the more disseminated aspects of seduction. Again, it is not even primarily a matter of a certain level of sensual fulfillment dispersed throughout the offerings of commercial products. More important than these is the vast, undifferentiated horizon of *potential* fulfillments.

Seduction "is made possible once the market succeeds in making consumers dependent on itself . . . . once men and women cannot proceed with the business of life without tuning themselves to the logic of the market."[22] This requires the "deskilling" we discussed in chapter 2. The disempowerment of deskilling is not perceived as an imposition; rather, it is experienced as the enriching of needs and agency. Whereas traditional nonmarket productive skills had a limited range of usefulness (namely, the support of the essentials of the domestic realm), the market provides a much broader range of fulfillments. With these offerings comes a sense of individual agency experienced in the ability to choose among them. Capitalism triumphed over communism by being able to meet not only people's basic physical needs (a task at which communism was sometimes more effective) but by being able to multiply needs and their fulfillment.[23] Seduction describes how this expansion of the market into all dimensions of human existence is experienced as pleasurable, as a manifold expansion of the modalities of fulfillment.

Many of the erosions we have spoken of in this book—the loss of communal enclaves of support, the loss of the power of cultural traditions and symbols to orient us in the world, the fragmentation of identity—involve a corresponding set of liberations. Of these, consider the one that is most easily associated with specific conscious choices: the exodus from the urban immigrant enclaves to the suburbs. In the space of a generation or two, American immigrants' children exchanged the "informal support mechanisms in the social worlds of the enclaves, based on reciprocity, duty and cultural tradition" for a more independent and vulnerable existence in the suburbs, where their ability to thrive was more and more linked solely to the level and stability of their income.[24] The social supports of the extended family were replaced by a host of appliances that supported the nuclear family in its single-family home.

When put that way, these choices were manifestly foolish: relationships were exchanged for wages and things. But Bauman's notion of seduction illuminates the more complex horizon of these choices, which rendered them attractive. Above all, market solutions provided possibilities or at least the ability to imagine them when their costs were too high. The security of traditional social supports is frequently stifling. Immigrant cultural traditions were robust precisely because of their intricate systems of gender, family, and social roles. Their protections entailed significant obligations. Being dependent on family for support in the broader world is wonderful when things go well, but dependence on family members brings with it vulnerability to their individual weaknesses as well as their fate in the broader eddies of economic and social turmoil. These burdens of "rootedness" stand in stark contrast to the unlimited horizon of potential fulfillment that marks seduction. The promises of the market ignore and replace (or pretend to) ascribed aspects of identity such as class, ethnicity, and race. Thus, in this context, the bewildering task of constructing an identity in the maelstrom of postmodern culture can be experienced as a liberation. It promises the freedom of constructing an identity of one's own that is not dependent on one's family of origin, ethnic background, or class. Even one's own past decisions recede in power as such identities seem endlessly revisable and replaceable should they fail or simply lose their appeal. Whatever the burdens that result from the commodification of the self, they are accompanied by the ever-present promise of self-renewal.

The dynamic of seduction shapes the experience of time in consumer cultures in a way that conflicts with commonsense assumptions about immediate gratification. As standards of living have risen in the advanced capitalist societies, their members have lived lives of ever-greater comfort and have been trained to seek an ever-wider range of gratifications. But there is a problem. As Freud argued, happiness is not a state that can be sustained. "It is from its nature only possible as an episodic phenomenon." He describes the paradoxical heartbreak of the hedonist. When the desired fulfillment is indulged in too often, the experience of pleasure fades to, at best, a "feeling of mild contentment."[25] Unlike many of Freud's insights, this one is readily corroborated with evidence from more empirical forms of psychology. In a set of experiments that have become classic in psychology, Wilhelm Wundt found a common pattern in responses to a wide range of stimuli. The response curve has the shape of an inverted U. When a novel stimulus is encountered, at first it is not enjoyed because of its unfamiliarity. Then, as it becomes familiar, it is experienced as pleasurable. If it is sustained, or repeatedly encountered, our response gradually fades into acclimated disinterest or active dislike.[26] Sustained levels of positive stimuli at best give feelings of contentment. Pleasure is associated with a change in state or intensity such as going from a level of deprivation to fulfillment.

Bauman argues that the consumer market has proved "to be more inventive than Freud was imaginative." It has managed to produce not simply passing moments of fleeting pleasures but the very "state of happiness which Freud deemed unattainable." It has done so by multiplying desires, arousing them faster than they can be fulfilled. "Objects of desire" are replaced more rapidly than the time it takes for consumers "to get bored and annoyed with their possession."[27] This state of happiness is a sustained state of desire and anticipation. In other words, consumer desire has very little at all to do with immediate gratification. On the contrary, it is about the constant search for gratification, which in the end proves to be more gratifying still. As Peter Sedgwick observes concerning desire among the romantics, they learned that "longing could give us as much pleasure as gratification."[28]

If consumer capitalism has proved more imaginative than Freud, its solution to satiation would have come as no surprise in classical Greece. Anne Carson highlights the importance of "lack" as the "animating, fundamental constituent" of the classical understanding of eros. Grammatically it is a noun, but it functions as a verb. It is, in Aristotle's words, "a reaching out for the sweet."[29] While it seems that the lover wants only the beloved, "this, of course, is not really the case." "That which is known, attained, possessed, cannot be an object of desire."[30] Desire and its pleasures, are constituted in lack. Sappho provides the tensive description of its fundamental nature. It is *glukupikron,* sweet and bitter, pleasure and pain; a lack that is enjoyable because the self is confirmed in the reaching out that flows from its experience of absence, need, and incompleteness. Consumer desire works in the same way. It strengthens the joys of seeking, of reaching out. The sufferings of particular lacks are endlessly overwritten with new desires. The bitterness of disappointment and frustration with particular objects of desire is endlessly glazed over by the sweetness of desire for new ones. With each cycle, the subject is reinforced in the habit of endless consumption, formed in the joys of endless desire. Thus, the insatiability of consumer desire arises not from confusion about the proper object of human longing, but as a result of formation in the daily commerce of advanced capitalist economies.

Misdirection

Consumer desire is elicited and sustained by a second dynamic that complements seduction. I will call this "misdirection," the systematic association of other needs and desires with commodity objects and the resultant channeling of the drive to fulfill these needs into acts of consumption. Misdirection can be thought of in terms of more psychological notions of fetishism. These are now described as "paraphilias," overdetermined sexual/emotional attachments to objects and practices outside the normal range of sexual behavior.[31] For consumerism, there are three major factors that drive this misdirection of desire: the decline of traditional social and cultural markers of identity and belonging, the rise of advertising, and the increasing complexity of commercial products.

The first of these factors, the decline of traditional markers of identity, was discussed in previous chapters. People engage in consumption in order to fulfill the social needs for identity and belonging. The erosions of modernity and postmodernity have made this task ever more difficult. As traditional markers of identity have been rendered less stable, people are increasingly driven to conspicuous consumption to fill the vacuum in their social identities.

We have considered how advertising exacerbated and exploited the erosion of traditional markers of identity by associating them with products. William Leiss has offered a more complex account of this process and its consequences. His analysis begins with the increasing complexity of modern commodities. Extremely few consumers have sufficient knowledge to make informed choices about the products they buy. We generally do not understand the detailed workings, and thus the pros and cons, of much that we buy—from antiperspirant to televisions. I was struck by this several years ago when purchasing a television. Beyond the small three-by-five-inch cards in the showroom listing the product's features and comparing the picture quality with the other sets on offer, there is virtually no information to be had. And given the short life span of many manufactured objects, *Consumer Reports'* evaluations are not useful for much beyond identifying manufacturers who have produced quality products in the past. As a result of these dynamics, decisions become less rational in the sense presumed by liberal economics and more dependent on advertising. Leiss argues that complexity provides the opening for the manipulation of needs by advertising. The shift from informational advertising to the use of emotional claims accompanies the rise in complexity of commercial products. As appliances and household and personal care products become more technologically and chemically complex, advertisements can no longer easily describe their advantages in everyday language, and thus the use of other methods of appeal comes to dominate.

Leiss analyzes in detail the consequences of this shift for the act of consumption. The association of more fundamental psychological and social needs with commodities leads to a fragmentation of these needs and values. "Each aspect of a person's needs tends to be broken down into progressively smaller component parts, and therefore . . . it becomes increasingly difficult for the person to integrate the components."[32] The integration of these fragmented needs is left to the commodities themselves. Consider how an attractive commodity such as a well-made watch appears. Luxury watches clearly serve as conspicuous displays of distinction, so let us focus on a less expensive, more "functional" example. Its case is carefully cast and machined from an impressive material—stainless steel or titanium. The window on the front—its "crystal"—is "hardened mineral glass" or even a disk of synthetic sapphire, impervious to scratching by anything but a diamond. The case is waterproof to five hundred feet. The mechanism is accurate to within one-tenth of a second per day. Few of these features are necessary for the rigors of most daily lives. Arriving within a few minutes of the time of a scheduled appointment is well within social standards of punctuality. Still, the watch, like a host of other "professional" quality appliances—from blow dryers to toasters—provides compensations far beyond its most literal use. The well-made thing is a fetish of competence, reliability, stability, and durability. When we wear and use such an item, we are reassured that we too are competent and capable. We are prepared to face not only daily life but extreme circumstances as well, where these exotic materials—titanium eyeglass frames, hard-anodized cookware—will prove their mettle, as will we.

We could multiply examples of commodities that engage other values: from lingerie to lawn furniture. As desires and values as diverse as belonging, success in sexual relationships and friendships, adventure, concern for the environment, and political and ethical commitments are attached to objects of consumption, the act of consumption becomes simultaneously overdetermined and undecidable. The act becomes overdetermined because so much is at stake. "Wholeness," the integration of values and needs, "tends to become a property of the commodities themselves."[33] The act of consumption becomes increasingly undecidable because the exploitation of other needs and desires by advertising erodes the "previously distinct categories of needs" which guided their resolution before their absorption into the market.[34] Thus, more and more is at stake in our acts of consumption, and we have fewer and fewer resources to guide us. Since consumer commodities can never deliver on the promised resolution of values, each decision becomes a fleeting still point in the marketing cacophony: values are stabilized and the anxiety of choice is relieved, but only momentarily. Then the inevitable failure of the commodity's promised synthesis drives us back into the marketplace for endless, futile repetitions.

> The dizzy pirouette of wants and commodities presents to the individual an ever-changing ensemble of satisfaction and dissatisfactions in terms of which there is no resolution, but only a continuous movement from a less extensive to a more extensive participation in market activity.[35]

Thus, there are two complementary dynamics that drive consumer desire, each deeply ensconced in our imaginations. Neither has much to do with the vulgar attachment to material things; in fact, both militate against such attachments. Leiss observes the paradox that in "high-consumption lifestyles" individuals become increasingly indifferent to particular wants and objects of consumption because of the increased amount of time "expended on the total activity of consumption."[36]

The Fragmentation of Desire

Having considered these two motives of consumer desire, we must now consider the texture of this desire in more detail. How is it focused? How does it structure our engagements with objects of desire? A famous set of ads from the 1980s for Calvin Klein's Obsession fragrances stands out as a metaphor for consumer desire. These are worth considering not only because they exemplify of the workings of seduction but also because they illuminate its psychological dimensions. The Obsession campaign was controversial at the time for its intense eroticism, and it stands out now as an early example of the many provocative campaigns Calvin Klein has used. Although the campaign involved celebrity model shots and intensely erotic images of couples *in flagrante delicto,* it is best remembered for several indecipherable images of tangled bodies. One is a vista of intertwined nude female bodies, limbs disorientingly interwoven, the center page break strangely cropped to suggest both continuity and discontinuity. Another is a grainy, chiaroscuro shot of a woman surrounded by an equally indecipherable tangle of limbs and faces that are, as far as can be guessed, male. The woman's face seems much more ecstatic than is warranted by the staid kiss the male on her right is placing on her extended thumb. The eroticism of both images is frankly orgiastic. While the gender imbalances might suggest homosexual transgression, they conform readily to gender role stereotypes. The first needs no male protagonist, as the (mostly headless) female forms are laid out for the pleasure of the implied male gaze. Because the gaze of the spectator is male, the second image requires an image of an orgasmic woman to convey the enjoyment of multiple male bodies. (In both, the perfume bottle is, not surprisingly, depicted and located in an unsubtly phallic manner.) They perform and depict, respectively, a decidedly pre-oedipal sexuality, an individual enveloped in a wall of undifferentiated pleasurable flesh. This lack of differentiation clearly builds on the gender-bending success of Calvin Klein's underwear line in the 1980s, which offered women's underwear designed in the fashion of men's cotton briefs, and in turn sexualized men's versions by mimicking the more revealing cuts of women's underwear. Ads for these often exploited the androgyny of the underwear by posing topless models in positions that heightened gender ambiguity. The ads presented beautiful expanses of semi-nude androgynous flesh. This use of eroticized but gender-ambiguous flesh evokes infantile pre-oedipal desire before the separation of the child's consciousness from the rest of the world and (in certain psychoanalytic narratives) from its mother's body. The images return us to the sensual enjoyment of the contact of flesh, before we separated the world into subject and object.

This is precisely the sort of subjectivity implicit in Bauman's notion of seduction. Here the self has no stable center but is an endless task of self-construction. The only stability to subjectivity is the body itself, which functions "as the material, tangible substratum, container, carrier and executor" of ever-changing "protean and fickle" identities. This explains, for Bauman, the popularity of exercise and health concerns as the dominant notion of self-cultivation. These serve to enhance "the capacity of the body for absorbing the input of sensuous impressions."[37]

Even more than the unstable self, however, these images convey the dispersed sorts of pleasure at the heart of seduction. As a horizon of fulfillment, the market offers possibilities that go beyond determinate categories. Pleasures can be attached to any object or activity. The liquidation of other realms (social, cultural, religious) is analogous to the fragmentation of bodies into flesh in these images. Their constituent parts are disassembled and dispersed for pleasurable use, recombined to suit the pre-oedipal desires of the consumer. In the process, their particularities are likely to be elided, like the faces of the women models in the first ad. When they do survive, they live on in a similarly disembodied manner, like the non-narrative pleasure on the face of the model in the second. Thus, in consumer culture, religions are broken down into commodified fragments that are abstracted from their traditional interconnections and the communities that connect them to a particular form of life.

Desire in this abstract, fragmented form can be endlessly multiplied without becoming disruptive. Since it is always focused "out there" on some new object, it renders people highly adaptable to systematic frustrations and injustices. Its licentiousness is not transgressive; it fosters no dangerous attachments to particular persons, things, or values. Provocations of dangerous desires—the face of the beloved or the suffering other, gross injustice, commitment to some particular campaign or movement—are given no time to take hold. Thus, it does not know thankfulness for the goodness of any thing or person. It is lured away and distracted from traces of singularity by images of airbrushed perfection free of the blemishes of particularity, narratives of scars and stretch marks, or intimations of mortality. Nor does it know sacrifice. For all its excesses, seduction is, in the end, practiced through purchase. Its limit is one's account balance, not death or self-donation. It is, in the end, surprisingly parsimonious, unfamiliar with any splendid expenditure, any reckless, gracious bestowal of one's life. It disciplines by locking people's lives into the pursuit of purchasing power, channeling dangerous desires into private consumption.

Outside of these private excesses, the mores of the professional middle class and instrumental reason reign. I was struck by the anger that students expressed in a discussion of Rachel Corrie's death in the Gaza Strip. Corrie, a college student working with the International Solidarity Campaign to Protect the Palestinian People, was run over by an Israeli bulldozer as she attempted to prevent it from destroying a Palestinian home. A short bio-piece in the *New York Times Magazine* that we were discussing ended invoking desire. Perhaps "she cared too deeply for her own good."[38] Students did not express anger in terms of the politics of the Israeli–Palestinian conflict, as I expected. Rather, they were angry about her irresponsible decision to "waste" her life. If she cared about the plight of the Palestinians, she should have pursued a career in diplomacy or policy. Not that they were necessarily selfish, but they had great difficulty imagining such a nonprofessional sacrifice.

The Obsession ads illuminate the dynamics of seduction, but they also give insight into the broader relationship between advertising and the formation of desire. This goes far beyond eliciting desire for a particular product. Indeed, of the countless ads we see each day—in print, on billboards, in buses, on taxis, and on television—only a fraction will elicit particular interest in a product, and fewer still will ever lead to a purchase. As we read the morning paper each day, articles on politics, the economy, and global conflict in the A-section are interspersed with ads for luxury items. Although we will never purchase these watches, jewelry, furs, and cars, they still have a profound effect on us by establishing a horizon of seduction. At the borders of everyday life, they array a promised land of pleasures—shiny, sleek, and seductive. Images of products we will never buy associated with flesh we will neither resemble nor touch nevertheless train us to fix our desires out there, beyond where we are. Always beyond the mundane particulars of our own place, relationships, and narratives.

This disconnection between the promised pleasures of seduction and the details of our mundane existence is an intrinsic part of consumer advertising and entertainment. T. J. Jackson Lears argues that ironic consumption of such seduction is long-standing in consumer culture. It dates at least to P. T. Barnum's open confession of pandering to "suckers."

> Twentieth-century advertizing institutionalized this joke by mass-producing a fantasy world of wish fulfilment. No doubt many ordinary Americans refused to embrace this world literally, but they were drawn into it for its entertainment value—the sensual appeal of its illustrations, the seductiveness of basking (however briefly) in the promise of self-realization through consumption. Many advertisements took their place alongside other mass diversions—the amusement park, the slick-paper romance, the movies. None demanded to be taken literally or even all that seriously; yet all promised intense "real life" to their clientele, and all implicitly defined "real life" as something outside the individual's everyday experience.[39]

This disconnection has a political consequence. There is something inherent in the pre-oedipal form of desire that impedes its ability to have a concrete effect. The psychoanalytic account of the oedipal crisis offered by Julia Kristeva is helpful for understanding the problem. She presents the oedipal crisis as more properly social and linguistic than sexual. It involves the child's coming to awareness of its distinct identity as separate from its mother. Kristeva speaks of a shift from the semiotic realm of infantile wholeness (where the child does not distinguish between its own body and that of the mother) to the symbolic realm, where identity is fractured and partial. The child constructs an identity metaphorically, by identifying with the father (or more precisely with his metaphorical difference from the mother). From this point on, the child must construct an identity in the foreign land of symbolic human language by using symbols that are imposed on it and that are never fully suited to its identity and desires. As a result, we bear within us a nostalgia for the lost fullness of pre-oedipal experience. Kristeva's position demarcates the political power of this oedipal nostalgia. It returns in adult life in desire, longing, sorrow, and mourning that can never be adequately expressed in the "symbolic," alienated language of the adult world. It appears therefore in disruptions of language—inarticulate cries, poetic twists and misuses, and so on. These challenge the ideological closure of everyday life by giving voice to needs and desires it either denies or cannot address. These subversions are, however, limited by their inarticulateness. Since they cannot be directly translated into the everyday language of the symbolic, they are, of their very nature, impractical; an ocean of desire seething beneath what can be directly said or demanded. The problem is that, in order to engage the particularities of politics, one must enter the realm of the symbolic.[40] The pre-oedipal character of consumer seduction is particularly well suited to draw off the disruptive potential of these desires. The endlessly deferred promise of their fulfillment draws us into seeking them in the marketplace. Herbert Marcuse made this point using a slightly different psychoanalytic narrative with his notion of "repressive desublimation," whereby the revolutionary unrest of the working class is siphoned off into the pursuit of mundane consumer pleasures.[41] The truncated politics of pre-oedipal desire is perhaps evident in conventional pornography. Those much-derided shallow plotlines serve an important function. They provide just enough of a setting amid everyday life for the rapid turn to undressing and sex to function as a symbolic exit from the burdens and complexities of daily existence (and sexual relationships).[42] Andrew Ross notes that, for all the marketing hue and cry about sexual explicitness, consumers of pornography have little tolerance for overly realistic portrayals of the vagaries of sexual encounters.[43]

The abstracting effects of seduction work far beyond pornography and the stylish sexualized ads of trendy designers. Consider the practice of catalogue shopping or watching a shopping channel. Again, we do this much more often than we actually purchase anything from them. Whether or not we want to make a purchase, the act itself is an imaginative exercise—a training in a specific *form* of desire. We consider how we would look in this shirt or that; what it would be like to own such a fine piece of clothing; how this electronic gadget would render our lives organized, keep us in contact with friends, or enhance our leisure; how this tool or gear would make us more proficient in a sport or hobby; how this kitchen or that bath would enhance our domestic bliss. Each of these is an analogue of the disembodied flesh of the Obsession ads, a possibility imagined in abstraction from or as an alternative to the details of our everyday lives. This contemporary form of window shopping is more influential than actually shopping for a purchase. Purchasing drags us immediately into mundane details. Do they have my size? Where would I wear this? Could I keep an all-white kitchen clean? Where would the kids sit in a car like that? Our practice of ads is much more akin to reading a travel guide for a journey we will never take. We find pleasure in the imagination more than in reality because that would require the burdens of planning. Make no mistake, such "practice of ads" is every bit as formative of our desires as more traditional religious disciplines and practices such as saying the rosary or sitting in meditation. Moreover, it is a practice to which we devote an immense amount of time. Rare is the religious practitioner who repeats a prayer or mantra as often in a day as the average person engages an ad.

If seduction plays upon the semiotic, misdirection is consonant with the symbolic. It builds on the more fundamental alienation we experience in negotiating our identities and desires in languages and cultures that always precede and construct us. It accentuates this alienation, however, by systematically twisting the symbols through which we express ourselves and upon which we focus our desire, in order to increase consumer demand.

CONSUMER AND RELIGIOUS DESIRES

With this sketch of the shape and texture of desire in consumer culture in mind, we can now turn to a consideration of its impact on religious desires. If our society is marked by a massive deployment of infrastructures and practices aimed at eliciting, inciting, and sustaining consumer desire, whither the desires long cultivated in the Christian traditions? What do consumer desires have to do with religious ones? What does, one might say, Madison Avenue have to do with Jerusalem? Notwithstanding the fact that major denominations and dioceses regularly employ ad agencies and publicity firms, clearly there is a conflict, but how to express it? One could attempt to distinguish these desires by their objects and argue that consumer desire (as well as its attendant frustrations and insatiability) is different from religious desire because it is focused on material things. While there is much to be said for this distinction, it does not take seriously the *form* of consumer desire. As we saw above, it is not particularly focused on the material and physical level. Its very insatiability is driven by the fact that it exploits more profound longings. As we pointed out above, the conflict between consumer desire and religious desire is not a head-on collision; it is something more akin to a train being sidetracked. We will consider three *loci* in the Christian traditions where desire is particularly at issue: the desire for God, the desire for the kingdom of God, and the desires associated with discipleship and vocation.

The Desire for God and the Desire for Goods

Augustine's anthropology provides the seminal insights for much of Christianity in this regard. Consumerism tempts us to become entangled in "the love of lower things," which causes our advance to be "impeded and sometimes even diverted, and we are held back" from our pursuit of higher things. Thus, rather than turning our hearts toward what can truly fulfill us, we squander our love on petty objects, rendering ourselves squalid in the process.[44] Consumerism seems a classic example of confusing what Augustine described as things to be "used" with those that are to be "enjoyed." The latter are things to which we can "hold fast . . . in love for its own sake." We should and, in the end, can only enjoy God. Nothing else can fulfill our desire. All other things are only to be used in our quest for our proper object of desire. The myriad cultivations of consumer desire seem quite literally to encourage us to enjoy lower things. Use value is eclipsed by other principles of desire (a curious overlap of marxist and Augustinian terminology).

Clothing becomes fashion; electronic gadgets become objects of desire in themselves rather than for their utility.

Consumer desire is neither about attachment nor about enjoyment. While by most standards of Christian anthropology, it is clearly a disordered desire, the disorder is not adequately described by the focus of desire on particular objects. Imelda Marcos owned thousands of pairs of shoes. Unless she was a person of exceptional intellect, it is unlikely that Marcos had detailed knowledge of the majority of the shoes she owned. Like most members of affluent consumer societies, she had far too many things to actually enjoy. Proper enjoyment is work that takes focus and time. Both diminish our levels of consumption. Seduction is not about *having* the perfect outfit, piece of jewelry, or CD. It is about *seeking* the perfect one, about ensuring that one has access to just the right one for just the right time. We have hundreds of CDs in our collections. More than we could ever realistically plan to listen to. With the exception of a few "devotees" or "fanatics" who structure their lives around their avocations, most sporting goods are only intermittently used. Thus, we can return to Imelda and realize that she was not all that unusual. She had enough shoes to wear three a day for a year without ever repeating. No doubt the planning and organization for such enjoyment would be burdensome. Her pleasure was in accumulating.

The dominance of this form of desire, which is fixated on consumption but not attached to things, poses a fundamental challenge to one of the seminal structures of Christian spirituality: the mystical ascent. Having its roots in Plato's discussion of the "ladder of love" in the *Symposium* and its Neoplatonic refinements, accounts of the mystical ascent by theologians and mystical writers are too numerous to list. Some of the most influential accounts are found in Gregory of Nyssa, Augustine, Pseudo-Dionysius, Bonaventure, Dante, and Teresa of Avila. It appears in other forms in more contemporary theology, such as twentieth-century debates over the "natural desire for God" in the work of Henri de Lubac and in transcendental forms of philosophy and theology such as Maurice Blondel, Joseph Maréchal, and Karl Rahner. In one way or another, all of these rely on the insight that the human person can never be fully satisfied with finite objects and, as a result, is constantly searching for more. However unwisely we may choose what to set our hearts on, we will eventually be spurred on to seek more, since we are made for fellowship with the divine and only that will satisfy the profundity of our desire. "You made us for yourself, and our hearts find no peace until they rest in you."[45] Christianity takes desire quite seriously. It trusts that, ultimately, it will lead us to God.

This is not to say that this tradition has never realized that many never undertake the quest or fail to achieve its ultimate goal. There are long-standing accounts of why most people are blinded to the true nature of their deeper longings by sin—thus locked in an endlessly frustrating attempt to sate spiritual desires with objects and actions that can never fulfill them. In this sense, consumer culture is really nothing new. The mystical path has always been a difficult one that involves sacrifice and renunciation. Little has changed in this regard, although rising standards of living seem to have been accompanied by a growing lack of interest in ascetic practices. As American Catholics have become more affluent and are less and less likely to have ever experienced involuntary hunger in their lives, the requirements for various liturgical and penitential fasting have been increasingly relaxed.[46] The Catholic fast before the Eucharist has been reduced from midnight the night before, to one hour, and the definition of a "fast day" for Lent and Good Friday has been reduced to one full meal and two partial meals. If physical privations have become paradoxically more difficult as ease of lifestyle has increased, the psychological and intellectual challenges of the mystical ascent have either remained constant or, in light of the liquidity of culture and belief, actually grown easier. We are much more accustomed to changing beliefs and accepting their limitations than our patristic and medieval forebears. We are much more ready to let go of our concepts of God.

The most pressing challenge of consumer desire, however, is not its difference from, but its profound similarity to, the form of the mystical ascent. Both share the same axiom, that particular objects cannot satisfy the depths of human longing. The mystical ascent tradition aimed to focus this dissatisfaction by generalizing it to entire classes of objects: material goods, other humans, intellectual concepts, and the like. Consumer seduction channels this fact of human nature in another direction: the endless seeking of fulfillments in more objects. The subject's desire is disseminated horizontally across an endless range of objects of the same class. The constant arousal of new desire short-circuits the lessons that could be learned from the disappointments with particular acts of consumption. Thus, just as it has found a way around Freud's pessimism concerning the possibility of maintaining happiness, it has also found a way to mitigate the spiritual reckoning that Christianity has long assumed was inevitable for the hedonist. We never tire of our earthly pleasures because their disproportion to our desire is constantly promised fulfillment by something else.

In addition to this endless substitution and eliciting of new desire, seduction undercuts the mystical ascent in another way. It has made desiring pleasurable in itself. Unlike Augustine, we do not experience restlessness, *inquies*, as a discomfort, as a spur to change the way we live our lives. Rather, we consider it a source of pleasure. Augustine hints at this in a passing metaphor. When describing enjoyment, he gives the example of someone in a foreign country on a journey home. They face the danger not only of being so beguiled by the beauties of the foreign land as to forget their goal of returning home, but also of getting caught up in "the delights of the journey and the actual traveling."[47] Thomas Aquinas spoke of this aspect of desire for temporal things: before they are "possessed, they are highly regarded and thought satisfying; but after they are possessed, they are found to be neither so great as thought nor sufficient to satisfy our desires, and so our desires are not satisfied but move on to something else."[48] We regret not our restless desires but their fulfillment. Intoxication, rather than a pleasurable state, begins to be interpreted as an inability to handle liquor, climax as sexual inadequacy. A common theme in the recent wave of popular sex manuals is the telling promise of "multiple" orgasms. While arguing the proper number is pedantic, the lack of specificity is of a piece with the temporality of seduction. What matters is that there is always the possibility of wanting and pursuing one more. We cannot assume that the monastic quest for *quies,* or rest in God, was ever unquestionably accepted as an ideal by all. There have long been many who were uninterested in such spiritual pursuits, and there have always been less Apollonian forms of religiosity. We can say, however, that the quest for such quietude seems particularly odd in the context of consumer culture, where the self is defined in terms of its capacity for experience. The ultimate goal of the spiritual quest for union with God, where all desire and anticipation cease in their absolute fulfillment, seems strangely unattractive. It sounds, dare we say, boring.

The fulfillment of the desire for God is not, however, so straightforward. The Song of Songs, the Hebrew text so heavily employed in Christian mystical traditions, portrays desire as marked by both fulfillment and lack, identity and discontinuity. Tod Linafelt finds these twin dynamics portrayed in the two "night scenes" in chapters 3 and 5. In chapter 3, the woman is driven by desire out into the streets at night to seek her love. She clings to him and brings him to her "mother's house." She takes to the streets in search again in chapter 5, but this time she is caught by the watchmen, beaten, bruised, and stripped. The chapter ends with her speaking to the daughters of Jerusalem, "If you find my lover, you will tell him that I suffer for love."[49] Gregory of Nyssa considered the bride's loss a model of desire for the inexhaustible divine Other, which no understanding or experience can ever fulfill. For Gregory, the spiritual life is marked by a progressive increase in desire as the soul presses closer to the ever-unreachable object of its desire. As he says in the *Life of Moses,* "Never to reach satiety of desiring is truly to see God."[50] To return to Augustine, although the *Confessions* concludes by reflecting on rest in the "Sabbath of eternal life," this is described in terms of the mystery of God's eternal creative activity as much as rest. The text ends not with the closure of tidy explanation but with hope that the meaning of this "will be opened to us." Charles Mathewes argues that Augustine's conclusion is an evocation of the Christian life as an endless, infinite "inquiry into God."[51] This perspective on desire is consonant with Karl Rahner's insistence that even after one's death and entry into the beatific vision, God remains incomprehensible mystery.[52] If this other Christian account of the fulfillment of desire differs from the first, it too is strikingly similar to the consumer construction of desire. The ever more intoxicated pursuit of an unattainable object, where fleeting, fragmentary experiences of union and fulfillment must be always left behind, can be transposed easily into the key of consumer seduction. If the sidetracking of the mystical ascent threatened to co-opt the desire for God into the service of consuming things, this form of mystical desire is most likely to reinforce consumerist religious habits: for example, the earnest quest of the seeker, moving from one tradition, vision, and practice to another in an endless and stunted attempt to encounter God. Discussing seekers in the context of the mystical quest suggests potentially profound connections between this postwar American phenomenon and venerable traditions of the religious pilgrim and wanderer. But in consumer culture, these committed endless departures are in danger of being reduced to the part-time dabbling of the religious consumer. We will return to these questions in our discussion of vocational desires later in the chapter.

The similarity of form between the desire for God and consumer desire provides the danger of a subtle sidetracking that threatens the transcendence of God—or more properly—our sense of it. When the desire for God is assimilated to the workings of consumer desire, its disruptions and subversions, its demand for something more than the status quo is harnessed into service of a system that provides only more of the same. Through misdirection, advertising exploits any available desire in order to hawk merchandise. All of these other rich desires are channeled into one action which can never fulfill them. Seduction uses the surplus of dissatisfaction as a spur to encourage only more consumption. Consumer desire mimics the restlessness of the mystical ascent, of our earthly pilgrimage, but safely defuses its judgment of classes of objects, actions, and pursuits. Thus, consumer desire draws the disruptive desire for the different, for union with a transcendent God, into the service of the consumer status quo. The similarity between consumer desire and traditions that emphasize the endlessness of spiritual desire suggests a different problem—the shunting of this profound restlessness into a shallow form of seekerism.

This absorption of the desire for something more into the service of the reinforcement of the status quo is evident in another facet of Christian desire—the desire for the kingdom of God. Let us turn then to a consideration of consumer desire and eschatology.

Consumer Desire and the Derailing of Eschatology

There are two dimensions of desire in Christian eschatology that are particularly likely to be derailed by consumer desire: the eschatological temporality of hope and the desire for justice. The synthesis of deferral and anticipation that marks seduction is likely to reduce eschatological hope to an impotent desire for improvement that, because it is by nature not invested in any particular object or program, can envision nothing new, only endless superficial changes in the present order. The absorption of concern for the other into commodification, likewise threatens to route the disruptive power of the eschatological and apocalyptic desire for justice into shopping. We will consider these problems in turn.

Stephen O'Leary has argued that one of the sources of the manifest political power of apocalyptic rhetoric is its "discursive construction of temporality."[53] It moves people to action by portraying the present moment as a time of decisive conflict between good and evil. John Caputo's presentation of the power of messianic time (employing the thought of Jacques Derrida and Maurice Blanchot) corresponds well to this description. He describes the destabilizing power of the messianic sense of temporality. It is constantly on the watch for the "justice to come." Messianic time is a fundamental disruption of the time experienced by the conscious subject, the irruption of an unexpected future and the constant judgment of the inadequacies of the present. It is a "structural wakefulness or openness to an impossible breach of the present, shattering the conditions of possibility by which we are presently circumscribed."[54] Its wary hopefulness is expressed in the cry of *viens*, "come." Messianism subverts linear time through its constant watchfulness for an event that will never occur. Each moment is held in tension with a fullness that it can never deliver. The temptation to gloss over the injustices of the present order is constantly challenged by desire for the justice to come. This structural wakefulness is always focused on the horizon of the future—hoping, crying *viens* and "incoming!"

Johann-Baptist Metz has written much about the ways in which the "dangerous" apocalyptic temporality at the heart of Christianity has been domesticated into the "evolutionary poisoned lassitude" of bourgeois religion.[55] He associates the failure of apocalyptic with the dominance of the "timelessness" of evolutionary time, which he considers the "secret Lord of late modernity."[56] Evolutionary time is a bad infinity in which anything can happen except for a serious interruption of the status quo, anything but the coming of salvation.[57] Time is seen as a "continuous process, which is empty and evolving towards infinity and within which everything is enclosed without grace."[58] The future is merely the present continued without end, and end here means not simply cessation but telos or goal. History is empty and meaningless because there is nothing outside of it. It runs on and on with nowhere to go. This sense of temporality destroys eschatological expectation. "'Bourgeois' religion steadily loses its messianic weakness, the fact that it still expects something. But the price hope pays for being detached from expectations that could ever be disappointed is high! Hope becomes a hope without expectations, and hope without expectation is essentially hope without joy."[59] The failure of the particular imminent expectation of the first generations of Christians is generalized into a general fatalism that nothing will ever change. In this atmosphere the great utopian projects of modernity corrode and people lack energy for anything but the most short-term of strategies. This closed, disenchanted universe is the realm of technological planning and pragmatic rationality in which expectation plays no role. The underlying fear is no longer the imminent end of history, but that history will never end.

Christianity loses much when it is recast in evolutionary time. Metz sees this as part of the attraction. The sense of "danger" and the demands for action driven by a sense of the imminence of judgment are eased. These are replaced by a "cult" of apathy and political disengagement. Christianity becomes a bourgeois religion of family and homeland that is purged of danger and risk. Along with these it loses as well the ability to offer any true consolation.[60]

The temporality of consumer desire contributes to the cultural force of evolutionary temporality. At first glance, they may seem to have little in common. Metz describes evolutionary time as closed and devoid of expectation. Consumer seduction, in contrast, is constituted against a horizon of possibility. It is always looking beyond the present for more fulfilling alternatives. Expectation is endlessly aroused. But, as we saw, this expectation is as shallow as it is widespread. Since desire is sustained by being detached from particular objects, consumer anticipation wishes for everything and hopes for nothing. It is precisely the form of hope that Metz associates with bourgeois religion—hope detached from concrete expectation. Joy is sought in desire itself; thus, satiety and fulfillment become sources of regret. As with Metz's description of evolutionary time, there is no room here for finality, for an end, for salvation. Consumer anticipation is at heart a way of accommodating the endless repeat of the same, of finding pleasure in a world without hope.

Seduction creates a temporality very similar to Metz's description of evolutionary time. Like the problem with consumerist desire more generally, however, it does so in a way that mimics the theological form of apocalyptic temporality. The inadequacy of the present moment is axiomatic. This inadequacy, however, ceases to be a source of anguish, scandal, or judgment. It is reduced to the baseline of deprivation against which pleasures are sought and measured. As we habitually turn to the future, apocalyptic expectation is absorbed into the confused quest of consumer desire. Radical, innovative, revolutionary—these are the words of ad copy. As Frank Kermode noted in 1965, the sense of "eternal transition" and "perpetual crisis" had become so pervasive that the apocalypticism of avant garde and modernist art lost its power to disrupt.[61] The problem is not simply a Christianity domesticated in suburban subdivisions, safely purged of disruptive desire and danger, its apocalyptic roots long forgotten. Rather, we face a domesticated Christianity where the forms of apocalyptic longing have been co-opted into the service of inciting consumer desire. In this form of bourgeois religion, the more properly apocalyptic needs of the poor and oppressed are not viewed with distaste and horror for challenging the illusory justice of the status quo. They lose their power to shock us because the inadequacy of the present moment is taken for granted. No one has enough. This, it seems, is the way of the world. It is, of course, outrageous to equate the experienced "need" of people making more than $200,000 a year with those living on less than a dollar a day. Nevertheless, there is more here than the shallow desire for things. With social identity and class location in constant, competitive flux, everyone must constantly struggle to maintain their own social location. Whatever the intellectual genealogy of the "ontology of lack" discussed by Radical Orthodox critics, this social structure is its proximate cause and support.

The abstraction inherent in consumer desire absorbs not only our own ability to determine how much is enough but also our ability to engage the needs of others seriously. This brings us to the second dimension of Christian eschatology that is derailed by consumer desire: the desire for justice. The range of biblical traditions from which Christian eschatology draws—Deuteronomistic history, prophetic eschatology, apocalyptic—are all marked by a profound desire for justice that drives their passionate rejection of the status quo. Exile, forceful occupation, and the suffering of the innocent call out to God for redress. Edward Schillebeeckx's description of negative "contrast experiences" characterizes well the eschatological scandal of suffering. Such experiences evoke protest, and our reaction bears within it a practical (if only incipient and vague) awareness of "the absence of what things ought to be like."[62] Both Metz and Caputo argue that apocalyptic perspectives challenge the status quo with the repressed suffering of the exploited and excluded. The needs of the suffering are apocalyptic. For them, there is no waiting for progressivist reforms, for a rising tide to lift all ships. Children are dying now. Their catastrophic need, if we face it, is an apocalyptic interruption.

We have just noted one way in which these desperate needs are diluted temporally into the broader lukewarm ocean of consumer desire. There is, however, another set of factors in consumer culture that undercuts the subversive power of encounters with suffering others in an equally significant way. John Berger has argued that in the postmodern world, space is increasingly becoming an important component of prophecy, alongside the traditional temporal dimensions.[63] Our "public" spaces are increasingly corporate owned and restricted to commercial use. Zoning laws (combined with their effects upon real estate prices) enforce a strict homogenization of neighborhoods. The fantasy lands of consumer desire are policed to keep suffering others from disrupting the party.

There is much to this argument, but it overlooks an important fact. Others, difference, and alterity are embraced and celebrated in consumer culture. Even suffering others appear in a variety of ways in the news and in other offerings of the popular culture industries. Far from being excluded, they are incorporated into consumer culture in a way that domesticates their challenge to the status quo. Two separate dynamics contribute to this domestication. The first is media spectacle, which embraces suffering as a source of intense experience. The second involves the spread of the habits of consumption into the political realm resulting in what bell hooks describes as the inclination to "eat the other."

Metz discusses the mollifying effects of spectacle. "Catastrophes are reported on the radio in between pieces of music. The music plays on like the 'passage of time' rendered audible, that rolls over everything mercilessly, and that nothing can interrupt."[64] This integration of suffering into the broader flow of the media diffuses its challenge to the dominant sense of evolutionary time. But there is more to the relation between suffering and spectacle. Human suffering is neither ignored nor comprehended as a necessary part of some larger ideational totality; rather, it is packaged and sold as media spectacle. The more apocalyptic, the more stirring the cry for justice, the better. Witness the profusion of "reality-based" television shows consisting of natural disasters and police, fire, and medical rescue footage. A character in Don DeLillo's novel *Mao II* speaks of the "emergence of news as an apocalyptic event . . . our desperation has led us toward something larger and darker. So we turn to the news, which provides an unremitting mood of catastrophe. This is where we find emotional experience not available elsewhere."[65] Suffering shares the same fate as other elements of culture in a commodified world. It becomes an abstract signifier, separated from its causes and valued for its intensity. Once again we see the peculiar complexity of the effects of consumer culture on religious concern. It is not simply that we are coddled, kept in gilded cages, battened on luxury, and incapable of facing the suffering of others. As much as that may be true, the problem is deeper. Our most laudable concerns for others are pulled into the flow of the media spectacle.

This reinforces the "cult of apathy" that Metz associates with the "evolutionary poisoned lassitude" of evolutionary time. People "do not want to take on dangerous responsibilities, they play possum, they stick their heads in the sand in the face of danger or they become voyeurs (spectators) of their own downfall."[66] The media's abstraction of images of suffering from analysis of its causes and the rapid pace of their endless substitution reduces viewers to stunned inaction. The news media are not in the business of analyzing causes and promoting debate on solutions. Rather, it is a marketer of intensities, of which the suffering other is a best-selling variety. This irruption of suffering alterity does indeed have the disquieting effect that theorists such as Caputo claim, but, in the absence of analysis of its causes and proposals to address it, it merely stupefies.

The irruption of alterity is disarmed in consumer culture for another reason. The other is easily drawn into the structures of marketing. This is not an entirely negative occurrence. Post-Fordist markets provide the possibility of catering to difference. Popular music tells the tale. Rock-and-roll music has its roots in the large-market demographics of Fordist marketing. African American musical styles provided the cultural material for white performers to repackage and sell to mainstream white culture. In order to be a star in a nationalized market, one either had to be a white Anglo American or suppress one's ethnic identity. The situation is much different now. The fragmentation of the market into subgroups allows for much greater diversity. Racial and ethnic difference need no longer be suppressed to gain access to the market. Indeed, these are exploited to distinguish products in a competitive marketplace.[67]

This incorporation of alterity into the market has a profound downside, however. Race relations in the United States provide an example. In chapter 3, we discussed the limits of "virtual solidarity"; now we can explore more deeply the confused desires that drive this behavior. Black feminist bell hooks speaks of "consumer cannibalism" to describe how the interplay between commodification and the formation of desire enacts a powerful domestication and disciplining of the object of desire. hooks analyzes white male sexual interest in black females in a culture where racism is still an active force. She uses Renato Rosaldo's notion of "imperialist nostalgia," which describes privileged classes' longing for what their predecessors have destroyed.[68] This arises from the intractable guilt of those whose present privilege is entangled in the atrocities of the past and is reinforced by the perceived banality and lifelessness of the dominant culture. These are manifest in the repeated waves of Western romanticization of the primitive and archaic. hooks argues that this nostalgia prevents interracial sexual desire from leading to anything but a pseudo encounter. The other is not engaged as a challenging, destabilizing other, but is used, "consumed," as a source of transgressive experience.

Such pseudo encounters undermine the political power of true encounters in two ways. First, the racism of the consuming male subject is reinforced by objectifying the other as a means to furthering his experience. The other is still being used here "to be both witness and participant in this transformation" of the desiring subject. "White males . . . claim the body of the colored Other instrumentally, as unexplored terrain, a symbolic frontier that will be fertile ground for their reconstruction of the masculine norm, for asserting themselves as transgressive desiring subjects."[69] Implicit within these expressions of desire is the assertion/ hope that the one desiring is therefore not racist. This is the second way in which such consumerist desire is not subversive. It implicitly supports the broader politics of race by constructing the interpersonal realm as an alternative venue for addressing racial division. "The desire to make contact with those bodies deemed Other, with no apparent will to dominate, assuages the guilt of the past, even takes the form of a defiant gesture." But in the end, because the interpersonal realm is no more free of the power politics of racism than any other, such an act is a denial of "accountability and historical connection."[70] Thus the self-deception at the heart of this construction of desire—that one truly desires the other as other— flows over into a broader denial of one's own historical and political context.

Just as white desire for intimacy with racial others can serve as a strategy for denial of the desiring subject's implication in racism, so also does the consumption of black culture serve a supportive role in larger-scale denial. Consumption of black music, art, and culture is, for hooks, an act by dominant white culture that "demands that the Other be offered as a sign that progressive political change is taking place, that the American Dream can indeed be inclusive of difference." Difference here is reduced to an easily commodified denominator. "The acknowledged Other must assume recognizable forms."[71] These forms are not merely simplified; they are domesticated. As Leiss observed regarding tourism, "the abrasive particles which might disrupt the flow of everyday normal experience" are filtered out "through layers of commodities."[72] This denial unearthed by hooks's analysis of the racial politics of "eating the other" can be generalized to other consumerist engagements with alterity. This broader manifestation is not simply a denial of a particular location within political conflict. It is also the attempt to respond to suffering, inequality, and injustice through consumption. Misdirection turns consumption into a virtual form of politics, through which people attempt to enact political, ethical, and religious convictions. This concern for others, however, draws us not toward some act of solidarity with them but to consume their culture.

Leon Wynter faults "*def* white people" for assuming that such acts of consumption constitute an adequate cultural politics to address the racial divisions that continue to mark American society.[73] There is much to his criticism; hooks shows well how transgressive desire is frequently neither transgressive nor true desire for the other. But our analysis suggests that at times these desires are desperately sincere; people do want interracial reconciliation, atonement, and solidarity. The problem lies in their attempts to enact these desires through consumption. Alex Kotlowitz sketches the tragedy of this sundering effect of commodified desire in an essay fittingly entitled "False Connections." Kotlowitz presents Chicago's Madison Street as an axis that both connects poor youth from the West side with rich youth who shop in the retail districts in the Loop and isolates them from each other. Shops on the western end of Madison Street hawk the latest fashion trends to the economically disenfranchised. These retail outlets serve as more than a source of revenue for fashion producers. Their sales are of interest also to the "cool hunters" who track their stylistic interests which are then often recycled back into marketing targeted at their affluent peers. On both ends of the street, young people want to dress like their cohorts a few miles away. Wealthy white kids wear baggy jeans and address their friends in street slang, while their poorer peers save their money for Coach wallets and two-hundred-dollar shoes. Here we have interest and desire for the other expressed through a system and set of practices that do not provide the possibility for encounter. "And so, in lieu of building real connections—by providing opportunities or rebuilding communities—we have found some common ground as purchasers of each other's trademarks. At best, that link is tenuous; at worse, it's false. It lets us believe we are connected when the distance, in fact, is farther than anyone cares to admit."[74]

Commodification trumps transgression. Any desire is imaginable and on offer, but in a form that insulates desire from its object. Politically potent transgression becomes increasingly unlikely in a "social order that seems to know no outside."[75] This co-optation of desire to reinforce the dominant social order makes all the more clear the importance of the alterity critique offered by Emmanuel Levinas and others, and tempers optimism that it can be easily engaged in consumer culture. We encounter not people but things—safely sanitized CDs wrapped in cellophane. These mediated encounters make little claim upon us. They are unlikely to lead to the "change of heart" demanded by the gospel (which Metz finds absent from bourgeois religion). The complex negotiations and self-critique that are part of true encounter with another are absent. We are saved the trouble of spending time with people who may not only smell different but may have radically different views of the world from ours, who may make demands on the way we see and act in the world. These mediated encounters, like the interracial sexual desire analyzed by hooks, reinforce rather than challenge the identity of the consumer.

As the music of another culture is brought into the single-family home, its closure against the outside world is covertly reinforced as the anguish we might be inclined to feel at the inequality and balkanization of the world is assuaged by the symbolic transgression of putting a CD in a "home entertainment center" and pushing play. The new information technologies, the commodification of culture, and the single-family home make virtual globe-trotting much easier than encountering the marginalized closer to one's own neighborhood. Encountering the others who live around and among us is much more difficult. Here we face the issue of the geography of consumption (the single-family home, the car stereo, demographically niched retail outlets) and political encounter. Unlike the symbolic solidarity of consumption, real solidarity requires the effort of departing from the well-worn channels of our lifestyle niches (not something marketers work much to convince us to do). We must make time in our daily routines, travel to parts of town we do not frequent, struggle with language barriers, wrestle with just what we want from or for these other people who have their own lives and projects. This is both inconvenient and excruciating. It is much easier to have them singing on the stereo as we write a check to a relief organization and go on living lives largely untroubled by their struggles.

So we see the subtlety of the effects of consumer desire on Christian eschatology. For all their obvious irreconcilable differences, they are not experienced as two conflicting perspectives. Consumer desire reorients the eschatological desire for justice from the outside. Imminent expectation is transformed into the endlessly deferred search for fulfillment; anguish with the injustices of the present is assimilated to the ubiquitous consumer experience of lack; the suffering of others becomes a source of intense experience; and our desire to respond is shunted into symbolic consumption. We will now turn to another locus of desire in Christian life: the desire implicit in discipleship for commitment and personal transformation.

Consumer Desire, Engagement, and Transformation of the Self

The final area of conflict between consumer desire and religious desire that we will consider concerns our desires for ourselves—our sense of discipleship and vocation, what we feel called to be and to do, and how we go about achieving that. Vocation involves commitment to a particular form of life and to the transformation of the self in order to sustain that commitment. The Benedictine vow of "stability" seems the perfect contrast to the rootlessness of contemporary America, yet other venerable traditions such as the Franciscan and the Dominican show how the wandering life of the mendicant is its own form of stable commitment. An insight from a more modern order, the Jesuits, links vocational commitment to desire. In an influential study of Jesuit spirituality, E. Edward Kinerk explores the importance of great "apostolic desires" in motivating and sustaining the mission of the Society. While these include desires for specific ministries, they are under-girded by more fundamental spiritual ones, such as the desire for holiness, the desire to share in the sufferings of Christ, and the desire to help souls.[76] Disciple-ship and desire are intertwined.

L. Gregory Jones's critique of consumer spirituality provides a helpful starting point for considering the relation between self-transformation and consumer desire. He contrasts the spirituality offered by Thomas Moore in his best-selling *Care of the Soul* with the sermons and spiritual treatises of Bernard of Clairvaux. The writings of Bernard provide a catalogue of elements of the spiritual life missing from Moore's work. For Bernard, as for orthodox Christianity, the spiritual life begins with a call from beyond ourselves that elicits our response. Thus the spiritual life is, from the start, a challenge to the self. As much as this call may confirm our deepest longings, for Bernard it also reveals the disorder of our current desires. For this reason, Bernard prescribes a series of practices for responding to this call. These begin with the recognition of the distance between our desires and God, a mourning of our being unlike God, which Bernard describes as a "sowing in tears." After embracing this mourning and correction, the disciple can then proceed to the disciplining of desire through alms, fasting, penance, and prayer.[77] This reformation of desire continues through earthly life, where God's presence is always accompanied by absence. While this graced struggle to discipline desire does lead to the development of good habits that incline the disciple to desire the good, in the end, "acting perfectly from delight is possible only in the next life."[78]

Jones contrasts Bernard's description of the spiritual life with Moore's, finding the latter lacking both a sense of call from outside the self and transformative practices. The first of these, tied to the fundamental Christian notion of grace, has enormous practical consequences. Bernard's founding of the spiritual life upon a call from outside establishes a telos, a goal for the spiritual life. It constructs the spiritual life as an ongoing journey of response to a transcendent God who is call-ing the believer to self-discovery and transformation. (Other traditions have alter-native diagnoses of what is "out of joint" in human existence and offer the correcting goal toward which progress can be judged.) In the absence of such a call from without, the spiritual life may still be understood as a journey, but it becomes, in Jones's words, an unguided one of the "ceaseless motion of self-discovery, or more likely, self invention." True spirituality is replaced with a "vague, self-referential . . . synthetic substitute."[79]

The loss of telos brings a loss of self-critique. Moore hopes to broaden his reader's understanding of spirituality by making available to them a wide range of values, narratives, symbols, and practices for use in the spiritual life. These include the riches of the Christian spiritual traditions and precisely the sorts of practices that Bernard advocated. Without a principle of external critique, however, the spiritual life becomes moored to a potentially deluded self and these practices cease to be transformative. Jones argues that the only criteria Moore offers for choosing among the diverse beliefs and practices he catalogues is "what the individual person finds useful. . . . There is no sense of formation, no need for reformation or transformation, except as it seems suitable to that individual 'I' waiting to emerge. In effect, Moore substitutes the random rituals of a religious tourist for Bernard's disciplined quest for self-knowledge through journeys toward God."[80] The self that goes unchallenged here is precisely the consumer self. It is on a quest not for self-transformation but for spiritual experience. Jones's criticisms are valid. Indeed, Moore himself has returned to a more tradition- and community-bound spirituality in his more recent work.[81] Jones's critique of Moore portrays well the tendencies and temptations of spirituality in consumer culture: a shallow engagement with the beliefs and practices of multiple religious traditions, where, because they are engaged in abstraction from the communities and practices that give them meaning and practical impact, they are less likely to challenge or transform the life of the seeker. The narcissism critique on which Jones relies does not, however, give an adequate account of the causes of these tendencies. For that reason, it is overly dismissive of the motives of such religious persons. This is evident in Jones's sharp conclusion that people today do not pursue the difficult path of Bernard's disciplined spirituality because of a "limitation of our willingness to have our everyday lives shaped by the grace of God."[82]

In the last chapter, we considered critiques of the "therapeutic culture" and the "culture of narcissism" from which Jones draws. While there was much to these analyses, their moralizing tone tends to underestimate the significance of the work that is carried out through consumption. Notwithstanding the infantile aspects of consumer desire, the consumer self engages in complex and important activities through consumption. In a socially fluid society, people establish individual identities as well as negotiate social belonging, solidarity, and difference through consumption. For this reason, dismissals of the consumer self as shallow and narcissistic are somewhat misguided and do not provide an adequate understanding of the problem that consumer desire poses for spirituality.

Awareness of the social background of such behavior helps us understand that it is not simply an expression of a culpable lack of commitment. It also helps us appreciate that, short of such rootless extremes, religious seekers often sustain profound commitments. The use of consumption to construct and communicate individual and social identity provides significant social mobility. Ascribed markers of identity such as class and ethnicity recede in significance, and individuals are free to construct a range of identities according to chance, opportunity, and interest. This increase in mobility and choice encourages religious behaviors similar to Jones's description of consumer spirituality. A society where we are so free to choose our adult identities inevitably produces seekers who move from tradition to tradition and lift elements willy-nilly without commitment to the overarching goals of any one tradition.

The increased mobility brought by the rise of consumption as a means of establishing and expressing identity is accompanied by a correlate increase in flexibility. Our identities become increasingly malleable, not just in our choice of social location but through time as well. Our freedom to choose how to present ourselves brings with it the freedom to revise such choices. Lyon describes this as one stereotype of the postmodern self.

> The popular image of the postmodern is of people flitting like butterflies from store to store and from symbol to symbol, constantly constructing themselves, trying on this fashion, that lifestyle. A sort of pastiche persona results, so the self—and life itself—becomes transient, ephemeral, episodic, and apparently insignificant. This is what we might call the "plastic self," flexible, amenable to infinite reshaping according to mood, whim, desire, and imagination. This self is most at home in Disneyland, where pleasures may be consumed continuously and personae donned like so many outfits.[83]

Despite its appeal and accuracy, like all stereotypes it does not tell the entire story. There is no denying that there are shallow seekers out there wandering from community to community and tradition to tradition, consuming experiences in a selfish attempt to get their "needs" met. Studies show, however, that a substantial proportion of those who switch religious affiliation do so for considered reasons (indeed, perhaps with greater consideration than those who remain in the traditions in which they were raised) and stick with their decisions.[84] The life of the wandering seeker is not an invention of the postwar generations; it predates both the boomers and Jack Kerouac by at least fifteen hundred years. It is in many ways an apt description of Augustine's life. He grew up in a pluralistic world, where multiple traditions offered differing accounts of human existence and flourishing. His search for truth and happiness led him to embrace and reject a number of ways of wisdom. It is uncontroversial to observe that his final commitment to Christianity was rooted in the fact that it confirmed his experience of the bondage of the will. Anthony Giddens's description of contemporary personal identity as a "reflexive achievement" of bringing "coherence to the finite life span, given changing external circumstances" through narrative reminds one very much of the Confessions.[85] There Augustine is fascinated with the details of his own life. Rather than something to be left behind and repressed as a mere connection to past sins and vices, the memory is mined for the details of God's workings in his life and his response to them. (This is not meant to imply that the Confessions is an autobiographical work in the modern sense or that Augustine understands the self in modern terms.) As in Bernard, the self is constituted in relationship to God's gracious call. Augustine's approach is simultaneously perfectly at home in and completely alien to consumer culture. Jones's analysis of Moore's spiritual writings suggests that while the autobiographical concern is welcome, the call from outside, the demand for transformation, is not. Despite his enormous book sales, and the presumed abundance of selfish narcissists, Moore does not speak for all religious seekers. Many understand the difficulty and seriousness of the quest for God, enlightenment, or spiritual transformation and would express discomfort with reducing this to the pursuit of "spiritual experience." Like Augustine, their self-concern does not equate with selfishness. In this regard, Robert Wuthnow has argued that being "self-oriented" overlaps with being morally reflective and asserts that self-oriented persons are more likely to engage in altruistic behavior.[86]

If it does not automatically lead to shallow narcissism, then, is there any problem with the plasticity of the postmodern self and its formation in consumer desire? Yes. There is a separate factor to the seeker phenomenon that is often assimilated to the critique of narcissism: a lack of long-term commitment to religious traditions, communities, and practices that hinders the development of spiritual transformation. It fits well with the critique of the shallow consumer self. We are always open to new and exciting experiences, but once the buzz of novelty wears off and we are left with the daily monotony of saying the rosary, reading the scriptures, and sitting in meditation, we move on, looking for something new to capture our attention and to relieve us of the burdens of discipline and the turmoil of self-transformation. Although this lack of fortitude and commitment is consistent with the narcissism critique, it has another cause. The underlying problem has to do with the form of desire cultivated in consumer culture.

The commonsense assumption about consumer desire—that it is desire for possession—might be consistent with religious commitment. Brand loyalty could correlate with denominational stability. As we saw in our discussion of seduction, however, from a thousand different directions we are constantly being tempted to consider something new. While individual manufacturers use advertising to cultivate brand loyalty and to channel consumption into integrated product lines, this takes place within the broader competition for consumer interest. Indeed, even those new structures of vocational stability—marketing niches—are not focused on a single path. Much effort is spent charting and exploiting the penumbra of particular desires. If you like mountain biking, chances are good you might be interested in hiking, snowboarding, or windsurfing. Chances are also good that someone will try to convince you to consider these other pastimes.

Consumer desire is not focused on particular things; it is constantly enticed to go beyond what has been acquired to consider something new. In the world of spirituality, one need not be a selfish narcissist who flees commitment to be interested in another tradition. There are countless profound spiritual traditions to consider. As the contemporary spiritual writer Ronald Rolheiser argues, our culture is one particularly unable to understand Kierkegaard's definition of a saint as someone "who can will the one thing."[87] This applies not simply to leaving the dissipations of the world behind for spiritual growth but also to choosing to commit to a particular path. We face a thousand good choices that require long-term investment and that are often mutually exclusive.

Thus, the so-called culture of choice is a factor in our lack of commitment. But just as the freedom to choose a life partner does not automatically result in infidelity, choice in itself is not a sufficient cause for our broader lack of commitment.[88] Both misdirection and seduction focus us on the instant of consumption. This has its analogue in the act of choosing a spiritual or religious tradition.

Advertising encourages us to choose and to purchase but not to keep and to use. Likewise, spiritually we are trained to seek, search, and choose but not to follow through and to commit. (This is not necessarily an unprecedented development; religious commitment has long been marked by initial enthusiasm followed by a subsequent slackening, as is evident in the development of complex formation programs for religious orders.)

This difficulty of sustaining commitment beyond the moment of choice is reinforced by the decline of social, cultural, and institutional religious infrastructures. As we argued in chapter 3, their decline has been accompanied by increased access to religious and spiritual traditions through market means. On the one hand, this has led to an enormous increase in the accessibility of these traditions and practices; on the other, it has placed commitment to their practice more and more in the hands of the individual believer. One can sample a range of spiritual practices at very little cost. A trip to the bookstore can provide introductions to and advanced guidance for various forms of prayer and meditation. One can buy the spiritual writings of mystics from Gregory of Nyssa to Evelyn Underhill, guides on the spiritual traditions of the Hasidim, Benedictines, Carmelites, Sufis, and Jesuits, written not by schlock popularizers but by master practitioners with years of experience. But for all the profundity and quality of this material, it leaves the spiritual consumer responsible for maintaining the discipline and sustaining their commitments. This spiritual consumer is constructed as an individual, in the single-family home, attempting to make sense of and to transform his or her life without the momentum provided by communal affiliation and support. One need not reduce the consumer's motives to selfishness to see the likelihood that such engagements with spiritual traditions are not likely to lead to long-term transformation.

Thus, "consumer spirituality" does reinforce our identities as consumers, but in a more complex way than the narcissism critique would have it. It is not simply that it reinforces our self-centeredness and immaturity, encouraging us to cloak our selfishness in the aura of spiritual wisdom. Rather, it offers us the transformative wisdom of many religious traditions stripped from their supporting communal infrastructures. In so doing, consumer spirituality distracts us from the structures that maintain our dissipation: the geography of our lives in isolated, single-family homes, where the primary connection to others is through the range of media and communications technologies; the flow of our time, which is driven by demands of the workplace and high consumption leisure; and the telos of our lives, which is always implicitly the need to secure a livelihood in a competitive economy.

Monasteries, friaries, ashrams, and houses of hospitality have always been alternative structures outside the mainstream. Their very structures critique the status quo. They have their own economies (although seldom fully independent), temporalities, and reasons for being. Thus, in Bernard's spiritual anthropology, the challenge to the self to respond to a transcendent God was enacted in a community of shared practices, where an abbot such as himself would offer sermons on the spiritual life. The importance of community, institutions, and rules are evident in some of the narrative conceits of Bernard's sermons (which were carefully crafted literary works). He punctuates his expositions on the nature of the spiritual life with references to the temporality and demands of the monastery. His first sermon concludes: "But the hour is passing and poverty and our Rule demand that we go out to work." The third, one of his most influential, on the three types of spiritual kiss, concludes with an interruption. The announcement of the arrival of guests obliges Bernard "to break off my sermon . . . so as not to neglect the duty of charity of which we have been speaking—lest we hear it said of us, 'They do not practice what they preach.'"[89] Consumer spirituality is interrupted as well, but by the structures of everyday life: the need to get ready for work in the morning, to return to the work world after a weekend retreat, to pay the Internet service provider to maintain access to a spirituality discussion group, and so on. This is not a new problem. In a well-marketed introduction to Buddhism available in malls and retreat centers around the world, Thich Nhat Hanh cites a Buddhist saying, "Hardest of all is to practice the Way at home, second in the crowd, and third in the pagoda."[90] The point is not that authentic, transformative spirituality can only be practiced in a monastery. Again, Bernard's sermons are crafted works, not unedited transcripts. They point out, however, the importance of the location and the lived structure of temporality for spirituality—precisely the aspects that are obscured by the consumer reception of such traditions. It is not a question of leaving Lefebvre's everyday life for Bernard's Clairvaux or Nhat Hanh's Plum Village, but of developing structures in daily life that can support the ideas, values, and practices that contemporary spiritual practitioners appropriate from these traditions.

One of the obstacles to establishing and maintaining such structures is the use of market-based access by retreat centers and religious communities. Thus, as with books and other spiritual media (and McDonald's), one can come and go as one pleases. There is little interpersonal cost to be negotiated for entry and, consequently, little for exit. In more traditional societies, it would take an enormous amount of work to negotiate entry into multiple religious communities, to learn their teachings, and to practice with their masters. The effort of progressing through systems of mystagogy and initiation brought with it concomitant support. There is more to this than "rational choice theory" attention to costs of access; teachings and spiritual practices had a communal or interpersonal context. This provided the two things that are destabilized by the commodification of culture: a culture in which beliefs, symbols, and practices had stable meanings and communal and institutional infrastructures that linked these meanings to the practice of life.

The narcissism critique accurately highlights some of the ways in which spiritual traditions are co-opted by consumerism, but it does not tell the whole story. Our desires to form our lives in discipleship and service are not, despite the fact that they so often go unrealized, mere self-delusion. The formation of consumer desire pulls them off track. Our "great apostolic desires" are formed within a culture where desire is endlessly elicited. We are constantly bombarded with more options to consider, and these are often quite profound ones. Whereas in other cultures, choice is or was narrowly circumscribed and rigidly enforced, in ours we are endlessly encouraged to reconsider. Furthermore, because of the misdirection by advertising of needs and desires toward consumption, our more profound desires are focused on the moment of decision. We are looking to choose the ideal vision, synthesis, or vocation that will bring everything together for us. Commitment becomes a momentary action of self-disposition, not a long-term process of self-transformation. The practice we are engaging in is consumption. Thus, it is hard for us to move on to the transformative practices of the tradition we choose. When we do manage to commit ourselves to the rigors of long-term disciplines, we do so increasingly as isolated individuals who encounter traditions in the abstract, not as part of a particular community. We live our spiritualities dispersed in the micro-monasteries of single-family homes. Unless we have the temperament and calling of the solitary, like a Carthusian, it is unlikely that we possess the strength of will or the grace to sustain the commitments we so sincerely wish to carry through.

CONCLUSION

The shape and texture of consumer desire is not what it is commonly assumed to be: a shallow attachment to things. It is much more complex. It is constituted in the never-fulfilled promise of consumption. It is about the joy of desiring itself, rather than possessing. Even the most banal objects are marketed through the invocation of profound values and desires. Thus, the conflict between consumer and religious desires is not direct and explicit. Consumer desire is similar in form to traditional religious desires. It resembles more profound longings for transcendence, justice, and self-transformation enough to be able to absorb the concepts, values, and practices of religious traditions into its own forms without apparent conflict. The subversions of the mystical quest, apocalyptic longing for justice, and the radical transformation of the self live on in sedate domestication in everyday life.

This account might seem unrelentingly pessimistic. Not only has consumer culture succeeded in turning countless people into shallow narcissists, but it has also encompassed those who attempt to hold out against its erosions by drawing from the wisdom of religious traditions. The aim of this book is not pessimistic, however, but practical. Rather than simply suggesting another way in which consumerism trumps religion, this analysis has shown the mechanisms through which it does so. By outlining the ways in which consumer culture systematically disarms the subversive potential of religious traditions, we are mapping the cultural terrain on which any contemporary religious retrieval must operate. The final chapter will develop a practical response to these problems. In order to do so, we must first consider some questions that have been haunting the account of commodification of culture. If consumption has become the dominant practice for engaging culture, what are people able to accomplish through it? Is the explosion of cultural agency that has accompanied the rise of consumer culture completely coopted into consumption, or, are people able to accomplish politically and religiously significant things through their consumption? The next two chapters will consider these questions.

CHAPTER 5

The Politics of Consumption

Although they are composed with the vocabularies of established languages (those of television, newspapers, supermarkets, or museum sequences) and although they remain subordinated to the predescribed syntactical forms . . . the trajectories [of consumers] trace out the ruses of other interests and desires that are neither determined nor captured by the systems in which they develop.

—Michel de Certeau, *The Practice of Everyday Life*

T HUS FAR OUR ANALYSIS OF THE EFFECTS OF CONSUMERISM UPON RELIGION has been undertaken from a "productivist" perspective. Its emphasis on the ways that systems of production and distribution influence the desires, dispositions, and actions of consumers has provided an enormously helpful means for understanding changes in the way believers and communities engage and hand on their traditions. For all its fruitfulness, however, this perspective has a critical blind spot concerning the activity of consumption. Its very value in unveiling the ways that consumer activity is determined by changes in the system of production leaves it poorly equipped to consider what consumers actually do when they consume—beyond paying for or salivating over whatever is on offer and treating everything else as an object of consumption. This temptation to portray consumers as mindless, passive dupes is a particular temptation in Christian theology, a discourse that has been formed in the conflict between elite and popular religion.

The tension between these two perspectives is not new. Don Slater notes that discourse on consumer culture has perennially been divided between terms such as "rational or irrational, sovereign or manipulated, autonomous or other determined, active or passive, creative or conformist, individual or mass, subject or object."[1] Clearly, our work thus far has emphasized the latter set of terms. But as we have done so, we have noted other aspects of consumption, such as its role in determining social status. We have also noted how advertising has associated it with meaning making. Having outlined the problems that flow from this association, we must now consider consumption from the other direction. If consumption has become the primary action through which individuals and groups establish identity and make meaning, then what sorts of identities, solidarities, and meanings are consumers able to fashion through consumption?

In this analysis, we will continue our examination of popular culture. At this point it will be helpful to clarify a distinction we have been using concerning the term "popular culture." The constructivist approach tends to dismiss popular culture as mindless and ideological, as in the classic essay "The Culture Industry" by Theodor Adorno and Max Horkheimer.[2] This makes a strong distinction between the organic popular cultures of traditional societies and the elite-produced, commercial popular culture. The dichotomous nature of this distinction is difficult to sustain but remains useful.

If marxist-inspired productivist accounts of culture are inclined to ignore the creativity and activity of the masses, we must also be wary of the temptation to assign agency or authorship of popular culture to an entire community or group. We encounter this difficulty when we attempt to distinguish truly "popular" culture from corporate cultural production. We know where it *does not* come from—Hollywood script writers—but it is much more difficult to specify whence it *does* originate. Popular or folk cultures are neither the production of undifferentiated, unified groups nor spontaneous productions of nonspecialists who, after writing, singing, or drawing, return to their ordinary lives. Without developing a complete theory of its origins, we can note that popular culture is generally the production of elites as well—poets, musicians, artists, visionaries, and the like, although ones with a much more immediate connection to the consumers and users of their work than producers of commercial popular culture. In many cases, however, we have no idea of the origins of popular cultural and religious beliefs and practices. Their designation as popular is a function of their dissemination and use: they are handed on and practiced by ordinary people. From this perspective, culture or religion is popular because it is practiced, used, engaged, and found meaningful by "the people"—however they may be defined. This, to some extent, unravels the dichotomy. Commercial popular culture has been and continues to be used popularly—from movie lines memorized verbatim by young professionals to religious and other imagery in film and music that people employ in their spiritual lives. The same can be said from the other direction—corporate cultural production draws from popular cultural production whenever it can.

I will use the terms "corporate cultural production" and "commercial popular culture" to refer to the products of the corporate culture industries. This includes products produced by professional writers and artists as well as traditional culture that is disseminated through corporate marketing channels and mass media for commercial purposes (e.g., "World Beat" music). The term "popular culture" will be reserved for either grassroots or traditional popular culture or the popular use of commercial popular culture.

Whatever our criticisms of consumer culture (and certainly the previous four chapters have offered many), we must find a way to engage it constructively as well as critically. Such a constructive evaluation requires a consideration of the agency of consumers. If consumption is a dominant social practice, we must consider what people are able to accomplish through it. Are beliefs and values completely reduced to disposable objects of consumption, or are people able to accomplish politically significant things through such consumption? Thomas Frank's account of the Doyle Dane Bernbach ad campaign for Volkswagen in the late 1950s and early 1960s serves as an example of the problem. Bill Bernbach, the creative genius behind the ads, appropriated the then pervasive "mass-culture" critique as a tool for advertising. Frank summarizes the move in mock ad copy "Alienated by the Conformity and Hypocrisy of Mass Society? Have We Got a Car for You!"[3] This is a textbook case of the commodification of dissent, yet there is more to the story. This ad campaign established the Volkswagen brand as a marker for nonconformity. The icon of 1960s counterculture, the flower-painted VW microbus, built on the significance Bernbach's campaign had established.

Thus, the relationship between commercial culture and consumption is more complex than the commodification critique would suggest. Attending to these aspects of consumption is crucial for any theological evaluation of the rise of consumer culture because it will help us understand consumption dialectically, not simply as decline but also as a potential moment of grace allied with other positive aspects of the current historical moment, such as the rise of literacy and increased intentionality in religious choice and commitment. This task requires theoretical perspectives that better illuminate the details of how consumers engage the objects they consume. The chapter will first consider sociological perspectives that explore the role of consumption in social status and differentiation. These will show how consumption—both the literal consumption of material goods and derivative forms of cultural consumption—provide the means for forming individual and group identity in contemporary society. It will then turn to literature on subcultures that explores the subversive ways that consumers employ consumer goods and commercial popular culture. This will provide a segue into cultural studies analyses of the act of consumption and the complex ways in which consumers engage cultural objects in postmodern, post-Fordist culture.

THE SERIOUSNESS OF CONSPICUOUS CONSUMPTION

The term "conspicuous consumption" was coined by Thorsten Veblen in his influential 1899 work *The Theory of the Leisure Class*. Much like the man himself, the term is better known for its polemical punch than for its broader analytical value. Veblen described the world that would later be associated with *The Great Gatsby*, where the wealthy established social status and power through ostentatious displays. Enormous homes, huge parties, expensive food, drink, clothing, cars, and travel served not simply as hedonistic excess but also as markers of class identity. The world Veblen described outlived the Gilded Age and the Roaring Twenties and has returned in every economic boom since. Although his critique of the leisure class still hits home after a century, its relevance for our investigation lies in its attention to the social significance of consumption.

Veblen based his notion of conspicuous consumption on what he considered a perennial disdain for productive or "brute" labor. The work of securing food, shelter, and clothing has been systematically devalued as female "drudgery" in favor of male "exploits" or "prowess" that involve the conflict of hunting or appropriating the work of others through war and domination.[4] The display of goods obtained through these means establishes the social status of the possessor. Veblen argued that in American society with its fluid class boundaries, the wealthy engaged in the difficult work of ostentatious consumption to mark their difference from the middle and working classes. This provided not only solidarity for the leisure class but also social discipline, as the lower classes, whose members were struggling enough to merely survive, were spurred on to imitate the lifestyles of the wealthy.

Harvard economist Juliet Schor offers a contemporary analysis of consumption that builds on this perspective. She describes a "new consumerism," where the status consumption of Veblen's leisure class has spread through the lower strata of society. (Indeed in Western countries only a handful of what Zygmunt Bauman terms "defective consumers" are excluded from it.)[5] This new configuration of consumption is still driven by class imitation. A variety of shifts in American society have accelerated competitive consumption: the decline of homogeneous neighborhoods, the mass entrance of married working-class women into white-collar office jobs, and growing inequalities in income distribution. The latter has driven a shift in the lifestyles represented in print and television advertising and programming, as marketers seek the business of the wealthy, ensuring that the lower-income majority "is aware of the status purchasing that has swept the upper echelons."[6] This perspective leads Schor to question the effectiveness of economic policies aimed at increasing income, since in a system where everyone is on the "positional treadmill" of "upscaling" to keep up with the Joneses, increased income does not bring increased satisfaction. Americans work ever longer hours, save less, and go deeper into consumer debt to buy ever more things, while consistently reporting less satisfaction with life.[7] Schor's updating of Veblen is essential for any contemporary critique of consumption and provides insight into the dynamisms of class imitation that drive our excessive consumption, which has such dour consequences for social inequality and the environment. However, as the summer sounds of Hip Hop in the Hamptons make clear, the hierarchical simplicity of class emulation has been supplanted by a much more complex, multi-directional exchange. A consideration of this complexity will bring us into territory more directly relevant to our interest in the fate of religious belief and practice in consumer culture.

PIERRE BOURDIEU AND DISTINCTION

The sociologist Pierre Bourdieu has undertaken a sustained reflection on the relationship between consumption and social differentiation in his influential work *Distinction: A Social Critique of the Judgement of Taste.* As the play on Kant's *Critique of Judgement* suggests, Bourdieu offers a sociological account of aesthetics. Cultural preferences can be mapped to social class and profession with a disturbingly high level of correlation. Bourdieu summons data that show labor and service workers interested in romance novels and the *Blue Danube*, office and technical workers interested in photography and *Rhapsody in Blue*, while professionals and educators prefer *Well Tempered Clavier*, modern art, and "reading philosophical essays."[8] Such correlations, however, do not tell the whole story. They suggest that culture is merely a mimetic reflection of society. Bourdieu's understanding of culture is more complex. He considers it a contested battleground where social classes and subgroups compete for the power of status or "social capital." They do so by exploiting "cultural capital" or distinction.

Distinction is both a system and an activity. It has an objective character as a hierarchal system of cultural material. Music, art, literature, food, drink, clothing, and the like are stratified into a system of class markers. Use of this system is not simply a matter of drinking the right wine. One must drink it in the proper way. This is the second sense of the term. Distinction is something one displays by knowing the proper glass for a Cabernet and what foods it should be served with, and indeed how to signal confidence by knowingly transgressing such standards. Culture is the realm in which groups contend for social status. They do so by defending and subverting the system of distinction (e.g., preserving high costs for access to elite culture such as opera or establishing a system of distinction for noncanonical cultural forms such as film or beer) and by displaying distinction in various domains of taste, whether those of their own class or another that can serve their interests.

Bourdieu's analysis adds to Veblen's by illuminating the complexities of the relationship between consumption and social identity. There is more going on than elites establishing their status through ostentatious displays of wealth and the lower strata of society parroting those above. Culture is a constant play of groups withholding, appropriating, and innovating in competition for social status. This provides a much more complex way to read the commodification of culture. Rather than the inexorable logic of the expansion of commodification to encompass all cultural production, we have an ongoing interplay between social groups. Groups employ various commodities (clothing, music, food, etc.) in an attempt to establish identity and status. On this spontaneous level, consumers exercise significant group agency, and the commodification of culture is not a pressing concern. But in a society such as ours, with an extensively developed and deployed commercial infrastructure, such cultural production is an attractive source of marketable distinction. Thus marketing firms and high-style manufacturers employ "cool-hunters" to spot emerging trends so that they can exploit them commercially.[9]

Corporate appropriation of subcultures has a depoliticizing effect. The sign value of the culture is used as a source of authenticity to be associated with the advertised commodity. To accomplish this, the style must be removed from the social and cultural relations where it had political force.[10] Subcultural styles are inevitably commodified, but the subcultures themselves continue their production and innovation. Political and cultural movements are not necessarily defused by the integration of their cultural capital into the marketplace. Just as once-avant-garde high culture is abandoned by elites when it becomes "middle brow," so other subcultures move on to other markers of identity, with cool hunters fast on their trail.

Thus, the function of clothing as a marker for political affiliation is not *necessarily* a sign of the commodification of dissent. In the 1980s, Birkenstock sandals became the quasi-official footwear of leftist Catholic religious. Many derided the use of eighty-five-dollar sandals as a sign of solidarity with the poor. But clearly the clunky ergonomic style of the dull beige suede sandals provided a pointed contrast to the glossy Gucci culture of the yuppie 1980s. Thus, far from being simply the commodification of politics, the use of Birkenstocks was a recapitulation of an ancient practice of religious choosing distinctive habits to signal their life commitments and establish subgroup solidarity. Updating this practice involved drawing distinctive dress from the commercial offerings rather than from the local cultural repertoire (e.g., women religious' use of widow's garb). Once the Birkenstock design was broadly marketed and imitated, it ceased to function as a sign of distinction and was absorbed into broader consumer culture. The difference between this and earlier distinctive habits such as the sixteenth-century Capuchin hood was the presence of a clothing industry constantly looking for new styles to appropriate and market, not the use of clothing as a marker for identity.

Indeed, such use of clothing plays a fundamental role in the identity of one of the religious groups most successful at avoiding consumerism—the Amish. The example is worth considering to distinguish the point being made from another possible interpretation that would read the Amish and strict Mennonites as being able to avoid excessive and ostentatious consumption because of their religious concern for simplicity and plainness. In this view, their religious beliefs and practices, such as conservative Mennonites painting chrome bumpers black, help them control fleshly desires for candy-apple red Ferrari Testa Rossas. Certainly their beliefs are important in holding the line against consumerism. As a group, however, they avoid consumerism by using the same social dynamics exploited by consumerism. Their taste for plainness in dress and automobiles is precisely a conspicuous display of distinction.

This account of the social significance of consumption frees us from the totalist pessimism of the commodification of culture. It portrays culture as a much more complex field of action. It does not do away with the power of the corporate culture industries to commodify culture, but it shows how this is but one action among many in the cultural sphere. Large corporations enjoy enormous advantages in dictating the meaning of style through their control of production and representation in advertising and entertainment media, but their control is not absolute. They work in a field with many players and rely on grassroots cultural production as a source of style. At times they also fear its unforeseen consequences, as when clothing or shoe manufacturers used to targeting staid, suburban consumers find their goods appearing on Hip Hop videos. (Of course, such anxiety and the racist reflexes that support it quickly dissipate when they realize that they have been dragged against their will into a much larger market.) The culture industries have great power, but they are not all-powerful.

However much this approach augments the limitations of the materialist accounts pursued in the first two chapters, it is subject to some vulgar materialist caveats. First, whatever the political potential of consumer agency, it must be noted that this is a sphere of action reserved for those with sufficient financial resources to purchase not only the basic level of necessities in a given society, but to engage in sophisticated, symbolic expenditures. To return to leftist use of Birkenstocks, the criticism of designer radicalism was on target insofar as the politics of those who wore them involved solidarity with people who could never afford high-priced European footwear. This location of cultural politics in the realm of consumption amounts to the imposition of a very high unofficial poll tax. Those who cannot afford lifestyle consumption are excluded. As Zygmunt Bauman has noted regarding the poor in a consumer society, "there is very little [they] can do collectively" to devise a meaningful alternative to an identity based on consumption. Even though they have unlimited time and many peers, the dominance of consumption as the socially sanctioned sphere of action and self-expression devalues whatever homespun culture they may develop from the start.[11] Inner-city youth culture targeted by cool-hunters is an obvious exception to the rule proven by their parents and by low-income groups in second- and third-tier cities, suburbs, and small towns across the country. There is very little in these cultures that can compete with the glitz of consumer fantasy brought in through glossy magazines, television, and cinema.

There is a second, related problem inherent in the shift of politics into the realm of consumption. It is a decidedly expensive and materially intensive means of establishing social capital. Even in its most refined forms, consumer culture places an enormous burden on environmental resources and productive capacity. Conspicuous consumption—no matter how politically significant—comes at the "all-too-real social, economic and political expense of other groups and other areas of society, nationally and internationally."[12] It is difficult to find a way to divert resources to the more basic needs of the poor in a political system that devotes so much of its resources to politically significant ostentation. This describes well American political history over the past twenty-five years: round after round of dismantling the New Deal safety net in order to reduce people's tax burden. Perhaps it is not that our ability to imagine the common good has become impoverished; rather we understand perfectly what it is about: a vast, safe, economically homogeneous middle class where blue-collar workers have similar lifestyles to professionals. We reject such lukewarm justice for the thrill of social competition, the chance to set ourselves apart, to display distinction. This is one of the central myths of consumerism: that our narrowly preprogrammed choices manifest our wisdom and good taste.

This returns us to the central tension in this account of socially significant consumption: consumer agency. We must consider in greater detail the survival of grassroots production and agency in consumer culture if we are adequately to understand how religious faith and practice are transformed in such a context. Bourdieu's position is one of many attempts to describe the cultural agency of individuals and groups. Others provide fuller accounts of the creative nature of consumption. To these we will now turn in order to clarify the nature and limits of individual and social agency in the context of consumer culture.

THE AGENCY OF CONSUMERS

Questions concerning the agency of consumers tie in directly with an important theoretical debate in the study of culture. On many fronts, scholars have been wrestling with the legacies of structuralism and various forms of poststructuralism that so emphasize the determinative aspects of social, cultural, and linguistic structures and the abstract workings of signifiers, language, textuality, and the like that creative human action becomes hard to imagine. In Martyn J. Lee's words, these thinkers are attempting to navigate between the extremes of conceiving the "the actor either as the fully conscious maker of social meaning, or merely as the slave to various external forces."[13] He quotes Bourdieu's description of the goals of his research program:

> My intention was to bring real life actors back in who had vanished at the hands of Lévi- Strauss and other structuralists, especially Althusser, through being considered as epiphenomena of structures. I do mean "actors," and not "subjects." An action is not just the mere carrying-out of a rule. Neither in archaic nor in our society are social actors regulated automatons who, like clockwork, follow mechanical laws existing outside of their consciousness.[14]

Bourdieu's account of the debate is well suited to a consideration of consumer culture because he does not ignore the insights of structuralism in attempting to correct for its weaknesses. He thus helps us locate the creative actions of consumers within the constraints of consumer culture.

Bourdieu is but one of many theorists pursuing these concerns. Others include Michel de Certeau, early British practitioners of what would become known as "cultural studies," their successors such as Stuart Hall and the Birmingham school, as well as American scholars such as John Fiske and Janice Radway. All of these share a common desire to take popular culture seriously as a locus of political opposition where minority and lower-class groups make subversive use of the dominant culture.

Michel de Certeau and Bricolage

Bricolage and pastiche. The words are frequently used interchangeably to designate the shallowness of postmodern culture. Both presume a setting amid the rubble of traditions, where people pick and choose among fragments of culture sundered from the contexts that gave them meaning. An Internet search for "bricolage" will yield a multitude of sites of two types. The first are French dealers of antiques, exotica, and kitsch. The second share the francophone inclination but are English-language academic sites devoted to postmodernism and cultural studies with glossaries and references to now-classic essays by Jacques Derrida and Michel de Certeau. While the terms "bricolage" and "pastiche" have some overlap in meaning and usage, they are not identical. We have spoken of pastiche as a style. Fredric Jameson associates it with the cultural logic of advanced capitalism, where the absence of any shared project or "natural language" makes satiric parody impossible. Instead there is the endless adoption and juxtaposition of styles and diverse symbols.[15] It offers the pleasures of *jouissance* arising from the playful composition and juxtaposition of signifiers sundered from the contexts that give them meaning. Bourdieu added a class location to this analysis by noting its attractiveness to the new cultural intermediaries for its usefulness in leveling traditional cultural hierarchies. If pastiche primarily denotes a style, bricolage refers more immediately to a practice or action, an action that presumes the political traction missing from Jameson's pastiche. We will consider the activity of bricolage as a signal term for the agency of consumers.

Claude Lévi-Strauss brought the term "bricolage" into academic discourse when he used it to explain the scientific workings of mythic reflection in *The Savage Mind*. The French term refers to expediency, adapting one's actions to the situation at hand. The *bricoleur* is the handyman in contrast to a craftsman or engineer, one adept at odd jobs and repairs who does not begin work with a planned-out project, dedicated materials, and accepted procedures, but must "make do with 'whatever is at hand,' that is to say with a set of tools and materials which . . . bears no relation to the current project." For Lévi-Strauss, this provides a metaphor for understanding the rational sophistication of primitive cultures. "Like 'bricolage' on the technical plane, mythical reflection can reach brilliant unforeseen results on the intellectual plane."[16] He distinguishes this from the modern scientific perspective, characterized by the methods of the engineer who works in a carefully defined field with specialized materials and methods.

Of the many theorists who have employed the term since Lévi-Strauss, Michel de Certeau has been the most influential. His idea of bricolage is best understood in terms of the whole of his project to explore the rationality and practices of daily life. His interest in the *quotidien* was indebted to Henri Lefebvre's work, but his project differed significantly.[17] Whereas Lefebvre was interested in exploring the new spaces and forms of life in the modern world, de Certeau's interest was not limited to the modern. His understanding of everyday life is closer to the concerns of social history: how ordinary women and men, those whose voices are heard only as the background "murmur" of official history, live their lives from day to day. De Certeau was particularly interested in the activities of groups who lacked power. His research provides a counterbalance to the determinism of structuralist accounts of culture, especially against totalist accounts of power such as Michel Foucault's. With the notion of bricolage, de Certeau sought to understand how the powerless made creative use of the culture imposed on them.

Consider the imposition of European culture and Christianity upon indigenous Americans.

> Submissive, and even consenting to their subjection, the Indians nevertheless often *made of* the rituals, representations and laws imposed on them something quite different from what their conquerors had in mind; they subverted them not by rejecting or altering them, but by using them with respect to ends and references foreign to the system they had no choice but to accept.[18]

They did this most famously through the various syncretistic religions they fashioned that preserved the content of their beliefs and practices in the form of European Catholicism. The great examples of this are the various Afro-Christian religions such as Santeria, Voudoun, and Condomble. The slaves were forbidden to practice their cultural and religious traditions and were forced to convert to Catholicism. Enslavement and deculturation did not, however, deprive them of agency. The slaves decided what they would do with the religion that was imposed on them. What they did was use it as a means to preserve their Yoruba religious traditions. Slaveowners and priests were happy to see them revering the Catholic saints, but what they were actually doing was revering the saints as representations of their traditional deities. Thus Mary, St. Barbara, and Lazarus were used to translate and preserve devotion to the great Yoruba Orishas: Oshun, Shango, and Babaluaiye.[19]

De Certeau explored the politics of the quotidian in studies of many different groups. In addition to colonized peoples, he considered North African immigrants in France, factory workers "whigging," or using factory tools and time for their own projects, dwellers of modern, planned cities making surprising, unplanned use of their environment, readers pursuing their own unauthorized meanings as they "poached" within texts, and consumers of mass culture. Over and over again, he insisted that consumers and the masses were not passive dupes, that "we must not take people for fools."[20]

All of these variations on bricolage are examples of what de Certeau called tactical practices. He distinguished tactics from strategies. The latter are exercised by

subjects with their own proper place, akin to a fortification, from which operations can be carried out. These include social or institutional domains such as gov-
ernments, church institutions, and academic disciplines, which have defined
territories, powers, and competencies. Tactics, on the other hand, are the "art of
the weak," who dwell within foreign territory, making do and getting by in terrains
and cultures not of their own design and beyond their control. They are "ruses,"
"surprises," and "clever tricks" whereby the weak work within the "order established by the 'strong'" by taking advantage of "cross cuts, fragments, cracks and
lucky hits."[21] Freud's reflections on slips in language provided the means for trans-
lating these martial reflections on tactics into the realm of culture. De Certeau
described them in rhetorical terms—the willful, creative twisting of language to
suit the needs of the situation. Tactical actions are "phrasings," the "practical
equivalents of wit." De Certeau considered the arts and ruses of the weak to be
literally primordial. Not only did he note their presence in ancient cultural traditions (Greek, Islamic, Chinese); he went so far as to suggest a link with the decep-
tions of plant and animal camouflage, speaking of a "permanence of a memory
without language, from the depths of the oceans to the streets of our great cities."[22]

De Certeau's belief in the ability of consumers creatively to use what they are
given is a welcome tonic to the patrician pessimism of intellectual critics of mass
culture. What sort of examples can we find of such tactical engagements with consumer culture? How do consumers use consumer products, which de Certeau
believes now function as the "lexicon of users' practices" that serve "other interests
and desires that are neither determined nor captured by the systems in which they
develop."[23]

Media studies undertaken from perspectives like de Certeau's seek to understand what viewers make of what they watch. Don Slater highlights the significance of this approach by contrasting it with structuralist analyses, such as those
of Roland Barthes or Judith Williamson. In Williamson's study of advertisements,
the politics are, literally, in the text. The composition of ad images and copy leads
the viewer to associate this or that image of femininity, comfort, or joy with the
product being marketed. An entire ideology can be spun out of the logic of these
image associations. It is assumed that readers of the ads are trapped in their logic.
Williamson later nuanced this identification between the logic of the ad and its
reception.[24] A classic study by Jane Clark and Diana Simmonds of women viewers
of Doris Day movies provides a contrasting perspective. They found that while
these films inevitably married Doris off in the end, this plot resolution required
that Doris be portrayed as unruly and energetic earlier in the film. A structuralist
analysis would suggest that this resolution of the plot results in an ideological closure with political effect: assertive and free-spirited young women must inevitably
be reduced to passivity and conform to traditional gender roles. They found, on
the contrary, that young women frequently identified with the autonomous and
brash role given to Day in the first parts of these films and ignored her later transformation into a passive female who finds happiness as the partner of a man.
Young female viewers took what they found useful from the film and ignored the

rest.[25] Similar patterns of creative use have been studied in women's reading of romance novels.[26] Another striking example of the active interpretation of culture is found in JoEllen Shively's sociological study of the contrasting Anglo and Indian receptions of the John Wayne film *The Searchers*. The film is unremittingly negative in its portrayal of Indians and the narrative structure all but forces the viewer to identify with Wayne's character, which both the Anglo and the Indian viewers do. The Indian viewers, however, value very different things about the film and the character. Whereas Anglo viewers prize it as a mythic story of European conquest of the American West, Indians emphasize the free-spirited lifestyle of the cowboys and Wayne's character's consonance with idealized Indian values.[27]

A classical Christian theological example of this can be found in the royal office of Christ. The image of Christ the King has often been used in unmistakably ideological fashion by elites in monarchical cultures. Its symbolism and rhetoric in statues and prayers would be simple subjects of an analysis such as Williamson's as a means of reinforcing earthly structures of authority. However, the title has always borne an opposing dynamic within it. Lower classes that know nothing of "polysemy" or Derrida have perennially heard the title as a relativization of earthly authority. It has served simultaneously as both the foundation for and subversion of the legitimacy of monarchs.[28]

Dick Hebdige's account of the "mods," "teds," and "rockers" in *Subculture: The Meaning of Style* combines de Certeau's appreciation of popular agency with Bourdieu's account of the use of consumption to establish social capital. He offered an ethnographic account of the dress, practices, and culture of 1960s British working-class youth. The "mods" embraced middle-class dress and pushed it to the sartorial extreme of dandyism. Their ironic mimicry of higher-class style both expressed disdain for its banality and served as a program to provide the necessary distinction to negotiate upward mobility.[29] This analysis of the creativity of consumers rests on the assumption of the polysemy of consumer goods, that things can have multiple meanings that can be exploited in a variety of ways. This sort of perspective is interested in different data than the economic analyses we have previously considered. Rather than structural changes in production and evolutions in advertising strategies, these thinkers focus on the activity of consumers. What do people do with consumer goods, advertisements, and commercial popular culture? Hebdige's account of the mods makes clear that mimicry of upper classes is a complex affair, involving both subversive mockery and opportunistic exploitation. The commercial response to this subculture through advertising and merchandising does not signal merely its co-optation and domestication. It is equally a manifestation of public recognition of the social capital attained by this subculture.

The Limits of Agency

Clearly there is something to this activity of consumers, but we must be sober in our evaluation. What are all of these actions worth? Does de Certeau's attention to tactics get us much more than young women sublimating their powerlessness into sly appropriations of Doris Day and Madonna or consumers making unauthorized uses of shopping malls in an era of declining real income?[30] If this widespread resistance to mass culture is a hopeful sign, its hopefulness is diluted by its dispersal. While it is essential to recognize the existence of such tactical actions, we must also recognize their profound constraints. Three problems emerge in this regard. They all involve de Certeau's distinction between tactics and practices. The first concerns the romanticization of subcultural resistance in de Certeau and cultural studies. The second concerns the relation of culture, politics, and space. The third involves the nature of the cultural objects people have access to in consumer culture.

De Certeau's distinction between tactics and strategies has been challenged as overly romantic, for harboring a polar conception of power that essentializes the masses as an organic, unified resistance. Certainly tactics and strategies are not dichotomized in war. They are two aspects of the same struggle. De Certeau's tendency to moralize the distinction renders strategic exercises of power suspect. John Frow argues that de Certeau relegates the oppressed to mere resistance, overlooking the possibility of their having a strategic structural impact on the system of domination.[31] Unfortunately, all too often this polar model of power corresponds to the concrete power dynamics in societies. Nevertheless, Frow is on to something in de Certeau's work. It clearly requires a mourning of the modern, revolutionary desire to remake or restructure civilization according to some rational ideal or model. De Certeau consistently contrasted the rationality of tactical practices with such strategic forms of knowledge. In evaluating this mourning of the revolutionary ideal, we must consider the decidedly mixed record of revolutions from political upheavals to urban renewal. De Certeau wrote at the end of a century of such revolutions, well aware that their ideals were seldom realized. Despite these failures, the people whom these revolutions were supposed to help found ways to make do and get by—much as they always had.[32]

The academic reception of de Certeau's theoretical perspective builds on a widespread fascination with subcultural resistance. In Slater's words, "If a subculture member dons an Italian suit *he* is a working-class hero engaging in creative and expressive *bricolage*; if anyone else does they are engaged in unthinking and conformist consumerism."[33] To evaluate this concern we must consider the asymmetry between various situations of cultural resistance.

We are used to thinking of resistance in terms of a marginalized subculture, often along the model of European colonial destruction of indigenous cultures. Clearly, globalized consumer capitalism continues the cultural violence of colonialism. Buddhists in Bhutan, Pentecostals in Colombia, and Muslims in the Middle East are profoundly troubled by the inability of local cultures to keep Britney Spears and the WWF at bay. Reruns of the soap opera *Dallas* spread via satellite networks like Rupert Murdoch's Star Network have probably influenced the attitudes and expectations of more people around the globe than the manners, culture, and lifestyle of British colonists. Notwithstanding the fact that, as of this writing, the White House is occupied by a former oil executive, commercial popular culture is profoundly different from previous Western colonial exports because what is being exported is no longer the lived culture of an imperialist nation. The commercial culture industries have absorbed the traditional cultures of the United States. We have no folk songs handed on from generation to generation. Our ancestral recipes are made with Minute Rice and Campbell's tomato soup. Consumer culture has transformed consumers into "immigrants" within a system too vast for them to escape. They cannot "go into exile elsewhere," because "there is no longer an elsewhere."[34]

Thus, we face a problem other than the West recognizing the legitimacy of other cultures. This is not a situation that can be described simply in terms of intergroup oppression. In situations where one group of people is systematically devaluing and destroying another group's culture, the ruses of the subaltern are almost by definition real political successes. They enable a group to preserve its cultural identity in a marginal position, to twist the oppressor's culture into the forms of its own. No matter how minor these successes are, the victories of the seemingly powerless are worthy of celebration. First-world consumers watching television are in a different situation. Their culture has been drawn into the structures of corporate cultural production. There is no elsewhere, no homeland, no home shrine honoring other gods. Their ruses are harder to value, because the "other desires" to which they turn corporate culture are not those of a shared culture, however precarious and marginal. Such habitations in foreign lands suffer from the dispersal of consumers; they do not automatically preserve a threatened community. Consumers may build a new one, but, as we shall see, that is a much more difficult task involving organizing, claiming space, and sharing a message.

This brings us to a second criticism concerning the relationship between culture and politics. As Tim Edwards argues, the term "consumer culture" and theoretical valuations of it are in constant danger of being co-opted into the very political abstraction we associated with commodification. For this reason, he prefers the term "consumer society," because it better situates the political significance of consumption alongside social and economic factors such as class and race.[35] Likewise, Slater fears that cultural studies approaches to consumption overcompensate for the pessimism of productivist accounts and end up completely sundering the freedoms of consumption from any links to production. Consumers' actions are read not simply as exploitations of the polysemy of consumer goods and media culture, but as potent and effective subversions of the hegemonic intentions of corporate producers.[36] In her account of anticorporate politics, Naomi Klein raises a similar concern about the optimism of so-called "culture-jammers." These contemporary heirs of Guy Debord ironically deface and rework advertisements and corporate logos. While these are important guerrilla tactics in the all-too-real war against the corporatization of the public sphere, they are obviously not enough in themselves. Such symbolic political tactics must build on more fundamental actions such as political organizing, critique, and alternative constructive proposals.[37]

Two examples of successful cultural political actions can help us sort out what is required for these to be effective: Foucault's analysis of the politics of the term "homosexual" and John Fiske's interpretation of the Murphy Brown/Dan Quayle incident. In his discussion of the category of homosexuality, Foucault spoke of the "tactical polyvalence of discourse," whereby even the most oppressive language can be twisted to subversive use. What began as a means of repressive classification of certain individuals as sexual deviants became the basis for a positive discourse of homosexuality that authorized claims of legitimacy, naturality, and demands for legal protection.[38] Suspicions of the romantic excesses of cultural studies notwithstanding, the politics of polysemy are well argued by American cultural studies icon John Fiske in his account of the debate concerning the meaning of "family" that was sparked by then vice president Dan Quayle's criticism of the television sitcom *Murphy Brown*. After being criticized by Quayle for devaluing fatherhood, the television character argued back by turning the Republican slogan of "family values" on its head. Taking a page out of the script of presidential State of the Union addresses, Brown concluded a show by calling out representatives of real families who did not fit the Republican model. "I'd like to introduce you to some people who might not fit the vice president's vision of the family, but they consider themselves families nonetheless. They work, they struggle, they hope for the kind of life for their children that we all want for our children, and these are the kind of people we should be paying attention to."[39]

Both of these examples show how the tactical uses of language can have political effects. Both are very much like de Certeau's description of consumption, yet each involves a control of space. Homosexual claims for civil rights did not arise out of a dispersed, simultaneous, spontaneous twisting of clinical language to political advantage. They were made by gay and lesbian communities in very specific places: New York's Stonewall district, the Castro in San Francisco, and so on, whose existence depended on a range of historical and cultural factors. Coming from very specific places, these acts were, in de Certeau's terms, somewhat strategic. These spaces were, however, claimed and practiced around tactical discursive plays that allowed people to think of themselves not simply as doing certain things, but as being certain kinds of people. Likewise, Murphy Brown's very real virtual politics depended on a strategic use of space. Candice Bergen (or her script writer), along with millions of others, saw through shallow talk of "family values" by a party that had been dismantling the social safety net in the United States for more than a decade. Like others, she likely contemplated a witty twist or two on the theme. It was not until this tactical twist was worked into the screenplay of a popular television series that it had impact beyond her imagination. The rhetorical twist spread to others, and the political power of the "family values" slogan was eroded.

The relationship between these tactical plays and the use of space is important. De Certeau used numerous linguistic metaphors to describe tactics: wit, tact, narrative, and so on. Concerns such as those of Slater and Edwards arise when these metaphors are taken literally. Narratives do not of themselves make new spaces, but human itineraries and other ways of "practicing" space do, however, have a narrative character.[40] People inhabit spaces by endowing them with meanings and putting them to use. Without spaces to inhabit, rhetorical misuses of dominant ideology, no matter how crafty or subversive, have little impact.

Space is a profound problem in consumer cultures. De Certeau's most compelling examples of tactical appropriation involve practices of space: for example, the myriad daily itineraries of city dwellers who act out significances and uses that are opaque to the comprehension and planning of urban administrators. Skateboarders appropriate the Euclidean plane beneath a dour Bauhaus tower for play; immigrants use a traffic island at a busy intersection to sell their traditional foods. What are we to make of the space for agency remaining in the consumer cultures of advanced capitalist nations? In de Certeau's analysis consumers are deprived of a proper place to act just as much as other marginalized groups.

> The child still scrawls and daubs on his schoolbooks; even if he is punished for the crime, he has made a space for himself and signs his existence as author on it. The television viewer cannot write anything on the screen of his set. He has been dislodged from the product; he plays no role in its apparition. He loses his author's right and becomes, or so it seems, a pure receiver.[41]

Where it not for de Certeau's ability to find meaningful agency on the tactical level, this dystopian vision would slide into Baudrillard's nihilistic totalism. On the tactical level, however, there is much to be valued in how seemingly passive consumers "use" what they watch on television.

> In reality, a rationalized, expansionist, centralized, spectacular and clamourous production is confronted by an entirely different kind of production, called "consumption" and characterized by its ruses, its fragmentation (the result of the circumstances), its poaching, its clandestine nature, its tireless but quiet activity, in short by its quasi-invisibility, since it shows itself not in its own products (where would it place them?) but in an *art of using* those imposed on it.[42]

This hopeful appreciation of the resistive use of mass culture must be tempered by the narrowness of the space of action. Whatever its genius, this agency suffers from its fragmentation and dispersal. Its unruly uses, sly subversions, and creative appropriations remain solitary endeavors, momentary coping mechanisms that hold the media flux at bay. This is perhaps the limit case of tactical action. These creative receptions have no initiative of their own; they respond to the pace set by the media and are as ephemeral as the media flow itself. In order to have more than momentary impact, they must be preserved and shared. This requires means of recording and sharing this cultural work. Indeed, without means of being communicated and joined to organized, communal practices, such resistance plays directly into the hands of consumer culture. Recall Zygmunt Bauman's argument that seduction replaces more ideological and disciplinary forms of social control. The capitalist system is now perpetuated through individual choice. Postmodern forms of culture contribute to this through their very "heterogeneity and fissiparousness." Fifties fears of "mass culture" have been replaced by the fragmenting, depoliticization of culture.[43] Thus, resistance requires a practice of space. The next two chapters will wrestle with points to evaluate the fate of religion in consumer culture.

The final problem with this conception of popular agency concerns the way in which people encounter cultural objects in consumer culture. Bricolage is haunted by pastiche because people encounter culture in a highly commodified form. If the bricoleur's genius is to construct surprising things from disparate objects, part of that ability depends on the complexity of the building blocks. Cultural objects' complexity arises from their interconnection with other symbols and beliefs and their associations with traditional logics and practices. It is precisely these interconnections that are stripped from objects when they are brought to the cultural marketplace by the corporate culture industries. They come shorn of their messy interconnections with their originating traditions and communities. They are not irregularly shaped pieces implying the context from which they were torn, but ground fine, like sand, able to conform to the shape of the cultural container into which they are poured, like Vera Hall's and Difang Kuo's voices in the music of Moby and Enigma. When the building blocks are so commodified, the bricolage they fund is less likely to be surprising or subversive of the status quo, since it is built with elements that offer little resistance to shallow appropriation.

CONCLUSION

The notion of the social importance of conspicuous consumption provides a helpful corrective to pessimistic marxist accounts of the commodification of culture. In contrast to Jameson's dystopia of a commodified postmodern world where culture is deprived of political friction, it shows how individuals and groups compete for social status through material and cultural consumption. Bourdieu's map provided a better way to analyze the plural power structures at work within society. Corporate cultural production exercises an increasingly powerful hold on the rest of culture, but does not completely dominate it. Subcultures still exist that engage it on their own terms. The culture industries are one very powerful structure within a complex social environment, and individuals and subgroups have other resources to employ when they engage it. Bourdieu provides a way to envision how culture is politically significant. De Certeau shows how people carry out these politics through the creative appropriation and use of culture. All of this provides the basis for reconsidering popular religion in consumer culture. If cultural consumption can be politically significant, then perhaps the activity of religious consumers warrants closer scrutiny as popular religious bricolage. The caveats just noted concerning popular agency will, however, have to be kept in mind. Religious bricolage will likely face the same pitfalls: dispersal, a lack of means to share popular cultural innovation, and the limitations imposed by commodified building blocks. With these ways of valuing popular religion and awareness of its limits, let us now turn to a consideration of religious agency in consumer culture.

CHAPTER 6

Popular Religion in Consumer Culture

MICHEL DE CERTEAU AND PIERRE BOURDIEU PROVIDE A WAY TO TAKE THE dispersed activity of consumers seriously as significant and potent political action. Our topic demands more. A full evaluation of the impact of consumer culture upon religious faith and practice must consider the theological significance of the practices of consumers. These topics are not unrelated. As theologians from Thomas Aquinas to Gustavo Gutiérrez have made clear, the encounter with God always takes place within the structures of human social and political existence. For this reason, the questions of oppression and agency we have been considering were already theologically significant. It is perhaps no coincidence that de Certeau, the great theorist of popular agency, was a Jesuit and a scholar of mysticism. We have considered the liberative potential of popular resistance, a topic that is certainly related to the Christian quest for salvation. There is more here than the issue of whether or not such actions should be considered "salvific." The question of popular agency and liberation brings us to our central concern: the possibilities and pitfalls of practicing Christian faith in a consumer culture. This chapter will consider how the cultural politics outlined by Bourdieu and de Certeau can help us attend to the ways Christianity is practiced in consumer culture as well as the constraints that are placed upon that practice. We will do so in dialogue with theological literature on "popular religion" as well as historical and anthropological studies of "lived religion." We will face a number of interrelated issues. How can popular religion be appraised theologically? Is it something that should be viewed as a passive object, the state of belief among the nonelite members of the church, merely to be evaluated in terms of its adherence to orthodoxy? Or should it be viewed actively, as a particular subculture (of the majority!) with its own dynamic form of life and perhaps its own inchoate theological reflection? If the latter, how should academic theology engage it—as a source for theological reflection that is integrated into academic methods and concerns or as an alternative theological system with its own logic, concerns, and practices? The relation between academic theology and popular religion cuts to the core of our concern with religious practice in consumer culture. While popular or lived religion lacks the reflective abstraction of academic theology, it is for the same reason much more insinuated into concrete practices. It takes place on the ground, in response to the ebb and flow of history.

THEOLOGY AND POPULAR RELIGION

The ambivalence of the word "popular" in contemporary usage has long marked theological attitudes toward popular religion. Notwithstanding exceptions such as Athanasius's appeal to the faith of the people in the Arian controversy or Francis of Assisi's idealization of peasant faith, for much of the history of the Christian tradition the word has had a negative connotation. The religion of the people has long been the "other" of elite clerical religion. It was the (literally) unruly blend of surviving paganism and superstitious, magical interpretations of Christianity against which high clergy and theologians in the Protestant and Catholic Reformations contended to bring a semblance of orthodoxy. Two centuries later, at the end of a century of modernization that had significantly eroded peasant culture, romantic theologians and other scholars adopted a much more positive view of the popular. This romanticizing of what was being lost was made possible in part because the peasantry had finally been subdued as a political force by centralized state power structures. Popular culture and religion no longer posed a challenge to elite control and could be revered, in de Certeau's words, as the "beauty of the dead."[1] This turn to the popular was reinforced by the emergence of European nationalism and the rise of notions of national character such as *Volk* and *Gemeingeist*. German National Socialism gave such profoundly negative resonances to this language that many twentieth-century theologians looked with great suspicion upon popular religion.[2] The 1968 conference of the Latin American bishops in Medellin followed in the tradition of Trent in particular and both reformations in general in viewing popular religion negatively, as a "semi-pagan" manifestation of an unevangelized culture. Medellin did make room for some positive evaluation of the theological content of popular religion, which, it held, could contain "stammerings of an authentic religious sense."[3] These were not, however, valued as Christian insights, but rather as variations on Justin Martyr's "seeds of the Word" in the world outside the church similar to the evaluation of non-Christian religions in the Vatican II Decree on Missionary Activity *Ad Gentes*.[4] Pope Paul VI changed attitudes toward popular religion by repeatedly expressing concern for the importance of culture. His 1967 encyclical on development, *Populorum Progressio*, called attention to the erosion of traditional cultures and ways of life by modernization and industrialization. His 1975 exhortation on evangelization, *Evangelii Nuntiandi*, called for an "evangelization of cultures," in which the gospel would permeate the particularity of a given culture rather than being offered as a "thin veneer" that ignores the concrete form of life.[5] The 1979 Latin American bishops' conference in Puebla built on these advances, offering a positive evaluation of popular religion as a legitimate "expression of the Catholic faith." It is a "people's Catholicism." "At its core, the religiosity of the people is a storehouse of values that offers the answers of Christian wisdom to the great questions of life." It is "capable of fashioning a vital synthesis."[6]

Contemporary North American Latino/Latina theologians have made extensive use of this more salutary evaluation of "popular religion" in their efforts to
bring theology from a Latino perspective into a critical and constructive dialogue
with North American theology undertaken from (non-Iberian) European perspectives. These theologians emphasize popular religion as an essential component of the catholicity of the church. Popular religiosity and elite theological
reflection are two aspects of the same ecclesial community. Orlando Espín and
Sixto García speak of "two strands of the Christian Tradition."[7] Espín justifies this
popular religious sensibility theologically in terms of the *sensus fidelium*, which he
defines as the "'faith-full' intuition" by which "Christian people *sense* that something is true or not vis-à-vis the gospel."[8] While these accounts resist casting the
popular in opposition to elite or clerical religious practice and traditions, they do
consistently specify that "popular" means not simply "widespread," or representative of the majority, but the religion of "the people" who are marginalized and
oppressed.[9] Espín contrasts the religion of the people with the positions of religious virtuosi, who are equated with educated, clerical elites.[10]

The work of these theologians provides a number of helpful insights for considering the popular. They argue that popular religion is a mediation of the Christian tradition as important and valid as learned theology and magisterial teaching.
Thus, it should be used as a source for theological reflection. Their use of traditional beliefs and symbols retrieves their overlooked or suppressed cultural power.
Espín's notion of socialized religious experience shows the loss to catholicity that
results from dismissing this reserve of theological experience.

There are, however, two related characteristics of this analysis that render it
problematic for application to consumer culture. First, it shares the emphasis on
subcultural resistance that the previous chapter found problematic. This is manifest in spatial references—"marginal," "peripheral," and so on. Espín's understanding of the importance of popular religion rests on its social location. Religion
is a "socialization of the experience of the divine." Popular religion is the experience of the divine of a subaltern class, whose experience is systematically devalued
by the hegemonic class.[11] By distancing "themselves from what is recognized as
normative by church and society" while simultaneously drawing from the beliefs
and symbols of the tradition, subalterns are able to "*critique* persons, groups, and
institutional structures which abuse and misuse the Christian tradition."[12] They
"find an access to God and salvation" and create a religious space that maintains
their identity and affirms the validity of their religious experience over against the
hegemonic regime.[13] I argued above, however, that this hegemonic/subaltern cultural mapping does not translate well to consumer culture, where much of popular culture has been absorbed by the corporate culture industries. But the North
American Latino example makes clear that there are certainly still instances of
such cultural conflicts. This is an important correction to the theories of the politics of consumption discussed above. Even in postmodern culture, religious traditions provide the possibility of an "other" place from which people can act to

engage wider culture. These practices are not entirely tactical; they involve a strategic component, because they work from an alternative cultural space provided by a religious/cultural tradition. If this theological use of popular religion continues the emphasis on *sub*cultural resistance, it also shows the importance of this resistance being sub*cultural.*

The second problem is related to the first. These theologians' use of the category of popular religion is primarily cultural. It is a way of describing the particular religious imagination, sensibilities, attitudes, and practices of Latin American Catholics. Their descriptions of popular religion tend toward ethnographic sketches of Latino Catholicism, from which they derive theological positions.[14] Because they are dealing with a long-established culture, these theologians do not devote much attention to the agency of specific individuals and communities who originated these beliefs and practices. A theological evaluation of popular religion in contemporary consumer culture must consider more explicitly the production of popular religion. For this we must turn to an example of popular religion of more recent origin.

ROBERT ORSI AND DEVOTION TO ST. JUDE

Robert Orsi's research on immigrant Catholicism offers more detailed insights into the nature of popular religious agency because it investigates a popular religious tradition of more recent origin. *Thank You, St. Jude* studies the devotion to St. Jude that flourished among second-generation immigrant daughters, who, unlike their parents, were torn not between the Old World and the New but between the culture of the urban immigrant enclaves and assimilated life in the suburbs. In their religious activity, members of this generation were negotiating their way in a world where they could no longer rely on the structures, symbols, and practices of their ancestral cultural traditions. St. Jude's devotees had to cope with precisely the cultural dynamics associated with twentieth-century consumer culture, such as the loss of the extended kinship structures of the immigrant enclaves and the emergence of the single-family home and the nuclear family.[15]

The recent origins of devotion to St. Jude allow a detailed consideration of the agency involved in its development. The shape of the devotion emerged from a complex interplay of clerical and lay creativity and practice. The National Shrine of St. Jude was founded in 1929 by James Tort, a Spanish Claretian priest who brought the devotion with him to Chicago from the Southwest. Tort and the Claretians exercised significant control over the cult as they drafted the prayers and theology of the Shrine, directed its operation, and officiated at its rituals. Nevertheless, as stewards of an emergent devotion that had to vie with other, more established devotions for interest and financial support, they had to attend to the desires and needs of St. Jude's (and their) clients. Thus, both the clerics and the faithful together developed the devotion. This dual agency was above all evident in the official publication of the shrine, *The Voice of St. Jude*, which made the devotion a national phenomenon. The *Voice* conveyed the Claretian's authority in articles and editorials. It also contained what would become the distinctive characteristic of the devotion: letters of petition and gratitude written to St. Jude by devout followers. Although the Claretians maintained editorial control over which letters would be published, the followers were the authors of the letters, and in many ways of the devotion itself—from imagining St. Jude's appearance to shaping the domain of his intercessory power. These expressions of devotion were handed on both through the official publications of the Shrine and through the personal networks that Jude's devotees constructed.

The conflict between the male clerics who oversaw the devotion and the mostly female devout who practiced it has all the characters and plot twists of the storied celebration of the ruses of the subalterns discussed in chapter 5. Although Orsi attends to this aspect of the devotion, he locates it within the broader context of changes in society, Catholic culture, and gender roles that swept the United States during the middle of the twentieth century. This gives a much more complex account of the effects of religious belief and practice. This thick description of devotion to St. Jude provides an entry into popular religion different from the epistemological/revelatory perspective of Latino theology. Here it is not so much a particular way of encountering the divine as it is a complex of practices, relationships, and desires that entwine and secure the beliefs of the devout in their lives. While these cannot be directly translated into a particular conception of God, they do implicate a number of theological themes such as suffering and providence, oppression and resistance, dependence and agency.

St. Jude's devout followers accomplished a wide variety of things through their devotions. Orsi stresses that the effects wrought by the devotion remain decidedly mixed and ambiguous. They cannot be tidily classified as purely liberative or simply repressive. When people pray, they are negotiating their situation in the world so that they can work within it. But, "as they work on the world like this, the world is also working on them."[16] Resistance and accommodation are combined in the same act. Orsi describes a number of issues the devout worked on in their interactions in the devotion. They dealt with hopeless situations in a way that helped focus their action; they resisted the professionalization of health care and the medicalization of human suffering; and they established networks of solidarity and support. In their narratives of petition and thanksgiving they were able to give voice to sufferings and desires that otherwise would have gone unspoken.

The Shrine promoted St. Jude as the patron of "Hopeless Causes and Things Despaired Of." In Orsi's analysis, "hopelessness" is more than catastrophe; it is an experience of being caught in the clash between expectation and reality. For example, if husbands, who were supposed to support their families and not be alcoholic or unfaithful, did not fulfill these expectations, women still had responsibility for holding the family together, either seeking employment themselves (while still being responsible for child care) or patiently suffering the deficient spouse. The notion of "hopelessness" allowed women to express the contradictions and conflicts that they faced. At the same time, praying to St. Jude also provided a covert way for them to continue to take responsibility for what lay outside their control. The devotion was a simultaneous formation in struggle and acceptance.[17]

This relation between hopelessness and the questioning of established ideologies is evident in the use of the devotion by those suffering illness. Doctors declaring patients "hopeless" is a common theme in the published letters. In turning to St. Jude, the devout were refusing to give scientific medicine the final word; they subordinated its practitioners to a higher authority. (This did, however, often result in risky medical decisions.) This conflict with the ascendant institution of modern medicine was about more than prognoses. This professionalization of health care was part and parcel of the wider erosion of kinship structures and traditional practices of medical and spiritual care. In its rise to authority and power, the medical profession had to systematically discredit or co-opt competing authorities such as folk healing arts, midwifery, and nursing—all of which were feminine domains. The presence of the devotion within the medical system reads like a textbook case of de Certeau's notion of tactical plays by which the powerless inhabit territory controlled by others. Patients and nurses did this by distributing prayer cards, wearing pins and medals (even into surgery), and maintaining shrines in hospital spaces or on the grounds. These practices challenged the hegemony of the medical profession and the medicalization of illness by contextualizing them within theological narratives.

In these practices we glimpse another important dimension of devotion to St. Jude: the establishment of networks of solidarity and support. Whether in the hospital, the neighborhood, or the office, the devotion was spread from person to person. It supplemented the kinship structures that were being lost in the suburban exodus, by providing a pretense for people to acknowledge others' suffering, to share their own experiences, and to offer hope. It empowered people to penetrate the isolating boundaries raised by illness and catastrophe. The display of a prayer card, medal, or statue in the workplace, hospital, or home provided a means of identifying and establishing contact with others on a level that touched their deepest struggles and concerns.

Implicit within many of these effects of the devotion has been what may be its most important function. It empowered the devout to speak, to give voice to their sufferings, needs, and desires at a time when secular and religious cultures heavily censored women's voices. It allowed them to voice sufferings otherwise unspeakable: illnesses of the female body, mental and emotional disturbances, marital discord, and so on. Orsi contrasts the complexity of the desires and needs that women, struggling with life in the suburbs, entry into the workforce, and raising children were able to express in the *Voice* with the gender stereotypes of the time, which dichotomized women into passive, silent, suffering victims or selfish, materialistic temptresses who were destroying community and family. The petitionary narratives of the devotion gave women caught in these unfulfillable expectations the opportunity to express their real situations and needs. Even more fundamentally, by providing the opportunity to speak about these forbidden topics, the St. Jude devotion empowered women to speak. Even if they never wrote letters to the *Voice* or if their letters were never published, the publication of the "narratives of grace" of ordinary people in the magazine legitimated women's right and ability to speak their own lives.[18]

This act of narration functioned as a spiritual practice that enabled the devout to clarify their problems and focus their desires. These narratives imbued their lives with meaning. They were not simply caught in the workings of impersonal forces; powerful, personal forces were at work in the world. Indeed, one of the most powerful of these, St. Jude, was on their side, interceding for them with the source of all power. Such devotions allowed women to focus their efforts to work in the world. Women replotted their lives through their petitions uttered out of hopelessness. In their devotions, women brought the insurmountable into focus and, along with it, their desire to overcome it. Petitions were a practice in the formation of desire. They provided the devout a space to imagine life and the world differently. In speaking the problem, they began to imagine its resolution. Petitionary narratives were framed by the "narratives of grace" told by others about how St. Jude's intercession had helped them. The devout would then compose their own narratives of thanksgiving that codified their negotiation of difficulties, gave them courage and a sense of continuity as they faced new ones, and authorized their own recommendations of St. Jude to others facing hopeless situations.[19]

Orsi's account of devotion to St. Jude reinforces many of the points we derived from Latino theology, such as the importance of culture in the practice of religion and the need to attend to broader popular mediations of religious traditions. Orsi also gives a complex account of the functions of religious symbols. To use an overworked metaphor, they function both vertically and horizontally. Vertically, they are expressions and evocations of experiences of the divine. Representations of St. Jude express divine concern for the struggles that believers face in their everyday lives. This corresponds well to Espín and Goizueta's attempt to derive a theology of God from Latino devotional culture. Orsi's account gives us insight into the interplay of elite and popular agency in the genesis of the theology of such devotions. Elements of the tradition offered by elites are given meaning and function by the way they are engaged and practiced by the people. Much of this takes place on the horizontal level, where the devout practice elements of religious traditions, insinuating their meanings into daily life. The devotion to Jude provided numerous examples of such applications and practices. Religious symbols function as social markers for solidarity as well as counterhegemonic symbols that offer an alternative schema of power. Wearing a medal into a hospital invokes belief in divine comfort and concern. It also establishes contact with other believers who can provide comfort and challenges the health care establishment's medicalization of illness. In devotion to St. Jude we also see the essential relation between practices and infrastructures. The all-important practice of narrating petitions and thanksgiving did not come about simply because of a belief in the value of petitions and thanksgiving or an exhortation to engage in such practices. Rather, it was supported by the shrine's publications, its ritual practice (placing petitions underneath the altar), and the personal interactions of the devout.

"LIVED" RELIGION AND THEOLOGY

These complexities bring us into a conversation concerning the best way to account for the everyday religious practices of believers. Thus far we have pursued this analysis under the rubric of "popular religion." This way of framing the question emerged from the study of the Protestant and Catholic Reformations in Europe. Both were elite attempts to address the perceived lack of orthodoxy among the Christian masses. The study of popular religion attempts to gauge how successful these reform movements were at changing the religious beliefs and practices of the people. In this context, the term "popular religion" signifies the space "between official or learned Christianity and profane (or 'pagan') culture," where believers could elude elite attempts at regulation and fashion their own religious culture.[20]

This approach generally assumes the politics of subaltern conflict with elites and it contrasts the ad hoc nature of popular religious production with the ordered, doctrinal distinctions of elite religion. Both of these assumptions have come under serious scrutiny. First, while it is clear in certain canonical examples (e.g., the religion of African slaves in the Americas, certain liberation theology evaluations of popular religion in Latin America) that popular religion is a locus of resistance to political and cultural oppression, in many other circumstances there is little evidence that the people imagine themselves in opposition to elites. Second, popular religion's presumed "other"—ordered, coherent, doctrinal knowledge with a linear correspondence to practice—is not that easy to find. Close examination of elite religious practice reveals patterns indistinguishable from bricolage. Jeffrey Stout's description of Thomas Aquinas in terms of bricolage should be a sufficient example. "His real accomplishment was to bring together into a single whole a wide assortment of fragments—Platonic, Stoic, Pauline, Jewish, Islamic, Augustinian, and Aristotelian." Aquinas's synthesis should be studied not only for the sources he used but also for how he used them, "how he reconfigured the fragments into a whole." Against Alasdair MacIntyre, Stout argues that the "coherent moral languages of earlier generations were themselves products of eclectic *bricolage*. . . . Thomistic Latin was made entirely of borrowed parts, designed to insert Aristotle into a canon intent on excluding him."[21] In Orsi's words, "People appropriate religious idioms as they need them, in response to particular circumstances. All religious ideas and impulses are of the moment, invented, taken, borrowed, and improvised at the intersections of life."[22]

The term "lived religion" describes this practical dimension of everyday religious belief and practice.

Lived religion involves a more multidimensional relation between belief and practice than is usually considered by theology. Religious symbols, beliefs, and practices function in a way akin to the cultural dynamics described by Michel de Certeau and Pierre Bourdieu. Rather than the linear relationship between doctrine and practice envisioned by theology (elites adjudicating issues of orthodoxy that are then disseminated to believers for application in practice), here we have religion providing complexities to the cultural terrain that can be employed in a variety of ways. Although this perspective is critical of an exclusively conceptual focus, the meaning "content" of religious doctrines matters. In both Latino popular religion and devotion to St. Jude, doctrines of divine providence and intercession were integrated into the way individuals faced crises and acted in the world. On this level, religious doctrines and symbols provide shelter from dominant mores and expectations. This is exemplified well by pastoral programs inspired by liberation theologies that aim to promote overlooked and suppressed subversive symbols and doctrines such as the Exodus, the kingdom of God, and the option for the poor.

Religious symbols and doctrines function in many less-direct ways as well. As Orsi's analysis of devotion to St. Jude makes clear, they provide a space for agency as much as a set of beliefs. They can serve as fulcrums about which cultural expectations and power positions can be subverted. These twists are often surprising and ironic, such as in Mary McClintock Fulkerson's account of women in conservative Pentecostal churches using manifestly misogynistic biblical texts and doctrines in a way that gives them authority in their congregations and allows them to transgress patriarchal limits on women's speech and bodily display.[23] They can function as practices and cover for developing unexpected desires. In the case of devotion to St. Jude, narratives of petition—textbook candidates for indictment as "alienating self-projection" by Feuerbach—function surprisingly as legitimations of narrative self-agency. Religious symbols also function as symbolic markers in social conflict. A shrine, an image, or a medal within the heart of a male-dominated, scientific-medical establishment legitimates women's power and serves as a countercolonization.

It is true that such uses of symbols and doctrines often involve conceptual misunderstandings, but such uses have formed the building blocks for the complex and unplanned masterpieces of religious traditions for millennia, despite the protest of elites (who were just as often engaging in similar activities themselves). Bricolage and syncretism are constitutional in religious traditions as the failure of attempts to retrieve the original unity of these traditions reveals. The assumption that bricolage is shallow and ignorant is frequently a manifestation of either (or both) a pessimistic theological anthropology or clerical/intellectual elitism that assumes that, when left to their own devices, the masses will inevitably corrupt the faith. Espín's association of the *sensus fidelium* with popular religion provides a theological check on this tendency. The Holy Spirit guides the church not simply through the hierarchy, but also through its presence in the entire community. Thus, the creativity and engagement of the community in its encounters with culture must be considered as potentially revelatory moments in the ongoing life of the tradition.

Elite dismissals ignore the very nature of bricolage. It is not simply the activity of ignorant people living in literal ruins—whether the young monk's devout illumination of a copy of a sacred manuscript (a diagram of a radio circuit) in Walter Miller's *A Canticle for Leibowitz* or the emotivist's use of the language of morality in the similarly postapocalyptic narrative that opens Alasdair MacIntyre's *After Virtue*.[24] Ravens and pack rats may build nests with stolen objects without concern for their cultural meanings, but humans do not. To return to the example of Santeria, it did not arise from random associations. Correlations between Yoruba Orishas and the Catholic saints were heavily influenced by symbolic and visual conventions that might seem shallow. For example, the association of St. Barbara with Shango is likely founded on the consonance between the cruciform hilt of her sword and his battle axe. There are, however, deeper associations. Domestic violence and death by lightning are present in both of their stories. Their domains of competence are similar as well. Both are associated not simply with lightning but also with emotional and political volatility. Barbara is the patron saint of artillerists.[25]

If bricolage often involves robust, meaning-based associations, learned theology often displays a logic similar to lived religion. Kathryn Tanner argues that academic theology frequently engages the Christian tradition and the present moment in an ad hoc, practical manner. "Rather than being a self-sufficient sort of cultural production formed in isolation from the wider culture in which theologians participate, theological discourse is a kind of parasitic cultural production" that depends on wider culture "for the materials with which it works."[26] Figures such as Paul Tillich and Karl Rahner drew heavily from the intellectual resources of their age to fashion theologies that had enormous popular and practical impact. Their contribution is best understood not by focusing on the content they shared with their contemporaries but by considering how they "used" this material; "the rhetorical surfaces of elite theological productions—their 'figures' and 'turns'—have to be taken more seriously than they usually are."[27]

Nevertheless, Tanner argues that academic theology remains distinct from "everyday theology."[28] It has a greater range of sources at its disposal, including both historical sources from the life of the tradition and contemporary syntheses. These sources give academic theology a wider range of materials to bring to bear on the contemporary problems the community faces. Academic theology also follows different rules. It values conceptual clarity and strives to apply doctrines consistently and systematically across the range of their relevance. These rules bring obvious advantages, but they entail weaknesses as well. Clarity and consistency come at the cost of abstraction. Lived religion is, by its nature, engaged in practice.

Academic theology is always in danger of succumbing to the comforts of theory by attending to its specialized rules to the exclusion of the practical concerns of the Christian community. Short of such extremes, by its very nature, academic theology transforms practical questions into intellectual ones. Application is not intrinsic to its responses; academic theology requires a secondary (and often infinitely deferred) moment of application.

For this reason, academic theology not only teaches and corrects but also learns from the everyday theology of lived religion. It can contribute much by recognizing the wisdom, the practical "doings," and "ways of operating" at work within the faith of the people.[29] Furthermore it can contribute its own analytical strengths to these inchoate practical responses, recognizing, reinforcing, and guiding the tactical responses already afoot in the community.

No matter how distinct their ways of proceeding may be, both learned theology and lived religion apply the tradition to the present moment in a manner that resembles bricolage, which suggests that this form of cultural agency is important to the ongoing life of religious traditions. We will thus turn to a consideration of the relation between bricolage and the handing on of the Christian tradition.

TRADITION AND BRICOLAGE

All along our discussion of bricolage has bordered on the topic of tradition. The previous chapter argued that shallowness arises not from the nature of bricolage itself, or from the fact that it is undertaken by the uneducated, but from the commodified nature of the cultural building blocks that people encounter in consumer culture. This is a result of the workings of corporate cultural production and fragmenting effects of the use of culture in marketing and advertising. The example of Latino popular religion makes clear, however, that the postmodern liquefaction of culture is not complete. There are surviving ancient (and perhaps new alternative) cultural systems that preserve robust traditions. Religious traditions along with their communal and institutional supports provide the material for a complex engagement with culture.

Thus, the impasse painted by de Certeau at the close of the last chapter is not absolute. Although the danger is clear, contemporary popular or lived religion is not adequately described in terms of the dispersed, isolated consumer silently resisting the onslaught of consumer culture in solitary tactical plays. Religious traditions still mediate "other desires" to which believers can twist the dominant culture. In his more explicitly theological writings, de Certeau used the term "articulation" to describe the Christian engagement with culture. "Articulation" here does not mean translation or reexpression but "to join flexibly" as in "articulated" buses or sculptures. The articulation or "writing" of the tradition in the present moment involves "insinuating" the desires and operations of Christianity into contemporary institutions, practices, and systems of knowledge. This takes the form not of a new expression or utterance but of a reconfiguration and reorientation of the surrounding culture according to logics and desires borne by the Christian traditions.[30]

Writing in the early 1970s, de Certeau shared the assumption of his contemporaries that secularization was a *fait accompli*. His understanding of it, however, directly anticipated the later refinements of the deregulation thesis (including references to sales of Bibles in secular bookstores). What had declined, he believed, was not the presence of Christian belief or language but the power of the church as an organized social body to control religious belief and behavior or "to organize operations" in the broader culture.[31] To use his later terminology, it had ceased to function as a place of strategic control.

Aware of the profound costs of this "shattering" of Christianity, de Certeau nonetheless embraced it as a situation that could return Christianity to its more authentic character of "Abrahamic" wandering.[32] De Certeau's enthusiasm for the final dissolution of Christendom was grounded in more than the revolutionary optimism of the time. It rested on his understanding of the nature of Christianity itself. He understood it not as a particular set of doctrines or institutions but as a particular kind of practice, a certain "style" of transgressing and exceeding limits—for example, siding with outcasts, going the extra mile, and so on. For de Certeau, there is no essence or original presence to the Christian tradition; it is a series of responses to a call. The ministry of Jesus itself was a response to the call of the Father. The Gospels do not mediate his presence but record this founding "rupture." The subsequent life of the tradition is a series of departures provoked by this ongoing call. Attempts to concretize and codify this response never capture the call itself, which always escapes representation. This is the form of speech of the mystic and the source of the endless reform movements in the church. Secularization helps the church learn the lesson of mystic speech; the "new Israel" joins the old "in exile and in the diaspora."[33]

Secularization signals the end neither of the call nor of responses to it, but merely the end of the highly institutionalized attempt to embody the response that was the church of Christendom. A reader of the mystics, de Certeau did not lament this kenosis of the gospel, the reduction of the church to a powerless "fable," a "fragile and floating text" no longer the "Book" stabilized by commentaries and theological treatises, but a "narrative of a belief" that is only a "drop in the ocean" of language.[34] The ecclesial strategies of Christendom falsely identified the gospel with the political interests and needs of a particular institution. The shattering of this institution freed belief from these false moorings to undertake its works of excess on social practices. A hierarchically organized Christendom is replaced with the myriad activities of countless believers articulating their beliefs through the workings of bricolage, rupturing established unities, transgressing conventional limits, bringing together what society assumes must be kept separate, for example, rejecting a safe middle-class existence, crossing class boundaries, working with outcasts for their civil rights.

Decades later, contemporary commentators have difficulty following de Certeau's literally utopian optimism. Jeremy Aherne worries about the danger of Christian practices becoming "anonymous, if not aphasic" (a neurological disorder where people lose their ability to use language), of losing their specifically Christian identity and thus, their ultimate motivation. Graham Ward argues that de Certeau's account must be supplemented by a thicker theological narrative, if it is not to fall into a "social destitution" that is merely nihilistic "endless dissemination" lacking any spiritual dimension.[35] De Certeau's position cannot be easily reconciled with a stabilizing narrative or authority, but his descriptions of the form of mystic speech need not be equated with prescriptive calls to abandon all the trappings of tradition, save the Gideons' task of distributing copies of the New Testament in secular settings. If the elements of Christian traditions cannot mediate a certain presence, they do preserve in myriad ways the departures that the call has provoked. They are an important source of the "other desires" de Certeau so often evokes. These witnesses to past departures inspire new ones.

As was noted in the previous chapter, bricolage works best with complex building blocks. When they are predigested and commodified, they are stripped of their alien logics and strange desires. Without this richness, agency is diminished along with the potential impact of popular production. Susan Ross argues that the loss of devotional practices deprived women of an important form of agency in post-Vatican II Catholicism. Mary McClintock Fulkerson notes that women lose power in clearly patriarchal Pentecostal communities when the theology of the community is liberalized.[36] I think that one can hold onto de Certeau's theological valuing of popular agency and argue that traditions, institutions, and stable communities remain valuable as locations (perhaps not strategic places) where the elements of the tradition are preserved and handed on with a level of complexity that would be stripped away if they were mediated by the culture industries. It is not a question of reestablishing a clerically administered Christendom, but of preserving the complexity of religious archives so that they might fund a richer and more potent articulation with the present moment.

CONCLUSION

This chapter built on the last by continuing to investigate the nature and power of popular agency. A consideration of religion made it clear that popular agency can accomplish more than the competition for social status and resistance. Latino popular religion and devotion to St. Jude illustrate that popular religion is both a source of religious creativity providing new religious expressions and a process in which extant religious beliefs, doctrines, and symbols are insinuated into daily life. These uses sometimes take the form of direct applications of doctrines (e.g., the doctrine of providence supporting practices of petition and intercession), but they frequently take more convoluted forms, as religious traditions provide complexities to the space of practice, themes around which ideologies can be pivoted, desires to which accepted values can be redirected, and practices through which agency otherwise denied can be expressed. Both the creativity of new religious expressions and insinuation of belief into daily life are essential tasks in the ongoing lives of religious traditions. Popular religious agency thus plays an important role in the lives of religious communities. It is fitting, therefore, that Espín associates popular religion with the guidance of the Holy Spirit through the *sensus fidelium*.

Thus, "spirituality" as the dominant configuration of religious belief and practice in consumer culture requires more respect. Its ad hoc syntheses are precisely bricolage. Its practical focus on what "works" is a textbook example of the practical dimension of religion studied by scholars of lived religion. The pluralism of sources employed by seekers in constructing their spiritualities is quantitatively, but not qualitatively, different from past eras of change in religious traditions. This chapter enables us to supplement the narcissism critique of spirituality with a more balanced assessment. There is some truth to stark denunciations of consumer spirituality, such as Michael Budde's argument that "do-it-yourself spirituality . . . is utterly incapable of radical practices aimed at peace, the option for the poor, or any demanding exercises in transcending self-interest. There is no Amos or Jeremiah, no 'Woe to you rich' in the canon of Sheila-ism."[37] But there also can be much of value in the unruly spiritualities of our religiously deregulated age. The "solidarity community" in Washington, D.C., provides a perfect example. It is a broad, loose, and diverse community of activists who are committed to radical politics. A great number (likely the majority) of them are as suspicious of orthodox religious institutions as they are of the military industrial complex and the institutions of global capitalism. Their religious beliefs thus manifest a decided "do-it-yourself" character. Their religiosity is a splendid bricolage of the radical elements of many traditions (that religious elites such as myself cannot help but note are doctrinally irreconcilable). Francis of Assisi is blended with Ghandi's satyagraha, Buddhism, Quakerism, songs of the civil rights movement, the symbols of left-wing Latin American Catholicism, a sampling of symbols and practices from a variety of world religions (with particular interest in goddess traditions), all topped off with a smattering of Bob Dylan. These unruly syntheses, however, ground profound practical commitments. With them, people craft religiously and politically committed lifestyles: living in troubled neighborhoods in solidarity with the poor, embracing lives of voluntary poverty, sustaining long-term ministries with the poor and educating the well-to-do, engaging in civil disobedience and serving time in federal prison because of it.

If this chapter provides the basis for a positive reevaluation of spirituality, it also offers a refined understanding of its shortcomings. Religious traditions provide the material and motivation for a complex engagement with culture. De Certeau's notion of "articulation" offers a way of understanding bricolage as directed toward "other desires" and values without rejecting its popular and spontaneous character. Popular religious agency depends on the resources of religious traditions for its practical engagements with culture. These are weakened when encountered in commodified form. The arguments of Latino theologians make clear that, despite the commodification of culture and the predations of a culture industry constantly on the lookout for material to exploit, cultural traditions have not been completely eroded. The example of devotion to St. Jude shows the importance of social and communications infrastructures. Shared beliefs, symbols, and practices provided the means for establishing contacts among the followers. The National Shrine and the *Voice of St. Jude* provided the means for disseminating the devotion and supporting its practice. Above all, the *Voice* provided the means and model for the devotees to narrate their own lives of suffering and grace. It provided a location for the exercise of agency and the sharing of its products.

Devotion to St. Jude provides insight into the mixed agency of popular religion. Although the devotion was marked by the polarities of a classic subaltern conflict—male clerical control of a devotion practiced primarily by women—the reality was more complex. If the devotion began with the offerings of the clerics, who constructed for themselves an important role in the rituals of the Shrine, its final shape and daily practice were much more dependent on the system of beliefs, imaginings, and practices that the devout wove out of its original form. The *Voice* was a model infrastructure for popular religion, as it was (to use telecommunications metaphor) a "full duplex" medium. It gave voice to both the clerics and the devout. The clerics reshaped the narratives of the devout through their editorial power, and the devout reworked the offerings of the clerics through their imagination, their practice, and the writing that provided the bulk of the *Voice's* content.

This mixed agency provides helpful guidance for considering the relation between theology and popular religion. Both share similar practical concerns about the relation of belief to the practice of daily life. Academic theology can both draw from and contribute to the everyday theology of lived religion. By attending to everyday theology, academic theology can gain an understanding of both the practical problems the Christian community faces and its intuitive theological responses to them. These can serve as touch-points for academic theology's own analyses and constructive proposals. Academic theology possesses resources and methods that can contribute to and strengthen popular religious agency in a number of ways that will be considered in the next chapter.

Next we will consider tactics for countering the pernicious effects of consumer culture upon religious belief and practice. We have suggested a number of important topics that such a tactical response should consider. It should, above all, strive to strengthen popular agency, both as it works to create new religious symbols and interpretations and as it works to apply extant ones to contemporary life. The vitality of popular religion depends on its access to the logics and desires mediated by religious traditions. This depends significantly on the complexity of the building blocks with which it works. The more these are mediated in commodified form by the corporate culture industries, the less likely they are to bear subversive desires and alternative logics. Thus, traditional communal communication structures will have to be considered as ways of preserving the complex connections among elements of traditions.

CHAPTER 7

Stewarding Religious Traditions in Consumer Culture

We cannot ignore the fact that it is impossible for a *written* act (ours), an ambition ... to seriously purport to found a new kind of relation.

—Michel de Certeau, *Heterologies*

NOW WE TURN TO A CONSIDERATION OF HOW TO RESPOND TO THE PROBLEMS posed by consumer culture. The analysis pursued by the previous chapters will be used to develop specific prescriptions for addressing the corrosive impact of consumer culture on religious practice. The burden of the previous chapters has been to illuminate the ways that consumer culture transforms religious belief and practice. The problem is not simply a clash of beliefs, values, or cultures that pits consumerism against Christianity. Although very real conflicts in values exist, the problem is deeper and more subtle. Rather than a conflict between cultures, we face a cultural infrastructure that is capable of absorbing all other cultures as "content" to be commodified, distributed, and consumed. This changes our relationship to religious beliefs and practices profoundly. They continue to be revered and celebrated, but are increasingly deprived of their ability to influence and shape our individual, interpersonal, and communal lives.

Consumer culture forms people in consumerist habits of use and interpretation, which believers, in turn, bring to their religious beliefs and practice. Thus, while theology can offer daring and radical counternarratives by drawing on the rich wisdom of religious traditions, these responses are subject to the same fate as other cultural objects within consumer culture. For that reason, Christian counternarratives, metanarratives, or even master narratives are in danger of becoming ineffectual and, more than that, of functioning as comforting delusions that are nothing more than a way for religious believers to convince themselves that, appearances notwithstanding, their religious faith is impervious to the erosions of commodification. Indeed such reassuring narratives are very marketable commodities in the cultural turmoil of advanced capitalism. Theology has to learn the lesson that the market has taught other subversives who have attempted to reach a mass audience: this system greets subversion and denunciation with

179

mercantile enthusiasm. It welcomes the most radical denunciations of the shallowness of our civilization and its global excesses in the same way the sated gourmand welcomes the tartness of a sorbet between courses of a heavy meal.

This is a very pessimistic account of the triumph of commodification over all resources for dissent. It is, however, more than that. As an account of the cultural dynamisms that defuse the subversive potential of religious and cultural traditions, it can guide our efforts to counter them. If theology is willing to supplement its retrievals of doctrine and narrative poesis with a serious consideration of the cultural context of the reception of its work, it can increase the likelihood that its visions for how life should be lived will be put into practice. How can theology do this if the products of its traditional skills—hermeneutics of retrieval and suspicion, conceptual clarification, and systematic elaboration—are susceptible to commodification? It can do so by engaging consumer culture on the level of practices and structures rather than meanings and beliefs.

This chapter will focus on the mundane, concrete structures and practices that form our habits of interpretation and use. It will consistently steer clear of conceptual and doctrinal retrievals and proposals. For that reason, it may be criticized for being insufficiently theological. Its theological standing is rooted in its consideration of how a particular religious community can respond to the challenges posed by consumer culture. Other authors, for example, Daniel Bell, have attempted a theological engagement with advanced capitalism in terms of the impact of its structures, practices, disciplines, and technologies on contemporary believers. Bell offers a constructive proposal of Christian forgiveness as potent therapy for countering capitalist desire. This presumes an embodied Christianity "as a fully material formation, as a true politics," where forgiveness is incarnated in particular technologies of reconciliation, repentance, and penance.[1] Yet Bell's concluding proposal remains highly conceptual, focusing on the relative adequacy of the "conceptions" of justice and forgiveness for "sustaining resistance to the capitalist order."[2] While such a proposal is recognizably theological and helpful for Bell's particular concerns, an engagement with consumer culture requires a much more concrete focus. This chapter will not offer a conceptual or narrative solution, but will focus on how the concrete structures and practices with which Roman Catholicism stewards its tradition can be used to resist the erosions of consumer culture.

Concern about the structures and practices through which beliefs are enacted is both familiar and foreign territory for theology. The relation between religious communities' doctrines and practices have seldom been straightforward. Thus, consumer culture presents a new instance of an old problem: the difficulty of enacting Christian belief in a system of practice. Consumer culture intensifies this long-standing problem. Since it is so adept at absorbing meanings, symbols, and narratives, a meaning-centered understanding of theology is particularly in danger of compromising the integrity of the Christian message because the cultural system does not offer an explicit, public ideology that theology can critique and embrace. Consider, in contrast, imperial Rome or European monarchical societies. The association of Christian doctrines and symbols with eminently visible and powerful institutions and their ideologies provided explicit contradictions that a hermeneutical or meaning-centered theological method could address. Since daily life in advanced capitalism is marked by a lack (although not complete absence) of explicit ideologies, theology, as critical reflection on the ongoing life of the ecclesial community, must pay particular attention to the details of how faith is insinuated into practice in this context.

The identity and agency of the theologian were secure in classical intellectual and hermeneutic approaches to theology. In these strategic conceptions of theology, the theologian's specialized training and skill made her the obvious person to clarify the consequences of symbols, narratives, and doctrines for Christian practice, which the community would then presumably put into action. In advanced capitalist societies, no religion or traditional culture maintains anything approaching a strategic control of the cultural field or, for that matter, control of the cultural formation of its own faithful. For that reason, a theological engagement with consumer culture must take place on the tactical level.

A turn to tactical practices raises important questions of agency for academic theology. Tactics involve a different kind of knowledge. Tactics are carried out on the ground and, as Michel de Certeau argued, are not easily penetrated by the gaze of elite knowledge. Thus, engaging consumer culture tactically will involve more than theologians telling people what to do. The last chapter explored ways in which theology can recognize and engage the practical wisdom evident in lived religion. For that reason, this chapter will highlight examples where contemporary believers are critically engaging the structures and practices that support consumer culture. But we saw that learned theology often has a tactical character as well. Thus, the bulk of this chapter will pursue a tactical engagement with consumer culture from the perspective of theology's location within the believing community.

There is a deeper theological significance to the use of tactics. Conceptions of culture are not theologically neutral.[3] Religious commitments incline theologians to particular conceptions of culture as well as models of theological production. A tactical approach implicates both of these. My openness to a tactical response is significantly informed by my location within the Roman Catholic Church. While for much of its history this tradition has been deeply wedded to eminently strategic models of the church's relationship to the world, this has been balanced by its respect for the presence of the Spirit in the community inspiring the *sensus fidelium*. Thus, it has the intellectual resources to notice and value the small, capillary actions of the members of the church in their daily lives. No matter how much it might secretly prefer the clarity of an officially Catholic state, it respects the political presence of its vast assembly of anonymous members. There is a second Catholic theological reason to accept a tactical response. The highly structured nature of the Roman Catholic Church severely limits fanciful flights of theological poesis. The theologian must always return to the inertia (in the neutral sense) of an enormous church with a highly structured institutional and doctrinal system, as well as myriad concrete cultural forms. The Protestant tendency to subsume ecclesiology to theological narrative is not easily sustained for Roman Catholic theology.[4] (This is not to say that Roman Catholicism does not have its own forms of linguistic idealism; however, these are more ideological justifications for the ecclesial status quo than utopian narratives of the ideal community.) The Roman Catholic tradition knows well the tension (and occasional rupture) between belief and practice. Catholic critiques of church and culture must return to the messy particularities of the ecclesial community. A tactical engagement with consumer culture will prevent us from wandering too far from these particularities by focusing on the resources that Roman Catholicism possesses for contesting the erosions of consumer culture.

This chapter will proceed in two stages. The first will consider tactics for countering commodification in general. If the commodification of culture arises from habits acquired in our daily commerce with fetishized commodities, then a tactical engagement must consider this mundane level. The second part will consider the commodification of culture and religion more specifically. After a brief discussion of general tactics for countering the commodification of culture, it will turn to two sets of tactics for countering the commodification of religion: reembedding and deepening agency. The first comprises a host of tactics that aim to strengthen the connections between cultural objects and their communal traditions in order to prevent them from becoming shallow postmodern signifiers. The goal of these tactics is to preserve more complex building blocks for popular religious bricolage. The second set of tactics concerns deepening and supporting the agency of believers. It focuses on giving believers a sense of authorization and obligation to function as traditional agents who work according to the logics of their religious traditions, as opposed to the free-lancing of the new cultural intermediaries.

COUNTERING COMMODIFICATION IN GENERAL

If the commodification of culture has its roots in our daily engagement with literal commodities, then theology must concern itself with the mundane details of everyday commodification. This means, for instance, that the rare concrete example in Karl Rahner's *Foundations of Christian Faith*—the unreflective consumption of a banana whose price is tied to "the pitiful lot of banana pickers, which is in turn co-determined by social injustice, exploitation, or a centuries-old commercial policy"—is relevant not only for theological reflections on original sin but also for theological hermeneutics.[5] It is relevant, at least, if we broaden our understanding of hermeneutics to include the relationship between "life practice and interpretation" that was presumed by patristic and monastic theologians and has been kept alive in contemporary theology by existential theological hermeneutics and liberation theology.[6] These connections are always in danger of being ignored by explanatory modes of understanding such as historical-critical analysis and religious studies approaches modeled on scientific rationality. Francis Schüssler Fiorenza questions whether such methods do not inherently "objectify and commodify" their objects of study by removing them from their traditional contexts, thus presenting them as consumer commodities, objects to be chosen by a sovereign consumer, rather than elements of a tradition or traces of an other that make a claim on us.[7] To return to commodities, each act of commodified consumption trains us to value and engage everything—including religious symbols, beliefs, and practices—in a similarly abstracted manner. Thus, insofar as academic theology believes that its work is relevant to the lived faith of the religious community that it serves, it must also give thought to countering cultural dynamisms that prevent it from informing the lives of contemporary believers.

Numerous authors have suggested tactics for countering consumerism. Juliet Schor, for example, offers nine principles for stopping the "upward creep" of consumer desire.[8] Our focus is not on consumption per se but on commodification and the cultural habits it engenders. Thus, many fine suggestions for fighting excessive consumption, such as living more simply, buying durable products, avoiding purchases that will require upgrades, and enacting a more robust luxury tax system are not relevant to our concerns. Several of Schor's other principles, such as developing awareness of the origins of products and the strategies used to sell them, are useful, however, because they work by directly engaging the commodity fetish and the structures that support it. These challenge consumerism by challenging commodification. Thus, these sorts of tactics are useful not only for countering the consumption of physical commodities but also for challenging the habits of interpretation and use that lead to the commodification of culture and religion.

We must be clear on the aims and scope of tactical practices. The counterpractices discussed in this chapter may also function as strategic practices within a Christian setting. Indeed, many of them are discussed by social ethicists. For example, buying fair trade goods and obtaining produce from local family farms are certainly consonant with a more authentically Christian economic vision. Setting up alternative economies whose rules better embody Christian notions of the good is a worthy task, and religious communities generally have more resources to pursue such programs than they realize (e.g., a mid-sized congregation could easily keep a local vegetable farm in business). When considered strategically, such practices seem insignificant symbolic gestures. When considered as tactical practices, however, they can be valued differently. Their success is measured not as miniscule enclaves amid regnant global capitalism but as meditative counterpractices that provide means for forming believers' imaginations against the logic of the commodity fetish, thus helping them swim against the broader tide of the commodification of culture that deprives religions of the power to inform a way of life.

This section will consider two groups of tactics. The first focuses on commodities themselves and works by attempting to penetrate the fog of the commodity fetish and reconnect it with its conditions of production. The second type involves labor and production. When people engage in their own production, they are better able to notice and value the labor that is involved in the other commodities they consume. This prevents physical commodities from being reduced to mere carriers of sign value, to incidental substrates of style. Analogues of these two types of tactics will prove valuable for countering the commodification of religion as well. For that reason they will appear again below in a discussion of strengthening the interconnections between elements of religious traditions and encouraging a sense of agency among believers that is rooted in tradition.

Unveiling the Commodity Fetish

If the practices of consuming food from nowhere and wearing clothes made by no one, which we do daily, train us to engage culture and religion as abstract objects of consumption, then cultivating habits of being mindful of the origins of foodstuffs or other commodities can help combat the impact of the consumer mentality on religion. It is extremely difficult to find out the conditions of production of most items. One is quickly thrown into the morass of corporate subsidiaries, outsourcing, and subcontracting through which products are produced in this post-Fordist, globalized economy. The very difficulty of the task is itself instructional. It shows how deeply mysterious contemporary commodities are beneath their appealing surfaces. While successfully connecting the product with its producer is essential for restoring the act of consumption to its full moral complexity, even the attempt to do so serves as a counterpractice to commodified habits of engaging and valuing things.

A pastoral letter by the Catholic Bishops of the South, "Voices and Choices: A Pastoral Message on Justice in the Workplace," is a model challenge to commodification on this front. It demystifies the origins of a staple ingredient in contemporary American cuisine: chicken, specifically, very cheap chicken. We are a long way from Herbert Hoover's day when a presidential candidate could promise "a chicken in every pot" as a sign of prosperity. In their pastoral, the bishops attempt to expose the "intolerable personal and community cost" of cheap chicken.

Chicken has become the ubiquitous inoffensive meat. Borderline vegetarians eat it, and it hovers in the penumbra of fish for Catholics during Lent. This culturally based innocuousness coincides with the heavily commodified presentation of chicken in the grocery store. As factory processing has grown exponentially in the past decades, chicken has increasingly come to be known by its most commodified form: glistening, coral pink, boneless, skinless breast meat. It appears more as a raw material than as the flesh of any particular living thing. Nothing save an occasional stray tendon betrays its origins in the chest of a living bird. Its low cost and convenience make any desire to skin and fillet one's own chicken seem pointless romanticism. It is a messy and somewhat dangerous task. The danger of this job is multiplied by orders of magnitude for the line workers in processing plants, who must rapidly and repeatedly dismember, skin, and bone chickens, while working in refrigerated temperatures. According to department of labor statistics, it is one of the most dangerous jobs in the United States.[9] Poultry workers suffer in addition from poor pay, exploitative labor policies, and lack of union representation.

In a series of vignettes, the bishops chronicle the details of the lives of the workers who process the chickens, the farmers who grow them, and the factory managers who are forced to make difficult decisions within an exploitative system. The pastoral letter is very effective in pointing out the hidden costs of cheap chicken. Workers are exploited and injured. Farmers are forced into contracts that saddle them with all of the risks and do not pay them enough to support their farms, forcing many into bankruptcy. Processing plants pollute the environment with chicken waste. Knowledge of the details of the system brings a proper moral depth to the decision to consume chicken. The bishops restore what was initially a choice based solely on convenience and price to its true complexity. The price of chicken is simultaneously too low and too high. Too low to provide a living wage and safe working conditions for those who must produce the meat, entirely too high when all of the off-the-books social costs are factored in. The bishops do not provide answers to these problems. They are content to raise consciousness of the problem as a first step. In this task they are clearly successful.

The bishops' attempt to demystify the origins of supermarket chicken is a model tactic for countering commodification. They offer their analysis of the poultry industry as an example for other businesses "in agriculture and manufacturing, which share the same challenges, whether furniture is being made, produce picked, or livestock raised under contract."[10] Whether undertaken on the communal or individual level, this tactic is worth pursuing for any of the countless commodities we purchase every day as a way of training our imaginations to be mindful of the origins of goods and consequently, to be mindful of the original contexts of elements of culture as well.

Since we consume so many things, it is helpful to pick one item that we consume—a banana, toilet paper, a cell phone—and research its origins, the natural resources it requires, its impact on the environment, the labor conditions under which it is produced, and so on. Bananas travel thousands of miles to tables, which consumes significant amounts of marine and jet fuel. Banana workers in Central America were able, after decades of bloody struggle, to obtain union representation and a higher (but still low) standard of living and decent working conditions. These gains have, of late, been undercut as banana plantations in Ecuador have come into production. Ecuador has few protections for organized labor and almost no union presence. The exploitation that results means that bananas are exported at a much lower cost. This has put pressure on Central American growers to cut labor costs or move their operations to Ecuador—all of this behind the veil of bunches of simple yellow bananas. With such knowledge, the special price of forty-nine cents a pound becomes less attractive. One could look for bananas with stickers that say Costa Rica or Honduras, instead of Ecuador. When such details are considered, bananas are no longer generic commodities. They are reconnected to their context. Unveiling the commodity fetish likewise fights the commodification of culture and religion by training our imagination to consider such connections between cultural objects and their originating traditions.[11]

The Craft Ideal

Consumerist habits of use and engagement are not simply about things; they are about how we relate to things. They are a matter of the habits of subjects as much as the status of commodified objects. Thus, our notions of agency are a source of potential tactics for countering commodified habits of use and engagement. Here we will consider the notion of the "craft ideal" which extols the virtues of traditional handcraft. By the craft ideal, I mean the practice of handcrafts, not the consumption of handmade goods (although that can, at times, contribute to unveiling the commodity fetish).

Nostalgia for preindustial craft traditions is long standing in the West. Its chief promoter is doubtless the Arts and Crafts movement, which crystallized around the mid-nineteenth-century writings of the Oxford don John Ruskin.[12] Ruskin offered a polemical and visionary mix of socialism, antimodernism, medieval nostalgia, and advocacy of the guild craft tradition that inspired a range of figures in the height of the movement during the two decades that spanned the turn of the twentieth century. William Morris was the most influential and best remembered of these. His encounter with Ruskin spurred him to expand his humanistic medievalism into a broad aesthetic and political program. Morris advocated the recovery of the figure of the master artisan. He himself retrieved and mastered the techniques of many lost crafts, including traditional textile dyeing, tapestry weaving, manuscript illumination, and bookmaking. The Arts and Crafts aesthetic rejected the added-on decorations popular in Victorian design such as veneers and faux wood finishes. Instead it emphasized functional designs and finishes that highlighted the intrinsic beauty of the materials, the functional elements of design (such as dovetail keys and through tenons) and the traces of the workers' labor such as hammer and tool marks.

Why did they do this? Their disdain for the shoddiness and shallow pretense of mass-produced goods was founded on a deeper respect for the nobility of labor. The guild system had preserved the economic value of skilled labor and the status of the craftsman and had provided a traditional system of skill and excellence. Industrialization, in contrast, subjected laborers to both economic and cultural privation—thus John Milbank's argument that Ruskin was "no mere medievalising reactionary." His aesthetic articulation of the craft ideal formed part of a social vision in which the worth of things was not reduced to abstract exchange value and substantive notions of the good could inform public life.[13] In fact, Morris played a role in the founding of what would become the British Labour Party. He was also a commercially successful designer and producer of interior decor products such as textiles and wallpaper. At the height of their popularity they were purchased enthusiastically by bourgeois who had little difficulty appreciating aesthetics that, for Morris, were organically tied to socialist politics they abhorred.

Any attempt to employ the craft ideal as a tactic must deal with its fate in consumer culture. By the First World War, the energy of the Arts and Crafts movement had been dissipated and the craft ideal "had largely been reduced to a revivifying hobby for the affluent." (Indeed, the showy "gentlemen's tools" produced for these well-to-do hobby artisans are much sought after by contemporary tool collectors.) T. J. Jackson Lears argues that the political aspirations of the movement were readily absorbed into the therapeutic paradigm. It gave "a sense of autonomy and a chance to confront the substantial reality of material things" to people who were alienated from the labor they expended in their day jobs. As is so often the case with consumer culture, the ideal ended up functioning in a way exactly opposite to the movement's goals, by reinforcing "the split between work for pay and work for joy."[14]

Jackson Lears's criticism of the fate of the craft ideal is trenchant but does not exhaust what can be said about its tactical value. The craft ideal has experienced several revivals since the height of its popularity in the 1910s, and it continues to inspire avocations to this day. While much of this can be critiqued as another manifestation of consumerism (e.g., home woodworkers who invest more energy in replicating Norm Abram's workshop than in actually making furniture), learning a handcraft builds awareness of the amount of labor that goes into making things. This knowledge, born of craft skill, is a very powerful tactic for countering commodification. It militates against the reduction of value to appearance without consideration of raw materials and labor.

This point was brought home to me by a friend, one of Jackson Lears's office workers, who is a quilt maker. Her craft knowledge gave her critical insight into the labor costs hidden beneath the popular and widely marketed handmade quilts in the early 1990s. At the time, the mail-order company Lands End offered a line of handmade quilts produced by an Appalachian co-op. The quilts were designed in traditional styles and were priced according to their complexity. Even the least expensive designs cost several hundred dollars. This high cost notwithstanding, given the enormous amount of labor each quilt required (even a moderately complex quilt requires about 240 hours of work), the hourly wage of the quilt makers was not particularly high. Quilts were something of a fashion fad at the time, and within a year discount retailers like Target were offering Chinese-made quilts. These were handmade as well, but at very low wages, and could be offered for less than fifty dollars.

Experience with the craft gave my friend a clear understanding of the enormous amount of labor that went into these products. It decommodified them.

What appeared to most people to be simply a nice bargain appeared to her as a shocking manifestation of the low wages the Chinese workers were paid. For the rest of us, the quilts were free to function as abstracted commodities. "Handmade" was as depthless a symbol as the traditional designs. Both readily signified nostalgia for a simpler time, when people "took the time" to make things by hand (as if they had a choice). No doubt millions were sold, and, in accord with the temporality of trends in interior design, they have by now been retired to storage closets, charities, and landfills. To one experienced in the difficulty of such work, the commodity fog could not obscure the twenty to thirty days of someone's labor that produced the quilt.

This insight into the origins of things, born of craft knowledge, carries over into the cultural realm as well, where it can foster respect for the communal origins of elements of tradition. Craft knowledge fights the commodification of culture in another way as well. This has to do with being trained as a practitioner in a tradition. Acquiring a craft is not merely a matter of technical knowhow and manual dexterity; it involves the acquisition of traditional knowledge and practical facility in knowing and applying the standards of the craft. Traditional practices and designs are not mere conventions or shallow fashions; their logic embodies the wisdom learned in generations of work with the material and tools. There are reasons for the classic shapes in pottery, the joints in woodworking, and the patterns in quilting. Some shapes, proportions, and patterns simply will not work with a given material. Excellence in a craft involves both knowledge of its rules and facility in their application. Awareness of such tradition-based limits of practice is precisely what is lost in the commodification of culture.

In this regard it is worth recalling that domestic production declined simultaneously with the loss of noncommercial popular culture. Certainly the growth of commercial cultural and entertainment offerings can explain their simultaneous decline, but perhaps there is something more that links them. Both traditional cuisine and folk culture required formation and agency in a tradition. Sometimes it was as mundane as chopping cabbage for the sauerkraut crock, but in each of these myriad domestic practices, people functioned as agents, not consumers. With the loss of crafts, experience of popular agency atrophied—agency in producing cuisine, agency in learning and handing on folk songs and culture, and agency in popular or folk religion. People now readily engage all of culture, including their religion, as an object for passive consumption, rather than active, tradition-bound engagement. The latter is precisely the sort of agency that must be strengthened within religious communities to counter the erosions of consumer culture.

Sacramentality against Commodification

To these general tactics for countering commodification, we can add a specifically religious one. Each religious tradition has its own resources; here we will focus on one of the central theological and cultural characteristics of Roman Catholicism: sacramentality. Richard McBrien describes a way of seeing "God in all things (St. Ignatius of Loyola): other people, communities, movements, events, places, objects, the environment, the world at large, the whole cosmos. The visible, the tangible, the finite, the historical—all these are actual or potential carriers of the divine presence."[15] Sacramentality, or the allied term "sacramental imagination," refers to a broad sensibility within Catholicism manifest in doctrine, liturgy, and popular culture.[16] Strong claims for the presence and influence of a sacramental imagination among ordinary Catholics presume the very cultural stability and formation that consumer culture is increasingly eroding.[17] The entire notion of a general "imagination" abstracted from particular ritual formation and religious culture can be criticized as an attempt to transcendentalize the ethnic particularity with which Catholicism was once so strongly associated. Nevertheless, the incarnational and analogical doctrinal logic and the sacramental liturgical practice of Catholicism do entail a certain sensibility. Sacramentality is an interesting example of a religious resource for countering consumer culture, because it challenges consumer culture not by critiquing consumption but by challenging the abstracting dynamisms of commodification itself.

In the past century, consumption has increasingly become centered on the meanings borne by things rather than on the things themselves. Advertising has shifted from arguing for the usefulness of products to associating them with unrelated values and desires. We expect the things we consume not only to meet the various needs of daily life in our affluent world but also to help us establish our personal identities and to signify and support our social standing. The Catholic "sacramental imagination" may have proved a useful imaginative support for the emergence of consumer culture. A religious culture accustomed to seeing material things as overdetermined bearers of meaning sets the stage for its members to enter the imaginative world of consumer capitalism. Terrence Tilley argues just this, that a debased parody of the sacramental imagination is perfectly at home in consumer culture. "When the analogical imagination is lost, the absurd becomes the Mysterious and commodities are transubstantiated into sacraments by the spiritually starved in a world empty of the presence of God."[18] Short of such extremes, one can see a misdirected form of sacramentality at work in the consumption of exotic foodstuffs and "varietal" products such as wines, liquors, coffees, and now even chocolates. The respect for the particularities of climate and soil claimed by connoisseurs provides cover for the real source of value of such items: their role in the display of distinction.

If sacramentality provided a cultural opening for consumerism in Catholicism, it may also provide the cultural basis, both in belief and practice, for an oppositional sensibility. Its deepest currents draw believers in another direction. By hallowing physical things, it endows them with importance. As mediations of the divine, they matter. This sensibility is the opposite of the oft-heard dismissal that something or other is "just a symbol." Rather, a sacramental sensibility values the particular thing precisely *as* a symbol—hence the quandary of what to do with old sacred images, statues, vessels, and the like. Rectories have closets that are veritable treasuries of sacred vessels, studded with mothers' jewels, remaining from the once vast numbers of clergy. Openly religious young Catholics often find themselves the unwitting recipients of an entire family's deposit of religious material culture. What to do with a generation's plaster and plastic statuary, rosaries, and religious images keyed to pieties that no longer resonate? The answer is seldom to simply throw them away. If they were "just symbols," material mediations not valued in themselves, they could be easily consigned to the dumpster or the precious metals recycler. But in the sacramental worldview, the mediation itself matters and the sacred aura adheres to the things themselves. Indeed canon law makes provisions for the proper disposal of such blessed religious items. They are to be burned or buried.[19]

Alongside the terms "sacramental imagination" and "sacramental worldview," I suggest a related term, "sacramental operation" (to use Michel de Certeau's terminology). By this I mean the connection that is forged between the mundane material of a sacramental sign and the theological realities it signifies. This sacramental operation has a subversive tactical value against commodity abstraction. It directly frustrates the abstraction inherent in commodification by tying the significance of symbols to their particularity. Many have long noted that liturgical ritual is a formation in particular values and dispositions: hospitality, receptiveness to the graciousness of existence and the mystery of suffering, anticipation of kingdom in its fullness, and so on. Such debates are ongoing and complex. Here I want to call attention to the most simple level of ritual's formation of the sacramental imagination.

Consider the Preparation of the Gifts in the current Rite of the Mass. It echos Jewish prayers of thanksgiving, linking the liturgical elements with creation and human labor: "Blessed are you, Lord, God of all-creation. Through your goodness we have this bread to offer, which earth has given and human hands have made. It will become for us the bread of life." The opening of the liturgy calls attention to the particularity of the bread and wine. "This bread" comes from the earth, "this wine" is the "fruit" of vines and worked by human hands.[20] This initial gesture lays the foundation for the main liturgical action that will follow, the eucharistic prayer. *These* are the gifts that the celebrant offers and asks the Father to make "holy by the power of your Spirit, that they may become the body and blood of your Son, our Lord Jesus Christ." *This* is the bread and wine that is identified with Jesus' actions at the Last Supper, when "he broke the bread, gave it to his disciples, and said: Take this, all of you, and eat it: this is my body which will be given up for you."[21] One of the foundational thrusts of the entire liturgy is that particular bread and wine becomes the sacrament of Jesus' body and blood.

This sacramental operation is at work across the other sacraments in various ways and in varying degrees of relevance for Catholic life. Consider marriage. One could argue that this sensibility was at work in the debates surrounding the so-called secondary end of conjugal sexuality—personal union. The long-standing emphasis on procreation as the sole good of sex was fundamentally at odds with the sacramental symbolism of marriage as figuring the love of God for the church. From a sacramental perspective it is important that the couple actually figure this loving union, and that the unitive aspect of one of the most powerful symbolic acts of marriage be appreciated as such, that the nature of the signifying act be taken seriously.

This sacramental operation provides a particular religious logic for countering commodification. Consider the awkwardness of praying the offertory over bread and wine that were produced under oppressive conditions. The reference to "fruit of the vine and the work of human hands" is destabilizing. Where indeed does the wine being offered come from? Where do those vines grow? How are they tended? How are the humans whose hands pick the fruit from the vine treated? Anyone with even a vague knowledge of the wine industry in the United States cannot ask these questions without being unsettled. This collision of the sacred and the profane in the offertory and throughout the eucharistic liturgy is not unlike the incarnation itself. God takes a stand in human history and we are forced to respond. With neither an abstract God nor an abstract Eucharist, we are not free to fence off areas of life as secular, profane, or spiritually irrelevant. Sacramentality is both a source of motivation and a particular operation that undoes commodification. This second aspect even provides the possibility for unraveling the symbolic function of commodities that, as we saw, threatens to domesticate sacramentality into the service of consumption. The more that the origins of commodities are cloaked within other values, the more vulnerable they become to the return of their repressed origins. Naomi Klein has argued that contemporary brand-centered capitalism is particularly vulnerable for this reason. The more Nike, Starbucks, and The Body Shop base their sales on image and values, the more vulnerable they become when their products are produced under conditions that contradict these values.[22]

The Body Shop is exemplary. Anita Roddick made the company into an international success story, promoting it as much more than a cosmetics company. It was in the vanguard of a new generation of "green businesses" that would make a profit while employing ethical and environmentally sound business practices. Not only did such businesses wish to do no harm; they would channel consumer demand toward products that actually helped the environment and preserved indigenous cultures. By building a brand image based on such ethical values, the company was setting itself up for a cataclysmic fall should it be found out that the products do not live up to the branded ideals. This is exactly what happened when a series of critical investigative journalists exposed the details of The Body Shop's practices. They revealed that the products contained only minute traces of natural ingredients, that the commercial chemicals they used were frequently tested on animals (covered by a carefully worded, widely displayed policy "against animal testing"), that natural ingredients purchased through fair trade channels were given infinitely more significance in public relations than was warranted by the actual amount used in the products, and so on.[23]

When the sacramental imagination insists that the signifier be consonant with the value being signified, it short-circuits advanced capitalism's shell game of values. This is a powerful critical force, much better suited to the symbolic density of advanced capitalism than dour utilitarian marxist invocations of "use value." The sacramental operation can outflank consumer capitalism on this front. All of those values and hopes pinned to commodities are taken seriously, as are the commodities themselves. They are taken seriously enough to drive inquiry behind the glossy faces of commodities and to fuel outrage when they are revealed to be not only false, but outright hypocrisy. In this sense the sacramental operation can also work against the liquidity of depthless signifiers in postmodern consumer culture by engendering a sensibility that connects symbols and values with their contexts.

We have considered a range of tactics, both general and religious, for countering the abstracting dynamisms of commodification. This level of engagement with consumer culture, perhaps more mundane than theology is used to considering, is essential because the daily practice of the consumption of commodities is also a formation in habits of use and interpretation that believers bring to their engagement with religious traditions. Having addressed this fundamental level of engagement, we can now consider tactics for countering the commodification of culture in general and the commodification of religion in particular.

COUNTERING THE COMMODIFICATION OF CULTURE

Although the commodification of culture arises from the interpretive habits acquired in the consumption of more literal commodities, it is not simply a superstructural epiphenomenon. It is supported by its own infrastructures and practices. As a particular way of relating to culture, it can be challenged on its own as well. Since it is an issue of particular cultural habits, such challenges will, to a large extent, involve cultivating the habits and dispositions of alternative cultures. Thus, the bulk of our reflections on resisting the commodification of culture will be reserved for the next section, which will focus on the resources of one particular tradition—Roman Catholicism—for resisting the erosions of the commodification of culture. That said, there are a number of habits and default practices in consumer culture that can be resisted on their own. These include relating to culture as an object of consumption, the abstraction of belief and practice, and the tendency to substitute consumption for other forms of ethical and political action.

Perhaps the most fundamental tactic for countering the commodification of culture is simple awareness of it as a problem. We are comfortable engaging cultures as abstract objects of consumption and enjoyment. The Enigma song "Return to Innocence" is the paradigmatic example. Millions bought the album and millions more enjoyed it without asking or caring what the sampled voice was singing about, let alone what language it was. Upon a moment's reflection, the problem becomes obvious. Thus, knowledge of the problem begins to challenge the workings of the commodification of culture.

A number of more specific tactics complement this general one. The first involves considering more deeply how to relate to foreign cultures. We currently presume that respect is best expressed by being "open" to and "appreciating" other cultures. This is well expressed in truly pluralistic societies, where members of each subculture are free to practice and display their own culture accordingly. It is less well expressed when people who are nonmembers consume and display the elements of a given culture. (I remain astounded by the display of a temple-sized Torah scroll in a classroom hallway of an "Inter-Cultural Center" on my campus.) The point here is not merely one of intercultural respect or manners. It is directly relevant to how people engage their own cultures as well. As the example that opened this book made clear, the decision to fly Tibetan prayer flags on my front porch impacts my engagement with the symbols of my own religious culture as much as that of Tibet. The traditional practices and beliefs that accompany the display of such objects recede in importance, and they are all reduced a bit more toward a decorative function in everyday life of advanced capitalism. This suggests that setting intentional limits on consumption, setting some things off limits for use and display may be a very valuable tactic for countering the commodification of culture. Appreciation and respect of others' cultures might be best expressed by not appropriating their symbols because one does not embrace or know the beliefs and practices that accompany them. There is more here than Lee Yearley's proposal of the virtue of "spiritual regret"—a respect of another tradition born of deep knowledge, that nonetheless does not result in a desire to embrace the given belief (although that certainly seems a virtue worth cultivating in a consumer culture).[24] The limits I am suggesting redound to our relationship to our own cultures. Consideration of the beliefs and practices that accompany cultural objects from foreign traditions simultaneously calls attention to the relationship among symbols, beliefs, and practices in one's own and thus serves as a challenge to the commodification of culture.

In addition to this general attitude toward elements of tradition, consumer culture also trains us to substitute consumption for other practices. The moment of consumer choice becomes so overdetermined that it replaces more traditional practices of commitment such as joining a community or organizing for change. Instead we read a book on a spiritual topic or express solidarity across racial lines by listening to other people's music. This again is an area where simply being aware of the tendency has tactical value. Once people are aware of the disconnection between their beliefs and the practices through which they attempt to enact them, they are freed to pursue more direct alternatives. Of course, these are often more difficult and time consuming, but they are certainly bypassed as long as people can unreflectively assume that symbolic consumption is sufficient and efficacious.

COUNTERING THE COMMODIFICATION OF RELIGION

This book has argued that consumer culture is not a "culture" in the sense that it enshrined a particular worldview and ethos. Rather it is a set of interpretive habits and dispositions supported by a variety of practices and infrastructures for engaging elements of any culture. Thus, a critical religious engagement with consumer culture must focus on this level of interpretive practice and infrastructures. This section considers the tactical potential of various resources of Roman Catholicism for resisting the erosions of consumer culture. Since each religious tradition has its own particular vulnerabilities and resources for resisting commodification, some of these tactics will be generalizable, others will not.

This section begins with a consideration of how religious communities' responses to commodification are both tactical and strategic. Then it develops two groups of tactics, which roughly reprise the complementary tactics of unveiling the commodity fetish and focusing on productive agency discussed above. The first group of tactics involves "reembedding" doctrines, symbols, and practices within their historical tradition and the ongoing life of the community. They challenge the reduction of cultural objects to shallow postmodern signifiers by reenforcing their connections with other doctrines, symbols, and practices. Religious communities can do much to ensure the practical influence of their beliefs by working to hand on and communicate their traditions in a manner that preserves these complex interrelationships. While these tactics presume communal limits on use and appropriation, the point is not to preserve religious traditions from unauthorized or unruly use. The aim is to support the workings of popular religion. Chapter 5 noted that bricolage is shallow not because of its popular origins, but because of the commodified nature of the cultural/religious "building blocks" that people have to work with. Thus, maintaining the complex connections between religious beliefs and religious traditions can be understood as a task in service of popular agency. These tactics are complemented by a second set that aims to encourage and deepen popular agency. These tactics range from a presentation of the tradition as the ongoing work of the community to careful attention to how liturgical space and communications infrastructures encourage or discourage popular agency.

The basic orientation of these responses will be tactical, insofar as they are a response to a situation that the religious community does not control. Religious communities lack control not simply because they do not have theocratic authority over their society but also because believers are not socialized solely within religious communities. As in most times, the community shares most of its culture with people outside of the church. Thus broader cultural habits, such as commodified habits of interpretation and use, are already within the church. Yet religious communities, especially highly institutional ones such as Roman Catholicism, possess robust alternative organizational, communications, and formation structures that can be used against the liquefying influences of consumer culture. For this reason, the responses of religious communities will have a somewhat strategic character, as they apply their own resources to oppose the cultural tide of commodification.

Embedding within Tradition and Community

The fundamental problem with the commodification of culture is that it trains believers to abstract religious doctrines, symbols, and practices from the traditional and communal contexts that give them meaning and connect them to a form of life. Such shallow retrieval of doctrines, prayers, symbols, and practices can be countered by tactically emphasizing their embeddedness in an ongoing, historical tradition. As with commodities in general, the more they are associated with their particular origins, the less susceptible they are to abstraction and shallow engagement. Tradition stabilizes the meaning of cultural objects, preventing them from sliding into weightless postmodern signifiers. The contemporary context is equally important. Beliefs, symbols, and practices have their meaning and function within a complex web of interrelationships. Communal practices and institutions connect them with a particular form of life. We will consider three potential tactical resources: theology, liturgy, and church communications infrastructures. Each of these resources can function tactically if envisioned and employed against the cultural tide of commodification.

Theology

I have consistently argued that theological argumentation is in itself an inadequate response to the erosions of consumer culture. This is the case if theology is conceived of as a strategic undertaking that works out questions of proper belief in principle by building an overarching system or offering a master narrative that positions everything else. These are indeed important tasks, but they have little effect unless they find some point of insertion into the lived religion of the broader religious community. If this connection to the community is taken seriously, these same tasks have great promise as tactics for reinforcing the connections among doctrines, symbols, and practices in order to fund a more complex popular engagement with the tradition.

Learned theology has a number of important resources for stabilizing the meaning of doctrines. Chief among these are access to the history of the tradition, facility in tradition's manner of reasoning, and experience in dealing with contemporary innovations in the tradition. Robert Schreiter summarizes the role of the professional theologian in relation to the local community as helping the "community clarify its own experience and to relate it to the experience of other communities past and present."[25] Theology's access to the complex history of the tradition can fight commodity abstraction by situating contemporary doctrines and practices within their historical origins and development. This is the theological equivalent of demystifying the commodity by revealing its conditions of production. In addition to highlighting the connections between contemporary lived religion and past tradition, theologians also bring past debates and distinctions into critical relationship with contemporary innovations and questions raised by other church communities. While not all contemporary problems can be resolved by a return to tradition, there are perennial ways in which Christian belief is inclined to go astray. Edward Schillebeeckx considered making both the positive and negative connections to be among the central tasks of the theologian. In his christological and ecclesiological writings, Schillebeeckx attempted to connect the inchoate reflection of the Dutch church (both mainstream and avant garde "critical communities") with supporting and clarifying material from the Christian tradition. One commentator described this model of theology as serving as a "theological midwife" for the birth of a new Christian experience.[26] We have seen that such connections between experience and religious traditions are particularly at issue in consumer culture. By making these critical connections between contemporary Christian experience and tradition, the theologian provides an important hedge against the habits of abstract appropriation in which believers are trained by consumer culture.

A particularly important connection that theology can make in this regard is between the dissatisfactions of contemporary believers and the internal pluralism and tensions of the tradition. This is important for training believers to think within a tradition as opposed to defaulting to the spirituality model, which inclines believers to presume that the only way to correct the perceived shortcomings of one religious tradition is to supplement it with the offerings of a different religious or secular tradition. Dissatisfaction with the status quo in a religious community is not necessarily a manifestation of a narcissistic consumerist refusal to allow a community or tradition to limit one's choices. Indeed, such desires for change are often the result of an inchoate sense that contemporary church practice is not consistent with the wisdom of the tradition. Calls for change also arise in those cases when a religious community faces a genuinely new situation for which there is no undisputedly obvious traditional response.

An example drawn from the classroom illustrates the point. Sexism is a concern students frequently express about their own religious traditions. Many also speak of some form of feminism, vague or specific, as a resource they employ to correct these problems. Yet I rarely encounter students who are aware of the work of theological feminists (save those students who have taken a course on the topic). Most readily assume that "religious" and "feminist" are simply separate categories and concerns that they must reconcile in their own personal syntheses. They are unaware of the long and complex tensions surrounding gender in their own traditions as well as the specific resources these traditions may offer in addressing feminist concerns. Ignorance of the internal pluralism of religious traditions forces people to turn to external pluralism (either by drawing from other traditions or, more severely, by switching to another tradition) to address concerns that may, in fact, be motivated by an inchoate grasp of the logic of their original tradition.

Learned theology can do much by making this internal pluralism available to everyday believers so that they can locate their own reasoning, concerns, and objections within the ongoing "argument" of their "living tradition."[27] The sociologist Michele Dillon has found that "pro-change Catholics" are able to offer complex arguments for their positions drawn from their theological traditions. She argues that this "interpretive autonomy" indicates a serious engagement with "their doctrinal tradition."[28] Grounding believers' desires for change within a tradition's internal pluralism and tension suggests the ongoing development of the tradition. Careful proposals for innovative reinterpretations of doctrines and practices for new situations further reinforce the perceived connections between doctrines and traditions. If people can better understand that their concerns are rooted in the tradition, they are more likely to consider solutions that are based on the logic of their tradition rather than one cobbled together out of fragments of multiple traditions, spirituality-style.

Learned theology also contributes to the stability of meanings through the tasks of systematic theology. Reflecting on the interrelationships among doctrines and symbols and working for their consistent application to practice directly address the problem of the habits of abstracted engagement. This need not, however, take the form of a rigid insistence on a set, proper meaning and application (although it certainly might). As we saw in chapter 6, both popular and learned uses of religious doctrines are seldom straightforward, transparent affairs. Nevertheless, even the surprising, unpredictable workings of bricolage depend on cultural objects bearing complex meanings and logics. By treating cultural objects seriously as elements of an overarching tradition, theology reinforces the interconnections that stabilize their meanings, thus preserving their power to inform a potent popular, lived religion.

No discussion of the potential uses of contemporary academic theology within the Roman Catholic Church can overlook the current theological polarization and hierarchical suspicion of theologians. Over the past three decades, the public status of theology has changed significantly. Growing up in the postconciliar period, I recall frequent invocations of "theologians" during homilies. These are seldom heard now. There was widespread interest in the opinions and insights of theologians on contemporary issues: scientific questions on the origins of the universe and of life, psychological conceptions of the human person and moral and spiritual questions, critical history and the status of the biblical texts, and so on. The homilies from that period by a priest at a local parish were so appreciated that his notes were transcribed by parishioners and published after his death. They are full of explicit references to and anonymous paraphrases of the great theologians of the time: Karl Rahner, Edward Schillebeeckx, Hans Küng, Gustavo Gutiérrez, and others. Criticisms that popular access to the range of learned opinion (which was never excessively broad) encouraged a naive laity to think that everything was up for grabs, miss a profoundly important point. People were fascinated with doctrinal debates and speculation. This enthusiasm was premised on the assumption that doctrines mattered. People were engaged in the ongoing conversations and arguments of their religious tradition.

Although apologists for the Vatican's concerted efforts to reign in this theological ferment during the reign of Pope John Paul II generally miss this important point, their program does highlight another important pole of theology's ecclesial function—the need for a socially accessible, shared consensus. Generations that turned to best-selling popularizations of academic theology with names such as *What Are the Theologians Saying?* were followed by others that turned to John Paul II's extensive and voluminous writings and to the new *Catechism of the Catholic Church* for an introduction to the basics of the faith. Whatever their inherent limitations, catechisms can provide a stable baseline of meanings and definitions.[29] The two positions represent complementary means of fighting shallow engagement by stabilizing the meanings of elements of religious traditions: engaged application of doctrine to matters of contemporary concern and stable communally shared meanings and applications.

Roman Catholicism may be in the midst of a crisis regarding a stable consensus on the meanings of central doctrines and beliefs. This can easily be overstated. There is little evidence of division on the most fundamental doctrines. Nevertheless, a range of cultural and intellectual upheavals over the past half-century have left Catholicism in a particularly unsettled state as it faces the onslaught of consumer culture. Catholicism in the United States has it share of the legacies of liberal Protestantism and its own forms of theological liberalism, manifested in a discomfort with particularity. But these intellectual currents must be situated alongside specific historical changes. Key among these is the turmoil of the postconciliar period. As John Henry Newman observed, it is probably impossible to have a significant church council without serious turmoil. In the case of Vatican II, however, this was exacerbated by concurrent upheavals in broader society. It overlapped with the cultural upheavals of the 1960s that followed upon the profound social and cultural shifts within American Catholicism resulting from the postwar suburban exodus and assimilation of Catholics to the American mainstream. In addition to these broader cultural changes, the often unresolved compromises and contradictions within the council documents themselves and the rise to power of forces opposed to many of the council's reforms have hindered the formation of a postconciliar consensus.

This lack of stable, shared consensus is not simply intellectual; it involves architecture, art, and music as well. This has been exacerbated by the emergence of a cultural expectation of change (and perhaps a religious music industry). Although their reasons may differ, contemporary conservatives and liberals agree that "Kumbaya" is out. Certainly a commodification critique finds much to fault in white suburban congregations' lugubrious attempts to mimic Carolina Sea Island dialects. The almost universal disdain expressed for this venerable workhorse of the folk mass canon, however, strikes me as overdetermined. It bears the sort of befuddled shame that people express when viewing pictures of themselves from the same period sporting polyester jackets with contrasting stitching and broad lapels. "Kumbaya" isn't the worst song ever sung. It is a pretty good reflection on providence and petition. Whatever their theological and artistic merits, it and similar music of its time were formative in the liturgical practice of postconciliar Catholics. Catholics growing up at the time have since gone through three or four subsequent cycles of hymnody, and they are only now approaching middle age.

Frequent calls are now heard for a return to Gregorian chant. That too is good in itself (perhaps better than some of what has come in the intervening years), but it doesn't address the problem of stability. My own parish has a song the assembly sings together following each baptism. It is a good song; no doubt some would find its melody and lyrics a bit on the sweet side. But it is a tradition, one that has been relatively stable for the seven years I have attended. It would be nice to believe that my own children might someday sing the song as adults welcoming others into the church as they were once welcomed, returning to that compact expression of the community's understanding of baptism. But in twenty years, odds are that something else will have replaced it. Perhaps something much better—be it Gregorian, Baroque, or hip hop (and I do not intend the last reference as a joke). The lack of a stable cultural repertoire prevents people from revisiting the set pieces (ideally classics, but realistically these are rare) of their tradition throughout their lives and finding new meaning and relevance as they mature, face crises, and develop their faith.

In light of this situation, the tactic of establishing a stable doctrinal and aesthetic tradition cannot be dismissed as a project suited only to restorationists. Edward Schillebeeckx challenged a Dutch "critical community" (a radical parish that had broken with diocesan authority) to the same task in 1981, noting that "the Christian identity of the messianic community" depends on a stable sense of tradition engaged with the "great Christian tradition." He cautioned that, "we cannot dispense with such a tradition without exhausting our resources."[30]

There are a number of obstacles to enacting this tactical use of theology. Obviously it is against the tide of the academic professionalization of theology. But as many theologians make clear with their careers, the two can be reconciled. Obtaining access to a popular church audience poses a more profound problem. Here theologians face the same dynamisms that assimilate religious leaders to the new class of cultural intermediaries. This involves both issues that are common to all communities and ones that are specific to particular churches and denominations.

On the general level, theologians' denominational identity and influence have declined with the deregulation of religion in general. With the decline of denominational presses and the expansion of secular publishing houses into the religion market, theologians attempting to reach a broad audience are placed into the market alongside popular religious authors who function much more directly as new cultural intermediaries. Thus, people are inclined to engage their work with consumerist habits of interpretation.

The problem of the status of the theologian is also linked to the loss of specifically ecclesial structures of communication, including theologians' role in training seminary professors and writing works for seminarians and the clergy. The importance of these paths of communication is evident in an experience I had in graduate school. A few months into my graduate program, I had the shock of realizing that, despite the obscure writing style and unfamiliar vocabulary of "supernatural existential" and "transcendental" words, which I generally misunderstood completely upon first (and second) reading, I already knew the Rahnerian synthesis quite well. The moment of epiphany came while I was gazing at the reference stacks, specifically at six large volumes bound in grey with burgundy titles—*Sacramentum Mundi,* the theological encyclopedia Rahner had edited. It was from one of these that my seventh-grade catechist, a married deacon, taught us during a fantastic year of Confraternity of Christian Doctrine classes, the only year I recall in any detail. Students with more than their share of delinquencies, who would go on to become farmers, truck drivers, white-collar professionals, and theologians were all engaged and interested. (All went very well until the pastor intervened, forbidding further use of the book, suggesting that it be burned.) My tacit knowledge of Rahner, however, arose more from years of preaching by priests who were educated in Rahner during their seminary training. Rahner's theology was mediated through those institutional structures of seminary teaching and parish preaching. The same was certainly true for other twentieth-century theologians such as Paul Tillich and Karl Barth. All of these theologians had influence far beyond the readership of their brief works aimed at popular audiences.

Theologians can do a great deal to correct consumerist habits of interpretation by employing the resources of academic theology in their writings. Still the question of access and interpretation is profound and cannot be completely overcome by theologians themselves. It requires serious attention to the ecclesial location of the theologian. In Roman Catholicism this crisis is exacerbated by a number of factors. As we discussed in chapter 3, the erosion of local ecclesial structures caused by deregulation has been accelerated by the centralizing policies of John Paul's pontificate. The tensions between theologians and the hierarchy during two and a half decades of restoration have also caused a great loss of influence for theologians. What is needed is some way of restoring the ecclesial status of the theologian. In an ideal situation, something like the *mandatum* would be a useful contribution to such a task (bracketing the very serious problems it poses in the academy). But in the current atmosphere of division there is suspicion that it will more likely be used as a means of censorship and control. These are not problems that can be resolved here, but the current tensions between the hierarchy and academic theologians are profoundly hindering academic theology from contributing to the stabilization of the tradition by denying it access to ecclesial channels of communication.

Liturgy

The eucharistic and other liturgies counter the abstracting effects of commodification in two ways. First, like theology, they serve to reinforce the interconnections among doctrines and symbols, thus stabilizing their meanings. In addition to this, liturgy is one of the fundamental places where doctrines and symbols are connected with practice. The ritual aspects of liturgy provide a way for participants to enact doctrines as members of a broader believing community.

The liturgy provides an example of the importance of context in shaping believers' attitudes toward the "content" of religious traditions. Consider the difference between studying a Bible at home on one's own and hearing it proclaimed to the gathered assembly in the mass. In the former, perhaps the edition was carefully chosen for its features from the offerings at Barnes & Noble. Choice of the biblical passage to be read is up to the reader. In the latter case, the text is chosen according to a lectionary cycle shared by communities around the world. Its proclamation is framed by ritual introductions and responses, and it is interpreted by an authorized leader. Our reading of de Certeau prevents us from equating the relative passivity of the congregation with passive reception. They continue to engage the text as individuals motivated both by the fecundity of the text and in an effort to compensate for the sometimes poor quality of the interpretations offered by said authorized leaders. But it is much more difficult to "disembed" the text from the congregation, the broader church community, and tradition in a pubic setting than in private, self-guided reading at home.

One context hinders commodification; the other encourages it. There are two factors in the difference: the first concerns the interests and obligations of the intermediaries; the second, structures and practices. Chapter 3 described how, for a variety of reasons, the social location of the new cultural intermediaries places them outside of traditional social structures and communal traditions. Thus, they have little interest in preserving the integrity of cultural traditions. They view them instead as open archives from which they can draw cultural material for use in their own creative offerings. Religious leaders expounding on their community's revered texts are in quite different situations. They are bound to interpret the text from within the context of the community's tradition and ongoing life. While at times the interests and burdens of this social location result in the censoring of unwelcome and perhaps prophetic opinions (which, as the second Gulf War has shown, come from congregations as much as the hierarchy), such neuralgic cases are extreme examples of a broader, more genial reality. Charged with expounding the meaning of a text to a particular community, the homilist must address the obvious connections and tensions between the text and the community's belief and practice. Thus, a Catholic homilist preaching on Peter's profession of faith in the sixteenth chapter of the Gospel of Matthew will inevitably make reference to the Petrine ministry of the pope. The lectionary selection includes Jesus both lauding Peter as the "rock" upon which he will build his community and denouncing him as "satan." Whether the homilist offers a pious celebration of the glories of the papacy, uses the text to critique the current exercise of the papal ministry, or merely mentions it in passing to move on to another point, in a Catholic setting the homilist will have to deal with the text's association with the community's doctrines and institutions. The text would be engaged in a very different way in a tradition without much interest in the Petrine ministry. Likewise, sermons on Paul's doctrine of justification by faith in the Letter to the Romans would be very different in Lutheran and Catholic settings.

This brings us to the second factor, the structural differences between encountering a biblical text in a community and at home. The ritual, communal, and institutional context of the liturgy provides an alternative structure to that of consumer culture: the private space of consumption in the single-family home and the sovereign choices of the individual consumer. In the liturgy, one is not free to yawn and move on to a more interesting passage, or to decide that it is irrelevant. The lectionary parcels out the texts. The symbols, doctrines, and practices of the community provide the context in which they are engaged. The liturgical ritual provides the thick context in which religious beliefs, symbols, and practices find their meaning. Speaking of the Eucharist, Terrence Tilley notes, "The significance or meaning of the doctrine of the Real Presence can be paraphrased or summarized theologically, but it cannot be fully understood except when it is connected with the ritual practices of the community that holds the doctrine."[31] Robert Schreiter's analysis of changes in Roman Catholic eucharistic practice and belief provides the example. Ritual change (e.g., the turning of the celebrant to face the congregation, the use of the vernacular and lay eucharistic ministers, and so on) has given rise to a change in the understanding of the Real Presence, resulting in an emphasis on its function as a communal meal over a sacral sacrifice.[32] These changes illustrate how the liturgical setting reinforces connections—interrelations between meanings and associations with practice—that can be used as a resource against the commodification of religion.

Liturgies have, however, been celebrated throughout the entire rise of consumer culture, and this has not prevented the commodification of religion from taking place (although that does not mean that liturgical ritual has not done much to stem the tide). Nevertheless, liturgy can be used as a resource in a tactical response to the commodification of religion, and it is more likely to succeed if it is consciously understood as serving such a purpose. In such a case, the conflicts between the logic of the liturgy and that of consumer culture can be highlighted and explained. Oft-cited frustrations with the liturgy such as the limits on homilies discussed above, repetitiveness, and so on can be engaged not simply as a manifestation of spiritual shortcomings on the part of impatient believers (an opportunity perhaps to remind people that Pascal associated boredom with human sinfulness), but as moments where believers (laity and clergy alike) experience the conflict between the habits fostered by consumer culture and those necessary for being formed by and stewarding the Christian tradition.[33] Here the analysis of this book is helpful for guiding pastoral sensibilities. The problem is best understood not in terms of moral weaknesses to be preached against (e.g., torpid passivity, a jaded demand for spectacle) but in terms of working against the consumerist habits of use and interpretation in which contemporary believers are formed from infancy. Such a tactical presentation is tremendously important in Roman Catholicism, where tensions between the hierarchy and the laity threaten to become the default interpretive framework for all conflicts between contemporary sensibilities and tradition.

Alternative Communication and Organizational Structures

Chapter 3 associated the commodification of culture with specific institutional changes in religious communities, such as the decline of denominational media (e.g., presses and publications) and traditional communications structures (e.g., the once robust diocesan infrastructures of Catholicism). The shift to the use of corporate media that accompanied this decline contributed to the penetration of consumerist habits of interpretation and use into religious communities, as believers brought interpretive habits and dispositions learned in consuming commercial popular culture to their own religious traditions. If this shift contributed to the commodification of religion, then it is likely that a proper use and revitalizing of these communal media institutions can challenge it by providing the means for disseminating religious doctrines and symbols so that they are more readily associated with traditional religious habits of use and interpretation. Michael Budde makes this point employing the terminology of media studies. He observes the need for "schemata" or frameworks for understanding and applying elements of religious traditions. These are not provided by the secular media, no matter how much religious content they mediate. "Christians can get 'well-developed schemas' about Christianity and Jesus only from Christians and the church. When they do not get that, they are more likely to become indistinguishable from the larger media-formed culture in which they live."[34]

This applies both to literal religious media infrastructures such as presses, newspapers, and television networks, and to the broader systems of communication dispersed throughout the community's structures, institutions, and practices, for example, the similar issues just addressed regarding the liturgy. Scott Appleby's analysis of the Catholic Church's role in the nonviolent "People's Revolution" that unseated the dictator Ferdinand Marcos in the Philippines highlights the political power of church communication and organizational structures.

> The Manila-based hierarchy, parishes throughout the country, and church-supported radio stations and newspapers served as a formidable communication and support network for the incipient revolutionaries. Sermons from the pulpit, newspapers, pastoral letters, Radio Veritas, and various Bible and spiritual discussion groups were all employed in the church's campaign. A network of priests, seminarians, and nuns carried messages among members of the opposition in hiding.[35]

Examples of the use of church communications and organizational infrastructures to support political change could be multiplied: the American civil rights movement, resistance to various dictatorial regimes in Latin America, the Polish anti-communist movement, South Africa's struggle against apartheid (along with less genial examples such as the breakup of the former Yugoslavia and the genocide in Rwanda). Such media and communications structures enable the community to organize and work toward countercultural goals.

The organizational structures of church communities also provide alternatives to the narrow niching of American society, anchored in the single-family home, supported by zoning laws, and strengthened by the cultural force of post-Fordist niche marketing structures. The marketing firm Claritas's widely used "cluster" system describes not only the sorts of people that live in my zip code but also my default circle of friends.[36] On further consideration, there is a curious, if not surprising, absence in the cluster description. The thousands of immigrants living in apartment complexes in my zip code do not appear (one shudders to think what cute descriptive name their cluster would be given). The well-worn pathways of my life in work, leisure, and socializing engage me with people that are pretty much like myself. I have four options for meeting the lower-income immigrants that I live near. They work as custodians at my office; I can dine at their restaurants; I encounter them as fellow parents at our public school; and I can meet them at church. The latter place is the only one where we meet on equal footing; and, consequently, the only place where I have been able to develop friendships outside of my own demographic niche.[37] One ordinary Sunday, in a local church, Our Lady Queen of Peace, I had an astounding experience of the power of ecclesial structures as alternatives to income niching when my family sat between a man named Federico and a woman named Lorenza. Federico was at that time the United States Secretary of Energy, and Lorenza worked in the cash economy. There is no shortage of desperately homogeneous parishes (and no shortage of cabinet secretaries not inclined to worship with the masses), but the parish system provides the possibility of an alternative social structure. It is hard to think of a comparable, alternative system that could bring those two people together as equals (incidentally Lorenza had met Henry Kissinger and other cabinet secretaries while working for a caterer). Certainly many churches have doctrines and values that would incline them to practice such equality. As Robert Cabié notes regarding the eucharistic assembly in the second century, "During the time of celebration they had to do a certain violence to the social order that reigned in their everyday lives. . . . The Eucharistic assembly. . . makes the Church visible as a community of love; in this way it once again challenges society with its inequities."[38] The example makes clear that this challenge to social stratification requires not simply strongly held beliefs but also quite mundane structures such as the parish. These structures can have enormous tactical value when they are viewed as more than administrative units and considered as possible alternative social spaces.

In this regard something should be said about small Christian communities and other grassroots movements that provide alternatives and challenges to the dominant social structure of the single-family home. Observers of such communities note the risk they face of becoming homogeneous, inward-focused groups of mutual support as opposed to mission oriented and outward directed.[39] That said, even as homogeneous groups of mutual support, they provide a mediating structure between the nuclear family and the parish. This is an area where tactical reflection should take the form of paying close attention to the efforts of grassroots intentional ecclesial movements that are trying to find alternative forms of life to the single-family home. The broader "co-housing" movement is interesting in this regard, as are the ongoing attempts by the Catholic Worker movement to form communities that include families.[40]

In addition to their usefulness in organizing and as alternative social structures, religious infrastructures can foster habits of interpretation that are more consistent with the community's tradition. The liturgical setting has some obvious symbolic means of encouraging a specific attitude toward the biblical text: the entrance procession, prayers uttered *sotto voce* before reading, the incensing of the Gospels, and so on. The Christian traditions hand on a host of practices for engaging the biblical texts: public proclamation, antiphonal recitation, *lectio divina* and other forms of spiritual reflection, and other practices. More literal media such as print and video likewise carry interpretative values. These are sometimes best sensed in the contrast with the visual conventions of secular and Catholic media, revealed in some religious media's distinctly "cheesy" feel. Images are selected not for their visual appeal but because they present valued moments in the life of the community: church leaders exercising their authority by officiating at a groundbreaking, visiting a community, or celebrating a religious ceremony; believers engaging in some good but visually banal activity; and so on. These subtle contrasts may connect with more critical engagements and rejections of contemporary media values. Chief among these are the logic of ubiquitous display and the imperative to achieve impact in a fast-changing media market. As many have warned, the gospel message is in danger of being drowned out or ignored if it is not presented in a manner that can compete in such an environment. But to present the message in such a context is to risk being determined by the rules of the media consumer marketplace. Success may come at the cost of commodifying the message itself.

The logic of consumer culture is one of access and display: everything should be available to everyone (who can pay). Value is established by appearance, whether social belonging and status through conspicuous consumption or the physical commodity's reduction to a carrier of sign value, a substrate for visible display. Everything that takes place should be brought into the all-encompassing spectacle. Pornography is hyped for its degree of "explicitness," even if, after the initial taboo of watching people have sex is crossed, greater and greater levels of visual biological detail are likely to have a rapidly diminishing erotic payoff.[41] Explicit violence in cinema is even lauded at times; the hyperviolent opening of *Saving Private Ryan* was praised as a lesson in the horrors of war. Sonograms of fetuses (and indeed embryos) are shared with friends and acquaintances and displayed on refrigerators and cubicle walls. To use Émile Durkheim's terminology, consumer culture favors positive rituals. These reinforce a sense of the sacred by bringing the faithful into closer contact with it—whether by entering a sacred space, impersonating a sacred figure, enacting a drama, proclaiming a narrative, or consuming a ritual meal. Negative rituals, which reinforce the sacred by restricting access to it, have less appeal in consumer culture, which does not understand ritual prohibitions or cultic abstinence. Save an admission fee, it knows no iconostasis or temple veil. Its icons and idols are not protected in an inner sanctum open only to ritually purified initiates, but displayed before all on the covers of magazines and on billboards.

A campaign by a group of conservative students at Georgetown in 1998 is illustrative of the reflex sensibility concerning religious display in a consumer culture. As part of their ongoing struggle to halt the perceived secularization of Georgetown, they petitioned the university to replace crucifixes in certain classrooms where they had been removed and to install them in newer buildings where they had never been displayed. The issue worked well for the group in garnering attention from the media and church leaders. It was at once deeply symbolic and trivial. Surely if Georgetown was still Catholic, it was not too much to ask that it display the crucifix. The administration could easily be flogged for being "ashamed of the cross." Catholic and non-Catholic faculty and students responded that, as a symbol, the crucifix had a particular history that was associated at times with oppression such as anti-Semitic pogroms. Thus, many non-Catholics feel uncomfortable in its presence.

The students organizing the campaign preferred a simpler framing of the question. The crucifix was a symbol of Georgetown's Catholic identity. To display it in classrooms was to openly embrace this identity, to refuse to display it was to renounce it. The debate thus focused on where and when was it appropriate to display such a symbol of Georgetown's identity, given that fact the some found it disturbing because of its negative historical resonances. This, of course, is about as literal an application of Durkheim's notion of totem as one could imagine.[42] The crucifix signified communal identity. The theological complexities of the symbol were largely absent from the debate, as were discussions of its liturgical use. The debate was framed in terms of consumer culture's logic of display. Symbols are meant to be seen. The Nike Corporation is not shy about its swoosh, displaying it on architecture, letterhead, every product it sells, its corpus of celebrity representatives, even on executive tattoos. If Georgetown is Catholic, surely it would want to display its symbol as well.

By framing the question in this way, the complex symbolism of the crucifix was flattened out. It is indeed a thoroughly odd, shocking religious symbol. A representation of a tortured body hung on the instrument of its execution symbolizes the high point of God's self-disclosure to humankind. It should be considered disturbing, not primarily for its historical association with atrocity (which, it is worth noting, occurred precisely at moments when it was functioning as a totem of group identity amid ingroup/outgroup violence), but for the paschal mystery which it represents. That this theological complexity never appeared in the debate (or was immediately misunderstood when proposed) shows the dominance of consumer display. It is not at all clear that the theological meaning of the symbol is best served by ubiquitous display. In the congested cultural marketplace of consumer culture, such widespread public display, while it may bring success in competing with other corporate/cultural symbols, wins such success at the cost of reducing the crucifix to the same level of significance as all the other shallow symbols in the marketplace. Nike's swoosh, Starbucks' mermaid, Target's logo—offer little reward to meditative contemplation. They bear no surplus of meaning and harbor no disturbing tensions or negations.[43]

A more secular example of a powerful symbol and its function in consumer culture is helpful for clarifying the problem and the nature of an adequate response. Billie Holiday's brooding reflection on lynching, "Strange Fruit," engages America's history of racial violence in a politically powerful way. There is, however, a danger that in listening to the song, we reduce its meditation on atrocity to an intense aesthetic experience of outrage and horror. The experience provides emotional catharsis, but when received in a recreational setting (whether in its original context of the Harlem club scene or now on CD played on a home stereo or in a car) it functions in a manner detached from the politics it evokes.[44]

What options do we have in a consumer culture to respond to such a cultural object without reducing it to a recreational commodity? Most obviously, we could simply refuse to consume it. By placing it off limits, one might in fact be better honoring its concerns. Although this tactic can easily slide into complicity with the silence of American culture on the topic of race, it need not. The song is well known and is encountered from time to time on jazz radio stations and in cultural programming. Turning off the radio at such moments can be an active response. Experiencing the song suggests a resolution that is not matched in the concrete details of most people's lives. Deprived of the aesthetic consolation of the lyrics and melody, one is left to face one's own unresolved place within the history of interracial violence and oppression in this country. In a consumer setting, such abstinence is a gesture of respect that keeps the political tension alive by refusing to resolve it through consumption.

There are less drastic, but more difficult tactics for resisting the reduction of a cultural object to a consumable commodity. One concerns context. To continue with my example, listening to "Strange Fruit" in a racially mixed discussion group on interracial violence would be another experience indeed, one that would immediately tie it to its referent and lessen the likelihood of its being reduced to the "cheap grace" of the tears of commodified outrage.

The same tactics are valuable for the preservation of religious symbols. If ubiquitous, ostentatious display and positive rituals are the dominant symbolic practices of consumer culture, perhaps aspects of the Christian traditions that more closely resemble negative rituals—those that attend to symbols and beliefs by holding them in reserve—can provide tactical resources. One example is the medieval chancel barrier or rood screen, which survives today mainly in the Orthodox iconostasis, which separates the sanctuary from the nave. These screens served to establish the importance of what took place within their boundaries by limiting access to it. More recent practices of this nature include the fading practice of the eucharistic fast and the emergent one of reserving the Eucharist within a dedicated chapel distinct from the main worship space of the church. The most obvious negative ritual in this regard is the practice of not receiving the Eucharist when in a state of serious sin. It is a paradigmatic example of honoring something by not consuming it. There are clearly problems with simplistically reestablishing some of these structures and disciplines: for example, recent moves to restrict the sanctuary to the ordained are widely regarded as having more to do with a problematic theology of ordination than with respect for the Eucharist. Alongside such particular problems lies a more fundamental one of openness and sharing of the salvation God bestowed on humankind in Jesus. Not all emphases on openness in contemporary churches can be reduced to a mindless adoption of consumer mores. Nonetheless, in such a context, openness is always in danger of being drawn into unwitting complicity with the erosions of consumer culture. Thus, we should consider using these negative ritual resources to counter the consumer convention of equating significance with ubiquitous display.

The goal is not, however, withholding for its own sake—some slavish application of Durkheim to the present moment. These negative aspects of ritual contrast with the dominant culture and are suggestive places to begin to construct a practice and logic of exposure that are more thoroughly Christian. They provide a way of practicing religious symbols that ties them to their traditional doctrinal and liturgical references. The answers to the problems faced in consumer culture lie not simply in acknowledging the sophistication of a given symbol but in treating it differently, by framing it in theologically informed contexts and practices. Returning to the example of the crucifix, what was lacking in the Georgetown debate was a compelling theological reason for placing the crucifix *as* a symbol of the paschal mystery in the classroom.

Religious communities have their own particular logics of display, which have different goals and time scales from those of the postmodern corporate media.

Doctrines and practices are the wealth of the community and are for that reason stewarded with care. Transformative engagement, rather than broad exposure, is the ideal. These goals may lead to an explicit choice to withhold religious doctrines and symbols (e.g., restrictions on reception of the Eucharist to full members of the community). A useful model for this tactic is mystagogy: the explanation of the sacramental life after candidates have been initiated into the church. While the practice of withholding such instruction was, in antiquity, dependent on the influence of mystery religions and the precarious situation of persecuted Christian communities, today its long history provides an alternative ethos of communication that helps maintain the connections between doctrines and symbols and the communities that avow and practice them.

There is more here than a negative logic of reserve. It is not simply that the crucifix is not best respected by display in a classroom but that it is better respected in the complex space of a chapel. The chapel is a place of active practices that encourage attention to the crucifix's complex symbolism. We adjust our demeanor upon entering the space, either through genuflecting or adopting a respectful silence. Even as practice inside churches has become more social, interactions within the nave are more subdued than elsewhere. Pauses in conversation are frequently marked by a return to attentive facing toward the sanctuary. Clearly, the quiet nonliturgical visit to a chapel provides an opportunity for serious meditation on the crucifix and what it represents. The eucharistic liturgy provides a rich set of practices which contextualize the symbol of the crucifix within a celebration of the paschal mystery. At such times, it is in much less danger of being reduced to a shallow signifier of group identity than when hanging on a wall in a classroom, between the exit sign and the clock (objects whose symbolism is likely more pressing in the classroom context).

All of these tactics fight the commodification of religion by challenging habits of interpretation and use that abstract elements of culture from their traditional contexts. They work by using religious communities' resources that emphasize the interconnections among various doctrines, symbols, and practices. Although this involves what Paul Heelas calls "tradition based limits on consumption," it should not be equated with limiting or discouraging engagement and agency.[45] The goal of these tactics is not to proscribe popular religious agency but to preserve the complexity of the elements that people engage in order to support this agency. Bricolage is much more likely to be subversive of the status quo when it is funded by complex building blocks. Having considered various tactics for preserving the complexity of elements of tradition, we must now turn to a more direct consideration of forming and strengthening popular agency.

Strengthening Popular Agency

The tactics just discussed focused on stabilizing elements of tradition. In addition to this focus on the objects of tradition, we must also consider the subjects who engage them. The two are not easily separated, because the fate of elements of tradition is determined to a great extent by the habits of interpretation and use with which believers engage them. As was noted above, consumer culture coincides with the emergence of widespread literacy. The combination of the two has led to an explosion of cultural agency and widespread cultural production. While this expansion of agency coincides with the erosions of consumer culture and other aspects of postmodernity, and popular religious production is at times shallow and ignorant, it is not necessarily so. Since widespread agency is not going to go away any time soon, the answer lies in embracing it and attempting to deepen it and bring it into the ongoing conversation of the Christian tradition. Efforts to resist or dismiss it are destined to fail.

The obvious desideratum is a community of well-formed practitioners of tradition who engage beliefs, symbols, and practices in a manner informed by its logic. This is in contrast to the default mode of agency in consumer culture: the freelancing new cultural intermediary, who draws from traditions with little knowledge of their intrinsic logics and goals and without a sense of obligation for preservation of traditions. In religion, this takes the form of spirituality. Again, the problem with these forms of cultural engagement is not that they are popular and unlearned. Neither popular religious agency nor syncretism is new. Indeed they lie at the heart of most great traditions. The problem is that when people are trained to lift cultural/religious objects from their traditional contexts, they are less likely to be influenced by the other logics, values, and desires mediated by the religious traditions. Therefore they are unlikely to construct syntheses which enable them to develop forms of life that differ from the status quo. How can this goal be accomplished, beyond cautions against cultural piracy and exhortations for people to think within traditions? In order for people to act as agents of a given tradition they must first of all have a sense of authorization to do so. They also require times, spaces, and practices in which they can do so. This section will explore tactical means for deepening popular agency: the way that the tradition is presented, the relationship between the clergy and the laity, the liturgy and church architecture, and communications infrastructures. We will consider both types of agency that we discussed in chapter 6: the creation of new doctrinal insights, symbols, texts, and practices and the application and insinuation of beliefs into practices and forms of life.

The Clergy and the Laity

While Roman Catholicism has many resources for countering the commodification of religion, encouraging broad agency is not its strong suit. The hierarchy defines itself in terms of leading and controlling the laity. This is practically primordial in the tradition, as bishops in the early church struggled against the continuing reverence for Roman and indigenous European religions among the faithful (as well as competing figures within the church such as the confessors and ascetics). This bipolar model of church polity—clerics and peasantry—continued in the medieval period and reached a high pitch during the Protestant and Catholic Reformations, both of which were, significantly, about christianizing the countryside in Europe, which, beneath a nominal Christian veneer, remained effectively pagan until the sixteenth century. In the period since the reformations, the Roman Catholic hierarchy has consolidated its claims to both lead and speak for the tradition and has deployed a worldwide administrative system to do so. In the modern period however, it has had to contend with the fundamentally new problem: the rise of an educated laity. This emergence was profoundly disruptive, as was evident in the waves of secularization that rocked Europe in the eighteenth and nineteenth centuries, which the Catholic hierarchy referred to, among other things, as "laicism." The ongoing consequences of the rise of lay literacy and agency are likely to be just as disruptive. The Roman Catholic hierarchy rightly perceives this as a crisis. Its reflex reaction—to reenact centralized clerical control—is likely to fail for two reasons: it presumes a stable, vital popular religion and it misidentifies a lack of open opposition with active, engaged faithfulness.

In the past, clerics concerned about the excesses of popular religion could presume its unremitting vitality. Thus they could limit their responsibility to censoring, correcting, and controlling it. This situation has changed profoundly over the past several centuries. In Europe, the masses lost interest in the church. In many historically Catholic countries, there is little popular religious excess remaining to be curbed. Globalization and consumer culture present a similar problem in the present moment. What is at stake now is the survival of particular religious cultures amid the cultural maelstrom of advanced capitalism—for all the reasons the preceding chapters have catalogued: traditional channels of communication swamped amid the explosion of communications; traditional systems of religious socialization weakened under the influence of highly differentiated age cohorts each with its own distinct "culture"; people no longer envisioning their beliefs and choices in terms of cultural, religious, and communal obligations; and so on. Studies of younger Catholics show that so-called cultural Catholicism—the presence of a Catholic sensibility or worldview among disaffected or nonpracticing Catholics—is becoming increasingly hard to find.[46] Censoring an incorrigible culture is one task, preserving a vulnerable one is quite another.

A centralized, hierarchical strategy will fail in a particularly Catholic way—by creating a "postmodern peasantry." The present moment threatens to reenact the stereotypical divide between the peasantry and the educated clerical elite. The clerics controlled the institutional church, administered the sacraments, and preached the gospel, but they did not control the religious lives of the folk. The people had their own religious culture. Although it was connected to official Christianity and made use of its spaces, rituals, and symbols, it did so in ways that the clerical elites did not entirely understand and had limited power to influence. Consumer culture tends to encourage a similar style of engagement by believers. Accustomed to engaging culture as a consumable commodity, believers today are quite comfortable belonging to a church whose teachings they do not completely accept. These habits contrast with those of the boomer generation, whose members were given to great autobiographical crises of commitment and to anguished existential conflicts with institutions and organized religion. Suspicion of institutions continues, but it is no longer accompanied by an all-or-nothing hermeneutic. Generations formed by the offerings of the corporate culture industries more than family or church have little angst about picking and choosing from a tradition's offerings. They are, for that reason, not likely to confront religious authorities or even engage them. They "question authority" quietly, as peasants have always done, by taking what they can use and simply ignoring the rest. In such a context, the current *revanchist*, centralizing strategy of the Roman Catholic hierarchy is destined to fail.[47] The only way to deal with the rise of literacy and cultural agency that marks consumer cultures is to embrace this change and attempt to work through it by deepening and strengthening lay agency.

A vignette from a recent study of young adult Catholics illustrates the need to authorize believers to reinterpret and apply elements of traditions to the present moment. The authors of the study lament that, for all their emphasis on the necessity of constructing a personal spirituality, few of the young adults interviewed reported constructing anything particularly unusual or profound. For example, despite widespread expressions of discomfort with consumer materialism, the authors note that "nobody linked austerity and asceticism with environmental concerns about materialism and overconsumption."[48] This failure illustrates what we have been discussing. Much more than a particular failure of imagination is at issue. It is emblematic of a deeper lack of positive religious agency that is rooted in a lack of a sense of authorization to engage in such a creative reappropriation.

The generation of Catholics who are in their thirties has been socialized to see themselves as active agents of their religious beliefs, but as Catholics they have not been socialized to think of themselves as agents of their tradition. They construct their own personal religious visions, like all of their peers, but they define these actions as private, not as something they will ever hand back to the tradition from which they have drawn. This passive engagement can be deepened if they are given the knowledge and authorization to creatively engage the tradition. While the latter is indeed more threatening to church authorities, it is ultimately less destructive. For all their divisiveness, the contemporary left and right in the Catholic Church in America still share enough in common to argue about what constitutes the tradition. Passive consumers will not pester bishops with demands for reform, not because they particularly agree with them but because the episcopate, and perhaps even the local parish, are simply not important to their faith.

This is not simply a progressive Catholic polemic about opening the church to the people, although much of it is consonant with such arguments. There is indeed much that is lost by not listening to the laity. As Paul Lakeland notes, "there is an enormous reservoir of lay practical wisdom on the challenges of living life according to the gospel, both theologically and ethically, that remains untapped because the clerical teachers of the church draw upon it little, if at all, and because those whose experience it is are hobbled."[49] Neither is it a question of contemporary sensibilities, which, in the words of the Vatican document on the Internet, expect "interactivity" from religion. The issue is how to deepen popular agency by strengthening its connections with the tradition. There is no question whether people will exercise such agency; they always have, and coming generations will likely do so more than ever. The question is whether they will understand their agency as tied to a particular community and tradition, or whether they will default to the style of the new cultural intermediaries, drawing from multiple traditions without a sense of responsibility to them. This form of agency is more difficult because it involves tensions with communities and tradition. For that reason it requires authorization and encouragement. Such agency also requires exemplars, spaces, times, and practices. If believers are to understand their innovations and applications as contributions made to a community and living tradition to which they are responsible, they must also have systems of communication through which they can share their contributions. Our tactical considerations will focus on all of these aspects.

Foregrounding the Living Character of Tradition

Religious doctrines, symbols, and practices have histories. Although Christianity believes the ultimate author of the Christian tradition is God, theologians from Irenaeus of Lyon to Yves Congar have insisted that this authorship is worked through the agency of the church community. Doctrines arose from human response to the divine initiative through processes of reflection, dialogue, and debate. Dogmas promulgated by church councils were formulated by particular thinkers. The tradition's symbols have been drawn from the scriptures, worked into liturgies, expressed and developed by artists, leaders, and other virtuosi.

Presenting the tradition as the work of the community over time serves as a valuable tactic for reembedding, as discussed above. Shallow appropriation depends on an ignorance of the communal origins of traditions, much as the commodity fetish hides the conditions of production of literal commodities. Emphasis on the communal origins of tradition serves to strengthen agency as well by foregrounding the connections between tradition and community. This provides a model of agency that is an alternative to the new cultural intermediary practice of engaging traditions as sources from which one can draw without incurring any obligation for their maintenance. When viewed as what has been handed on from previous generations of the community, tradition is more readily perceived as entailing responsibility. Contemporary believers are responsible for seriously engaging what has been handed on, for working to interpret and apply it to the present moment, and for preserving and handing it on to the generations that will follow.

If doctrines are presented as arising from the work of persons within particular communities in response to particular challenges, they will be more difficult to abstract than if they are presented as disembodied "official" positions that depend on hierarchical dominance for their continued existence. This, of course, is a particular problem for Roman Catholicism, given its modern myth of the pope as the prime agent of the tradition. Although theologians and ecclesial insiders know or debate the names of the ghost writers of papal encyclicals, to the rest of the church these documents are presented as a given pope's epochal achievements, life's work, or masterpiece. As Herman Pottmeyer has argued, Catholicism has a developing theology of ecclesial agency. The premature ending of the First Vatican Council made it seem as if the pope were the only full "subject" in the church. Vatican II corrected this by restoring the College of Bishops to its proper teaching role.[50] While this council also did much to address the active contribution of the rest of the church outside of the several thousand members of the hierarchy, much work remains to be done to make this a functioning part of Catholic culture and practice.

Catholicism does have important resources in this regard. This need corresponds rather well to the Catholic doctrine of the communion of saints and its elaboration in the myriad stories of the lives of the saints. Reverence for the saints bears a broad and deeply communal understanding of the ongoing life and development of the Christian tradition. In Elizabeth Johnson's words, the symbol of the communion of saints

> signifies that those who seek the face of the living God today belong to a great historical company, an intergenerational band of the friends of God and prophets that includes the living and the dead, joined in community with the cosmic world, all connected in the gracious, compassionate love of Holy Wisdom who, in the midst of historical struggle, sin and defeat, continuously renews her gift of saving, healing grace.[51]

Stories of the saints recount individuals and communities developing new forms of life and models of ministry, as well as challenging the church to reform in times of crisis. They provide a way of situating the heritage of the church within the conflicts and struggles of individuals and communities in different times and places, thus connecting their reception with the active agency of contemporary believers.

The Liturgy and Agency

We discussed the liturgy above as a means of stabilizing the meanings of religious doctrines and practices. Here we will consider how the liturgy can serve as a setting for lay practice and a formation for lay agency outside the liturgy. The liturgical reforms of Vatican II that aimed at eliciting the "full, conscious, and active participation" of the assembly in the liturgy are perfectly suited for countering a passive consumer model of liturgical engagement.[52] Here the congregation is envisioned not as a group of passive consumers who are served by the celebrant but as active agents praying together the central prayer of the church. They are expected to know what they are praying and why.

This ideal is not, however, always achieved in reality. Despite the fact that the majority of believers know the liturgy well enough to participate in it actively and the fact that the liturgy has a logic that allows it, to some extent, to work as its own catechesis, there is still widespread ignorance of the basic parts of the liturgy and their purpose. This is a serious hindrance to the liturgy's functioning as a practice through which the laity exercise agency. However much an improvement the *Novus Ordo* liturgy may be over the Tridentine one in terms of encouraging lay participation, it is still widely perceived as boring and repetitive. Much of this could be due to poorly planned and implemented liturgies. It may also simply be due to the fact that full, conscious participation is enormously difficult to achieve in any oft-repeated and widely practiced ritual.

Another cause of frustration lies closer to the issue of agency. Control of the liturgy remains in the hands of the celebrant and other "professionals." The congregation has little input into how the liturgy is celebrated. Priests have great control over the pace, emphasis, and flow of the liturgy. They are able (if forbidden) to modify the eucharistic prayer at will, to interrupt the flow of the liturgy to make points both profound and banal, and above all publicly to share their insights into the scriptures and contemporary events in the homily. Liturgists and musicians likewise have the opportunity to contribute personally to the shape of the liturgy through choice of music and the use of their talents. Their choices are profoundly important. Music that functions as an integral part of the liturgy, whether carefully chosen settings of psalms and hymns or an entire musical setting of the mass, provides the possibility for a much more engaged celebration by the assembly. Celebrants' respect for the assembly's role, especially for the periods of silence built into the liturgy, which interweave individual and communal prayer, can do much to foster the active engagement of the assembly in the liturgy.

The very fact that so much depends on the choices and wisdom of the celebrant and music director highlights how passive the assembly is, however much this may be in conflict with the theological understanding of the liturgy. The congregation's input remains profoundly limited. They are encouraged to make the prayers their own, through the disciplined and graced struggle to keep "their minds attuned to their voices" as they pray.[53] As active and profound as their "interior" participation may be, there are very few ways for laypersons to manifest their exterior engagement. Above all, there is very little they can do if the presider or music director does not do his or her job well. All compensations remain individual and private; the assembly has no way of taking up the slack in such cases.

In this regard, the recent revision of the *General Instruction of the Roman Missal* (the official set of rules that govern how the liturgy is to be celebrated) missed a profound opportunity to recognize the *sensus fidelium* as manifested in the life of the church. It repeatedly emphasizes the ideal of "full active participation," but does so in a manner that discourages or discounts the active agency of the community. This can be seen in the manner in which it addresses liturgical posture. The emphasis is on uniformity, which "is a sign of the unity of the members of the

Christian community gathered for the sacred Liturgy."[54] The *Instruction* calls for greater attention to liturgical law regarding liturgical posture "for the common spiritual good" rather than an expression of "personal inclination or arbitrary choice."[55]

Divergent practices might, however, be much more than expressions of arbitrary consumerist preference. They can also be a sign of a tension being worked out in the life of the community. Even in this highly bureaucratic moment in the life of the Roman Catholic Church, *Lex orandi, lex credendi* might be applicable to more than official liturgical texts. Perhaps these divergent practices manifest a certain wisdom, born of the logic of the tradition and the liturgy. It is interesting that so many American communities default to the international norm of standing during the eucharistic prayer, in contrast to the "exception" granted to the American church to kneel throughout (an exception that was deemed "laudable" by the revised *Instruction*). Similarly popular reformulations of prayers to deal with gender manifest a definite logic and wisdom. Gender-neutral language appears in places that refer to the human race and to the church and where God is addressed in the abstract.

Although theologically I am in favor of both of these changes, my point is formal. Had these popular developments not been viewed as evidence of confusion but considered positively as a source in the deliberations for the revision of the *Instruction,* and had this fact been publicized, it could have had a profound impact on the way in which people envision their participation in the liturgy. The common practice of congregations holding hands while reciting the Lord's Prayer is an example of an accepted, if unacknowledged, use of a popular liturgical innovation. While such attention might encourage organized campaigns to change the liturgy, it could equally encourage a sense of responsibility born of agency, rather than unwillingness to respect rubrics born of frustration. If the liturgy is in flux, then our decisions about how to practice it become quite important, a place where believers exercise their responsibility to hand the faith on to following generations. Short of taking the developing practice of the community seriously as a source in its own deliberations, the *Instruction* could have, alongside its call for the congregation to follow whatever instructions are given by the celebrant, deacon, or lay instructor (in order to preserve unity), called for such figures, especially the ever-more-common visiting celebrant to learn and conform to the practices of the local community. The freedom of visiting clergy to follow their own practices without concern for those of the local community suggest that liturgical practice is indeed a matter of "personal inclination or arbitrary choice"—but only that of clerics.

Popular frustration with the liturgy may also manifest a deeper problem concerning the contrast between consumer sensibilities and those required for the stewarding of the Christian tradition. Concern about personal inclination and choice on the part of celebrants and members of the assembly is clearly justified in consumer cultures. Formation as an agent of the Roman Catholic tradition may involve learning precisely those habits that are most off-putting in the Roman rite: participation in an objective and highly formal ritual. Bruce Morrill argues that the liturgy is a site of conflict between the "market-driven values of private possession, individual convenience and personal comfort" and the demands of being part of an ancient and ongoing communal tradition, which requires the ability

> to engage in shared symbols, to give oneself generously and, to some degree, recklessly to the authority and "otherness" in a common practiced tradition, to accept initial or even sustained discomfort with the necessarily unconventional, poetic words and actions of rituals that place us in conscious contact with the divine.[56]

There is much to be said for this argument. Nonetheless a fundamental asymmetry remains between the passive scripted style of liturgical agency and the active, creative application of the wisdom of the tradition to daily life envisioned for the laity outside of the eucharistic gathering.

Agency and Space

In chapters 5 and 6, we argued that in order for consumption to be understood as a politically potent "use" of culture, it requires space as a location for action. Examples included women's use of devotion to St. Jude to resist the dominance of the scientific medical establishment in hospitals and Pentecostal women's preaching upon openly patriarchal scriptures in a way that uses them to achieve authority in their churches. We will discuss how liturgical space, its literal geometry as well as the practices carried out there, can support popular religious agency.

The liturgical reforms following Vatican II had an unintended consequence that conflicted with their goal of active engagement. In their effort to center Christian prayer life on the Eucharist, they all but eliminated a traditional locus of lay agency: devotions. Whatever their individual theological shortcomings—not to mention the profound general problem of diverting attention away from the eucharistic prayer—devotions provided a much more active set of practices for the laity to engage in during the liturgy. Devotions provided an eclectic set of practices, whose fittingness and pace the devotee decided and controlled. Devotionalism is one of the places where popular religion inserts itself visibly into the spaces of official religion. While clearly many devotions were authored and sponsored by clerics and religious orders, as a set of rituals practiced by the laity, they provided a place where the innovations and modifications of the community could be publicly manifested and where community members were actively involved in handing on practices and beliefs to others.

This loss of time for lay practices during the liturgy was exacerbated by the simplification of worship space to support the ritual focus on the eucharistic liturgy. The various spaces that were lost—side altars, shrines, sundry statuary, and the like—provided material for engaged reflection and imagination precisely as they distracted from the central liturgy. They contributed greatly to making the church interior a complex, practiced place; a place where people actively engaged religious symbols (icons, statues, waters, oils, the reserved Eucharist) and practiced beliefs (providence, grace, the paschal mystery, the communion of saints).

Equally important, these were sacred spaces that the laity were authorized to enter. The loss of these spaces greatly restricted the area within church buildings where the laity could exercise their own practices with official sanction. All that remains in most contemporary churches are the stations of the cross in the nave and statues of Mary and Joseph flanking the altar. With the exception of special ministries, authorized lay use of the space is limited to participation in the liturgy from the pews and quiet reflection or devotions at other times. The liturgical focus on the eucharistic prayer not surprisingly resulted in an architectural focus on the main altar and sanctuary. These two factors—the loss of space for lay believers to practice, and the architectural focus on the altar—combine to make agency within church space seem primarily a clerical affair.

Without going into a full review of the complex debates concerning church architecture, we can note how a number of factors coalesced to reinforce precisely what the liturgical reform aimed to correct: the reduction of the laity to passive onlookers and outsiders to the liturgical action.[57] The ritual emphasis on the main altar combines with the simplification of church interiors, especially those that preserve a widespread pre–Vatican II geometry that arrays all of the sites of action—ambo, altar, baptismal font, tabernacle—across the axis where the communion rail once stood between the sanctuary and the nave. Whether one traces the origins of this geometry to the classical basilica or to Renaissance theater, it finds its overwhelming resonance today with television viewing. It thus provides a ready invitation for believers to bring habits of interpretation and engagement learned in commercial popular culture to their engagement with their religious traditions.

The pernicious effects of this simplification cannot be blamed solely on the movement to reconceive church space in the vernacular of modern architecture. Certainly its drive for simplicity of form and its disdain for extraneous decoration contributed to the postconciliar "stripping of the altars," but its emphasis on the relationship between form and function combined well with the ideals of the liturgical movement to produce churches with much more complex, practicable interiors. Tabernacles were moved to separate meditation chapels; baptismal fonts were given a separate and more prominent focus within the main chapel or in a separate dedicated space. Their use can return much of the complexity of ancient church spaces as the congregation moves from place to place during baptismal liturgies. The stark division between the nave and the sanctuary was eased by placing the pews in an arc around the altar, or fully in the round, presenting the congregation as an active participant in the ritual. All of this provides a very different geometry and space for practice than television. Involvement in the liturgy becomes a spacial practice, the congregation an actively visible agent as opposed to a group of spectators noticed only when they block the "view" or have loud children.

Another space for people to exercise religious agency is provided by small Christian communities. We noted above their significance for providing a mediating structure between the single-family home and the parish. From the perspective of agency, such groups provide a less formal setting that is still explicitly ecclesial for community members to practice their faith. They provide opportunities for leadership by both men and women. Their practices, such as reflection on the scriptures, faith sharing, and theological reflection allow laypersons to actively express their insights and questions in ways not possible in the liturgy. Their smaller scale enables each member to be actively involved. Bernard Lee notes that many laypeople experience small Christian communities as "the first place where they have felt free to speak or have become aware that they have something to say." He argues that small Christian communities supply the communal contexts for "transmitting and maintaining the faith" that were once provided by "extended families and neighborhoods of an earlier time as mechanisms for transmitting and maintaining faith."[58] They do so precisely as places where people are empowered to actively and openly engage and work through the beliefs and symbols of their faith. They also provide a setting in which people's religious wisdom and insights can be shared with other members of their community. This brings us to a consideration of another spatial issue: communication infrastructures.

Communication Structures

In chapters 5 and 6, I argued against dismissing contemporary popular culture as inherently shallow and politically ineffective, but accepted that it frequently is for two specific reasons. First, popular cultural production in consumer cultures is hindered by the highly commodified nature of the cultural building blocks with which people work. The tactics aimed at reembedding cultural objects discussed above addressed this problem. The second reason for the disarming of popular culture concerns the ability of agents to share what they produce. Whether they are slyly resisting cultural hegemony, subversively using elements of the dominant culture against itself, or engaging in creative retrievals and applications of elements of religious traditions—no matter how ingenious they are—their impact is limited by their ability to influence others. This second aspect of the connection between practice and space was illustrated by Michel de Certeau's specter of the isolated, silent television viewer. While this spectator can resist what is presented and turn it to private use that escapes the surveillance and discipline of the system, unless there is a way to mark this resistance, it remains little more than a coping mechanism. The examples of the emergence of homosexuality as an identity and the *Murphy Brown* incident illustrated how such subversive twists can have a broader political impact if there are means by which they can be shared and linked to practice. Here we will consider how these same issues of space apply to supporting popular religious agency in consumer culture. This will complement the tactics discussed above for preserving the traditional and communal connections of religious doctrines and symbols by emphasizing the importance of developing structures that allow popular agency not only to draw from but also to contribute to the ongoing life of the Christian tradition.

This point became clear in a colloquium about the religious imagination and peacemaking in the wake of the terrorist attacks of September 11.[59] The conversation considered means to positively influence the popular religious imagination. Several participants asked, Where are the great leaders and reformers of today? Where are the contemporary peers of Francis of Assisi, Catherine of Siena, and Martin Luther King? What is striking about this pressing question is how unlikely it is that we would know. In the past, reformers, prophets, and leaders could establish a reputation in their local communities that would serve as a foundation for their broader influence. Francis's idiosyncratic holiness became known first in the small town of Assisi. His choice of poverty was scandalous because everyone knew he was the scion of a wealthy merchant. When he appeared at church dressed in rags, he was recognized, if reviled. There may be countless people like him today, but should they appear at a local church, in most cases, no one would know who they are. Since most parishioners know very little about each other, it is likely that the person's intentional choice of lifestyle would be written off to misfortune or mental illness. At best, that person would be welcomed warily to donuts after mass and perhaps be directed to the social outreach office. The problem lies not in our callousness, but in the scale of our communities, where word of mouth and reputation are no longer sufficient starting points for popular religious virtuosi to become recognized and respected by the religious community. Those who do, like Mother Teresa, do so as media spectacles, sundered from the life of local communities.

The politically charged days following September 11 provided an example of the problem. America witnessed a rare outpouring of personal political and religious statements. It was one of the few times in recent memory when public symbolic display seemed to matter. Politics collided in an open manner as people blithely placed flags in all their neighbors' yards (some of whom had to politely demur). People placed signs in their yards and car windows. Many of these were predictable, if heartfelt, expressions of support for the victims. Some were convoluted and anguished as people struggled to express complex feelings not easily reduced to bumper-sticker length. Others were marvelously eloquent. One stands out in memory. It was painted by children, and read "God—Allah Bless Us All"— a marvel of concise sophistication that managed to respond religiously to the trauma of the attacks and challenge the predictable knee-jerk religious nationalism. Within a week or two, these home-grown messages disappeared. They were replaced by commercially produced window and bumper stickers, the sophistication of which was limited to the number of exclamation points following "United we Stand!!!" or "These colors don't run!" Clearly there were better messages, but simplistic nationalistic slogans are what were offered to the post–September 11 mass market, and, after a too brief display, the genius of the grassroots went into hiding again. This loss was the result of a lack of communications infrastructure. The best and most insightful statements did not flourish because there were no means for their wisdom to be recognized and spread.

The same holds true for the religious imagination. There is no reason to believe that people are any less profound today than ever, and certainly no theological reason to believe that they are less responsive to grace than they were in the past. So it is likely that there are great religious geniuses out there, countless wise elders, mystics, poets, and prophets sitting in the pews.[60] In fact, there are certainly more of these today than ever who are literate and articulate. But unlike reformers past, such as Catherine of Siena, today's religious geniuses will probably not have their letters read by the pope, or for that matter, by their own bishops. Indeed, this may be because so many are now educated and there are too many writing. Yet these are the sorts of people who formed the vast, anonymous authorship of the Christian traditions in days past. How can this dispersed genius be supported and brought into the tradition today?

Communications channels are needed to allow this grassroots creativity to be shared with the broader community, sifted, evaluated, and brought into dialogue with the ongoing tradition. Roman Catholicism stands out as a religious community with the resources to address this problem. Unfortunately, its massive system of communication is still understood and used primarily in terms of the traditional task of clerical control of the unruly excesses of the masses. Thus the great advances in communication and information technologies over the past decades have generally resulted in an increase of centralized, conservative control. The rise of easy, accessible global communications (post, phone, fax, e-mail, and the like) has greatly increased the ability of local conservative activists to petition Rome to address the perceived heterodoxy of their local bishop and to stop innovations. It has not significantly increased the ability of average Catholics to communicate their insights, concerns, and frustrations to church leaders or to communicate among themselves. These existing communications infrastructures could be an enormous asset if they were used to provide a way of propagating, sharing, and deepening the discourse within the church. A new understanding and a new ethos of communication are needed in the church that will attend to the new issues that are emerging as a result of consumer culture and globalization. The stability and robustness of local communities can no longer be taken for granted. Extant communications channels should be reoriented toward supporting and disseminating the reflections, questions, struggles, and innovations of the local community.

Most American dioceses have their own newspapers. With a shift in ethos, these could be transformed into the infrastructure for a more substantial local ecclesial culture, just as small community newspapers serve as the foundation for civic culture. While it is understandable and important that bishops use them as channels to communicate with and instruct the laity, this tends to hinder their function as papers. Despite frequent claims of editorial independence, most of these media currently function suspiciously like "company" papers. The featured columnists remain clerical and conservative. "Ask Father X" columns are common (and valuable for providing commentary on the theological and cultural minutiae of Catholicism). The fact that the preponderance of columnists are conservative is not a problem in itself, but it suggests that critical or dissenting perspectives may seldom appear in official diocesan media. This is unfortunate, because there is still much to be discussed and reflected upon beyond the neuralgic (and dogmatically peripheral) points that divide the Catholic Church. The editorial narrowness of these papers symbolizes a much deeper unwillingness or lack of concern to foster and support dialogue within the Catholic community.

In addition to making better use of its existing media infrastructures, Catholicism sorely needs new structures of communication on the local level. However careful we need to be to avoid romanticizing the neighborhoods and extended families of immigrant Catholicism, it is clear that the contemporary Roman Catholic parish stands isolated without communal connections to broader society to a much greater degree than it did in the past. It is located in a very different geography, where connections with the daily life of the congregation are not easily made. The church needs places where the community can argue and think through contemporary problems. A place where people can "think" Catholic with others in facing the issues of the day. No doubt people currently bring their faith to bear in their responses to the ethical, cultural, and political issues they face, but they do so in an isolated manner, with few opportunities for drawing from the wisdom of others. The individualism of this decision making is encouraged by the lack of a cultural space in which to publicly practice such analysis and application. Whatever the many strengths of the guidance provided in these matters by professional intellectuals, Catholic journals of opinion, and bishops, without a place to practice such discernment and decision making, the model of the passive religious consumer will continue to dominate.

The issue of communication and popular religious production goes beyond discursive issues of doctrine and decision making. Religious traditions are also a matter of imagination and ritual, of devotional and lifestyle practices. On a level that still concerns the dissemination of discrete objects, we must consider less-didactic forms of cultural production, such as music, poetry, art, and devotional writing. Local churches and dioceses could encourage and support popular agency by providing venues for the sharing, performing, and displaying of such creative works. This could provide a way around the ideological impasse that currently limits the range of what is published in diocesan newspapers.

The appointments of church worship and community space provide another locus for the exercise of popular agency. Art, sculpture, liturgical linens, vestments, banners, even liturgical furnishings have long provided a place for artistic expression in the church, and they continue to provide the possibility for members of the local community to function as creative agents within their communities. Indeed, church art has long been one of the few ways in which the laity could contribute to the public expression of the church. The decoration of church interiors, how-ever, has in recent centuries become a mass-produced affair—from the poly-chrome plaster statuary of the St. Sulpice district in Paris and Barclay Street in New York, which dominated church interiors from the nineteenth century through the first half of the twentieth, to the subdued earth tones of the staid modernist/neo-Gothic cast-polyester resin statues that have replaced them in the past half century.[61] Whatever the artistic merits or theological vitality of either, mass-produced art in church interiors reinforces the passivity of the community by confirming the clerical pattern of limiting expression to elites. There is, of course, the problem of the quality of the work of local artists. Indeed, much of it might be at best second- or third-rate—like many homilies, much pastoral lead-ership, and, yes, theology. This is a plea for bad art. It is worth asking why this is such a pressing concern, in contrast to the quality of liturgy or preaching. Few of us, whether artists, theologians, priests, or bishops, produce masterworks, and most of us must accept the fact that we will achieve second-rate status at best. That this is more easily accepted in homilies than in art suggests that the decoration of church interiors is heavily influenced by the logic of conspicuous display. Con-temporary church art functions analogously to the interior decoration of the single-family home, as a display of the community's good taste. For that reason it is a rich location in which to challenge such a passive understanding of decora-tion, by making it a place where the community actively expresses its own appro-priation and articulation of its traditional symbols.

CONCLUSION

This chapter has proposed a tactical response to the problems posed by consumer culture. These tactics involve both supporting popular religious responses and learned consideration of the key points where the commodification of culture affects a religious tradition in order to plan a response. As the opening quotation from de Certeau suggests, there is no guarantee that such tactics will work. We must not confuse the resolution of a scholarly thesis with success in cultural politics. Tactics for reembedding must swim against a massive cultural tide of commodification. Even though Roman Catholicism possesses very robust institu-tional structures and communication networks, these are dwarfed in size and scope by the corporate culture industries. Tactics are indeed the art of the weak.

The program of deepening agency likewise faces very serious hurdles. The emergence of a literate laity is an epochal shift for Roman Catholicism, as the var-ious initiatives, failures, renewals, and reversals over the past century make clear. It requires a radical redefinition of the identity of the clergy, the hierarchy, and the laity. It is one thing to censor and stifle an intransigent popular religiosity among the laity; it is quite another to form the laity in the dogmatic, liturgical, and spir-itual depths of the Catholic tradition. In light of the difficulty of the shift, it is understandable that the hierarchy would be inclined to turn to the global south, where (for the time being) a more traditional division of communal agency is still tenable. I have argued that a clerical response to consumer culture is bound to fail because it replicates the very passive reception that is problematic in consumer culture. If a cleric-centered response is bound to fail, that does not mean that a lay-centered one will necessarily succeed. Although the church is composed of the most educated laity in its history, for a variety of reasons the church has not kept pace with the explosion of literacy. People are more learned than ever, but this increase in knowledge has largely come from secular sources. Filling this gap will be difficult but certainly not impossible. All sectors of the advanced capitalist societies are highly educated and capable of understanding complex knowledge. Theologians who teach undergraduates have much to offer here, as they spend a significant amount of their careers considering what can be taught to intelligent nonspecialists (students in introductory courses have only high school degrees). Catholicism desperately needs adult education on a scale that is daunting.

Beyond the difficulty of bringing the laity up to speed in theological literacy, there lies another hindrance for the tactic of deepening agency. It is not clear that the majority of believers are particularly interested in taking an active role in their religious communities. While clericalism benefits from lay passivity, it is not its only cause. Many believers are quite content with a form of religious practice that combines consumerism and professional middle-class sensibilities. This sees the priest as the religious expert who provides professional services to his clients. As long as he is reasonably competent, or at least kind and innocuous, they are happy to leave knowledge and stewardship of the tradition to him. They have their own professional competences (not necessarily white collar) and see themselves not as agents of the Christian tradition but as members of a community whose passivity approximates that of consumers of professional services. Clerical malfeasance on the scale that has rocked the Roman Catholic Church in America over the past two years will bring calls for reform. But in the absence of such glaring problems, people are happy to return to the passive status quo.

The tactics proposed in this chapter, which work on both the individual and the communal level, although they are of a more concrete and practical nature than theology is accustomed to considering, are a necessary component of any contemporary theological method or theological hermeneutics. Just as patristic hermeneutics embraced ascetic issues of self-transformation and the authority of the hierarchy, so contemporary hermeneutics can make room for meditative practices that fight the tide of commodification and for considerations of how the church can best employ its systems of communication to preserve its heritage in the cultural maelstrom of advanced capitalism.

Conclusion

CONSUMER CULTURE IS A PROFOUND PROBLEM FOR CONTEMPORARY religious belief and practice. Beyond the excesses of consumerism lie cultural dynamisms that incline people to engage religious beliefs as if they were consumer commodities. Framing the problem in this way provided a way to get beyond moralizing condemnations of selfish materialism and criticisms of the narcissism of consumer spirituality. Although the world has plenty of selfish narcissists, the real problem with consumer culture lies in the structures and practices that systematically confuse and misdirect well-intentioned people seeking to do good things such as show solidarity with others, find spiritual transformation, and practice their sincerely held religious beliefs. We have catalogued a host of such structures: alienated labor, the single-family home, post-Fordist marketing structures, corporate popular culture, and more. We can summarize the problem by considering two central structures and practices: the substitution of consumption for traditional religious practices, and the distribution of elements of religious traditions in commodified form.

When consumption becomes the dominant cultural practice, belief is systematically misdirected from traditional religious practices into consumption. This makes the moment of choice the fundamental means of self-actualization, implicitly presuming that the object being chosen, whether a banal commodity or a profound spiritual tradition, will in itself resolve all of the difficulties the consumer faces. Traditional practices of self-transformation are subordinated to consumer choice. This results in a divorce between belief and practice, as people sincerely and mistakenly assume that they are acting on the beliefs they are choosing.

When members of consumer cultures sincerely embrace religious traditions, they encounter them in a fragmented, commodified form. Beliefs, symbols, and even practices come abstracted from their connections to one another. They are therefore less likely to bring with them the strange logics and desires of their traditions that might draw believers' lives away from conformity with the status quo. Thus, religious belief is always in danger of being reduced to a decorative veneer of meaning over the vacuousness of everyday life in advanced capitalist societies.

Yet consumer culture brings opportunities as well. It accompanies and facilitates a great explosion of cultural agency. The doors of the archives of traditions have been opened to the masses. People have more access to cultural material than ever and more people are able to engage it creatively and produce their own. In addition to this, people accomplish important social and political tasks through consumption and display. This positive aspect of consumer culture provides the possibility for the tactic of deepening agency. We need not retreat to monasteries to ride out the new dark ages while the barbarians wreak bricolage. The path lies forward, through this explosion of agency, by embracing and forming it.

This book offers three lessons for theology, not all of which are necessarily new. If it is to respond to the challenges posed by consumer culture, theology must attend to the structures and practices that connect belief to daily life, attend to the lived, everyday theology of believing communities, and adopt the task of helping communities preserve and sustain their traditions in the face of the erosions of globalizing capitalism.

Theology must consider the structures and practices through which religious belief is insinuated into daily life. This requires a level of attention to cultural processes to which theology is unaccustomed. As we argued in chapter 7, if theological hermeneutics is going to address the relation between interpretation and the practice of daily life, it must pay much closer attention to the secular practices that inform our general attitudes toward culture as well as specifically ecclesial practices and structures of communication.

In the introduction, I noted that this book would not offer a thick theological narrative in order to focus on the habits of interpretation with which contemporary believers receive such narratives. This book has outlined the obstacles theology faces in sharing its discourse and has suggested some tactics for overcoming these problems. The Christian tradition does indeed have many rich resources for alternative forms of life. Hopefully, the tactics suggested in the last chapter can help those be presented in a way that is more likely to resist their assimilation to consumerist religion. Such retrievals and learned applications are primordial in theology, and they will certainly always have their place.

At the end of this work, however, I find myself asking other questions. In order to address the status of popular religion in consumer culture, I drew from Latino theology, Orsi's social history, and discussions of lived religion. These methods of valuing popular agency contributed to our consideration of tactics. The interface between belief and practice in a consumer culture is being worked out by countless believers. Theology needs more detailed knowledge of what is happening on this level. To give but one example, the Eucharist places a form of consumption at the center of Roman Catholic sacramental practice. How does this affect Catholic believers' understanding and practice of other consumption? How is it influenced by a culture where consumption is such a dominant practice? Our comfort with consciousness- and performance-enhancing substances from caffeine to Prozac resonates well with the overdetermined nature of consumption discussed in chapter 4. What similarities and differences do believers see between such consumption and their reception of the Eucharist? It is easy enough to argue that consumer practices are debased parodies of, or deficient alternatives to, traditional religious

practices. As is generally the case with such contrasts between religion and consumer culture, however, such evaluative distinctions are much less helpful than
they are obvious. Questions remain: What similarities and distinctions function
in the lived religious practices of believers in consumer culture? How is the
Eucharist affected by consumption? Does the Eucharist affect the way people consume in any way?

These sorts of questions are very difficult to answer. They require methods
beyond the training of most theologians, and the subtleties involved make them
resistant to quantitative social-science methods.[1] Cultural studies approaches
address such difficulties by readings texts or works of art as proxies for popular
belief and practice. These provide alternative entries to the issue, but they are still
engaging the work of elites (although not academics) who can be easily cited in
footnotes. The problem calls for something akin to the immersive methods of
ethnography, whereby the anthropologist spends extended time with members of
a culture, attending to the implicit logics of their practices and the texture of their
daily lives. The idea of theologians' being immersed in and listening to the believing community is not new. It requires not only listening to the community for the
questions that theology can answer, but, as Schillebeeckx, Schreiter, and Tanner
have argued, attending to the constructive theological moves already being taken
in the everyday theology of the believing community. If the tactic of deepening
religious agency is to be embraced, theology will have to develop its skills and
methods for attending to the lived religion of believing communities.

Consumer culture presents another new (but likewise not unprecedented)
problem for theology and the church. Our analysis has shown that the danger of
cultural erosion in globalizing capitalism is not something faced only by fragile,
dominated cultures; it also endangers the Western traditions at the heart of the
societies that have originated and profit from globalization. Thus, many of the
concerns of theologies of mission and inculturation are now relevant to first-
world cultures. In this light, the particularities of religious traditions—communities, cultures, institutions—which a generation ago were taken for granted or
glossed over by transcendental methods take on grave importance as the infrastructures through which belief is mediated and sustained. Their stability and
indeed existence can no longer be taken for granted. Thus, I would place myself
somewhere in the middle of the debate between Jeffrey Stout and Alasdair
MacIntyre.[2] With Stout I call for attention to and respect for the wisdom and vitality of popular bricolage. With MacIntyre I note the importance of robust cultural
traditions to fund cultural agency.

This book has attempted soberly to chart the perils posed by consumer culture
for religious belief and practice and to suggest tactics for addressing them. The
previous chapter noted the particular factors in Roman Catholicism that hinder a
tactical response. The most fundamental obstacle, however, is the ambiguous
nature of consumer culture itself. It is a decidedly soft target. It maintains no
gulags and deploys no death squads (although it accepts both outside of its

charmed circle). It works by seduction. Critiquing consumption is a hard enough sell, although many members of advanced capitalist societies are frustrated with the endless spiral of consumption and work that grips their lives. The commodification of culture is even harder to argue as a problem to organize opposition against. While it is easy enough to evoke outrage at the cultural appropriations of pop music artists, it is much more difficult to criticize the numerous ways in which we do similar things in our daily lives. Consumer culture is experienced by most people as a liberation. It liberates them from the constraints of closed cultures, small communities, and tightly scripted class, gender, and social roles. It liberates them from the inevitable limitations of local authorities such as parents, teachers, pastors, bishops, and even spouses, friends, and fellow parishioners. A trip to Barnes & Noble or the Internet brings myriad options and imaginative opportunities that compensate for the inevitable and—this must not be understated—sometimes very serious burdens of a finite, located human existence. Arguing against that is tough going indeed.

This book has shown the downside of consumer culture: a situation where culture is deprived of political friction, where each individual is free to pursue his or her own religious synthesis, whether ingenious and inspired, or banal and conforming—but all of these are imprisoned in the private realm of individual insight, while globalizing capitalism goes about its business unopposed. This aspect of consumer culture must be brought into ecclesial and public discourse to balance the very legitimate attractions of consumer culture. Rhetoric in this regard must be thoroughly dialectical. One-sided criticisms of consumerist religious narcissism engender only resentment. As I have lectured on this material in churches and universities, taught it to undergraduates and shared chapters with colleagues, I have found that criticisms such as those of spirituality offered in chapter 3 engender very emotional opposition, no matter how many caveats are attached. When they are presented in concert with an appreciation of popular religious agency as well as the problem of the domestic captivity of religious belief in consumer culture, however, people are more inclined to consider the problem (even college students deeply suspicious of authority). When the problems of consumer culture are presented dialectically, as a moment of both great opportunity and risk, of potential grace and evil, people are more willing to consider making sacrifices to combat these problems. In this book, I have offered such a dialectical account. It is my hope that it will help call attention to the problems posed by consumer culture and inspire a response to them.

Notes

INTRODUCTION

1. Robert Bocock, *Consumption* (New York: Routledge, 1993), 118.

2. Frank Koller, "Pop Group Enigma's Use of Taiwan Folk Song Stirs Debate," *All Things Considered*, National Public Radio (June 11, 1996). For a press release concerning the lawsuit, see http://www.taiwanfirstnations.org/Difang.htm, accessed June 4, 2003.

3. Thomas Frank, "Advertising as Cultural Criticism: Bill Bernbach versus the Mass Society," in *The Consumer Society Reader*, ed. Juliet B. Schor and Douglas B. Holt (New York: New Press, 2000), 375–95.

CHAPTER 1
HOW TO THINK ABOUT CONSUMER CULTURE

1. See John Kavanaugh, *Following Christ in a Consumer Society: The Spirituality of Cultural Resistance,* rev. ed. (Maryknoll, N.Y.: Orbis, 1991). Michael Budde's valuable work deserves mention here. In *The (Magic) Kingdom of God: Christianity and the Global Culture Industries* (Boulder, Colo.: Westview Press, 1997), he offers an extended structural account of the influence of the culture industries on Christian faith and practice. He consistently places emphasis, however, on the narrative and value content of corporate mass culture. Thus, while his analysis is similar to the one I offer in this book, his conclusions are more akin to those of the value critique of consumerism I am seeking to supplement. I regret that Budde's most recent work, *Christianity Incorporated: How Big Business Is Buying the Church* (Grand Rapids: Brazos Press, 2002), coauthored with Robert Brimlow, appeared too late for me to engage here.

2. "Message of His Holiness Pope John Paul II for the Celebration of the World Day of Peace" (January 1, 1999), #2. Available at www.vatican.va.

3. Philip P. Pan, "Worked Till They Drop: Few Protections for China's New Laborers," *The Washington Post*, May 13, 2002, A9.

4. John Paul II, *Centesimus Annus* (Washington, D.C.: United States Catholic Conference, 1991), #36.

5. Craig Gay, "Sensualists without Heart: Contemporary Consumerism in Light of the Modern Project," in *The Consuming Passion: Christianity and the Consumer Culture*, ed. Rodney Clapp (Downers Grove, Ill.: InterVarsity Press, 1998), 19-39.

6. Graham Ward, *Cities of God* (New York: Routledge, 2000). D. Stephen Long, *Divine*

Economy: Theology and the Market (New York: Routledge, 2000). Chapter 4 below will consider the work of these authors in greater detail.

7. The example of Morris is valuable because of its provocative ambiguity. His combination of prophetic denunciation of the destructiveness of industrial capitalism with romantic retrievals of medieval craft traditions and aesthetic sensuality render him perennially attractive to Catholics with countercultural convictions. Nevertheless, as the biographer Fiona MacCarthy notes, Morris the proprietor never managed to operate his own factories according to his ideals (e.g., his influential essay "A Factory as It Might Be"). See *William Morris: A Life for Our Time* (London: Faber & Faber, 1994), xviii. Such a criticism is easy enough to level against any visionary actively involved with the world, let alone a person of such prodigious activity as Morris. It retains force insofar as his establishment customers continued to find both his products and nostalgic romanticism desirable even if they despised his partisan politics.

8. "Bullsh*t on Parade: Rage against the Machine and Michael Moore Battle New York," *Spin* (May 2000): 56.

9. Clifford Geertz, "Thick Description: Toward an Interpretive Theory of Culture," in *The Interpretation of Cultures: Selected Essays* (New York: Basic Books, 1973), 5.

10. Geertz, "Religion as Cultural System," in *Interpretation of Cultures,* 89.

11. Ibid., 95.

12. Talal Asad, "Anthropological Conceptions of Religion: Reflections on Geertz," *Man* 18, no. 2 (1983): 245.

13. Ibid., 255 n. 2.

14. Ibid., 245.

15. Ibid., 242.

16. Michel Foucault, *Discipline and Punish: The Birth of the Prison* (New York: Vintage, 1979) and *The History of Sexuality* (New York: Vintage, 1980).

17. This is in contrast to Alasdair MacIntyre's teleological notion of social practices "as coherent, complex" forms of "socially established human activity" oriented toward their own internal goods (*After Virtue*, 2nd ed. [South Bend, Ind.: University of Notre Dame Press, 1984], 187). Consumption is not a practice in MacIntyre's sense. In fact, it is a textbook case of the opposite, because it is incorrectly and instrumentally oriented to goods outside itself (e.g., we buy a sports car to display our youth and virility.)

18. Foucault noted, "when I read . . . the thesis, 'Knowledge is power,' or 'Power is knowledge,' I begin to laugh, since studying their *relation* is precisely my problem. If they were identical, I would not have to study them and I would be spared a lot of fatigue as a result. The very fact that I pose the question of their relation proves clearly that I do not *identify* them" ("Critical Theory/Intellectual History," in *Politics, Philosophy, Culture*, ed. Lawrence D. Kritzman [New York: Routledge, 1988], 43).

19. Kathryn Tanner, *Theories of Culture: A New Agenda for Theology* (Minneapolis: Fortress Press, 1997), 47.

20. Robert Schreiter uses the terms "integrated" and "globalized" concepts of culture in *The New Catholicity: Theology between the Global and the Local* (Maryknoll, N.Y.: Orbis, 1997), 46ff. He borrows the first term from Margaret Archer, *Culture and Agency: The Place of Culture in Social Theory* (Cambridge: Cambridge University Press, 1989).

21. Daniel Cottem, *Text and Culture* (Minneapolis: University of Minnesota Press, 1989), 36; quoted in Tanner, *Theories of Culture,* 47.

22. Tanner, *Theories of Culture,* 61.

23. Ibid., 74, 76.

24. Francis Schüssler Fiorenza, "Pluralism: A Western Commodity or Justice for the Other?" in *Ethical Monotheism Past and Present: Essays in Honor of Wendell S. Dietrich*, ed. Theodore Vial and Mark Hadley, Brown Judaic Studies 329 (Providence, R.I.: Brown Judaic Studies, 2001), 298–99.

25. Tanner, *Theories of Culture*, 113.

26. Ibid., 116.

27. Wendy Griswold, *Cultures and Societies in a Changing World* (Thousand Oaks, Calif.: Pine Forge Press, 1994), 11.

28. Mike Featherstone, *Consumer Culture and Postmodernism* (London: Sage, 1991), 119.

29. John Milbank, *Theology and Social Theory: Beyond Secular Reason* (Oxford: Blackwell, 1990).

CHAPTER 2
THE COMMODIFICATION OF CULTURE

1. Robert Bocock, *Consumption* (New York: Routledge, 1993), 35.

2. Ibid., 44–49.

3. Karl Marx, *Economic and Philosophic Manuscripts of 1844*, in *The Marx-Engels Reader*, ed. Robert C. Tucker (New York: Norton, 1972), 60.

4. Ibid., 62, 63.

5. Sut Jhally, *The Codes of Advertising: Fetishism and the Political Economy of Meaning in the Consumer Society* (New York: St. Martin's Press, 1987), 26.

6. Marx, *Capital*, in *Marx-Engels Reader*, 215.

7. Marx's assumptions concerning the obviousness of use value have received much criticism. See Susan Willis, *A Primer for Daily Life* (London: Routledge, 1991), 1–23.

8. Jhally, *Codes of Advertising*, 28.

9. Marx, *Capital*, 216.

10. Ibid., 217.

11. Jhally, *Codes of Advertising*, 29.

12. See Guy Debord, *The Society of the Spectacle* (1967; repr., New York: Zone Books, 1994). This insight was utilized in *Gaudium et Spes* §35 (see *Vatican Council II: The Conciliar and Post-Conciliar Documents*, ed. Austin Flannery [Northport, N.Y.: Costello, 1979]) and was reiterated by Paul VI in *Populorum Progressio* §14 (Washington, D.C.: United States Catholic Conference, 1967). John Paul II has employed it repeatedly; see, e.g, *Redemptoris Hominis* (Washington, D.C.: United States Catholic Conference, 1979), §16; *Sollicitudo Rei Socialis* (Washington, D.C.: United States Catholic Conference, 1987), §28; *Centesimus Annus* (Washington, D.C.: United States Catholic Conference, 1991), §36.

13. Marx, *Capital*, 217.

14. Ibid.

15. Dean Hoge et al., *Young Adult Catholics: Religion in the Culture of Choice* (Notre Dame, Ind.: University of Notre Dame Press, 2001), 156.

16. Aglietta is a member of the "regulationist" school. The regulationists view the development of capitalism as a series of dynamic equilibriums. From time to time, the chaos of the market settles into a relatively stable state. These periods of equilibrium depend on a

variety of macroeconomic factors, which the regulationists term a "regime of accumulation." These involve questions of labor, standards of exchange, the relationship between segments of the economy, the distribution of wages, profits, taxes, and so on. Equilibria are also sustained by a given "mode of regulation," which includes the system of law, government regulation and cultural factors. See Ash Amin, "Post-Fordism: Models, Fantasies and Phantoms of Transition," in *Post-Fordism: A Reader*, ed. Ash Amin (Oxford: Blackwell, 1993), 8.

17. Taylor published his proposals in *Shop Management* and *Principles of Scientific Management* (bound together [with separate pagination] in Frederick Winslow Taylor, *Scientific Management* [New York: Harper & Row, 1947]).

18. Harry Braverman, *Labor and Monopoly Capital: The Degradation of Work in the Twentieth Century* (New York: Monthly Review Press, 1975), 91–98. See Taylor's own frank account in *Taylor's Testimony before the Special House Committee* in *Scientific Management*, 79–85.

19. Taylor, *Shop Management*, 98.

20. Taylor, *Principles of Scientific Management*, 36.

21. Braverman, *Labor and Monopoly Capital*, 134.

22. See, for example, Braverman's review of the literature concerning the development of the steam engine as the work of craftsmen/mechanics, and argument about how little contemporary scientific theory could contribute to that process (ibid., 155–58).

23. Ibid., 133.

24. Taylor, *Principles of Scientific Management*, 60–61.

25. Ibid., 43–44.

26. Alfred Dupont Chandler, *Giant Enterprise: Ford, General Motors and the Automobile Industry* (1964), 29, as quoted in Stuart Ewen, *Captains of Consciousness: Advertising and the Social Roots of the Consumer Culture* (New York: McGraw-Hill, 1976), 23.

27. Ewen, *Captains of Consciousness*, 226.

28. Simon Nelson Patten, *The New Basis of Civilization* (1907; repr., Cambridge, Mass.: John Harvard Library, 1968), 215. As quoted in T. J. Jackson Lears, *No Place of Grace: Antimodernism and the Transformation of American Culture, 1880–1920* (New York: Pantheon, 1981), 54.

29. Raymond Williams, *Keywords: A Vocabulary of Culture and Society* (New York: Oxford University Press, 1976), 68–70; Don Slater, *Consumer Culture and Modernity* (London: Polity Press, 1997), 174–83.

30. Michel Aglietta, *A Theory of Capitalist Regulation: The U. S. Experience* (London: NLB, 1979), 159–60.

31. Martyn J. Lee, *Consumer Culture Reborn: The Cultural Politics of Consumption* (New York: Routledge, 1993), 89.

32. For a discussion of the political factors, see chapter 8 of Gary Cross, *Time and Money: The Making of Consumer Culture* (New York: Routledge, 1993); and Mike Davis, *Prisoners of the American Dream* (London: Verso, 1986).

33. E. P. Thompson, "Time, Work-Discipline, and Industrial Capitalism," *Past and Present* 38 (December 1967): 97; as quoted in Ewen, *Captains of Consciousness*, 8.

34. Ewen, *Captains of Consciousness,* 58.

35. *Ladies Home Journal* (April 1920), as quoted in Ewen, *Captains of Consciousness*, 38.

36. Ewen, *Captains of Consciousness*, 47.

37. E. Rothschild, *Paradise Lost: The Decline of the Auto-Industrial Age* (London: Allen Lane, 1973), as quoted in Slater, *Consumer Culture and Modernity*, 192.

38. Slater, *Consumer Culture and Modernity*, 192.

39. See Elaine Hochman's discussion in "From Geist to Gadgets: The Bauhaus Attempts to Change," in *Bauhaus: Crucible of Modernism* (New York: Fromm International, 1997), 131–51.

40. Lee, *Consumer Culture Reborn*, 95.

41. Ewen, *Captains of Consciousness*, 107.

42. James M. Alexander, "Raymond Loewy," in *Contemporary Designers*, ed. Colin Naylor (London: St. James Press, 1990), 343.

43. Aglietta, *Theory of Capitalist Regulation*, 159.

44. Albert Borgmann, *Technology and the Character of Contemporary Life* (Chicago: University of Chicago Press, 1984), 40–48.

45. Ibid., 117–18.

46. Lee, *Consumer Culture Reborn*, 91–92; Betty Friedan, *The Feminine Mystique* (New York: W. W. Norton, 1963), 206–32.

47. Mary McClintock Fulkerson, *Changing the Subject: Women's Discourses and Feminist Theology* (Minneapolis: Fortress Press, 1994), 200–206, quotation from 205.

48. Bocock, *Consumption*, 89–112.

49. Juliet Schor, *The Overspent American: Upscaling, Downshifting, and the New Consumer* (New York: Basic Books, 1998), 43–63.

50. Mark Massa, *Catholics and American Culture: Fulton Sheen, Dorothy Day, and the Notre Dame Football Team* (New York: Crossroad, 1999), 227.

51. Zygmunt Bauman, *Intimations of Postmodernity* (New York: Routledge, 1992), 49.

52. Henri Lefebvre, *Everyday Life in the Modern World* (New Brunswick: Transaction Books, 1984), 40, 42.

53. Ibid., 38.

54. *Communist Manifesto*, in *Marx-Engels Reader*, 338.

55. Lefebvre, *Everyday Life in the Modern World*, 38.

56. Ibid., 29.

57. Georg Simmel, *The Philosophy of Money* (London: Routledge & Kegan Paul, 1978), as quoted in Mike Featherstone, *Postmodernism and Consumer Culture* (London: Sage, 1991), 26.

58. Lefebvre, *Everyday Life in the Modern World*, 90.

59. Ibid., 105.

60. Ibid., 91.

61. Ibid., 39.

62. Peter Marshall, *Demanding the Impossible: A History of Anarchism* (London: Fontana Press, 1992), 550.

63. "The first phase of the domination of the economy over social life brought into the definition of all human realization the obvious degradation of *being* into *having*. The present phase of total occupation of social life by the accumulated results of the economy leads to generalized sliding of *having* into *appearing*" (Guy Debord, *The Society of the Spectacle* [New York: Zone Books, 1994], #17; also available online at www.nothingness.org/SI).

64. Ibid., #12, #1.

65. Steven Best, "The Commodification of Reality and the Reality of Commodification:

Baudrillard, Debord and Postmodern Theory," in *Baudrillard: A Critical Reader,* ed. Douglas Kellner (Oxford: Blackwell, 1994), 47.

66. Debord, *Society of the Spectacle,* ##4, 42, 34, 36.

67. Sadie Plant, *The Most Radical Gesture: The Situationist International in a Postmodern Age* (London: Routledge, 1992), 12.

68. Ibid., 13.

69. Debord, *Society of the Spectacle,* #44.

70. Guy Debord, "Methods of Detournement," http://library.nothingness.org/articles/SI/en/display/3, accessed January 12, 2003. Originally published in *Les Lèvres Nues* 8 (May 1956).

71. Best, "Commodification of Reality," 60.

72. Douglas Kellner, *Jean Baudrillard: From Marxism to Postmodernism and Beyond* (Stanford: Stanford University Press, 1989), 24–25.

73. Baudrillard, *For a Critique of the Political Economy of the Sign,* 185.

74. Kellner, *Jean Baudrillard,* 68.

75. Jean Baudrillard, *The Gulf War Did Not Take Place* (Bloomington: Indiana University Press, 1995).

76. Christopher Norris, *Uncritical Theory: Postmodernism, Intellectuals & the Gulf War* (Amherst: University of Massachusetts Press, 1992).

77. Kellner, *Jean Baudrillard,* 74.

78. Fredric Jameson, *Postmodernism, or, the Cultural Logic of Late Capitalism* (Durham, N.C.: Duke University Press, 1997), 47.

79. Ibid., 398, 387.

80. Ibid., 8–9.

81. Ibid., 9.

82. Ibid., 17.

83. Ibid., 19; idem, "Postmodernism and Consumer Society," in *The Anti-Aesthetic: Essays on Postmodern Culture,* ed. Hal Foster (Seattle: Bay Press, 1983), 117.

84. Jameson, *Postmodernism,* xvii.

85. Ibid., 317.

86. Ibid., 26.

87. Ibid., 27.

88. Terry Eagleton, "Capitalism, Modernism and Postmodernism," *New Left Review* 152 (July/August 1985): 71.

89. Lee, *Consumer Culture Reborn,* 101–4.

90. Ash Amin, "Post-Fordism: Models, Fantasies and Phantoms of Transition," in *Post-Fordism: A Reader,* ed. Ash Amin (Oxford: Blackwell, 1993), 1–39.

91. See Michael Storper, "The Transition to Flexible Specialization in the US Film Industry: External Economies, the Division of Labour and the Crossing of Industrial Divides," in *Post-Fordism,* ed. Amin, 195–226.

92. It must be noted that these changes in labor management in the advanced capitalist countries do not lessen the global economy's reliance on alienated, industrial labor. This outsourcing to the third world or "peripheral Fordism" depends on a "primitive capitalism" that lacks the labor rights of Fordism. It should also be noted that some industries, especially the growing service sector, have only recently begun their Fordist phases. For example, the fast food industry continues to flourish using the most draconian of Taylorian management practices (Lee, *Consumer Culture Reborn,* 117).

93. Brett Williams, *Upscaling Downtown: Stalled Gentrification in Washington, D.C.* (Ithaca, N.Y.: Cornell University Press, 1988), quoted in Susan Christopherson, "The Fortress City: Privatized Spaces, Consumer Citizenship," in *Post-Fordism*, ed. Amin, 414–15.

94. Lee, *Consumer Culture Reborn*, 135.

95. Wade Clark Roof, *Spiritual Marketplace: Baby Boomers and the Remaking of American Religion* (Princeton: Princeton University Press, 1999), 67.

CHAPTER 3
CONSUMER RELIGION

1. Moby, "Natural Blues," *Play*, V2 Records, 1999. Printed on the back of the CD case: "Warning: Unauthorized reproduction of this recording is prohibited by federal law and is subject to criminal prosecution." Hall and other singers sampled by Moby can be found on *Sounds of the South*, Atlantic, 1961. The Lomax family, currently attempting to locate heirs of the various artists, disputes that it has been reimbursed for the use of the material from the album, which in addition to the royalties on album sales, also includes payments for use of the song in national ad campaigns. See Richard Leiby, "For Blues Artists, A Sad Refrain: Forgotten Musicians Reap Nothing from Platinum Sampler of Their Songs," *The Washington Post*, August 9, 2000, C1.

2. Richard Harrington, "Moby *Songs: 1993-1998* Elektra," *The Washington Post*, October 27, 2000, N14.

3. Katherine Bergeron, "The Virtual Sacred," *New Republic* 212, no. 9, February 7, 1995, 29–34. Note, as well, Bergeron's observation that it is likely that many purchasers never actually played the album.

4. Tom Beaudoin, *Virtual Faith: The Irreverent Spiritual Quest of Generation X* (San Francisco: Jossey-Bass, 1998), 39.

5. Ellie Weinert, "'Sadeness' Creator Settles Sample Suit," *Billboard* 14 (September 1991).

6. Bergeron, "Virtual Sacred," 32.

7. Don DeLillo, *Underworld* (New York: Scribner, 1997), 86–89.

8. "At the Family Worship Center, the music belonged to the people. But there was barely a whisper of a difference between it and that devil's music played by Jimmy's cousins Jerry Lee Lewis and country crooner Mickey Gilley" (Ann Rowe Seaman, *Swaggart: The Unauthorized Biography of an American Evangelist* [New York: Continuum, 1999], 16).

9. David Lyon, *Jesus in Disneyland: Religion in Postmodern Times* (Cambridge: Polity Press, 200), 49.

10. Andrew Greeley, "Like a Catholic: Madonna's Challenge to Her Church," *America* 160, no. 18, May 13, 1989, 447–50.

11. Scott Cohen, "Madonna," *Penthouse*, August 1985; quoted in Mark Bego, *Madonna: Blond Ambition* (New York: Harmony Books, 1992), 106.

12. An essay by Christopher Kiesling on Sunday rest offers an example of the reflex association of sacramentality and consumption. Seeking a positive portrayal of Sunday shopping, he associated it with the paschal mystery celebrated in the Sunday liturgy: "[M]ay not a leisurely shopping tour be . . . a way of celebrating [a] share in Christ's victory over the difficulties of human existence?" ("Sunday Rest: A New Approach," *Homiletic and Pastoral*

Review 68 [October 1967]: 23–29; 68 [November 1967]: 113–21, quotation from 120–21). I thank Sandra Yocum-Mize for the reference.

13. William L. Portier, "In Defense of Mt. Saint Mary's: They are Evangelical, Not Conservative," *Commonweal* 127, no. 3, February 11, 2000, 31–33. We will consider such tactical uses of tradition in chapter 5.

14. R. Laurence Moore, *Selling God: American Religion in the Marketplace of Culture* (New York: Oxford University Press, 1994), 234–35.

15. The executive producer is an evangelical Christian and attempts to craft an explicitly Christian message in each episode. If viewers are "not hearing the name of Jesus they are hearing the truth of Jesus" (Becky Garrison, "Prime Time Faith: Q&A with Martha Williamson," *Clarity* 2, no. 5 [April/May 2000]: 28).

16. Wade Clark Roof, *Spiritual Marketplace: Baby Boomers and the Remaking of American Religion* (Princeton, N.J.: Princeton University Press, 1999), 95.

17. Neil Gaiman, *American Gods* (New York: William Morrow, 2001), 243.

18. Eugene McCarraher, *Christian Critics: Religion and the Impasse in Modern American Social Thought* (Ithaca, N.Y.: Cornell University Press, 2000), 144. The description could not be as easily applied to Karl Rahner's Catholic theology.

19. John D. Caputo, *The Prayers and Tears of Jacques Derrida* (Bloomington: Indiana University Press, 1997); idem, *On Religion* (London: Routledge, 2001).

20. Francis Schüssler Fiorenza, "Pluralism: A Western Commodity or Justice for the Other?" in *Ethical Monotheism Past and Present: Essays in Honor of Wendell S. Dietrich*, ed. Theodore Vial and Mark Hadley (Providence, R.I.: Brown Judaic Studies, 2001), 278.

21. William Dinges, "American Catholics and the Joseph Campbell Phenomenon," *America* 168, no. 6, February 20, 1993, 14.

22. McCarraher, *Christian Critics*, 145.

23. Dinges, "American Catholics and the Joseph Campbell Phenomenon," 19.

24. Paul Heelas, "The Limits of Consumption and the Post-modern Religion of the New Age," in *The Authority of the Consumer*. ed. Russell Keat, Nigel Whiteley, and Nicholas Abercrombie (London: Routledge, 1994), 112.

25. Philip Rieff, *The Triumph of the Therapeutic: Uses of Faith after Freud* (New York: Harper & Row, 1966), 261.

26. Christopher Lasch, *The Culture of Narcissism* (New York: Norton, 1978), 7.

27. Ibid., 12.

28. T. J. Jackson Lears, "From Salvation to Self-Realization: Advertising the Roots of the Consumer Culture, 1880-1930," in *The Culture of Consumption: Critical Essays in American History, 1880-1980*, ed. Richard Fox and T. J. Jackson Lears (New York: Pantheon: 1983), 6. Lears's account is developed more fully in *No Place of Grace: Antimodernism and the Transformation of American Culture, 1880-1920* (New York: Pantheon, 1981).

29. Lears, "From Salvation to Self-Realization," 11.

30. Ibid., 13–14.

31. Ibid., 11.

32. Ibid., 19, 22.

33. Ibid., 21. Lears is paraphrasing Henri Lefebvre. For a more theoretical discussion of how advertising erodes the meaning of the cultural symbols it employs, see Robert Goldman and Stephen Papson, "Advertising in the Age of Accelerated Meaning," in *The Consumer Society Reader*, ed. Juliet Schor and Douglas Holt (New York: New Press, 2000), 81–98.

34. Vachel Lindsey, *The Art of the Motion Pictures,* as quoted in Lears, "From Salvation to Self-Realization," 18.

35. Robert Bellah et al., *Habits of the Heart: Individualism and Commitment in American Life* (New York: Harper & Row, 1986), 221, 236.

36. Wade Clark Roof, "God Is in the Details: Reflections on Religion's Public Presence in the United States in the Mid-1990's," *Sociology of Religion* 57, no. 2 (1996): 154.

37. Wade Clark Roof, *A Generation of Seekers: The Spiritual Journeys of the Baby Boom Generation* (San Francisco: HarperSanFrancisco, 1993), 8.

38. Roof, *Generation of Seekers,* 131; Catherine Albanese, "Religion and the American Experience: A Century After," *Church History* 57, no. 3 (September 1988): 337–51.

39. Robert Wuthnow, *After Heaven: Spirituality in America since the 1950s* (Berkeley: University of California Press, 1998), 1–19.

40. Wade Clark Roof, *Spiritual Marketplace: Baby Boomers and the Remaking of American Religion* (Princeton, N.J. : Princeton University Press, 1999), 48.

41. Ronald Inglehart, *Culture Shift in Advanced Industrial Society* (Princeton, N.J.: Princeton University Press, 1990), as quoted in Roof, *Spiritual Marketplace,* 58.

42. Susan Harding, *The Afterlife of Stories* (Berkeley: University of California Press, forthcoming), as quoted in Roof, *Spiritual Marketplace,* 42.

43. Roof, *Generation of Seekers,* 259–60.

44. Nancy Ammerman, "Golden Rule Christianity: Lived Religion in the American Mainstream," in *Lived Religion in America: Toward a History of Practice,* ed. David Hall (Princeton, N.J.: Princeton University Press, 1997), 196–216. Her characterization of this group as "Golden Rule Christians" is an attempt to correct the more derogatory connotations of "lay liberals" used in Dean Hoge, Benton Johnson, and Donald Luidens, *Vanishing Boundaries: The Religion of Mainline Protestant Baby Boomers* (Louisville, Ky.: Westminster John Knox, 1994).

45. Roof, *Spiritual Marketplace,* 109.

46. Elizabeth Brusco, "The Reformation of Machismo: Asceticism and Masculinity among Colombian Evangelicals," in *Rethinking Protestantism in Latin America,* ed. Virginia Garrard-Burnett and David Stoll (Philadelphia: Temple University Press, 1993), 143–58, as quoted in Lyon, *Jesus in Disneyland,* 23.

47. Lyon, *Jesus in Disneyland,* 34. See *The Desecularization of the World: Resurgent Religion and World Politics,* ed. Peter Berger and Jonathan Sachs (Grand Rapids: Eerdmans, 1999); David Lyon, *The Steeple's Shadow: On the Myths and Realities of Secularization* (Grand Rapids: Eerdmanns, 1987).

48. Roof, *Spiritual Marketplace,* 89–90.

49. The religious book market has experienced explosive growth. Statistics from the Association of American Publishers reported a 59 percent increase in sales of books in the Bible/religion/spirituality category between 1992 and 1994. A Gallup study projects an 82 percent increase in book sales in religion/spirituality by 2010. The next largest predicted increase is in investment books, which comes in far behind with a 59 percent projected growth. See Phyllis Tickle, *Re-Discovering the Sacred: Spirituality in America* (New York: Crossroad, 1995), 18.

50. Moore, *Selling God,* 266ff.

51. Lyon, *Jesus in Disneyland,* 34; Roof, *Spiritual Marketplace,* 87.

52. Mike Featherstone, *Consumer Culture and Postmodernism* (London: Sage, 2000), 118–19.

53. Guy Debord, *Society of the Spectacle* (Detroit: Black and Red, 1977), #1.

54. Chester Gillis, *Roman Catholicism in America* (New York: Columbia University Press, 1999), 1–2.

55. Donald Lopez, *Prisoners of Shangri-La* (Chicago: University of Chicago Press, 1998), 199.

56. Ibid., 184–90. Lopez highlights the importance of the Dalai Lama's attempts to discourage and suppress propitiation of Shugden, a deity protective of the Geluk sect.

57. Ibid., 11.

58. "John Paul II, Woman's Role in the Church" (September 3, 1995), in *Pope John Paul II on the Genius of Women* (Washington D.C.: United States Catholic Conference, 1997), 35–36.

59. Michael Budde, *The (Magic) Kingdom of God: Christianity and Global Culture Industries* (Boulder, Colo.: Westview Press, 1997), 98.

60. John Paul II, *Redemptoris Missio* (Washington, D.C.: United States Catholic Conference, 1990), §37.

61. John Paul II, "Message for the 24th World Communications Day 1990," as quoted in Pontifical Council for Social Communications, "The Church and Internet" (February 28, 2002), §7.

62. Pontifical Council for Social Communications, *Aetatis Novae: On the Twentieth Anniversary of Communio et Progressio* (February 22, 1992), §8.

63. John Paul II, "Message for the 35th World Communications Day 2001," §3.

64. Pontifical Council for Social Communications, "The Church and the Internet," §11.

65. John Paul II, "Address to the Bishops of the United States," Los Angeles, September 16, 1987, §5, as quoted in "The Church and the Internet," §9.

66. Ibid. No mention is made of the long-standing and once widespread tradition of "spiritual" reception of the Eucharist. See Gary Macy, "The Eucharist and Popular Religiosity," in *Proceedings of the Catholic Theological Society of America* 52 (1997): 39–58. This tradition, along with eucharistic adoration, is particularly attractive to Internet sites. See for example the Web site maintained by the Monks of Adoration, an Augustinian monastic community in Venice, Florida. Their Web site features a webcam image of the eucharistic tabernacle in their chapel, updated every minute, twenty-four hours a day, at http://www.monksofadoration.org/chapel.html.

67. George Weigel, *Witness to Hope: The Biography of Pope John Paul II* (New York: HarperCollins, 1999), 491.

68. Lyon, *Jesus in Disneyland*, 138.

69. Roof, *Spiritual Marketplace*, 86ff.

70. Featherstone, *Consumer Culture and Postmodernism*, 43–44. See Pierre Bourdieu, *Distinction: A Social Critique of the Judgement of Taste*, trans. Richard Nice (Cambridge, Mass.: Harvard University Press, 1984), 359–69.

71. Budde, *The (Magic) Kingdom of God*, 107.

72. David N. Power, *Sacrament: The Language of God's Giving* (New York: Crossroad, 1999), 36.

73. John Allen, Jr., "Mahony Appeals to Rome about Angelica," *National Catholic Reporter* 134, no. 13, January 30, 1998, 5.

74. Ibid.

75. As of January 1, 2000, Los Angeles had 4,121,601 members of the Catholic Church (*Official Catholic Directory* 2000 [New York: P. J. Kennedy, 2000], 455).

76. Richard Gaillardetz, "The New E-Magisterium," *America* 182, no. 16, May 6, 2000, 8.

77. Dean R. Hoge, William D. Dinges, Mary Johnson, and Juan L. Gonzales, *Young Adult Catholics: Religion in the Culture of Choice* (Notre Dame, Ind.: University of Notre Dame Press, 2000), 154–57.

78. Ibid., 163.

79. Featherstone, *Consumer Culture and Postmodernism*, 26; Budde, *The (Magic) Kingdom of God,* 79.

80. Bourdieu, *Distinction,* 359.

81. Ibid., 370.

82. Featherstone, *Consumer Culture and Postmodernism*, 19.

83. Mark Massa, *Catholics and American Culture: Fulton Sheen, Dorothy Day and the Notre Dame Football Team* (New York: Crossroad, 1999), 56. A rather obvious counterargument to Massa's claim is the fact that one would be hard pressed to find a person from that or a subsequent generation that entered religious life who would not cite reading Merton as influential in their formation.

CHAPTER 4

DESIRE AND THE KINGDOM OF GOD

1. Tim Edwards, *The Contradictions of Consumption* (Philadelphia: Open University Press, 2000), 191.

2. *State of Food Insecurity in the World,* 2002 (Rome: Food and Agriculture Organization of the United Nations, 2002), 6, ftp://ftp.fao.org/docrep/fao/005/y7352e/y7352e01.pdf, accessed January 31, 2003.

3. Betsy Taylor and Dave Tilford, "Why Consumption Matters," in *The Consumer Society Reader,* ed. Juliet B. Schor and Douglas Holt (New York: New Press, 2000), 468, 472.

4. Bernadette D. Proctor and Joseph Daleker, *Poverty in the United States: 2001* (Washington, D.C.: U.S. Census Bureau, 2002), 4, 6, 9. Food insecurity is defined as being "uncertain of having or unable to acquire, enough food to meet the basic needs of all their [household] members." See Mark Nord et al., *Household Food Security in the United States,* Food Assistance and Nutrition Research Report No. 21 (Washington, D.C.: USDA, 2000), 11, http://www.ers.usda.gov/publications/fanrr21/, accessed January 31, 2003.

5. Don Slater finds the abstraction of the notion of "basic needs" from the particulars of culture to be problematic. "It is only at the most horrific extremes of inhumanity, economic catastrophe, war . . . when—as we say in these circumstances—'people have been reduced to animals,'" that we recognize these basic needs. Even at the extremes of human deprivation and suffering, people still desire and act in culturally specific ways, such as keeping kosher in the face of starvation (Don Slater, *Consumer Culture and Modernity* [London: Polity Press, 1997], 134).

6. John Paul II, *Centesimus Annus* §36; Karl Marx, "Economic and Philosophical Manuscripts," in *Early Writings* (Harmondsworth: Penguin/New Left Review, 1975), 355, quoted in Slater, *Consumer Culture and Modernity,* 104.

7. Slater, *Consumer Culture and Modernity,* 136.

8. Graham Ward, *Cities of God* (New York: Routledge, 2000), 75.

9. Daniel M. Bell, Jr., *Liberation Theology after the End of History: The Refusal to Cease Suffering* (New York: Routledge, 2001).

10. D. Stephen Long, *Divine Economy* (New York: Routledge, 2000), 4.

11. Ibid. 144.

12. Ibid. 262.

13. John Kenneth Galbraith, *The Affluent Society* (Boston: Houghton Mifflin, 1958), 158; Slater, *Consumer Culture and Modernity*, 50.

14. Joe Dominguez and Vicki Robin, *Your Money or Your Life: Transforming Your Relationship with Money and Achieving Financial Independence* (New York: Penguin, 1999).

15. Neil McKendrick, John Brewer, and J. H. Plumb, *The Birth of a Consumer Society: The Commercialization of Eighteenth-century England* (London: Hutchenson, 1983); Colin Campbell, *The Romantic Ethic and the Spirit of Modern Consumerism* (Oxford: Blackwell, 1989).

16. Peter Sedgwick, *The Market Economy and Christian Ethics* (Cambridge: Cambridge University Press, 1999), 85.

17. Ibid., 87.

18. Craig Gay offers a similar analysis in "Sensualists without Heart: Contemporary Consumerism in Light of the Modern Project," in *The Consuming Passion: Christianity and the Consumer Culture,* ed. Rodney Clapp (Downers Grove, Ill.: InterVarsity Press, 1998), 19–39.

19. Sedgwick, *The Market Economy and Christian Ethics*, 83.

20. Zygmunt Bauman, *Intimations of Postmodernity* (London: Routledge, 1992), 14, 51.

21. Ibid., 50–51.

22. Ibid., 98.

23. Ibid., 169.

24. Robert Orsi, *Thank You, Saint Jude: Women's Devotion to the Patron Saint of Hopeless Causes* (New Haven, Conn: Yale University Press, 1996), 51.

25. Sigmund Freud, *Civilization and Its Discontents* (New York: Norton, 1962), 25.

26. For a summary of Wundt's research and a discussion of its relevance to the economics of consumer demand and satisfaction, see Tibor Scitovsky, *The Joyless Economy: The Psychology of Human Satisfaction,* rev. ed. (Oxford: Oxford University Press, 1992), 34–79.

27. Zygmunt Bauman, *Work, Consumerism and the New Poor* (Buckingham: Open University Press, 1998), 39.

28. Sedgwick, *Market Economy and Christian Ethics,* 83.

29. Aristotle, *Rhetoric* 1.1370a6, quoted in Anne Carson, *Eros the Bittersweet* (Normal, Ill.: Dalkey Archive Press, 1998), 63.

30. Carson, *Eros,* 62, 65.

31. *Diagnostic and Statistical Manual for Mental Disorders*, 4th ed. (Washington, D.C.: American Psychological Association, 1994), 522–23.

32. William Leiss, *The Limits to Satisfaction: An Essay on the Problem of Needs and Commodities* (Toronto: University of Toronto Press, 1976), 18.

33. Ibid., 19.

34. Ibid., 88.

35. Ibid., 27.

36. Ibid., 16.

37. Bauman, *Intimations of Postmodernity*, 194.

38. Deborah Sontag, "One Last Sit-In," *New York Times Magazine,* April 6, 2003, 80.

39. T. J. Jackson Lears, "From Salvation to Self-Realization," in *The Culture of Consumption*, ed. Richard Fox and T. J. Jackson Lears (New York: Pantheon, 1983), 28.

40. Julia Kristeva, *Revolution in Poetic Language* (New York: Columbia University Press, 1984), 68.

41. Herbert Marcuse, *One Dimensional Man* (Boston: Beacon Press, 1964), 56ff.

42. See Henri Lefebvre's discussion of nudity and everyday life in *The Critique of Everyday Life* (New York: Verso, 1991), 34–35.

43. Andrew Ross, "The Popularity of Pornography," in *The Cultural Studies Reader,* ed. Simon During (London: Routledge, 1993), 241. Then again, there are entire genres of pornography that play on the tensions and difficulties of everyday sexual relationships. See Jane Juffer's discussion of "The Redshoe Diaries," in *At Home with Pornography: Women, Sex and Everyday Life* (New York: New York University Press, 1998), 221.

44. Augustine, *On Christian Teaching,* trans. R. P. H. Green (New York: Oxford University Press, 1997), 9.

45. Augustine, *Confessions,* trans. R. S. Pine-Coffin (New York: Penguin, 1961), 21.

46. *Pace* the widespread problems with eating disorders. See Patrick T. McCormick, "How Could We Break the Lord's Bread in a Foreign Land? The Eucharist in 'Diet America,'" *Horizons* 25, no.1 (1988): 43–57.

47. Augustine, *On Christian Teaching,* 9.

48. Thomas Aquinas, *Commentary on the Gospel of John* (Albany: Magi Books, 1980), 242.

49. Tod Linafelt, "Biblical Love Poetry (. . . and God)," *Journal of the American Academy of Religion* 70, no. 2 (June 2002): 323–45 (Linafelt's translation from p. 329).

50. Trans. Bernard McGinn, *The Presence of God: A History of Western Mysticism,* vol. 1, *The Foundations of Mysticism* (New York: Crossroad, 1995), 141.

51. Charles T. Mathewes, "The Liberation of Questioning in Augustine's *Confessions,*" *Journal of the American Academy of Religion* 70, no. 3 (September 2002): 539–60.

52. Karl Rahner, "The Concept of Mystery in Catholic Theology," *Theological Investigations* (Baltimore: Helicon Press, 1966), 4:36–73.

53. Stephen D. O'Leary, *Arguing the Apocalypse: A Theory of Millennial Rhetoric* (New York: Oxford University Press, 1994), 14.

54. John Caputo, *The Prayers and Tears of Jacques Derrida* (Bloomington: Indiana University Press, 1999), 96.

55. Johann-Baptist Metz, "Theology Today: New Crises and New Visions," *Proceedings of the Catholic Theology Society of America* 40 (1985): 13. My discussion of Metz is indebted to J. Matthew Ashley, "Apocalypticism in Political and Liberation Theology: Toward an Historical *Docti Ignorantia,*" *Horizons* 27, no. 1 (spring 2000): 22–43.

56. Metz, "Theology Today," 13.

57. Johann-Baptist Metz, *Faith in History and Society: Toward a Practical Fundamental Theology,* trans. David Smith (New York: Crossroad, 1980), 175.

58. Ibid., 170. Graham Ward's account in *Cities of God* is similar, but makes no reference to Metz.

59. Johann-Baptist Metz, "Messianic or 'Bourgeois' Religion," in Johann-Baptist Metz and Jürgen Moltmann, *Faith and the Future: Essays on Theology, Solidarity, and Modernity* (Maryknoll, N.Y.: Orbis, 1995), 19.

60. Metz, "Theology Today," 12.

61. Frank Kermode, *The Sense of an Ending: Studies in the Theory of Fiction* (Oxford: Oxford University Press, 1966), 101, 121.

62. Edward Schillebeeckx, *God the Future of Man* (New York: Sheed & Ward, 1968), 136.

63. John Berger, *The Look of Things* (New York: Viking, 1974), 40, as quoted in Edward

W. Soja, *Postmodern Geographies: The Reassertion of Space in Critical Social Theory* (London: Verso, 1989), 22.

64. Johann-Baptist Metz, *Glaube in Geschichte und Gesellschaft: Studien zur einer praktischen Fundamentaltheologie*, 5th ed. (Mainz: Matthias Grünewald Verlag, 1977), 166; Eng. trans. by J. Matthew Ashley (New York: Crossroad-Herder, forthcoming).

65. Don DeLillo, *Mao II* (New York: Viking Penguin, 1991), 72.

66. Metz, "Theology Today," 13.

67. But as Anne DuCille has noted, as much as advanced capitalism seems to "adore" difference, it continues to "abhor" it as well. In order for difference to appear, it must be commodifiable, reducible to terms simple enough to be signified in slight modifications of mass-produced goods. Her study of various attempts by Mattel to market African American versions of Barbie demonstrates that the commodification of difference ends up reinforcing both racial stereotypes and racial subordination ("Toy Theory: Black Barbie and the Deep Play of Difference," in *The Consumer Society Reader*, ed. Juliet Schor and Douglas Holt [New York: New Press, 2000], 264–66).

68. Renato Rosaldo, *Culture & Truth: The Remaking of Social Analysis* (Boston: Beacon Press, 1989).

69. bell hooks, "Eating the Other," in *Consumer Society Reader*, ed. Schor and Holt, 345–46.

70. Ibid., 346.

71. Ibid., 347.

72. Leiss, *Limits to Satisfaction*, 22.

73. Leon Wynter, commentary on *All Things Considered*, National Public Radio, Friday, February 28, 2003. See Wynter's *American Skin: Pop Culture, Big Business and the End of White America* (New York: Crown, 2002).

74. Alex Kotlowitz, "False Connections," in *Consuming Desires: Consumption, Culture and the Pursuit of Happiness*, ed. Roger Rosenblatt (Washington D.C.: Island Press, 1999), 65–72.

75. Hal Foster, "Readings in Cultural Resistance," in *Readings: Art, Spectacle, Cultural Politics* (Port Townsend, Wash.: Bay Press, 1985), quoted in hooks, "Eating the Other," 347.

76. E. Edward Kinerk, S.J., "Eliciting Great Desires: Their Place in the Spirituality of the Society of Jesus," *Studies in the Spirituality of Jesuits* 16 (November 1984): 7–8.

77. L. Gregory Jones, "A Thirst for God or Consumer Spirituality?" in *Spirituality and Social Embodiment*, ed. L. Gregory Jones and James J. Buckley (Oxford: Blackwell, 1997), 7.

78. Ibid., 8.

79. Ibid., 4.

80. Ibid., 11, 15.

81. Thomas Moore, *The Soul's Religion: Cultivating a Profoundly Spiritual Way of Life* (New York: HarperCollins, 2002).

82. Jones, "Thirst for God," 23. Daniel Bell echos Jones's strong language (*Liberation Theology after the End of History*, 97).

83. Lyon, *Jesus in Disneyland*, 92.

84. Roof, *A Generation of Seekers*, 258–59. Steven Warner, "Work in Progress toward a New Paradigm for the Sociological Study of Religion in the United States," *American Journal of Sociology* 98, no. 5 (March 1993): 1077.

85. Anthony Giddens, *Modernity and Self-Identity* (Cambridge: Polity Press, 1991), 215, quoted in Lyon, *Jesus in Disneyland*, 89.

86. Robert Wuthnow, *Acts of Compassion: Caring for Others and Helping Ourselves* (Princeton, N.J.: Princeton University Press, 1991), 116.

87. Ronald Rolheiser, *The Holy Longing: The Search for a Christian Spirituality* (New York: Doubleday, 1999), 8.

88. See Michelle Dillon's discussion of the sociological literature on this topic (*Catholic Identity: Balancing Reason, Faith and Power* [New York: Cambridge University Press, 1999], 244).

89. Bernard of Clairvaux, *Selected Works*, trans. Gillian Evans (New York: Paulist Press, 1987), 215, 224.

90. Thich Nhat Hanh, *The Miracle of Mindfulness* (Boston: Beacon Press, 1975), 26.

CHAPTER 5
THE POLITICS OF CONSUMPTION

1. Don Slater, *Consumer Culture and Modernity* (Oxford: Polity Press, 1997), 33–34.

2. Theodor Adorno and Max Horkheimer, *The Dialectic of Enlightenment* (London: Verso, 1999), 120–67.

3. Thomas Frank, "Advertising as Cultural Criticism: Bill Bernbach versus the Mass Society," in *The Consumer Society Reader*, ed. Juliet B. Schor and Douglas B. Holt (New York: New Press, 2000), 379.

4. Thorsten Veblen, *The Theory of the Leisure Class: An Economic Study of Institutions* (New York: Macmillan/Mentor, 1953), 27–29.

5. Zygmunt Bauman, *Work, Consumerism and the New Poor* (Buckingham: Open University Press, 1988), 39.

6. Juliet Schor, "The New Politics of Consumption," in *Do Americans Shop Too Much?* (Boston: Beacon Press, 2000), 10. This essay is a précis of her fuller argument, *The Overspent American: Upscaling, Downshifting, and the New Consumer* (New York: Basic Books, 1998).

7. Schor, "New Politics of Consumption," 24.

8. Pierre Bourdieu, *Distinction: A Social Critique of the Judgement of Taste* (Cambridge, Mass: Harvard University Press, 1984), 16–18.

9. Malcolm Gladwell, "The Coolhunt," in *The Consumer Society Reader,* ed. Schor and Holt, 360–74.

10. Robert Goldman and Stephen Papson, "Advertising in the Age of Accelerated Meaning," in *The Consumer Society Reader*, ed. Schor and Holt, 91.

11. Bauman, *Work, Consumerism and the New Poor*, 39–40.

12. Tim Edwards, *The Contradictions of Consumption* (Buckingham: Open University Press, 2000), 30.

13. Martyn J. Lee, *Consumer Culture Reborn* (New York: Routledge, 1993), 31.

14. Axel Honneth, Hermann Kocyba, and Bernd Schwibs, "The Struggle for Symbolic Order: An Interview with Pierre Bourdieu," *Theory, Culture and Society* 3, no. 3 (June 1986): 41.

15. Fredric Jameson, *Postmodernism, or, the Cultural Logic of Late Capitalism* (Durham, N.C.: Duke University Press, 1990), 17.

16. Claude Lévi-Strauss, *The Savage Mind* (Chicago: University of Chicago Press, 1966), 17.

17. Simon During discusses the relationship between Lefebvre's and de Certeau's use of "everyday life." See "Introduction," in *The Cultural Studies Reader*, ed. Simon During (London: Routledge, 1993), 24–25.

18. Michel de Certeau, *The Practice of Everyday Life*, vol. 1 (Berkeley: University of California Press, 1984), xiii.

19. Joseph Murphy, *Santeria: An African Religion in America* (Boston: Beacon Press, 1988).

20. De Certeau, *Practice of Everyday Life*, 176.

21. Ibid., 37–38.

22. Ibid., 38, 40.

23. Ibid., 31, xviii.

24. Judith Williamson, *Decoding Advertisements: Ideology and Meaning in Advertising* (London: Marion Boyars, 2000), 6. Whereas she had originally employed the notion of bricolage to describe the use of images and symbols by ad composers, the Punk movement (which appeared a year after her original publication) convinced her that such creative restructuring of "stolen and inverted symbols" was also at work in popular reception of advertisements and systems of style.

25. Jane Clarke and Diana Simmonds, *Move over Misconceptions: Doris Day Reappraised* (London: British Film Institute, 1980), quoted in Slater, *Consumer Culture and Modernity*, 167.

26. Janice Radway, *Reading the Romance: Women, Patriarchy, and Popular Literature* (Chapel Hill: University of North Carolina Press, 1984).

27. JoEllen Shively, "Cowboys and Indians: Perceptions of Western Films Among American Indians and Anglos," *American Sociological Review* 57, no. 6 (December 1992): 725–34.

28. Kathryn Tanner, "Theology and Popular Culture," in *Changing Conversations: Religious Reflection and Cultural Analysis*, ed. Dwight Hopkins and Sheila Greeve Davaney (New York: Routledge, 1996), 112.

29. Dick Hebdige, *Subculture: The Meaning of Style* (London: Methuen, 1979); idem, *Hiding in the Light: On Images and Things* (London: Methuen, 1989). See Slater, *Consumer Culture and Modernity*, 165–73.

30. John Fiske, *Reading the Popular* (New York: Routledge, 1991), 13–42, 95–114.

31. John Frow, "Michel de Certeau and the Practice of Representation," *Cultural Studies* 5, no. 1 (1991): 58.

32. Tony Shirato argues that Frow's criticism overlooks the tactical nature of de Certeau's theoretical work and, for this reason, expects of his discourse the very dynamics it seeks to subvert. See "My Space or Yours? De Certeau, Frow and the Meanings of Popular Culture," *Cultural Studies* 7, no. 2 (1993): 282–91.

33. Slater, *Consumer Culture and Modernity*, 172.

34. De Certeau, *Practice of Everyday Life,* 40.

35. Edwards, *Contradictions of Consumption*, 30.

36. Slater, *Consumer Culture and Modernity*, 168.

37. Naomi Klein, *No Logo: Taking Aim at the Brand Bullies* (New York: Picador, 2000), 295ff. For culture jamming, see Kalle Lasn, *Culture Jam: The Uncooling of America* (New York: Eagle Brook, 1999).

38. Michel Foucault, *The History of Sexuality,* volume 1, *An Introduction* (New York: Vintage, 1978), 100–102.

39. *Murphy Brown* episode aired on September 21, 1992, quoted in John Fiske, *Media Matters: Everyday Culture and Political Change* (Minneapolis: University of Minnesota Press, 1996), 72–73.

40. De Certeau, *Practice of Everyday Life,* 91–110, 115–30.

41. Ibid., 31.

42. Ibid.

43. Zygmunt Bauman, *Intimations of Postmodernity* (London: Routledge, 1992), 48–53, quotation from p. 52.

CHAPTER 6

POPULAR RELIGION IN CONSUMER CULTURE

1. Michel de Certeau, "The Beauty of the Dead: Nisard," in *Heterologies: Discourse on the Other* (Minneapolis: University of Minnesota Press, 1985), 121–36.

2. See, for instance, Edward Schillebeeckx, "Offices in the Church of the Poor," in *La Iglesia Popular: Between Fear and Hope,* ed. Leonardo Boff and Virgil Elizondo, *Concilium* 176, no. 6 (1984): 105; and Johann-Baptist Metz, *Faith in History and Society: Toward a Practical Fundamental Theology* (New York: Seabury, 1980), 136.

3. *The Church in the Present Day Tranformation of Latin America in the Light of the Council,* II (Bogotá: CELAM, 1970), 123, quoted in Michael Candelaria, *Popular Religion and Liberation* (Berkeley: University of California Press, 1990), 21.

4. Candelaria, *Popular Religion and Liberation,* 21.

5. Pope Paul VI, *Populorum Progressio* (Washington, D.C.: United States Catholic Conference, 1967), §10; idem, *Evangelii Nuntiandi* (Washington, D.C.: United States Catholic Conference, 1975), §20.

6. *Puebla Document,* §§444, 448 in *Puebla and Beyond,* ed. John Eagleson and Phillip Sharper (Maryknoll, N.Y.: Orbis, 1979), 184, 185.

7. Sixto J. García and Orlando Espín, "'Lilies of the Field': A Hispanic Theology of Providence and Human Responsibility," *Proceedings of the Catholic Theological Society of America* 44(1989): 75.

8. Orlando Espín, *The Faith of the People: Theological Reflections on Popular Catholicism* (Maryknoll, N.Y.: Orbis Books, 1997), 65–66.

9. Ibid., 162; Roberto S. Goizueta, *Caminemos con Jesús: Toward a Hispanic/Latino Theology of Accompaniment* (Maryknoll, N.Y.: Orbis, 1995), 18–32.

10. Espín, *Faith of the People,* 112–13. While Weber did discuss the role of "dogmatics" in establishing the credentials of elites such as priests and theologians in strongly institutional churches, his original use of the term "religious virtuosi" did not primarily concern intellectual, clerical elites. The term appears in his discussion of asceticism and mysticism. Although he did cite the learned religious elitism of the Pharisees (in contrast to the ʿam haʾaretz, the "people of the land") as an example, his other examples tended toward monks and ascetics, including the decidedly anti-intellectual *poverello,* Francis of Assisi. See Max Weber, *The Sociology of Religion* (Boston: Beacon Press, 1963), 162–63, 195–96.

11. Espín, *Faith of the People,* 93–99.

12. García and Espín, "Lilies of the Field," 73; Goizueta, *Caminemos con Jesús,* 29.

13. Sixto García and Orlando Espín, "Hispanic-American Theology," *Proceedings of the Catholic Theological Society of America* 42 (1987): 115.

14. See the eight theological elements Espín derives from an analysis of Latino devotion to the crucified Christ and Our Lady of Guadalupe (*Faith of the People*, 71–78), as well as Goizueta's analysis of the latter and the Triduum celebration at San Fernando Cathedral in San Antonio, Texas (*Caminemos con Jesús*, 32–46).

15. Robert Orsi, *Thank You, St. Jude* (New Haven: Yale University Press, 1996), 13–14.

16. Ibid., 187.

17. Ibid., 208–9.

18. Ibid., 121–30.

19. Ibid., 131–41.

20. David Hall, "Introduction," in *Lived Religion in America*, ed. David Hall (Princeton, N.J.: Princeton University Press, 1997), viii.

21. Jeffrey Stout, *Ethics after Babel: The Languages of Morals and Their Discontents* (Boston: Beacon Press, 1988), 76, 218.

22. Robert Orsi, "Everyday Miracles," in *Lived Religion in America*, ed. Hall, 8.

23. Mary McClintock Fulkerson, *Changing the Subject: Women's Discourses and Feminist Theology* (Minneapolis: Fortress Press, 1994), 285–97.

24. D. Stephen Long compares the two works to make much the opposite point, that cultural traditions are easily corrupted. See *Divine Economy: Theology and the Market* (New York: Routledge, 2000), 219–20.

25. Joseph Murphy, *Mixed Blessings: Indigenous Encounters with Christianity* (Boston: Beacon Press, forthcoming).

26. Kathryn Tanner, "Theology and Popular Culture," in *Changing Conversations: Religious Reflection and Cultural Analysis*, ed. Dwight Hopkins and Sheila Greeve Davaney (New York: Routledge, 1996), 113.

27. Tanner, "Theology and Popular Culture,"115. See her more extended discussion in *Theories of Culture: A New Agenda for Theology* (Minneapolis: Fortress, 1997), 61–92.

28. Tanner, *Theories of Culture*, 69–71.

29. Tanner, "Theology and Popular Culture," 107, quoting de Certeau, *Practice of Everyday Life*, 89.

30. Michel de Certeau, "The Weakness of Believing: From the Body to Writing, a Christian Transit," in *The Certeau Reader*, ed. Graham Ward (London: Routledge, 2000), 215–43; idem, "How Is Christianity Thinkable Today?" *Theology Digest* 17, no. 4 (Winter, 1971): 344.

31. De Certeau, "Weakness of Believing," 218.

32. See Frederick Bauerschmidt, "The Abrahamic Voyage: Michel de Certeau and Theology," *Modern Theology* 12, no. 1 (January 1996): 1–26.

33. Ibid., 236.

34. Ibid., 237.

35. Jeremy Aherne, "The Shattering of Christianity and the Articulation of Belief," *New Blackfriars* 77, no. 909 (November 1996): 501; Graham Ward, "The Voice of the Other," ibid., 527–28.

36. Susan Ross, "God's Embodiment and Women," in *Freeing Theology*, ed. Catherine LaCugna (San Francisco: HarperSanFrancisco, 1993), 190–92; Mary McClintock Fulkerson, *Changing the Subject*, 389–91.

37. Michael Budde, *The (Magic) Kingdom of God: Christianity and Global Culture Industries* (Boulder, Colo.: Westview Press, 1987), 87.

CHAPTER 7
STEWARDING RELIGIOUS TRADITIONS IN CONSUMER CULTURE

1. Daniel M. Bell, Jr., *Liberation Theology after the End of History: The Refusal to Cease Suffering* (New York: Routledge, 2001), 162.

2. Ibid., 124.

3. Kathryn Tanner, *Theories of Culture: A New Agenda for Theology* (Minneapolis: Fortress, 1997), 61.

4. See Russell R. Reno "The Radical Orthodoxy Project," *First Things*, no. 100 (February 2000): 37–44; and Gavin Hyman's more extensive critique of John Milbank in *The Predicament of Postmodern Theology: Radical Orthodoxy or Nihilist Textualism* (Louisville: Westminster John Knox, 2001), 65–94. Hyman's constructive proposal employs de Certeau's notion of tactics, but in a manner much more textualist than my own.

5. Karl Rahner, *Foundations of Christian Faith* (New York: Crossroad, 1978), 110–11.

6. Francis Schüssler Fiorenza, "Systematic Theology: Task and Methods," in *Systematic Theology: Roman Catholic Perspectives*, vol. 1, ed. Francis Schüssler Fiorenza and John P. Galvin (Minneapolis: Fortress Press, 1991), 15.

7. Francis Schüssler Fiorenza, "Pluralism: A Western Commodity or Justice for the Other?" in *Ethical Monotheism Past and Present: Essays in Honor of Wendell S. Dietrich*, ed. Theodore Vial and Mark Hadley (Providence, R.I.: Brown Judaic Studies, 2001), 289–92.

8. Juliet Schor, *The Overspent American: Upscaling, Downshifting, and the New Consumer* (New York: Basic Books, 1998), 144–67.

9. Christopher D. Cook, "Fowl Trouble," *Harper's* 299, no. 1791 (August 1999): 78.

10. Catholic Bishops of the South, "Voices and Choices" (November 15, 2001), 1, available at http://www.poultry-pastoral.org.

11. Albert Borgmann's notion of "focal practices" is also a potential tactic in this regard. See his *Technology and the Character of Contemporary Life* (Chicago: University of Chicago Press, 1984). For a theological appropriation, see Richard Gaillardetz, *Transforming Our Days* (New York: Crossroad, 2000).

12. The following account is indebted to Fiona MacCarthy, *William Morris: A Life for Our Times* (London: Faber & Faber, 1994), and T. J. Jackson Lears, *No Place of Grace: Antimodernism and the Transformation of American Culture 1880–1920* (New York: Pantheon, 1981), 60–96 (chapter 2).

13. John Milbank, *Theology and Social Theory: Beyond Secular Reason* (Oxford: Blackwell, 1990), 199–200.

14. Jackson Lears, *No Place of Grace*, 65.

15. Richard P. McBrien, *Catholicism*, New Edition (New York: HarperCollins, 1994), 10.

16. The literature on the topic is vast. The following works are but a representative sampling: Bernard Cooke, *Sacraments and Sacramentality* (Mystic, Conn.: Twenty-Third Publications, 1994); Nancy Dallavalle, "Neither Idolatry Nor Iconoclasm: A Critical Essentialism for Catholic Feminist Theology," *Horizons* 25, no. 1 (spring 1998): 23–42; Andrew Greeley, "Catholics, Fine Arts and the Liturgical Imagination," *America* 174, May 18, 1996, 9–14; Anthony Godzieba, "Caravaggio, Theologian: Baroque Piety and Poesis in a Forgotten Chapter of the History of Catholic Theology," in *Theology and Lived Christianity*, ed. David M. Hammond (Mystic, Conn.: Twenty-Third Publications, 2000), 206–30. David

Hollenbach, "A Prophetic Church and the Catholic Sacramental Imagination," in *The Faith That Does Justice*, ed. John Haughey (New York: Paulist, 1977), 234–63; Mary Catherine Hilkert, *Naming Grace: Preaching and the Sacramental Imagination* (New York: Continuum, 1997); Susan Ross, *Extravagant Affections: A Feminist Sacramental Theology* (New York: Continuum, 1998); Terrence Tilley, *Inventing Catholic Tradition* (Maryknoll, N.Y.: Orbis, 2000); David Tracy, *The Analogical Imagination: Christian Theology and the Culture of Pluralism* (New York: Crossroad, 1984).

17. For a critical consideration of its relationship to popular culture, see Vincent J. Miller, "A Genealogy of Presence: Elite Anxiety and the Excesses of the Popular Sacramental Imagination," in *Sacramental Presence in a Postmodern Context*, Bibliotheca Ephemeridum Theologicarum Lovaniensium 160 (Leuven: Leuven University Press, 2001), 347–67.

18. Terrence Tilley, *Inventing Catholic Tradition* (Maryknoll, N.Y.: Orbis, 2000), 131.

19. *Code of Canon Law: Latin-English Edition* (Washington, D.C.: Canon Law Society of America, 1998), §1171.

20. *Sacramentary* (New York: Catholic Book Publishing, Co., 1985), 370.

21. Ibid., 552 (Eucharistic Prayer III).

22. Naomi Klein, *No Logo: Taking Aim at the Brand Bullies* (New York: Picador, 1999), 345–63.

23. Jon Entine, "Shattered Image: Is the Body Shop Too Good to Be True?" *Business Ethics* 8, no. 5 (September/October 1994): 23–28. Saulo Petain, "Broken Promises," *Brazzil* 8, no. 128 (December 1996): 16–18.

24. Lee H. Yearley. "New Religious Virtues and the Study of Religion." Fifteenth Annual University Lecture in Religion at Arizona State University, February 10, 1994, available at http://www.asu.edu/clas/religious_studies/home/1994lec.html, accessed June 8, 2003.

25. Robert Schreiter, *Constructing Local Theologies* (Maryknoll, N.Y.: Orbis, 1985), 18.

26. William L. Portier, "Interpretation and Method," in *The Praxis of Christian Experience*, ed. Robert Schreiter and Mary Catherine Hilkert (San Francisco: Harper & Row, 1989), 22.

27. Alasdair MacIntyre used both terms to describe tradition; see *After Virtue: A Study in Moral Theory*, 2nd ed. (Notre Dame, Ind.: University of Notre Dame Press, 1984), 222. My understanding of "living tradition" is drawn from Edward Schillebeeckx, "Liturgy and Theology," in *Revelation and Theology*, vol. 1 (New York: Sheed & Ward, 1967), 211–22. Schillebeeckx has developed the term throughout his career; see his reflections in the initial section of *Church: The Human Story of God* (New York: Crossroad, 1990).

28. Michele Dillon, *Catholic Identity: Balancing Reason, Faith and Power* (New York: Cambridge University Press, 1999), 253.

29. See the debates on the issue in *World Catechism or Inculturation?* ed. Johann-Baptist Metz and Edward Schillebeeckx, *Concilium* 204 (Edinburgh: T & T Clark, 1989).

30. Edward Schillebeeckx, *For the Sake of the Gospel* (New York: Crossroad, 1990), 170–71.

31. Tilley, *Inventing Catholic Tradition*, 69.

32. Schreiter, *Constructing Local Theologies*, 67–68.

33. See Tilley's attempts to develop an understanding of practice that encompasses both repetition and innovation in *Inventing Catholic Tradition*, 62–65.

34. Michael Budde, *The (Magic) Kingdom of God: Christianity and Global Culture Indus-*

tries (Boulder, Colo.: Westview Press, 1987), 86. See his discussion of religious formation in this regard, pp. 115–24.

35. Scott Appleby, *The Ambivalence of the Sacred: Religion, Violence and Reconciliation* (Lanham, Md.: Rowman and Littlefield, 2000), 235.

36. See Michael J. Weiss, *The Clustered World: How We Live, What We Buy, and What It All Means about Who We Are* (Boston: Little, Brown, 2000). Claritas maintains a Web site that offers sample information for each cluster named: "You Are Where You Live." See http://cluster2.claritas.com/YAWYL/Default.wjsp?System=WL.

37. The neighborhood public school provides an atmosphere of equality for children, but language barriers and differences in education and culture segregate parents. White-collar middle-class American parents run the PTA and volunteer their administrative skills out of their hectic schedules. Working-class immigrant parents contribute food for festivals and have little time to volunteer out of their even more hectic schedules. Many work two or three different jobs.

38. Robert Cabié, *The Eucharist*, rev. ed., vol. 2 of *The Church at Prayer*, ed. A. G. Martimort (Collegeville, Minn.: Liturgical Press, 1986), 19.

39. For the tension, see Bernard J. Lee, *The Catholic Experience of Small Christian Communities* (New York: Paulist, 2000), 136–47; and Robert Wuthnow, *Sharing the Journey: Support Groups and America's New Quest for Community* (New York: Free Press, 1994), 231–48.

40. Margot Patterson, "Finding Family at the Catholic Worker," *National Catholic Reporter,* March 7, 2003, 11–13, 15.

41. *Pace* Linda Williams's argument that pornography's popularity is a result of its function to make sex "visible" in a manner analogous to Foucault's argument that modern "sexuality" required that sex be transformed into discourse. See *Hard Core: Power, Pleasure, and the "Frenzy of the Visible"* (Berkeley: University of California Press, 1999).

42. See Emile Durkheim, *The Elementary Forms of the Religious Life* (New York: Free Press, 1965), 337–65.

43. Part of the university's solution involved placing "multicultural" crucifixes in selected classrooms. Part of the logic behind this was to address the association of the "standard" classroom crucifix style with the anti-Semitism of the Oberammergau passion play. These included the crucifix from John Paul II's crozier, an African crucifix, and the Franciscan crucifix of San Damiano. This policy can be questioned from the perspective of the commodification of culture. Why "multicultural"? Does Georgetown not have its own culture?

44. Indeed the song and its original context of performance are ambiguous themselves. See David Margolick's discussion of Holiday's politics and the sexual undertones of her performances of the song in *Strange Fruit: Billie Holiday, Café Society, and an Early Cry for Civil Rights* (New York: Running Press, 2000).

45. Paul Heelas, "The Limits of Consumption and the Post-modern Religion of the New Age," in *The Authority of the Consumer*, ed. Russell Keat, Nigel Whitely, and Nicholas Abercrombie (London: Routledge, 1994), 112.

46. Dean Hoge, William Dingis, Mary Johnson, and Juan Gonzales, *Young Adult Catholics: Religion in the Culture of Choice* (Notre Dame, Ind.: University of Notre Dame Press, 2001), 222.

47. Robert Schreiter uses the term to describe the latter part of John Paul II's pontifi-

cate. He describes it as a centralizing strategy that responds to erosions of modernity and globalization by attempting to "regain territory that has been lost" using modern communications technologies to reinforce a hierarchical church command structure (*The New Catholicity* [Maryknoll, N.Y.: Orbis, 1997], 21–23).

48. Hoge et al., *Young Adult Catholics*, 163.

49. Paul Lakeland, *The Liberation of the Laity: The Search for an Accountable Church* (New York: Continuum, 2003), 201.

50. Hermann J. Pottmeyer, "Kontinuität und Innovation in der Ekklesiologie des II. Vatikanums," in *Kirche im Wandel,* ed. Giuseppe Alberigo, Yves Congar, and Hermann J. Pottmeyer (Düsseldorf: Patmos, 1982), 89–110. See his expanded discussion in Hermann J. Pottmeyer, *Towards a Papacy in Communion: Perspectives from Vatican Councils I and II* (New York: Crossroad, 1998).

51. Elizabeth Johnson, *Friends of God and Prophets: A Feminist Theological Reading of the Communion of Saints* (New York: Continuum, 1998), 244.

52. *Sacrosanctum Concilium,* in *Vatican Council II: The Conciliar and Post-Conciliar Documents,* ed. Austin Flannery (Northport, N.Y.: Costello Publishing, 1975), §14.

53. *Sacrosanctum Concilium* §11.

54. *General Instruction of the Roman Missal: Including Adaptations for the Dioceses of the United States of America* (Washington, D.C.: United States Catholic Conference, 2003), §42

55. Ibid.

56. Bruce Morrill, "Hidden Presence: The Mystery of the Assembly as Body of Christ," *Liturgical Ministry* 11 (winter 2002): 35.

57. *Sacrosanctum Concilium,* §48.

58. Lee, *Catholic Experience of Small Christian Communities,* 85, 128.

59. "Peace and the Christian Imagination," *Woodstock Report* no. 69 (March 2002). The proceedings were published as "Imagining God's Presence: A Woodstock Theological Center Afternoon of Conversation," *Woodstock Occasional Paper* (Washington, D.C.: Woodstock Theological Center, 2002).

60. Schreiter, *Constructing Local Theologies,* 18–19.

61. Colleen McDanell, *Material Christianity: Religion and Popular Culture in America* (New Haven, Conn.: Yale University Press, 1995), 168–70.

CONCLUSION

1. See James D. Davidson's discussion of the difficulty of measuring the doctrinal beliefs of Catholics concerning the Eucharist ("Yes, Jesus Is Really There: What Do Catholics Mean When They Say They Believe In the Real Presence?" *Commonweal* 128, no. 17 [October 12, 2001]: 14–16). Colleen McDannell's analysis of the use and consumption of "Lourdes water" in relationship to nineteenth-century water cures and homeopathy is similar to the question I pose. McDannell does not, however, give much attention to Catholic conceptions of the Eucharist or sacramentality (see *Material Christianity: Religion and Popular Culture in America* [New Haven: Yale University Press, 1995], 142–52).

2. Jeffret Stout, *Ethics After Babel: The Languages of Morals and Their Discontents* (Boston: Beacon, 1988); Alasdair MacIntyre, *After Virtue,* 2nd ed. (South Bend, Ind.: University of Notre Dame Press, 1984).

Index

Abstraction of religious traditions, 10
Ad Gentes (Vatican II Decree on Missionary Activity), 165
Adorno, Theodor, 147
Advertising: choice and, 142; Drano advertisement, 87; Obsession campaign, 121–23, 125; print, 87–88, 109, 113; shift in, 189; Volkswagen campaign, 8, 148. *See also* Marketing
Aetatis Novae (1992 Pastoral Instruction), 99
Agency of consumers, 210–23; explosion of, 9–10; interpretive habits and, 29–30; and politics of consumption, 153–63; power of popular religious, 176–78
Aglietta, Michel, 39–40, 42
Aherne, Jeremy, 176
Albanese, Catherine, 89
Alienation, 32–35
American Gods (Gaiman), 82–83
American Psycho (film), 15
Ammerman, Nancy, 90
Appleby, Scott, 203
Aquinas, Thomas, 8, 50, 128, 164, 171
Armstrong, Karen, 104
Articulation, 174–75, 177
Arts and Crafts movement, 12, 45, 186–87
Asad, Talal, 20
Asceticism, 114
Augustine, 8, 12, 110, 126–27, 129, 140–41
Automated production line, 41–42
Avalon (film), 49

Baby boomers, 71, 89
Bakker, Jim and Tammy, 82
Balasuriya, Tissa, 102
Banana workers, 185–86
Barth, Karl, 200
Battle for Los Angeles, The (album/CD), 19
Baudrillard, Jean, 33, 60–63, 72
Bauhaus, 45
Bauman, Zygmunt, 53, 116–18, 122, 149, 152, 162
Beaudoin, Tom, 76

Beliefs: consumer culture and, 20–23; cultural objects and, 26–27; culture and, 20–24, 162; Foucault and, 21–23; practices and, 1–2, 195; symbols and, 195
Bell, Daniel, 112
Bellah, Robert, 88
Benedictine Monks of Santa Domingo, 74
Berger, John, 133
Bergeron, Katherine, 76–77
Bernard, 138–39, 142–43
Blondel, Maurice, 127
Bocock, Robert, 1
Body Shop (cosmetics company), 191
Boesky, Ivan, 15
Bonaventure, 127
Borgmann, Albert, 47–48
Bourdieu, Pierre, 9, 95, 100, 103, 116, 150–53, 162, 164, 172
Bourgeois religion, 131–32
Brancusi, Constantin, 45
Bricolage: de Certeau and, 154–57; politics of consumption and, 154–58, 163; Slater and, 158; Stout and, 171; term of, 9, 154; traditions and, 174–76
Brooks, David, 2
Budde, Michael, 98–99, 104, 177, 203
Buddhism, 4, 96–97

Cabié, Robert, 204–5
Campbell, Colin, 114
Campbell, Joseph, 83–84, 103
Capitalism: advanced, cultural logic of, 63–66; consumer culture and, 18–19; excesses of, 18–19; green businesses and, 191–92; high-consumption lifestyles and, 11–12; twentieth-century, 39–54
Caputo, John, 83, 131, 133–34
Care of the Soul (Thomas Moore), 138
Carson, Anne, 119
Catherine of Siena, 9, 12, 220
Catholic Worker movement, 50, 205
Catholicism. *See* Roman Catholicism

251